MUNGO'S CITY
A GLASGOW ANTHOLOGY

Mungo's City

A GLASGOW ANTHOLOGY

Edited by
BRIAN D. OSBORNE
and
RONALD ARMSTRONG

First published by Birlinn Limited
Unit 8, Canongate Venture
5 New Street
Edinburgh,
EH8 8BH

ISBN 1 84158 025 2

British Library Cataloguing in Publication Data
A catalogue record for this book is available
from the British Library.

Typesetting and origination by Textype Typesetters, Cambridge
Printed and bound in Great Britain by
Creative Print and Design Wales, Ebbw Vale

Contents

1
FOREWORD

'Gleska! Someday when I'm in the key for't, I'll mak' a song aboot her.' So reflected Neil Munro's pawky Glaswegian waiter and Kirk beadle, Erchie Macpherson. Indeed the variety of Glasgow life and experience has been so rich and so much has been written about it as to almost defy containment in one volume.

The simple fact that the city has enjoyed so many names and has been the subject of so much imagery in itself suggests the wealth of human experience that has gone on in her streets and squares, homes and factories, theatres and marketplaces. The realisation that authorities differ on the meaning of the very word 'Glasgow' adds to this impression of richness and variety. James Cleland, writing in *The Annals of Glasgow* claims that the name means grey smith or dark glen while it is more usually believed to mean dear green place. Even the city's patron saint rejoices in two names – Kentigern and Mungo.

Whether Glasgow is to be seen as 'the dear green place' or 'dark glen'; is to be lauded as an economic power-house, the 'second city of the Empire' by nineteenth-century enthusiasts; condemned as a depraved nest of razor gangs (by the 'no mean city' school of writers) or even seen in Professor Sydney Checkland's imagery as the Upas Tree – an oriental tree that flourished mightily but choked all growth around it – the city has clear claims to have something of its literary richness celebrated in this anthology.

Glasgow has enjoyed a remarkable flourishing of poetry and fiction in the second half of the twentieth century. Edwin Morgan, Alasdair Gray, and James Kelman, are just some of the writers who have put Glasgow at the forefront of contemporary writing. This contemporary richness is perhaps all the more remarkable when it is realised how few novels of the first rank took Glasgow for their setting before our own day. While there are memorable episodes in Scott and Galt it took the twentieth century to find in the lives and experiences of Glaswegians material with which to make great fiction. This does not mean however that there is nothing worth anthologising before the twentieth century – what it does mean is that the anthologist's net has to be cast wider than simply fiction.

In addition we have been very conscious that the Glasgow novel, the Glasgow short story and the Glasgow poem have found able analysts, advocates and scholars in Moira Burgess and Hamish Whyte. This anthology makes no attempt to compete with their collections and critical works, nor does it attempt the daunting task of giving an adequate representation to the rich modern treasures of Glasgow writing.

Our focus in this anthology has rather been to look more widely at the past of Glasgow and draw on all the types of writing, prose and poetry, journalism and analysis, fiction and non-fiction, which the city has evoked over the last eight centuries. We would argue that much of the modern city, however bright and glamorous the contemporary façade, is rooted in the past. To understand today's Glasgow aright one has to know something of the Glasgow of yesterday, and especially the Glasgow of the eighteenth, nineteenth and early twentieth centuries, a period when Glasgow was changing from being, in Daniel Defoe's words, 'the cleanest and beautifullest, and best built city in Britain, London excepted' to the dark, sooty, all-consuming city of a million souls.

One of the advantages of this selection policy is that we have been able to rescue from the obscurity of library stacks much interesting and revealing writing which deserves a wider audience than it all too often gets.

In order to impose a structure on this wealth of material and to assist readers in making connections for themselves we have arranged our selections of writings (which, of course, include the perceptions of both Glaswegians and visitors) in seven thematic chapters. Throughout it has been our object to choose extracts that are substantial and satisfying in length as well as being rich in interest, and to provide where appropriate, introductory notes and analysis to help the reader to appreciate the background and context of the extract. In addition to the commentary on the individual passages each of our chapters – City of Culture, Bishop's Burgh, Merchant City, the Clyde made Glasgow, Jock Tamson's Bairns, The Hampden Roar, and The Revolutionary Moment – has an introduction outlining the theme of the chapter and providing further illustration.

As in any anthology the selection is no more than the summary of the editorial tastes and prejudices. We have included what interested, engaged or amused us, we have grouped material in arbitrary ways and brought together some improbable bedfellows. It is our hope that this anthology will give pleasure to many, and that in enjoying it readers may also gain (in a painless way) a better understanding of the past, present and perhaps the future of the dear green place.

Let Glasgow Flourish! – which (as Nicol Jarvie tells Francis Osbaldistone in *Rob Roy*) – is 'judiciously and elegantly putten round the town's arms, by way of a by-word'.

Brian D. Osborne
Ronald Armstrong
August 1999

2
CITY OF CULTURE
Introduction

When it was announced that Glasgow had won the title of 'European City of Culture' for 1990 some eyebrows were raised, not least in cities whose challenge for the title had been unsuccessful. Glasgow, it was agreed, was a renowned manufacturing city, a great commercial centre – but a 'City of Culture'?

While it is true that as a deliberate policy the City Council and other agencies had re-invented Glasgow as a cultural centre – cleaning buildings, building a concert hall – even, finally, housing the Burrell Collection, it is equally true that Glasgow has long enjoyed an active cultural life. A university city which claimed the services of such enlightenment giants as Adam Smith, Francis Hutcheson and John Miller (to take examples from only one period in the city's history) could hardly fail to be a vital and vibrant centre of intellectual activity. Indeed as early as the sixteenth century it was observed that:

> . . . there was no place in Europe comparable to Glasgow for guid letters during these yeirs for a plentifull and guide chape mercat of all kynd of languages, artes, and sciences.

It must however be recorded that one distinguished visitor to the city and its university at the height of the eighteenth-century enlightenment – Dr Samuel Johnson – was much less impressed by the standards of Scottish and Glasgow university education:

> The students, for the most part, go thither boys, and depart before they are men; they carry with them little fundamental knowledge, and therefore the superstructure cannot be lofty.

The Doctor went on to observe:

> Men bred in the universities of Scotland cannot be expected to be often decorated with the splendours of ornamental erudition, but

> they obtain a mediocrity of knowledge, between learning and ignorance, not inadequate to the purposes of common life . . .

Such views must have made his breakfast with the professors of the university a somewhat tense social gathering. On his visit to Glasgow Johnson also met with Andrew and Robert Foulis, who established a fine printing and publishing house in Glasgow noted for the production of the Greek and Latin classics. The Foulis brothers maintained the reputation of Glasgow for combative debate, and James Boswell records that:

> Though good and ingenious men, they had that unsettled speculative mode of conversation which is offensive to a man regularly taught at an English school and university. I found that, instead of listening to the dictates of the Sage, they had teazed him with questions and doubtful disputations.

Even Johnson, who seldom found much to praise in Scotland, noted that the city's Cathedral had survived 'the rage of Reformation' and Andrew Aird's nineteenth-century description of this key Glasgow building (included in our chapter on 'The Bishop's Burgh') and of the old College, reminds us of both what has survived and what has been lost of early architecture in the city.

While theatre had some of its earliest roots in the Church the Scottish Reformation undoubtedly cast a blight over the development of the drama and the troubled story of theatre in Glasgow is told by John Strang. One clergyman noted for a controversial interest in the theatre was the Musselburgh minister, Alexander Carlyle. Despite his strong Edinburgh connections Carlyle also studied at Glasgow and his account of intellectual life there in the 1740s does remind us that Glasgow was not simply a growing centre of commerce and industry.

The aspect of the culture of Glasgow which evidently most appealed to William McGonagall was its civic sculpture – enthusiastically if ineptly praised in his poem 'Glasgow'. The statues of Glasgow – particularly the remarkable assemblage in George Square – have indeed always attracted much notice, not all of it necessarily favourable. Neil Munro, in his Erchie Macpherson story *How Jinnet saw the King*, has King Edward VII visiting the city in 1903, emerging from Queen Street station: 'Whitna graveyaird's this?' he asks, lookin' at the statues. 'It's no a graveyaird, it's a square, and that's the Municeepal Buildin', somebody tells him.

Neil Munro, twenty years later has, in another Erchie story, a truly surreal fantasy about the same George Square statues:

> Under the new movement for brightening' up Glaska the authorities is gaun to put a' the statues on wheels and hurl them to different sites in the city twice a year. The priceless gift o' Art is to be brung hame to the toilers o' Brigton Cross and Maryhill.

From such visions we turn to Andrew Aird's account of the development of art in Glasgow down to the end of the nineteenth century and to 'James Hamilton Muir's' sharp-eyed account of the city's architecture at the start of the new century.

Glasgow's celebrations of her reign as 'City of Culture' and the events of the 1988 Garden Festival were remarkable, but perhaps not quite as spectacular as the series of exhibitions which were held in the city in 1888, 1901, 1911 and 1938. Our survey of the 'City of Culture' concludes with a tale of a country visitor to the 1911 Scottish Exhibition of National History, Art and Industry. In all the emphasis on cultural benefits, endowment of art galleries, foundation of Chairs of Scottish History, and similar high-minded objectives, the element of sheer pleasure and high-spirited fun that these events produced should not be overlooked. Jimmy Swan's 'Country Customer' certainly carried back to Galloway more than just educative influences – the Manhattan Cocktails and bottles of 'buzz-water' played their part. Truly, culture is an all-embracing term.

'The Old College'

from Glimpses of Old Glasgow

ANDREW AIRD (1819–1899)

Andrew Aird published two volumes of reminiscences related to his own professional life, Letterpress Printing in Glasgow During the Last Fifty Years *(1882) and* Reminiscences of Editors, Reporters and Printers During the Last Sixty Years *(1890) as well as the more general* Glimpses of Old Glasgow *(1894) from which our extracts on one of the city's lost architectural treasures are taken.*

If, against all the odds, the Cathedral has survived as a vital part of the city's built environment, its neighbour – the University – disappeared in a remarkable act of architectural and cultural vandalism. Founded in 1451 by Bishop Turnbull, new buildings for the University were erected in the mid-seventeenth century on the High Street. Admittedly in the course of time this site became congested and less suited to academic needs, but it is nonetheless regrettable that the University consented to have the handsome historic buildings, described as the finest works of seventeenth-century architecture in Scotland, swept away to make room for a railway goods yard. Two fragments of the old College were salvaged and incorporated into Sir George Gilbert Scott's new buildings, opened at Gilmorehill in 1870, although even this token gesture depended on the generosity of a private benefactor, Sir William Pearce, the Govan shipbuilder.

THE UNIVERSITY

The grand central building of the High Street was the College or University. In 1459 this ancient seat of learning stood on the north side of the Rottenrow. In 1539 and 1658 were erected the buildings of the College in High Street, so long renowned. It must have had a splendid appearance when first built. Its frontage was 305 feet, and with its four quadrangular courts had space equal to 10,000 square yards. Its old plain steeple was in height 135 feet. Within the north court were houses for the professors. At the west end of the College Park stood the far-famed

Hunterian Museum, admired as a splendid specimen of classical building. The contents of the museum were bequeathed by Dr W. Hunter, a native of East Kilbride, born in 1710. The building cost £8,000. The books, coins, paintings, etc., collected during a long and very industrious life, were valued at £65,000, but additional contributions have since raised their value to £130,000. But all material glory gradually fades away, and so did the glory of the College buildings and their surroundings. The locality became densely populated and unhealthy, and the character of the inhabitants more unsavoury; the classroom accommodation also became too limited, and for the majority of the students the position was inconvenient. Accordingly new buildings became necessary. An opportunity being afforded through the North British Railway requiring the ground in High Street for a station, the senatus were enabled to secure a site further west. Through the proceeds of the sale and the gifts of many generous donors the present noble pile of the University on Gilmorehill was reared and opened in 1870. The cost of its erection amounted to nearly half-a-million sterling. By the thoughtful foresight of one of Glasgow's wealthy citizens, the handsome gateway of the old College was preserved, and rebuilt at one of the entrances to the present University.

Immediately behind the old College and Hunterian Museum, was the College Green or Gardens for the relaxation of the students. In 1850 the Senatus leased to a company this green for outdoor amusements. The entrance was made from Blackfriars Street. Athletic games, balloon ascents, fireworks, with bands of music, were provided. It was largely taken advantage of for a time, but the scheme did not succeed.

To the south of the old College stood Blackfriars' Church, with its ancient graveyard. The whole has been swept away for utilitarian purposes, so that a new church for the parish had to be built in Dennistoun. From the City Improvement Act and railway necessities almost the whole of the buildings on the east side of the High Street have been taken down. In *Hogg's Instructor* of 5th April, 1845, it is stated that Thomas Campbell the poet, author of 'Pleasures of Hope', 'Wyoming,' and 'Ye Mariners of England,' 'was born in the High Street, about a stone-cast from the University of which he was afterwards thrice elected Lord Rector. The house in which he first saw the light stood on the opposite side of the College, close to what is now the east end of George Street, and has long since been taken down to make way for improvements in that part of the city.'

'Early Theatre in Glasgow'

from Glasgow and its Clubs

JOHN STRANG (1795–1863)

John Strang was the son of a prosperous Glasgow wine merchant. He travelled extensively on the Continent, translated from the French and German and wrote on a variety of artistic, literary and political topics. His 1831 pamphlet Necropolis Glasguensis *was largely responsible for the creation of the city's private burying ground – the Necropolis. His analyses of the census returns for the city in 1841, 1851 and 1861 and his account of Glasgow for the 8th edition of the* Encyclopaedia Britannica *are evidence of his deep interest in his native city – an interest also revealed by his best-known work,* Glasgow and its Clubs *(1856), which gives an engaging picture of social and intellectual life in Glasgow and the west of Scotland in the eighteenth and early nineteenth century. Strang was awarded the honorary degree of Doctor of Laws by Glasgow University in recognition of his literary and public services.*

Strang's account of the vicissitudes of the dramatic art in Glasgow is interesting in that it reminds us of the origins of theatre in church-based productions of the mysteries. Strang outlines the perversity of the Glasgow Reformers in rejecting the theatre, and other arts: '. . . in the earlier days of their Protestant career, they made choice of the very antithesis of everything practised by other Christian communities.'

He tells of the long period when the drama was absent from Scotland and the problems of reintroducing it in such an unpromising setting, where, even in the mid-eighteenth-century promoters of a theatre could not obtain ground within the city.

Of course Glasgow was not alone in its opposition to theatre – the Musselburgh minister, Alexander Carlyle of Inveresk, tells how he was, in 1756, arraigned before the Presbytery of Dalkeith for attending an Edinburgh playhouse to see John Hume's famous tragedy Douglas. *Carlyle and the playgoers of course triumphed in the end. He relates how, in 1784, when the great actress, Mrs Siddons, was playing in Edinburgh, the General Assembly of the Kirk had to arrange all its important business on the alternate days when Mrs Siddons was not appearing.*

By the 1880s, when Groome's Ordnance Gazetteer *appeared and gave an overview of theatre in Glasgow, things had moved on considerably. The Dunlop Street theatre of which Strang wrote had gone to make way for railway development, but Glasgow now enjoyed the Theatre Royal in the Cowcaddens – 'inside the structure is worthy of the city'; the Gaiety Theatre on West Nile Street – 'the bright and successful home of comic opera and burlesque'; the Royalty Theatre on Sauchiehall Street – 'the home of sensation and melodrama'; and the Royal Princess's in the Gorbals – 'chiefly devoted to melo and sensation drama'. Hengler's Cirque in West Nile Street completed the theatrical resources of the city – apart that is from music halls, of which the contributor rather stuffily remarked: 'They do not call for particular notice.' Of the above theatres the Theatre Royal still exists – restored to use as a theatre and opera house after years as the home of Scottish Television, and the Royal Princess's is, of course, now the Citizens Theatre.*

EARLY THEATRE IN GLASGOW

To those who ignorantly imagine, as certainly some do, that dramatic entertainments in Scotland are of modern origin, it will doubtless appear strange to learn, that perhaps nowhere in Christendom was acting more early introduced, or more regularly practised, either as a means of extending religious truths or of affording amusement to the populace, than where such a cathedral as that of Glasgow was to be found, with its chapter of ecclesiastics and its accessories of monks and monasteries. The theatre sprung from the church; originally the subjects were scriptural – the clergy the composers – the church the stage – and Sunday the time of exhibition. In the performance of the religious *mysteries of* early times, as these were called, through which the Saviour's history and the leading traits of saints were palpably portrayed, we find that the people not only took the greatest delight, but would leave their homes, and hurry, at particular seasons, over the length and breadth of the land, to be present at any spot where a temporary stage was erected, either within doors or in the open air. Wherever, in fact, there were friars to enact the 'Fall of Man', the 'Judgment of Solomon', or the 'Marriage of Cana in Galilee', there was no want of an attentive and enthusiastic audience. Toward the commencement of the sixteenth century, the performance of even such sacred pieces, however, as those to which we have alluded, had begun to be undertaken by lay performers; and so common and popular had these entertainments become, particularly on the Sabbath-day, that every means was used by the early reformers of the Church to put them down. Previous, however, to any Church anathema having been issued, it also appears that these exhibitions had been extended from religious subjects to more mundane matters, called *moral plays* or *moralities*, and were given to the multitude in almost every town in Scotland, to which there was usually attached a place for the purpose, called the *Play-field*.

Until the Reformation, matters continued in this condition; but immediately after that event the Church not only prohibited religious *mysteries*, but likewise all profane dramas; and the people, in the west of Scotland at least, at once obeyed the dictum of their ecclesiastical leaders, and abandoned this formerly cherished pastime as a deadly sin.

In consequence of this change in the opinions of the people, it is certainly true that for many years previous to the Revolution of 1688, there was no city in Scotland whose inhabitants were more imbued with religious fanaticism, or in which were to be found parties among whom the Solemn League and Covenant was more zealously looked upon as a test of faith and good citizenship than in Glasgow. For the cause of Protestantism, in contradistinction to Popery, several of her denizens had fearlessly suffered at the stake; and many more had risked their lives and fortunes on what was then deemed equally important, in standing forth as the determined defenders of what they accounted the purer portion of Protestantism, viz. Presbyterianism, against the then dominant power of Prelacy. It may be easily conceived, therefore, that anything which partook, in the slightest degree, of the outward characteristics of the abettors either of book and bell, or of surplice and liturgy, was most religiously and anxiously avoided. Religion, in fact, in the eyes of the worthies of the west, was only considered true and to be admired when seen stripped of its gaudy trappings and its established forms, and consequently was looked upon as being more and more pure as it appeared more severed from the mummery of the mass, and the music of a chanted ritual. In spirit and in conduct it may be truly affirmed, that from the days when Archbishop James Beaton was obliged to flee to Paris, carrying with him the archives and valuables belonging to his diocese, till nearly the middle of the last century, the citizens of Glasgow generally displayed not a few of those ascetic and morose characteristics which belonged to the purest cast of the Puritans; while, in the earlier days of their Protestant career, they made choice of the very antithesis of everything practised by other Christian communities. In particular, they regarded Art, in her character of the handmaiden of Religion, as altogether sinful and detestable, and would have willingly followed to the letter the conduct of the other architectural spoliators in Scotland, had they not been prevented, by the worthy craftsmen of the City, from pulling down the only Scottish Cathedral which still happily remains, in all its pristine beauty, as the best monument of the taste of our ancestors.

It will not be difficult to comprehend how anything in the least degree allied to the exhibitions once so universally practised in all Roman Catholic countries, first by monks and friars, and thereafter by laymen, would be at all tolerated by a people imbued with the moody and morose temperament which the ascetic and self-denying creed, then so generally adopted by Glasgow citizens, must have naturally engendered and maintained. The result, in fact, was, that such *Mysteries* as those of Coventry, which at one time had been the delight of all whose habitations encircled an Episcopal or Archiepiscopal palace – as well as the later dramatic exhibitions of 'Robin Hood' and the 'Abbot of Unreason,' and other more mundane affairs, not only soon ceased – but what was more, their successors, as exhibited in the plays of Ben Johnson, Ford, and Shakespeare, were regarded as little less than an abomination and a sin. The truth is, that while in the sister kingdom the theatre had been long patronised and encouraged, not only by the Court but by the people, we find that in Scotland there were no regular stage-plays performed, even in the Scottish capital, during the Augustan age of Queen Anne. In short, it was not till after the turmoil occasioned by the Union and the Rebellion of 1715 had passed away, that players would be listened to in Scotland. We find, therefore, that the drama was not re-introduced into Edinburgh till about the year 1727, when it was first tried in the Tailors' Hall, Cowgate, and thereafter, in 1746, on the boards of the Canongate theatre. In Glasgow, it appears, there was no effort made to re-introduce what Voltaire calls the 'chef d'œuvre de la société', (if we except the itinerant performances attempted in Burrel's Hall, on the east side of upper High Street, in 1750) till the year 1752, when a wooden theatre was erected within the precincts of the Castle-yard, and attached to the ruined walls of the episcopal palace. Within this humble and miserable building, so unlike the gorgeous halls now dedicated to Thalia and Thespis, had the then denizens of Glasgow an opportunity of first listening to a British drama, and of gazing on such celebrities of the day as Digges, Love, Stamper, and Mrs Ward! The histrionic efforts of those persons, however, were unable to cope with the prejudices engendered by the Puritanical preaching of the period against all such pastimes, particularly among the lower orders of the people; and, moreover, as it happened that the celebrated George Whitefield had arrived about that time, and was holding forth in the immediate neighbourhood of what he designated the 'temple of Satan', a feeling was roused in the vulgar mind to such an extent against the erection, that the excited populace attacked it with stones and other missiles, if not to its destruction at least to its injury.

If such be an index to the feelings of the great mass of the inhabitants of Glasgow, with respect to the stage, in the year 1752, it appears that these had not materially altered ten years afterwards; for, although five of the leading gentlemen of the City then agreed to erect a theatre at their own expense, such was the prejudice then existing against the acted drama, that not a single individual who had ground within the Burgh would grant them a site. They were obliged, in consequence, to go in search of one beyond the royalty; and having at last obtained a piece of ground in Alston Street, a theatre was erected thereon, and was ready to be opened in the spring of 1764. The proprietors thereupon entered into arrangements with the Edinburgh company, the opening night was fixed, and the celebrated Mrs Bellamy was announced for the occasion. Previous to the night of opening, however, the theatre was wilfully set fire to, through the preaching of a Methodist, who, among other things, told his hearers that he had dreamed, the preceeding night, that he was in the infernal regions at a grand entertainment, where all the devils in hell were present – when Lucifer, their chief, gave for a toast the health of Mr Miller, who had sold his ground to build him a house upon! While the infuriated fire-raisers, upon this instigation, fearlessly proceeded to carry into effect what they deemed a duty to Heaven, it was fortunate that they only partially succeeded in their project of destruction; the stage and the theatrical wardrobe being the chief loss sustained through the frantic and disgraceful arson. In spite, however, of the destruction of these most important parts of the theatre, the manager made a bold effort to open his house on the day fixed; and having fortunately got a temporary stage erected, the curtain rose for the play of the *Citizen*, and the farce of the *Mock Doctor*, in which Mrs Bellamy, Mr Reddoch, and Mr Aiken took the prominent parts.

From this period till 1780 this theatre was successively managed by Mr Ross, the lessee of the Edinburgh company, by a Mr Williams, and by Mr Wilkinson of York; and, just when it was about to be opened by Messrs Bland, Mills, and Jackson, it was burned to the ground. This unfortunate event took place on 5th May, 1780, and it has always been alleged, and certainly not without very good reason, that it owed its destruction to design, and to the rancorous hatred that still lingered in the minds of a certain class of the people against the stage and its abettors. The proprietors of the ground on which the theatre stood, having stated that it was not their intention to rebuild it, Mr Jackson, who had been its lessee, at once decided on erecting one at his own cost and on his own responsibility; and, with that view, he purchased a site in Dunlop Street, and proceeded in making arrangements for the building. In this, however, he met with difficulties, arising from the prejudices of some of the proprietors in its immediate neighbourhood, and from the fear that such a building would injure the value of their adjoining tenements. But, although the objections urged showed the narrow-mindedness which then existed, they were found too futile to hinder him from going on with his undertaking. The consequence was that the foundation-stone of the Dunlop Street theatre was laid on the 17th February, 1781, and the house was opened in January 1782.

From this time, whether from the altered opinions of the people, or from the judicious management of Mr Jackson, it appears that the theatre became more and more patronised; and well was it worthy of the support of every admirer of the dramatic and histrionic art. Never, perhaps, were the dramas of Shakespeare, the tragedies of Otway and Rowe, or the comedies of Cumberland and Sheridan, produced more effectively than on these boards, and never were the characters better sustained. When we mention that, many times and oft, Mrs Siddons, the Kembles, and George Frederick Cooke enacted the leading personages of the Tragic, while Mrs Jordan, Miss Farren, Miss Duncan, Mr King, Jack Bannister, Rock, and Irish Johnston, were the representatives of the Comic muse, on the Dunlop Street stage, it will be readily conceived how so many in Glasgow were then found to acknowledge the truth of one of Thomson's 'Winter' amusements, when he says:

Dread o'er the scene the ghost of Hamlet stalks,
Othello rages, poor Monimia mourns,
And Belvidera pours her soul in love;
Terror alarms the breast; the comely tear
Steals on the cheek; or else the comic muse
Holds to the world a picture of itself,
And raises sly the fair impartial laugh.

Although Mr Jackson from time to time endeavoured both to improve and enlarge the Dunlop Street theatre, it was found, soon after the commencement of the present century, to be altogether too small and paltry for the growing theatrical taste of Glasgow. The consequence was that a subscription was opened for the erection of a more spacious house; and, in the course of a very short time, no less a sum than £7,000 was raised for this purpose. Ground was at once feued from the Corporation, near the head of Queen Street, for a site; and an edifice was erected thereon, which, whether for exterior or interior elegance, was scarcely surpassed by any of the London theatres, and for which a patent was obtained from the Crown. This house was opened by a most excellent company in 1804; and it is only just to say, that from the time when the curtain first rose till 1829 – when it was shrivelled up amid the flames which consumed the house, and reduced all within to ashes – theatrical 'stars' were not lacking to wake the feelings or rouse the laughter of those who visited it. It was here that Kean first enunciated in Scotland, amid breathless silence; 'Now is the winter of our discontent made glorious summer!' – that Miss O'Neil, as *Mrs Beverly*, roused the feelings to such a pitch, as nightly to cause ladies to be carried out insensible from the boxes – that Miss Stevens's syren voice first charmed the Glasgow musicante – that John Sinclair aided her in the duets in *Rob Roy* and *Guy Mannering* – that Miss M. Tree drew forth a never-failing encore after her 'Home, sweet home!' – and that Madame Catalani first, and many times afterwards, exhibited the powers of her unrivalled vocalisation, and excited that never-to-be-forgotten burst of patriotic approbation, when pouring out, in triumphant notes, above band and chorus, 'Britannia rules the waves!'

After the destruction of the theatre in Queen Street, the Dunlop Street theatre, which latterly afforded two places of amusement, was purchased by Mr J.H. Alexander, who, having also acquired the patent, commenced its improvement, and reopened it on the 14th December, 1829. The following are one or two stanzas taken from the prologue, written for the occasion by Mr William Anderson of the *Glasgow Courier*:

And now the stage, too long upon the wane,
Here, where your fathers met, resumes its reign;
Here, Young and Kemble charm'd the admiring age;
Here, Siddons swept, like glory, o'er the stage.
Within these walls your father felt the mind,
That roused to rapture, and entranced mankind.

The renewed taste which had gradually sprung up for the public stage, had also excited within the breasts of several of the citizens, at least the younger portion of them, a love for private theatricals. Even during the last century there were but few parents who permitted their sons and daughters to enact the tragedy of *Douglas*, or the Scottish drama of the *Gentle Shepherd*; while, about the commencement of the present century, we remember several distinct bands of private performers who really got up some of the plays of Shakespeare, and more particularly the '*Miller of Mansfield*' and the '*Vintner in the Suds*,' in a very creditable manner, not forgetting all the adjuncts of scenery, footlights, and music. With the progress of the century the love for this pastime seems to have increased; for we find that, in the year 1828, this species of entertainment – which was at one time so liberally patronised by the early sovereigns of England, and so fondly practised by its gay and gallant aristocracy – was successfully exhibited in the mansion of a gentleman living in the neighbourhood and intimately connected with Glasgow. We allude to a temporary stage which was tastefully erected in the dining-room of Craigend Castle, at that time possessed by Mr James Smith, and to the histrionic talents of a fashionable party of amateurs of the 'sock and buskin', who were assembled in that hospitable house, to enact *How to Shy Her*, a five-act comedy, written for the occasion by Mr Alexander Dunlop of Clober, who, with the spirit of an Alfieri, played the hero of his own piece, and received as many plaudits from the gay group of listeners who crowded the boxes and pit of the elegant saloon, as had been bestowed on the poet of Asti by the pope, the princes and cardinals who attended the private representation of *Saul*. The drama thus introduced into private society, created, at the time, no little gossip and some little squeamishness, upon the part of those who were accustomed to breathe a pure Calvinistic atmosphere; but, upon the whole, the practical result of introducing theatricals into the domestic circle was felt to be productive of no more injury to public morals or private delicacy than any other recreation incident to our social intercourse. To all lovers of the histrionic art, it must never be forgotten that, to a private theatre and to private actors, the drama owes as much as to the public stage and to hired players. The Italian comedy might, perhaps, never have existed, had it not been fostered by the princes, the marquises, the counts, and even the cardinals of past ages. The French theatre, too, is equally indebted for its progress to the taste of its monarchs and the passion of its nobility for private *spectacles*. While the British drama might very probably have remained in a state little removed from the mere pageantry of the mask, had not Thalia been welcomed at Windsor, and the Arundels, Cliffords and Howards, of former days been proud to 'saw the air' as her votaries. Many of our earliest plays, indeed, were written for the temporary proscenium of some private mansion; and not a few of the latest successful efforts of the dramatic muse were first enacted by private performers.

'Intellectual Life in Eighteenth-Century Glasgow'

from Autobiography

ALEXANDER CARLYLE (1722–1805)

Alexander Carlyle's Autobiography *is one of the best and liveliest sources for information on social, cultural and intellectual life in eighteenth-century Scotland. Alexander Carlyle, or 'Jupiter' Carlyle as he was frequently called (a reference to his having sat as a model for the King of the Gods to the Scottish artist, Gavin Hamilton) was the son of the Minister of Prestonpans in East Lothian and spent almost sixty years as Minister of Inveresk Parish in Musselburgh.*

After attending Edinburgh University, Carlyle went to Glasgow University in the winter of 1743 and he gives a valuable account of academic and social life in the Glasgow of the day. It is interesting to note that the distinctions between Edinburgh and Glasgow seem to have been well established, even then. Carlyle reflects on the superiority of an Edinburgh education, not so much in learning as in: '. . . knowledge of the world, and a certain manner and address that can only be obtained in the capital'. Carlyle's strictures on the residents of Glasgow being far behind Edinburgh: '. . . not only in their manner of living, but in those accomplishments and tastes that belong to people of opulence, much more to persons of education', should perhaps be taken with some reserve. Glasgow's tastes in architecture were, for example, remarkably advanced. One of the first examples of the Palladian villa in Britain – Shawfield, in the Trongate – had been built in 1712 for Daniel Campbell. After a Glasgow mob sacked the villa in 1725 (over Campbell's support for the extension of the Malt Tax to Scotland) it was sold to one of Glasgow's prosperous West Indian merchants. Shawfield was to be the temporary home of Prince Charles Edward Stuart when he stayed in Glasgow on his retreat from England in 1745.

The University (or College as it was then generally known) that Carlyle attended was, of course, the old foundation in the High Street, in the ancient heart of the city near the Cathedral. The Glasgow of his day was still a small, though increasingly prosperous, town. Carlyle tells of Robert Simpson, the Professor of Mathematics, who almost never left the College grounds, except on a Saturday to walk into the country, to the village of Anderston. The 'village of Anderston', which was laid out in 1725 and was created a burgh in 1824, has of course has long since been swallowed up by the westward development of the city, being annexed by Glasgow in 1846.

INTELLECTUAL LIFE IN EIGHTEENTH-CENTURY GLASGOW

In November 1743 I went to Glasgow, much more opportunely than I should have done the preceding year, for the old Professor of Divinity, Mr Potter, who had been a very short while there, died in the week I went to College; and his chair, being in the gift of the University, was immediately filled by Mr William Leechman, a neighbouring clergyman, a person thoroughly well qualified for the office, of which he gave the most satisfactory proof for a great many years that he continued Professor of Theology, which was till the death of Principal Neil Campbell* raised him to the head of the University. He was a distinguished preacher, and was followed when he was occasionally in Edinburgh. His appearance was that of an ascetic, reduced by fasting and prayer; but in aid of fine composition he delivered his sermons with such fervent spirit, and in so persuasive a manner, as captivated every audience.† This was so much the case that his admirers regretted that he should be withdrawn from the pulpit, for the Professor of Theology has no charge in Glasgow, and preaches only occasionally. It was much for the good of the Church, however, that he was raised to a station of more extensive usefulness; for while his interesting manner drew the steady attention of the students, the judicious choice and arrangement of his matter formed the most instructive set of lectures on theology that had, it was thought, ever been delivered in Scotland. It was no doubt, owing to him and his friend and colleague Mr Hutcheson, Professor of Moral Philosophy, that a better taste and greater liberality of sentiment were introduced among the clergy in the western provinces of Scotland.

Able as this gentleman was, however, and highly unexceptionable not only in morals but in decorum of behaviour, he was not allowed to ascend

* Mr Neil Campbell was minister of Roseneath, and through Argyll influence was appointed Principal of Glasgow University in 1728 in succession to Principal Stirling. He died in 1761.

† A portrait of Leechman from a painting by W. Millar, very characteristic, and in harmony with this description, is prefixed to an edition of his Sermons: London, 2 vols. 8vo, 1789. – J.H.B.

his chair without much opposition, and even a prosecution for heresy. Invulnerable as he seemed to be, the keen and prying eye of fanaticism discovered a weak place, to which they directed their attacks. There had been published at Glasgow, or in the neighbourhood of Dr Leechman's church, in the country, before he came to Glasgow, about that period, a small pamphlet against the use of prayer, which had circulated amongst the inferior ranks, and had made no small impression, being artfully composed. To counteract this poison Leechman had composed and published his sermon on the nature, reasonableness, and advantages of prayer; with an attempt to answer the objections against it, from Matthew, xxvi. 41. In this sermon, though admirably well composed, in defence of prayer as a duty of natural religion, the author had forgot, or omitted to state the obligations on Christians to pray in the name of Christ. The nature of his subject did not lead him to state this part of a Christian's prayer, and perhaps he thought that the inserting anything relative to that point might disgust or lessen the curiosity of those for whose conviction he had published the sermon. The fanatical or high-flying clergy in the presbytery of Glasgow took advantage of this omission and instituted an inquiry into the heresy contained in this sermon by omission, which lasted with much theological acrimony on the part of the inquirers (who were chiefly those who had encouraged Cambuslang's work, as it was called, two years before), till it was finally settled in favour of the Professor by the General Assembly of 1744.* Instead of raising any anxiety among the students in theology, or creating any suspicion of Dr Leechman's orthodoxy, this fit of zeal against him tended much to spread and establish his superior character.

I attended Hutcheson's class this year with great satisfaction and improvement. He was a good-looking man, of an engaging countenance. He delivered his lectures without notes walking backwards and forwards in the area of his room. As his elocution was good, and his voice and manner pleasing, he raised the attention of his hearers at all times; and when the subject led him to explain and enforce the moral virtues and duties he displayed a fervent and persuasive eloquence which was irresistible. Besides the lectures he gave through the week, he, every Sunday at six o'clock, opened his class-room to whoever chose to attend, when he delivered a set of lectures on *Grotius de veritate Religionis Christianæ*, which, though learned and ingenious, were adapted to every

* *Cambuslang's Work*: Revivals in the Parish of Cambuslang in Lanarkshire in the year 1742. They were the occasion of abundant controversy; but the fullest account of them will be found in *Narrative of the extraordinary Work of the Spirit of God at Cambuslang, Kilsyth, etc.*, written by Mr James Robe and others. – J.H.B.

capacity; for on that evening he expected to be attended, not only by students, but by many of the people of the city; and he was not disappointed, for this free lecture always drew crowds of attendants.

Besides Hutcheson and Leechman, there were at that period several eminent professors in that University; particularly Mr Robert Simson, the great mathematician, and Mr Alexander Dunlop, the Professor of Greek. The last, besides his eminence as a Greek scholar, was distinguished by his strong good sense and capacity for business; and being a man of a leading mind, was supposed, with the aid of Hutcheson, to direct and manage all the affairs of the University (for it is a wealthy corporation, and has much business), besides the charge of presiding over literature, and maintaining the discipline of the College.

One difference I remarked between this University and that of Edinburgh, where I had been bred, which was, that although at that time there appeared to be a marked superiority in the best scholars and most diligent students of Edinburgh, yet in Glasgow, learning seemed to be an object of more importance, and the habit of application was much more general. Besides the instruction I received from Drs Hutcheson and Leechman, I derived much pleasure, as well as enlargement of skill in the Greek language, from Mr Dunlop's translations and criticisms of the great tragic writers in that language. I likewise attended the Professor of Hebrew, a Mr Morthland,* who was master of his business. I had neglected that branch in Edinburgh, the professor being then superannuated.

In the second week I was in Glasgow I went to the dancing assembly with some of my new acquaintances and was there introduced to a married lady who claimed kindred with me, her mother's name being Carlyle, of the Limekiln family. She carried me home to sup with her that night, with a brother of hers, two years younger than me, and some other young people. This was the commencement of an intimate friendship that lasted during the whole of the lady's life, which was four or five and twenty years. She was connected with all the best families in Glasgow and the country round. Her husband was a good sort of man, and very opulent; and as they had no children, he took pleasure in her exercising a genteel hospitality. I became acquainted with all the best families in the town by this lady's means; and by a letter I had procured from my friend James Edgar, afterwards a Commissioner of the Customs, I also soon became well acquainted with all the young ladies who lived in the College. He had studied law the preceding year at Glasgow, under

* Mr Charles Morthland was appointed to the chair of Oriental languages in 1709, and held it till his death in 1744.

Professor Hercules Lindsay,* at that time of some note. On asking him for a letter of introduction to some one of his companions, he gave me one to Miss Mally Campbell, the daughter of the Principal; and when I seemed surprised at his choice, he added that I would find her not only more beautiful than any woman there, but more sensible and friendly than all the professors put together, and much more useful to me. This I found to be literally true.

The city of Glasgow at this time, though very industrious, wealthy, and commercial, was far inferior to what it afterwards became,† both before and after the failure of the Virginia trade. The modes of life, too, and manners, were different from what they are at present. Their chief branches were the tobacco trade with the American colonies;‡ and sugar and rum with the West India. There were not manufacturers sufficient, either there or at Paisley, to supply an outward-bound cargo for Virginia. For this purpose they were obliged to have recourse to Manchester. Manufacturers were in their infancy. About this time the inkle manufactory§ was first begun by Ingram & Glasford,** and was shown to strangers as a great curiosity. But the merchants had industry and stock, and the habits of business, and were ready to seize with eagerness, and prosecute with vigour, every new object in commerce or manufactures that promised success.

Few of them could be called learned merchants; yet there was a weekly club, of which a Provost Cochrane was the founder and a leading member, in which their express design was to inquire into the nature and principles of trade in all its branches, and to communicate their knowledge and views on that subject to each other. I was not acquainted with Provost Cochrane at this time, but I observed that the members of this society had the highest admiration of his knowledge and talents. I became well acquainted with him twenty years afterwards, when Drs Smith and Wight were members of the club, and was made sensible that

* Professor Hercules Lindsay was the first Professor of Law to deliver lectures on the *Institutes of Justinian* in English.

† 'In a word, 'tis one of the cleanest, most beautiful, and best built cities in Great Britain.' – Defoe's *Tour*, 1727.

'Glasgow is, to outward appearance, the prettiest and most uniform town that I have ever seen, and I believe there is nothing like it in Britain.' – Burt's *Letters from the North of Scotland* (published 1754).

‡ 'The tobacco lords distinguished themselves by a particular dress, like their Venetian and Genovese predecessors, in scarlet cloaks, curled wigs, cocked hats, and bearing golds-headed canes.' – Strang's *Glasgow and its Clubs*.

§ Inkle manufacture was introduced in 1732 by Mr Alexander Harvey, who brought over from Haarlem two looms and a Dutch workman.

** Messrs Ingram started the first calico print-field at Pollockshaws about 1742.

too much could not be said of his accurate and extensive knowledge, of his agreeable manners, and colloquial eloquence. Dr Smith acknowledged his obligations to this gentleman's information, when he was collecting materials for his *Wealth of Nations*; and the junior merchants who have flourished since his time, and extended their commerce far beyond what was then dreamt of, confess, with respectful remembrance, that it was Andrew Cochrane who first opened and enlarged their views.*

It was not long before I was well established in close intimacy with many of my fellow-students, and soon felt the superiority of an education in the College of Edinburgh; not in point of knowledge, or acquirements in the languages or sciences, but in knowledge of the world, and a certain manner and address that can only be attained in the capital. It must be confessed that at this time they were far behind in Glasgow, not only in their manner of living, but in those accomplishments and that taste belong to people of opulence, much more to persons of education. There were only a few families of ancient citizens who pretended to be gentlemen; and a few others, who were recent settlers there, who had obtained wealth and consideration in trade. The rest were shopkeepers and mechanics, or successful pedlars, who occupied larger warerooms full of manufactures of all sorts, to furnish a cargo to Virginia. It was usual for the sons of merchants to attend the College for one or two years, and a few of them completed their academical education. In this respect the females were still worse off, for at that period there was neither a teacher of French nor of music in the town. The consequence of this was twofold; first, the young ladies were entirely without accomplishments, and in general had nothing to recommend them but good looks and fine clothes, for their manners were ungainly. Secondly, the few who were distinguished drew all the young men of sense and taste about them; for, being void of frivolous accomplishments, which in some respects make all women equal, they trusted only to superior understanding and wit, to natural elegance and unaffected manners.

There never was but one concert during the two winters I was at Glasgow, and that was given by Walter Scott, Esq. of Harden, who was himself an eminent performer on the violin; and his band of assistants consisted of two dancing-school fiddlers and the town-waits.

The manner of living, too, at this time, was but coarse and vulgar. Very few of the wealthiest gave dinners to anybody but English riders, or their own relations at Christmas holidays. There were not half-a-dozen

* For information regarding Cochrane, Simson, and the other Glasgow celebrities mentioned in this chapter, the reader is referred to *Glasgow and its Clubs*, by Dr Strang, and to the *Cochrane Correspondence*, printed in 1836 for the Maitland Club.

families in town who had men-servants; some of those were kept by the professors who had boarders. There were neither post-chaises or hackney-coaches in the town, and only three or four sedan-chairs for carrying midwives about in the night, and old ladies to church, or to the dancing assemblies once a fortnight.

The principal merchants, fatigued with the morning's business, took an early dinner with their families at home, and then resorted to the coffeehouse or tavern to read the newspapers, which they generally did in companies of four to five in separate rooms, over a bottle of claret or a bowl of punch. But they never stayed supper, but always went home by nine o'clock, without company or further amusement. At last an arch fellow from Dublin, a Mr Cockaine, came to be master of the chief coffeehouse, who seduced them gradually to stay supper by placing a few nice cold things at first on the table, as relishers to the wine, till he gradually led them on to bespeak fine hot suppers, and to remain till midnight.

There was an order of women at that time in Glasgow, who, being either young widows not wealthy, or young women unprovided for, were set up in small grocery-shops in various parts of the town, and generally were protected and countenanced by some creditable merchant. In their back shops much time and money were consumed; for it being customary then to drink drams and white wine in the forenoon, the tipplers restored much to those shops, where there were bedrooms; and the patron, with his friends, frequently passed the evening there also, as taverns were not frequented by persons who affected characters of strict decency.

I was admitted a member of two clubs, one entirely literary, which was held in the porter's lodge at the College, and where we criticised books and wrote abridgements of them, with critical essays; and to this society we submitted the discourses which we were to deliver in the Divinity Hall in our turns, when we were appointed by the professor. The other club met in Mr Dugald's tavern near the Cross, weekly, and admitted a mixture of young gentlemen who were not intended for the study of theology. There met there John Bradefoot, afterwards minister of Dunsire; James Leslie, of Kilmarnock; John Robertson, of Dunblane; James Hamilton, of Paisley; and Robert Lawson, of London Wall. There also came some young merchants, such as Robin Bogle, my relation; James and George Anderson, William Sellar and Robin Craig. Here we drank a little punch after our beefsteaks and pancakes, and the expense never exceeded 1s. 6d., seldom 1s.

Our conversation was almost entirely literary; and we were of such good fame, that some ministers of the neighbourhood, when occasionally in Glasgow, frequented our club. Hyndman had been twice introduced by members; and being at that time passing his trials as a probationer before that presbytery in which his native town of Greenock lay, he had become well acquainted with Mr Robert Paton, minister of Renfrew, who, though a man well accomplished and of liberal sentiments, was too much a man of worth and principle not to be offended by licentious manners in students of divinity. Hyndman, by way of gaining favour with this man, took occasion to hint to him to advise his nephew, Robert Lawson, not to frequent our club, as it admitted and encouraged conversation not suitable to the profession we were to follow. He mentioned two instances, one of which Lawson said was false, and the other disguised by exaggeration. Lawson, who was a lad of pure morals, told me this; and as the best antidote to this injurious impression, which had been made chiefly against me, I begged him to let his uncle know that I would accept of the invitation he had given through him, to pass a night or two with him at Renfrew. We accordingly went next Saturday, and met with a gracious reception, and stayed all next day and heard him preach, at which he was thought to excel (though he was almost the only person who read in those days, in which he truly excelled); and being a very handsome man, his delivery much enhanced the value of his composition. We heard him read another sermon at night in his study, with much satisfaction, as he told us it was one of his best, and was a good model; to this we respectfully assented, and the good man was pleased. When we took leave on Monday morning, he politely requested another visit, and said to me, with a smile, he was now fortified against tale-bearers. These societies contributed much to our improvement; and as moderation and early hours were inviolable rules of both institutions, they served to open and enlarge our minds.

Towards the end of the session, however, I was introduced to a club which gave me much more satisfaction – I mean that of Mr Robert Simson,* the celebrated Professor of Mathematics. Mr Robert Dick, Professor of Natural Philosophy, an old friend of my father's, one evening after I had dined with him, said he was going to Mr Robert's club, and if I had a mind, he would take me there and introduce me. I readily accepted the honour. I had been introduced to Mr Robert before in the College court, for he was extremely courteous, and showed civility to every student who fell in his way. Though I was not attending any of his classes, having attended M'Laurin in Edinburgh for three sessions, he received me with great kindness; and I had the good fortune to please him so much,

* Dr Robert Simson was born in 1689 at Kirktonhall, Ayrshire, and was elected to the chair of Mathematics in Glasgow University in 1711. He died in 1768.

that he asked me to be a member of his Friday's club,* which I readily agreed to. Mr Simson, though a great humorist, who had a very particular way of living, was well-bred and complaisant, was a comely man, of a good size, and had a very prepossessing countenance. He lived entirely at the small tavern opposite the College gate, kept by a Mrs Millar. He breakfasted, dined, and supped there, and almost never accepted of any invitations to dinner, and paid no visits, but to illustrious or learned strangers, who wished to see the University; on such occasions he was always the cicerone. He showed the curiosities of the College, which consisted of a few manuscripts and a large collection of Roman antiquities, from Severus' Wall or Graham's Dyke, in the neighbourhood, with a display of much knowledge and taste. He was particularly averse to the company of ladies, and, except one day in the year, when he drank tea at Principal Campbell's, and conversed with gaiety and ease with his daughter Mally, who was always his first toast, he was never in company with them. It was said to have been otherwise with him in his youth, and that he had been much attached to one lady, to whom he had made proposals, but on her refusing him he became disgusted with the sex. The lady was dead before I became acquainted with the family, but her husband I knew, and must confess that in her choice the lady had preferred a satyr to Hyperion.

Mr Simson almost never left the bounds of the College, having a large garden to walk in, unless it was on Saturday, when, with two chosen companions, he always walked into the country, but no farther than the village of Anderston, one mile off, where he had a dinner bespoke, and where he always treated the company, not only when he had no other than his two humble attendants, but when he casually added one or two more, which happened twice to myself. If any of the club met him on Saturday night at his hotel, he took it very kind, for he was in good spirits, though fatigued with the company of his satellites, and revived on the sight of a fresh companion or two for the evening. He was of a mild temper and an engaging demeanour, and was master of all knowledge, even of theology, which he told us he had learned by being one year amanuensis to his uncle, the Professor of Divinity.† His knowledge he delivered in an easy colloquial style, with the simplicity of a child, and without the least symptom of self-sufficiency or arrogance.

* Some ten years later than the date of Dr Carlyle's visit to the Friday Club, Professor Simson founded the Anderston Club at an hostelry in the village of that name kept by 'ane God-fearing host – John Sharpe.' Among the members of this club were Adam Smith, Professor Leechman, Professor Dick, Robert Bogle, David Hume, and other of Caryle's friends. – Strang's *Glasgow and its Clubs*.

† Professor John Simson.

His club at that time consisted chiefly of Hercules Lindsay, Teacher of Law, who was talkative and assuming; of James Moore, Professor of Greek on the death of Mr Dunlop,* a very lively and witty man, and a famous Grecian,† but a more famous punster; Mr Dick, Professor of Natural Philosophy, a very worthy man, and of an agreeable temper; and Mr James Purdie, the rector of the grammar-school,‡ who had not much to recommend him but his being an adept in grammar. Having ben asked to see a famous comet that appeared this winter or the following, through Professor Dick's telescope, which was the best in the College at that time, when Mr Purdie retired from taking his view of it he turned to Mr Simson and said, 'Mr Robert, I believe it is *hic* or *hæc cometa*, a comet.' To settle the gender of the Latin was all he thought of this great and uncommon phenomenon of nature.

Mr Simson's most constant attendant, however, and greatest favourite, was his own scholar, Mr Mathew Stewart, afterwards Professor of Mathematics in the College of Edinburgh, much celebrated for his profound knowledge in that science. During the course of summer he was ordained minister of Roseneath, but resided during the winter in Glasgow College. He was of an amiable disposition and of a most ingenuous mind, and was highly valued in the society of Glasgow University; but when he was preferred to a chair in Edinburgh, being of diminutive stature and of an ordinary appearance, and having withal an embarrassed elocution, he was not able to bring himself into good company; and being left out of the society of those who should have seen through the shell, and put a due value on the kernel, he fell into company of an inferior sort, and adopted their habits with too great facility.§

With this club, and an accidental stranger at times, the great Mr Robert Simson relaxed his mind every evening from the severe studies of the day; for though there was properly but one club night in the week, yet, as he

* Mr Dunlop had the power of 'giving to his pupils a taste and stimulus for the work of the class, vital enough to impel them to prosecute the study from a love of it in after life.' – Stewart's *Glasgow University, Old and New*.

† 'When interpreting Homer to his class, he [Dr Moore] never looked at the book, and from numerous references which he made to parallel passages in his favourite author, it appeared that he could repeat most accurately the whole *Iliad* or *Odyssey*.' – Bower's *History of Edinburgh University*.

‡ The Grammar School stood in Greyfriars' Wynd, formerly Grammar School Wynd, on the west side of the High Street. It was built in 1601 and abandoned in 1782 for a new building in George Street.

§ Writing of Professor Stewart after he became professor at Edinburgh, the Rev. Dr Somerville says: 'He was of a disposition so bashful and sensitive that the slightest irregularity or approach to rudeness in the behaviour of the students disconcerted him. The misconduct of any of these boys – for such most of his pupils were – instead of meeting with a reproof from the professor, made him blush like a child.' – *Memoirs of My Life and Times*.

never failed to be there, some one or two commonly attended him, or at least one of the two minions whom he could command at any time, as he paid their reckoning.

The fame of Mr Hutcheson had filled the College with students of philosophy, and Leechman's high character brought all the students of divinity from the western provinces, as Hutcheson attracted the Irish. There were sundry young gentlemen from Ireland, with their tutors, one of whom was Archibald M'Laine, pastor at the Hague, the celebrated translator of Mosheim's *Ecclesiastical History* (who had himself been bred at Glasgow College). With him I became better acquainted next session, and I have often regretted since that it has never been my lot to meet him during the many times I have been for months in London, as his enlightened mind, engaging manners, and animated conversation gave reason to hope for excellent fruit when he arrived at maturity. There were of young men of fashion attending the College, Walter Lord Blantyre,* who died young; Sir Thomas Kennedy, and his brother David, afterwards Lord Cassilis;† Walter Scott of Harden; James Murray of Broughton; and Dunbar Hamilton, afterwards Earl of Selkirk. The education of this last gentleman had been marred at an English academy in Yorkshire. When his father, the Hon. Basil Hamilton, died, he came to Glasgow, but finding that he was so ill founded in Latin as to be unfit to attend a public class, he had resolution enough, at the age of fifteen, to pass seven or eight hours a day with Purdie the grammarian for the greater part of two years, when, having acquired Latin, he took James Moore, the Greek scholar, for his private tutor, fitted up rooms for himself in the College, and lived there with Moore in the most retired manner, visiting nobody but Miss M. Campbell, and letting nobody in to him but Lord Blantyre and myself, as I was his distant relation. In this manner he lived for ten years, hardly leaving the College for a few weeks in summer, till he had acquired the ancient tongues in perfection, and was master of ancient philosophy: the effect of which was, that with much rectitude and good intention, and some talent, he came into the world more fit to be a Professor than an Earl.

* Walter, eighth Lord Blantyre. He had a reputation as a scholar, and 'has the sweetest temper in the world, and to all appearance will be a very great honour to his country.' He, however, died in 1751 at the age of twenty-five.

† David, tenth Earl of Cassillis. Passed Advocate in 1751, and succeeded his brother Sir Thomas in 1776.

'Glasgow'

WILLIAM MCGONAGALL (1825–1902)

While William Topaz McGonagall is perhaps better remembered for his celebrations of Dundee and the 'silvery Tay' he also turned his deathless pen to the praise of Glasgow, and no celebration of this 'city of culture' would surely be complete without McGonagall's survey of civic sculpture. Those wishing to compare notes with McGonagall should note that the statue of William III was moved from the Trongate in 1923 and may now be found in Cathedral Square. The fountain McGonagall praises in Kelvingrove Park is the Stewart Memorial Fountain, dating from 1872, and celebrates the arrival of the city's pure water supply from Loch Katrine in 1859.

GLASGOW

Beautiful city of Glasgow, with your streets so neat and clean,
Your stately mansions, and beautiful Green!
Likewise your beautiful bridges across the river Clyde,
And on your bonnie banks I would like to reside.

Chorus:
Then away to the West – to the beautiful West!
To the fair city of Glasgow that I like the best,
Where the river Clyde rolls on to the sea,
And the lark and blackbird whistle with glee.

'Tis beautiful to see the ships passing to and fro,
Laden with goods for the high and the low;
So let the beautiful city of Glasgow flourish,
And may the inhabitants always find food their bodies to nourish.

The statue of the Prince of Orange is very grand,
Looking terror to the foe, with a truncheon in his hand,
And well mounted on a noble steed, which stands in the Trongate,
And holding up its foreleg, I'm sure it looks first-rate.

Then there's the Duke of Wellington's statue in Royal Exchange
Square –
It is a beautiful statue I without fear declare,
Besides inspiring and most magnificent to view,
Because he made the French fly at the battle of Waterloo.

And as for the statue of Sir Walter Scott that stands in George's
Square,
It is a handsome statue – few can with it compare,
And most elegant to be seen,
And close beside it stands the statue of Her Majesty the Queen.

Then there's the statue of Robert Burns in George Square,
And the treatment he received when living was very unfair;
Now, when he's dead, Scotland's sons for him do mourn,
But, alas! unto them he can never return.

Then as for Kelvin Grove, it is most lovely to be seen
With its beautiful flowers and trees so green.
And a magnificent water-fountain spouting up very high,
Where people can quench their thirst when they feel dry.

Beautiful city of Glasgow, I now conclude my muse,
And to write in praise of thee my pen does not refuse;
And, without fear of contradiction, I will venture to say
You are the second grandest city in Scotland at the present day!

'Progress in Art'

from Glimpses of Old Glasgow

ANDREW AIRD (1819–189?)

Andrew Aird published his reminiscences of life in Glasgow and the changing face of his native city, Glimpses of Old Glasgow, *in 1894. It is now conventional wisdom that Glasgow has arguably the finest civic art collection in Britain and the popularity of the Glasgow school of painting grows ever greater. Aird's account of the early days of the city's collection, particularly the role of the gift of Archibald McLellan, and of the development of artistic life and artistic organisations in Glasgow, sets this story in context.*

It is particularly interesting to note that Aird, writing as a septuagenarian in 1894, was sufficiently open to new tendencies to applaud the current state of art in the city. He enthuses about the 'vigorous' School of Art and the young artists: 'known and esteemed all over the world for the boldness and originality of their conceptions, and the power with which they express their ideas'. The School of Art, founded in 1840, had entered on a new lease of life with the appointment in 1885 of the visionary Fra Newberry as director.

Late nineteenth-century Glasgow saw a great flowering of artistic talent. The 'Glasgow Boys' and their associates, such as James Guthrie, W.Y. MacGregor, E.A. Walton, Joseph Crawhall and John Lavery had emerged in the 1880s and met with considerable support and patronage from Glasgow art-dealers and private collectors. They were to be followed by the group of artists, designers, craftworkers, and designers fostered by the School of Art, such as the Macdonald sisters and Charles Rennie Mackintosh, who made the 'Glasgow Style' a byword in the international avant-garde.

Neil Munro relates how in 1890 the Director of London's Grosvenor Galleries came to Glasgow to investigate the news of striking developments in the city and arranged a special show of Scottish (predominantly Glaswegian) painting in London. Many of these Glasgow paintings later transferred to an exhibition at Munich, supplemented by such key works of the Glasgow School as Lavery's Tennis Party *and George Henry's* Galloway Landscape. *In an article reprinted in* The Brave Days *Munro wrote:'The success of what was now definitely known to the*

Continent as the "Glasgow school" *called the attention of artistic circles all over the Continent to Scottish art in general.' From being something of an artistic backwater Glasgow had moved to centre stage.*

PROGRESS IN ART

The art history of Glasgow is generally assumed to date only from the period, in 1753, when the brothers Robert and Andrew Foulis, the famous printers, established their Academy of Art. Art and art patronage, there is no doubt, existed in the city before that time, and we are not without evidence of earlier appreciation and encouragement of artistic work. Limiting our remarks to painting, we find that in 1670 the Town Council ordered from London two portraits – one of Charles I, the other of the reigning monarch, Charles II, for the adornment of the Town Hall. The city was already apparently in possession of a portrait of James VII, painted in 1618; and these works, with the portraits of the later monarchs down to George III, are still with us, and may be seen in the Corporation Galleries in Sauchiehall Street. But of serious impulse towards the development of a local school of artists there was nothing till the Foulis brothers launched their long-projected scheme. The Academy continued to exist for twenty-two years – from 1753 till 1775; but, pecuniarly, its existence was disastrous. Premature and ill-starred as it was, however, its artistic outcome was not unworthy of the efforts and sacrifices of the gifted and broad-minded men who directed it. Several men who attained artistic eminence owed their training to the Foulis Academy, and of these may only be mentioned David Allan, the painter, and James Tassie, the gem engraver. Had the Academy done nothing more than develop the bent and talents of the latter gifted but imperfectly-appreciated artist, it would have justified its existence.

But the Foulis' ideas and their academy were in advance of the times in Glasgow, and for about half-a-century afterwards we hear little more of art education and encouragement. It happens that in 1812, more probably from political motives than from any artistic impulse, the city became possessed of a very remarkable statue of William Pitt, the work of John Flaxman. That work – Flaxman's *chef-d'œuvre* – we have still with us in the Corporation Galleries. It is esteemed the most successful single figure produced in modern times; and, indeed, one of the finest pieces of sculptured portraiture of any period.

In 1821 there was formed in the city an 'Institution for promoting and encouraging the Fine Arts in the West of Scotland'; but this body with the long name had but a short life, for it expired after holding two or three exhibitions. Next in 1825 there was formed the Dilettanti Society, which was endowed with more vigorous vitality. In 1828 it held its first exhibition in rooms in the Argyle Arcade: among those contributing on that occasion being John Graham, later known as John Graham Gilbert, Horatio M'Culloch, and Daniel Macneee, three young men who were destined to become well and widely known. Graham Gilbert, needing no incentive but his love of art, became one of our foremost figure painters; and the fine collection of old masters he brought together, bequeathed to the city by his widow, contains many of the gems of the Corporation Galleries. M'Culloch, at the time of his premature death, was the acknowledged chief of landscape painters in Scotland; and it need only be said of Macnee, that prince of raconteurs, that, devoting himself exclusively to portraiture, he rose to the presidential chair of the Royal Scottish Academy, and worthily wore the knighthood which accompanies that honoured position. Launched under conditions so favourable, the Dilettanti Society held five annual exhibitions in the Argyle Acade, then five others in Buchanan Street; and, in 1838, it also died of inanition.

But out of the ashes of the Dilettanti Society grew up the West of Scotland Academy – an institution devised on an ample scale with members, associates and all the lofty and exclusive privileges of a Royal Academy excepting the charter. The role it was called on to play, however, was in no way different from that of its predecessors: being a mere exhibiting body. For fourteen years – from 1840 till 1853 – it carried on a series of annual exhibitions, first in the rooms formerly occupied by the Dilettanti Society in Buchanan Street, and subsequently in the Argyle Arcade. The academy was conducted under the permanent presidency of Graham Gilbert. John Mossman, the eminent sculptor, was one of its most active promoters and supporters. Among those who rallied around it were Daniel Macnee, Robert Greenlees, A.D. Robertson, Gilfillan, and J. Milne Donald – the latter a man whose landscape art has exercised no small influence on the school of painters yet among us.

Into the management of the affairs of the West of Scotland Academy, no lay element was allowed to intrude. The body which succeeded it as organiser of exhibitions in Glasgow – the Institute of Fine Arts, which still flourishes in our midst – is composed principally of laymen; but its council consists of a mixed board of artist and lay members. As an exhibiting body its activity began in the year 1861, when its first exhibition was held in the Corporation Galleries, rented from the Parks and Galleries' Committee of the Town Council. The Institute has had, on the whole, not only a useful, but a flourishing career. It continued to occupy the Corporation Galleries with its annual exhibitions till 1879; and in 1880 was held its first exhibition in its own permanent home in Sauchiehall Street. Among its most devoted friends are to be reckoned the late John M'Gavin, who bequeathed to its funds a sum of £5,000; and Mr D.E. Outram, under whose will the institute benefited by a like amount. With a fine building, with an increasing appreciation of art among an increasing constituency, and with a vigorous and original school of local artists, the Institute of Fine Arts may well be pleased with its achievements, and content with its position.

As a factor in the art activities of Glasgow, the Art Club also deserves honourable mention. Begun in a very unpretentious manner in 1867 as a kind of sketching club, holding monthly meetings for mutual improvement and criticism, it grew continuously and gradually till it acquired a small home in Bothwell Circus. In 1886 the club was reconstituted on an enlarged basis; a lay section consisting of art amateurs was formed, the club leased commodious premises at 151 Bath Street, and there it entered on a prosperous career as a social institution. These premises were soon found to be too cramped for the necessities of the institution, and the club acquired the two houses, 187 and 189 Bath Street, which, altered and adapted in a clever manner, now form its home. Life classes are supported by the club for its artist members. Occasional lectures are delivered on art subjects, and on several occasions the club has organised special exhibitions of pictures; but the important feature of the institution is the bringing together in social intercourse, of the artists of the West of Scotland, and the influential sections of the public desirous of fostering art, and who seek the guidance of artists and experts.

Let us now go back to the time when the Dilettanti Society and the West of Scotland Academy were struggling to support and develop a native school among us. At that time there were several collectors in Glasgow, but none more eager, more persistent, and more successful in building up a collection of the old masters of the various European schools than Mr Archibald M'Lellan, coachbuilder and magistrate of Glasgow. The time was favourable for such an undertaking, for in the early half of the century the works of the great pioneers of art were comparatively neglected, and what would now cost a king's ransom could then be picked up at a comparatively modest cost. But the task undertaken by Bailie M'Lellan required an independent judgment, a trained eye, and an extent of knowledge then and now rarely found. All these M'Lellan possessed. With rare penetration he built up his collection, which became fully worthy of the high aim of its founder, which was nothing less than the establishment of a municipal gallery of art adequate for the great city Glasgow was destined to become. With a view to this great public benefaction M'Lellan built the spacious and beautifully proportioned range of galleries in Sauchiehall Street, where the pictures yet remain, and he bequeathed his entire collection to the city. Unfortunately, when he died in 1854, his affairs were found to be involved, principally owing to an extensive building scheme he had entered into in connection with the erection of his galleries; and it became necessary for the town to pay something for the property, or to lose entirely the benefit of the bequest. After much haggling and acrimonious debate the property was, in 1856, acquired for £44,500, being £19,500 for the pictures, and £25,000 for the extensive block of buildings. The purchase was stigmatised as a job; the pictures were pronounced by men who knew no better, to be rubbish and second-rate copies; and the property acquired unwillingly, was administered in a grudging spirit. After a few spasmodic and feeble attempts to make the collection publicly useful, the institution fell into entire neglect; the halls were used for concerts, balls, bazaars and dinners – for all purposes but their legitimate use; and the pictures were looked on as an encumbrance – a hindrance to the free use of the halls for commercial purposes. In this way the existence of the M'Lellan pictures was almost forgotten; but notwithstanding this strange neglect, several notable gifts and bequests were made towards the strengthening of the collection. Among these may be noted the gift, subsequently increased by a bequest of a large number of ancient and modern pictures, from a well-known citizen, Mr William Euing. A still more important addition was made to the galleries in 1877, when by the death of Mrs Graham Gilbert of Yorkhill the Corporation succeeded by her bequest to the fine series of old masters collected by her previously deceased husband, as well as to a large number of his own works. On the receipt of this valuable gift an earnest effort was made to improve the condition and usefulness of the institution,the collections were placed under a trained and experienced curator, a code of regulations was adopted, a proper catalogue was compiled and printed, and by degrees the galleries began to take their proper place, not only among the art institutions of the city, but among the galleries of the world. The Glasgow Gallery has, indeed, since the appointment of the curator, in 1877, been discovered, and now it is recognised, all the world over, that the city possesses a collection worthy to rank with the great Continental galleries, embracing some pictures of the first importance in the history and achievements of art. One or two of the pictures in the M'Lellan collection alone, were they now brought to the hammer, would bring more than the

'Architecture'

from Glasgow in 1901

JAMES HAMILTON MUIR

'James Hamilton Muir' was a pseudonym adopted by three young Glasgow men for their fascinating and evocative survey of Glasgow at the start of the twentieth century. The book was illustrated by Muirhead Bone (1876–1953), who rose to prominence and a knighthood as an artist particularly noted for his etchings and drawings of shipyard scenes in both World Wars. Muirhead Bone's older brother James (1872–1962) and Archibald Hamilton Charteris (1874–1940) completed the personnel of 'James Hamilton Muir'. James Bone went on to have a distinguished career in journalism, becoming London editor of the Manchester Guardian *and was made a Companion of Honour in 1947. Charteris became Challis Professor of International Law in the University of Sydney.*

The examination of architecture in Glasgow *in 1901 is a fascinating glimpse of the artistic views of the three men. This can be seen in their recognition of the work and merits of Alexander 'Greek' Thomson and of James Sellars. What is equally fascinating is their hostility to the art nouveau movement which gave Glasgow what we now think of as its defining building – Charles Rennie Mackintosh's Glasgow School of Art. Under the heading of the 'new' art they note: 'Some few things here and there show a weedy, "arty" influence, and in certain places the strange idea seems to obtain that the vegetable is the architect's pattern.' Their strictures on the shortcomings of Gilbert George Scott's university buildings on Gilmorehill: 'Its hundred little prickly turrets confuse the eye and distract the attention . . .' and their reservations about the City Chambers: 'Of the marble staircase within the buildings it is not the part of a friend of architecture to speak', underline the youthful vigour and iconoclasm of 'James Hamilton Muir'.*

ARCHITECTURE

In accounting Glasgow heedless of her looks, and contemptuous of effect, one must guard against the unfairness of sweeping generalisations. For, undeniably, Glasgow's appearance on the whole is the most consistently dignified of any industrial city save London. Building here is everywhere of a certain massiveness and weight, though, perhaps, in saying so much one is making a virtue of necessity. The cost of building in Glasgow is high, and a house must needs be built well and solidly from the very outset; it is never, or rarely, altered, and so our streets lack the improvisations that enliven by their variety and whimsicality the perspective of London or Liverpool, and afford endless interesting 'bits' for the picturesque sketcher, who never cranes his neck in Glasgow streets. From the day it is built until the day it is demolished the Glasgow house receives no attention or adornment. Spring surprises no painters on tall ladders making our façades look French and fine, or picking out with neat, white lines a stone jointing that doesn't exist, or painting the rose-brick doubly red after the absurd fashion of London. Our stone is *real* stone, and – there is No Stucco. The thing results in a terrible uniformity, unrelieved by a single note of colour. The gaudy signs which give the Strand its flaunting character, or the tints which make the slender tall slips of painted, flower-clad houses in the London West End appear to Scotsmen as foreign as Florence, are here quite wanting. We do nothing, though sometimes nature comes to our aid and enlivens our blank façades with touches of green; but this is only in the suburbs or where the parks are. So you may find in such places as Scotstounhill and Bearsden pretty boulevard streets; but sobriety, not to say downright gloom, is the key-note elsewhere. Modern brick becomes so shabby in a town that stucco and paint and flower-boxes are quite necessary alleviations. Stone, on the other hand, is accounted so dignified a material that in theory it requires no adjuncts of any sort to effect a beautiful result. But, alas, we reckon without smoke, and universal dulness is the penalty we pay for belief in unadorned stone. Our consolation we find in this, that although the fresh paint and flowers of Mayfair make it a gayer and pleasanter place than Kelvinside, yet brick and stucco and musty paint make immense tracts of London horrible with a frowsiness that is happily impossible in Glasgow. Yet, if it is true that we never sink to very great depths, it is unfortunately as true that we never rise to very great heights. Glasgow might be defined as a High Average, with much in it that an architect would dismiss from notice as good family pudding. There are whole districts in the Northern and Eastern suburbs of woeful monotony – street lengths ruled into pigeon-holes for working families. But though the giant uniformity of these districts is not without a certain impressiveness when seen through the glasses of memory, one has a pride in knowing that there are streets upon streets in our town without a building in them that is mean or undignified. Yet the town has suffered in its architecture from being, not a royal and aristocratic capital, but the home of traders. There has been no wilful personality at work in it; the rights of each citizen have to be considered too much to allow of great clearances for the spacious site of a nobly proportioned building. 'Canniness' is an admirable virtue in a man or a municipality, but it chills achievement in architecture. No one but a Hausmann can mend the matter of site, but in the proportions and style of the buildings themselves it would seem that 'canniness' is giving way to a worthy civic emulation among the great mercantile companies. The last few years have seen a change come over the town; today the eye is uplifted at every turn by great picturesque erections of red stone that are adding a kind of jocund quality to the life of our streets, like good-humoured red-faced giants in ranks of rather pallid men. Within a radius of half a mile from the Exchange there is much that is balanced and well relieved, and the newest comers are breaking up the skyline with an almost startling variety of profile, while the sparing use of the emphasis of detail upon wide, tranquil spaces lends it the sudden brilliance of a good 'attack' in music. There is to be noted, also, a growing tendency to accentuate the constructional lines. The style has become not only simpler, but more varied, and almost everywhere the belief that honesty lies at the root of good art is refreshingly evident. Some few things here and there show a weedy, 'arty' influence, and in certain places the strange idea seems to obtain that the vegetable is the architect's pattern. But it must be said, on the whole, that architecture is distinctly promising in the West of Scotland. Where the good seed first took root it is hard to say. Throughout the city there are a few buildings of great classic age that are extremely dignified. Adam's Royal Infirmary is one, and its sensitively felt proportions have no doubt been among the things that helped. St George's Church, in Buchanan Street, is rather weighty too, and the old Justiciary Court at the entrance to the Green seems like a page from Méryon's sketch-book, so intently do the little prison windows under the shadow of the cornice regard you.

These are works of the early nineteenth century, and after them came the nondescript, dubious things that choke our streets with dullness. Perhaps the first Glasgow architect of the new era (in which styles are arbitrarily chosen and combined, and depend for effect more on artistic feeling than on correct classic detail) was 'Greek' Thomson, a man consumed with a passion for bizarre arrangements of Greek and Egyptian ornament. He was a contemporary of crinolines and 'Mid-Victorian Art', and much of his work smacks of old-fashioned 'antique', but he brought together some effects so novel and personal, that a fevered admiration for him invariably attacks every young enthusiast that enters a Glasgow architect's office. And such a work as the Great Western Terrace in Kelvinside almost persuades one to enlist under his flag. The sureness and precision in its simple arrangement say their say with the absoluteness of a masterpiece. Yet the thing is like a divinely proportioned factory. In Union Street there is a work from the same hand, of a very different kind – a sumptuous cornice that seems in the dullest weather to be playing with a light and shade, entrapped, some brilliant day, amid the many facets of its rich members. The most original church in Glasgow – a little domed one in a back street of Queen's Park – is his, and the great thing that perpetually astonishes the travellers on their car-tops proceeding along Bothwell Street – a façade that rises imperious as an Italian cathedral from a low muddle of workshop roofs – is his also. James Sellars, an architect who belonged to our own time, probably helped the modern revival of mercantile architecture more than any other man; his New Club in West George Street is a faultlessly graceful piece of work. St Andrew's Halls, standing in an open space with the verandah down, would be hailed as a wonderful discovery by the people who pass it today without a look. Sellars will long be remembered as a designer of ironwork – no stock pattern would satisfy him; his grilles, panels, and gates are wonders of grace and suppleness.

Among its public buildings Glasgow has none that is quite as satisfactory as the St George's Hall of Liverpool. But we must remember that we have no city square to afford the same imposing site. The greatest we have is that occupied by the University, though not in the way one could dream of. The building is the work of a man who was competent enough, but who was a scholar rather than an instinctive artist. We should be proud to have a house designed by him, feeling sure that it would be a thing of dignity. But the task which was set him by this great site and the memories of our ancient University, was beyond his powers, and 'the classic pile on Gilmorehill' is not as wonderful as the guide-books say. As the crown of a considerable eminence, it lacks a great movement, a notable gesture. Its hundred little prickly turrets confuse the eye and distract the attention; the tower itself has been described by a youthful critic as 'a needle stuck in a cork', and certainly a heaviness in the building, which is sufficient to be dull and not weighty enough to be impressive, combines with a certain scantiness in the proportions of the spire to produce this impression. It is doubtful if Scott realised the exceptional position which his building was to occupy; something in the long lines of the front elevation suggests that he did, but the side elevations seem to be apologies for usurping a vantage-ground. There is a fatal desultoriness in the composition, and the whole has the look of a work that has grown too great for the hands of the designer. The detail is harmonious and well considered, and is the work of a scholar, and yet the reflection one is left with is this – that for a great national effort such as the building of our University, a man is required who is more than merely competent. And when we recollect that another opportunity of the kind may not occur in ten generations, we have a right to be irritated. If we are asked what *should* have been, naturally we find ourselves on more difficult ground; but this much at least might be said, that to add little mock heights to a height that is already great is a contradiction of well-established principles; the explosive little turrets everywhere give the lie to the gently swelling hill on which they rise, and nullify it into a great garden plot. Had the design been some long classic building lying along the hill-top, crowning it, then the hill would have its due importance, and the University would have seemed a temple to go up into.

Equal with the University in interest are the Municipal Buildings in George Square. The style is classic; the general appearance is imposing, and sufficiently suggestive of a great city's Palace of Common Good. The elevation to the Square is not, however, quite successful. The three storeys under the pediment are almost identical in treatment and size, and the eye, wandering in search of some distinctive feture, finds rest nowhere. The entrance is insignificant, the order missing its effect by being used so liberally elsewhere. The screen walls where the figures sit are well arranged, and the domed corners are quite gracefully designed, and form perhaps the most satisfactory parts of this elevation; the rusticated basement is a little meagre and diffident. The thinness of effect in the whole façade, which may be owing to the smallness of the order used, makes the whole composition appear timid, and wanting in openness and relief. The tower, when seen from a distance, has a certain fineness, but above the cornice, where it breaks into the round, there is detail that fatigues the eye. The inevitableness of art is scarcely to be found in it. The side elevations of the buildings are much more satisfactory, and the treatment of the George Street entrance very nearly merits unqualified praise. The scale of the orders is increased here with so great a gain in dignity that one is sorry that the front to the Square is not here where this is, and this open to the Square. Of the marble staircase within the buildings it is not the part of a friend of architecture to speak.

It is a proof of the waywardness of these notes that no mention has yet been made of the ancient Cathedral. Truth to say, it is so far from our midst and so seldom in our thoughts, that of the citizens many have never seen it, and most have never stepped to the echoes in its marvellous crypt.

For the man on 'Change it has no existence, and one may take it for certain that he never was there, unless he attended in his capacity of Bailie or Councillor at a rare official 'kirking' of the Corporation. It is impossible to deny that the Cathedral in these days is badly hit. The once considerable eminence upon which it stands has been made utterly insignificant to-day by the diversion of the sacred trout stream Molendinar from its 'rocky gorge' to an underground sewer, and by the levelling up of the valleys around it. No one is to blame, for the Moledinar, apparently, fell of itself into its present low estate, helplessly, without agency – as Tolstoi says that battles are lost or won. It became unbearable, and was put away underground – that is its history, its epitaph. Perhaps its old neighbour, the Cathedral, will one day see itself disposed of by a process as summary. As it is, it looks irritated by the continual pointing that robs the stone of its effect. The tall chimney stalks stand round it, an implacable cordon, as though bent on smeeking it out; behind it the graveyard of the Necropolis becomes every year more like broken glass crowning a Brobdignagian wall; in front of it a great expanse of poor's-house granolithic (by courtesy called Cathedral Square) provides a platform for the atheist, the evangelist, or the 'boss union-smasher'; and across this space, on the site of the Archbishop's Palace, are now the close-mouths of Castle Street, and its windows are outraged by the vilest stained glass that ever came out of Germany. Truly the Cathedral of Glasgow is fallen on evil days. Yet it still means a haven, a Holy Place, in the wilderness of the East End; and to enter its gaunt nave and climb down the ancient stairs and (till you find your prison eyes) fumble in the dark and think of the age that hewed these stones, the age to which light and clearness were nothing, and only an emotion mattered – to do this is to be rid of much intolerableness in the life of modern Glasgow, and to be at rest at 'Founder's Tomb'. I can never bring myself to pronounce coldly on its architecture; the spot is too strange and sacred for that. But travellers have given their word for it that the crypt is unique in Britain. After the Cathedral, the finest church in Glasgow is that of Blythswood Parish, in Bath Street. Its spire is almost a miracle of beautifully modulated members, and it springs from a stately street with the happiest grace.

There remain to be considered the Government buildings in Glasgow, and in this connection the chronicle is of very small beer. You see at once that the town has no official sanction for being the Second City in the Empire, for the Government Buildings are patched, and shabby, and meagre. The Post Office, a great dull, staring place, is suburban when compared with that of Manchester or Edinburgh or Liverpool. And the

Custom House is a solemn little thing, placed, not as in Dublin or Greenock, on an open quay which affords a promenade to observers of the harbour life, but in an out-of-the-way corner which only highly-trained civil servants can readily find.

But the city, as well as the Government, can fritter away ornamental opportunities, as Park Terrace shows. The buildings are admirable, and seem from almost any point to crown the hill, but the great staircase leading up to Park Church is quite spoiled for lack of openness. Had it led with the same noble flight of steps from the Prince of Wales' Bridge to the guns in the park, it had been as gallant a piece of architecture as the famous stairway in Verona.

Every city has the Albert Memorial it deserves, and the People's Palace is ours – a sad bungle of a worthy and honest idea. The part of Glasgow most like a desert is the Green, and so, to educate the masses and light them along the straight path of taste, the Palace was erected there, in the hope that people of sensibility would never see it. And the Corporation doubtless were proud of the trump card they played in closing it on Sundays against any wandering critic from another town, whom the dulness of the city might drive eastwards in search of exercise for his judgment. In the East End the Corporation was hardly on its mettle, but at Kelvingrove it made an effort, like Mrs Dombey, and the new Art Galleries were born. No British municipality has erected so important a palace of art, and one could wish that this one deserved better the praises of the discerning. The interior may be all that is promised, but the outline has neither breadth nor majesty. True, the glittering hydra-headed Exhibition does it no reverence, and the judgment can hardly be absolute till that is removed; but meanwhile it is architecture looking worried in a hundred different ways.

Yet, lest one is thought to be captious, the æsthetic debt which one owes to the Corporation may be here acknowledged. We are thankful for the loving (though recent) attention to the Corporation Galleries, the courageous purchase of Whistler's portrait of Carlyle, the decoration of the Banqueting Hall in the Municipal Buildings, the provision of municipal greenhouses, and the care for the parks. And if the wandering critic from the South is disposed to smile at the meagre list, let him look about him in his own city, at the new panels of the London Royal Exchange, at the city collection of Manchester and Liverpool, and he will acknowledge that Glasgow cannot look to other towns for leading and light.

'The Adventures of a Country Customer'

from Jimmy Swan, the Joy Traveller

NEIL MUNRO (1863–1930)

Jimmy Swan, traveller in soft goods, ladies' fashions and joy, is, sadly, the least well-known of Neil Munro's comic creations. A contemporary of Para Handy and Erchie Macpherson, Jimmy travels widely, representing the great Glasgow drapery warehouse of Campbell & MacDonald in the small towns of Scotland. On occasion however, as in this story, he has a home match to play.

This story, published in 1911, celebrated the third in the great series of Glasgow Exhibitions, held in the city's Kelvingrove Park. The first, in 1888, had as one of its aims the raising of funds to create a Civic Art Gallery and Museum; the second, in 1901, saw the inauguration of the resulting Kelvingrove Museum. The third – the one in which Jimmy had his adventure with a country customer, the Scottish Exhibition of National History, Art and Industry – was intended to raise funds to endow a Chair of Scottish History and Literature at Glasgow University.

The International Exhibition of 1888 – 'the Groveries' as it was popularly but unofficially called, attracted great crowds to the city from all over Britain to enjoy the mixture of 'educative influences' and popular entertainment. It was opened by the Prince and Princess of Wales (later Edward VII and Queen Alexandra) and received a visit from Queen Victoria. On the last Saturday of the Exhibition 118,000 people visited Kelvingrove to enjoy the final moments of a six-month long experiment in civic gaiety which raised £46,000 towards the cost of a new art gallery and museum to house the city's growing collections.

The habit of Exhibitions was well and truly established, and when the Kelvingrove Art Gallery and Museum was to be opened it was a natural step to repeat the experiment, this time with a stronger international flavour. Britain's colonies and dominions were represented by individual pavilions and foreign countries provided lavish displays – not least a complete Russian village.

In 1911, regardless of the effects on Jimmy Swan's health, Glasgow went in again for another season of mixed mental stimulation and reasonably decorous jollity. As Jimmy Swan observed in a nostalgic story about the Exhibitions published in 1924:

The 1911 Exhibition at Kelvingrove still found the natural appetite of Glasgow for art, education, and a high old time unabated; but I had to miss a lot of the attractions for the sake of my commercial reputation.

Among these attractions were village sets representing folk-life in countries from all parts of the world, including Laplanders with a herd of reindeer. One of these was 'An Clachan' – a Highland village complete with a village inn – 'An Tigh Osda' – serving such traditional Highland beverages as tea and non-alcoholic heather ale, but, as Jimmy's country customer found out, there was ample provision elsewhere on site for those whose tastes ran to more potent drinks. The manifold attractions of historical displays, Miss Cranston's catering, band concerts, reindeer and 'mysterious river rides' meant that the 1911 Exhibition, boosted by one of the best summers on record, attracted over nine million paying visitors.

Glasgow had to wait another seventeen years for its next taste of exhibition fever – the 1938 Empire Exhibition. This time the site was in Bellahouston Park on the south side of the Clyde, and the abiding image of the 1938 Exhibition was Tait's Tower – the tall silver centrepiece feature named after the architectural mastermind of the event, Thomas S. Tait. Like the Garden Festival of 1988 the 1938 Empire Exhibition was designed to aid in the depressed city's regeneration, in its case by attracting new industry to Glasgow.

THE ADVENTURES OF A COUNTRY CUSTOMER

Now that the Exhibition has the gravel nicely spread, and the voice of the cuckoo is adding to the monotony of a rural life, there is going to be a large and immediate influx of soft-goods men from places like Borgue in Kirkudbrightshire and Lochinver in the North. They will come into town on the Friday trains at Exhibition excursion rates; leave their leatherette Gladstone bags at Carmichael's Temperance Hotel or the YMCA Club, have a wash-up for the sake of our fine soft Glasgow water; take a bite, perhaps, and sally forth to the Wholesale House of Campbell & MacDonald (Ltd.) ostensibly to see what can be done in cashmere hose, summer-weight underwear, and a large discount on the winter bill. Strictly speaking they know nothing about Campbell & MacDonald, having never seen them, even if they have any existence, which is doubtful; the party they are going to lean on is Mr Swan the traveller, who covers Lochinver and Borgue two or three times a year, and is all the Campbell & MacDonald that the rural merchants know.

Mr Swan came through our two former Exhibitions with no apparent casualties beyond a slight chronic glow in the countenance and a chubby tendency in the space between the waistcoat pockets where he keeps his aromatic lozenges and little liver pills respectively. For an hour's convivial sprint through the various Scottish blends with a hurried customer in from Paisley, or a real sustained effort of four-and-twenty hours with a Perthshire man who is good for a £250 order, Mr Swan is still the most reliable man in Campbell & MacDonald's. He can hold his own even with big strong drapers from the distillery districts of the Spey; help them to take off their boots and wind their watches for them and yet turn up at the warehouse in the morning fresh as the ocean breeze, with an expenses bill of £3 10s 4½d which the manager will pass without the blink of an eyelash. The City of Glasgow, for the heads of the retail soft goods trade in Kirkudbrightshire and the North, is practically Jimmy Swan and a number of delightfully interesting streets radiating round him. In Borgue and Lochinver he has been recognised affectionately since the 'Groveries' year as a Regular Corker and Only Official Guide to Glasgow, and no one knew better than himself when the turf was turned up again in Kelvingrove, just when the grass was taking root, that 1911 was going to be a strenuous year.

'I feel I'm getting a little too old for the game,' he said to his wife with a sigh.

'You ought to have got out of the rut long ago, Jimmy,' said Mrs Swan. 'It isn't good for your health.'

'A rut that's thirty years deep isn't a tramway rail, Bella,' he rejoined, 'and anyhow, I'm not in it for the fun of the thing, but mainly because I like to see you in a sealskin coat. But mark my words! this is going to be a naughty summer for your little Jimmy; every customer I have from Gretna to Thurso is going to have some excuse to be in Glasgow sometime when the Fairy Fountain's on.'

The first of the important country customers turned up on Friday afternoon. He came from Galloway, and ran all the way from the station to the warehouse so as not to lose any time in seeing Mr Swan, who was just going out for a cup of tea. 'Why! Mr MacWatters! Delighted to see you!' said Jimmy, with a radiant smile kneading the customer's left arm all over as if he were feeling for a fracture. 'Come right in and see our manager! He was just saying yesterday, "We never see Mr MacWatters' own self," and I said: "No, Mr Simpson, but I'll bet you see his cheques as prompt as the cheques of any man in Campbell & MacDonald's books!" I had him there, Mac, had him there.'

The manager was exceedingly affable to Mr MacWatters, but vexed that he had not sent a postcard to say he was coming, 'I should have liked,' he said, 'to take you out to the Exhibition, but unfortunately I have a Board meeting at three o'clock – of course I could have the meeting postponed.'

'Not at all! not on my account!' said the Galloway customer with genuine alarm and a wistful glance at Jimmy. 'I just want to look over some lines and leave an order, and then—'

'But my dear Mr MacWatters, you must see the Exhibition, and you must have a bit of dinner, and – Perhaps Mr Swan would take my place?'

'Delighted!' said Jimmy, heartily.

Mr MacWatters was introduced to some attractive lines in foulards, Ceylons, blouses, and the like, and said he would think it over and give Mr Swan his order at his leisure.

'Very good!' said the manager, shaking him by the hand at leaving. 'I'm sure you'll have a pleasant evening and enjoy the Exhibition. You will be immensely struck by the Historical section: it will show you what an intensely interesting past we have had; and I'll wager you'll be delighted with the picture gallery. Then there's Sir Henry Wood's Orchestra – I wish I could be with you. But Mr Swan will show you everything; you can depend on Mr Swan.'

Five minutes later Jimmy and his country customer sat on tall stools in a lovely mahogany salon, and Jimmy was calling the country customer Bob, an affability which greatly pleased any man from Galloway. It was Bob's first experience of the mahogany salon; his business relations with the firm of Campbell & MacDonald didn't go back to the 'Groveries', and he had so far only the assurance of the soft-goods trade in Galloway that in Glasgow Jimmy was decidedly a good man to know.

In Galloway it is drunk out of a plain thick glass, with a little water, and it is always the same old stuff. In this mahogany salon, Jimmy appeared to control magical artesian wells from which the most beautiful ladies, with incredibly abundant hair, drew variegated and aromatic beverages into long thin glasses that tinkled melodiously when you brought them against your teeth. Jimmy gave his assurance that they were quite safe, and the very thing for an appetiser, and the man from Galloway said he never dreamt you could get the like of that anywhere except on the Continent. He added, reflectively, that he really must take home a small bottle. Pleased with his approval, Jimmy prescribed another kind called a Manhattan Cocktail, and the country customer enjoyed it so much that he started feeling his hip-pocket for his purse that he might buy another. But Jimmy said, 'On no account, old man! Leave this to me, it happens to be the centenary of the firm.' So the country customer carefully buttoned up his hip-pocket again, and consented to have another cocktail solely out of respect for the firm.

It was now decided by Jimmy that they could safely have a snack upstairs where the band was, and the country customer, being a corporal in the Territorials, walked upstairs carefully keeping time to the music, but somewhat chagrined that he had not divested himself, somewhere, of his yellow leggings.

They began with 'hors d'oeuvres', which tasted exactly like sardines, then they had soup, of which the country customer had a second helping after which he looked round for his cap and was preparing to go. But Jimmy laughingly said the thing was just starting, and a banquet followed which reminded the country customer of the one they had had at the Solway Arms Hotel in 1903 when the Grand Lodge deputation visited the local brethren.

When the fish had passed, Jimmy picked up a List Price card or catalogue affair and said something about a bottle of 'buzz-water'. Concealing his disappointment, the country customer, who never had cared for lemonade, said he didn't mind. It turned out to be quite a large bottle with a gilt neck, and except for a singular tendency to go up the nose, it was the most pleasant kind of lemonade he had ever tasted. He was surprised that Jimmy hadn't ordered two bottles and said so, and Jimmy, begging his pardon, promptly did so.

This stage of the proceedings terminated with cups of black coffee and two absurdly minute glasses of a most soothing green syrup strongly recommended by Jimmy as an aid to digestion. There was also a large cigar.

'I think,' said Jimmy, in dulcet tones, with the flush of health upon his countenance, and a roguish eye, 'I think we will be getting a move on, and as one might say, divagating towards the Grove of Gladness.'

They had just one more, seeing it really was the centenary of the firm, and the country customer, as he walked downstairs, was struck by the beautiful convoluted design of the marble balustrade.

In the very next moment the country customer asked 'What is this?' and Jimmy responded, 'It is the Scenic Railway. Feel the refreshing breeze upon your brow!' They were dashing with considerable celerity past a mountain tarn, and the country customer expressed a desire to stop for a moment that he might lave his fevered temples in the water. Far off a band was playing a dreamy waltz. A myriad lamps were shining in the night, and restlessly flitting from place to place. The air had a curious balminess that is not felt in Galloway. It was borne home to the country customer that he must there and then tell Mr Swan – good old Jimmy

Swan! – about Jean Dykes in Girvan, and how he loved her and meant to marry her if he could get another extension of the lease of his shop at present terms, but before he could lead up to this subject with the necessary delicacy, he found himself on a balcony looking down on an enormous crescent of humanity, confronted by a bandstand and a tumbler.

'The firm,' Jimmy was saying solemnly, 'has always appreciated your custom. Our Mr Simpson says over and over again "Give me the Galloway men; they know what they want, and they always see that they get it!" he says, "Whatever you do, Mr Swan, pay particular attention to Mr MacWatters, and put him on bedrock prices." I have always done so, Galloway has been, as you might say, the guiding-star of my business life.'

The country customer, profoundly moved, shook Jimmy by the hand.

'Where are we now?' he asked, and the balcony began to revolve rapidly. He steadied it with one hand, and tried to count the myriad lights with the other. They, too, were swinging round terrifically, and he realised that they must be stopped. He became cunning. He would pretend indifference to them as they swung round him, and then spring on them when they were off their guard. 'Where are we now?' he repeated.

'The Garden Club,' said the voice of Jimmy, coming out of the distance. 'Try and sit up and have this soda-water.'

Next morning, sharp at nine, Mr Swan came into the warehouse with a sparkling eye, a jaunty step, a voice as mellifluous as a silver bell and a camelia in his button-hole.

'Morning! Morning!' he cheerily said to the Ribbons Department, as he passed to the manager's room.

'Old Swan's looking pretty chirpy,' said the Ribbons enviously. 'He's been having a day at Turnberry or the Coast.'

Jimmy laid a substantial order for autumn goods for Galloway and a bill of expenses for £3 9s before the manager.

'Ah! just so!' said the manager. 'And how did Mr MacWatters like the Exhibition?'

'Immensely impressed!' said Jimmy.

'It is bound to have a great educative influence. Great! And such a noble object – Chair of History! What did Mr MacWatters think of the Art and Historical sections?'

'He was greatly pleased with them particularly,' said Jimmy. 'I have just seen him off in the train, and he said he would never forget it.'

The manager placed his initials at the foot of the expenses bill and handed it back to Jimmy who proceeded at once to the cashier's department.

3
THE BISHOP'S BURGH
Introduction

In this chapter we take the image of Glasgow's cathedral as a symbol of Scots virtues and of the city itself, forming a firm rock-like foundation. This church of St Mungo is small by English and Continental standards, yet gives a wonderful sense of the soaring Gothic canopy above the Caledonian forest of pillars and columns. The builders' dramatic positioning of the cathedral cut into the banks of the Molendinar burn is overwhelmed by the modern perspective, in which the massive cliff of the Victorian Royal Infirmary building dwarfs St Mungo's and gives the impression of a miniaturised cathedral.

Mungo's part in the story of Glasgow, apart from giving his name to the cathedral, is as the focus of the founding myth sometime in the sixth century. A symbolic representation of this myth is woven into the picture with the images of the city's coat of arms. The vividness of the imagery, with the bell, the fish, the tree and the ring, has inspired novelists and poets, and Glasgow weans too had it as part of their lore:

Yon's the tree that never grew,
Yon's the bird that never flew,
Yon's the fish that never swam,
Yon's the bell that never rang.

So since all cities need a founding myth, we begin this section of the anthology with extracts from the twelfth century Life of St Kentigern, written by a monk of Furness in the North of England. It is St Kentigern's Life, because, although we know little about him, we do know that the saint appears to have been called both Mungo and Kentigern at different times and by different people.

The chosen extracts, four in all, deal with various incidents in Kentigern's career and the circumstances in which the various symbols played their part. The final episode, which links the fish and the ring, is definitely the raciest of the tales. We discover that Queen Rederech of Strathclyde becomes involved with a young warrior, in an adulterous relationship quite reminiscent of the Arthurian episodes concerning Guinevere and Lancelot.

Next we leap forward into the medieval period and focus on the thirteenth-century cathedral and include the description of it in an early history of the city of Glasgow by John Gibson, Merchant in Glasgow, published in 1777. Gibson was writing in post-Reformation days, but in the first of two extracts from this history he gives a nice account of the complex structure of the building, with the lower level of the Blacader Aisle and the Laigh Kirk. The Laigh Kirk contains some remnants of an earlier medieval church, but there is nothing from Kentigern's time. The second extract explains the reasons for the almost miraculous escape of the building from the iconoclastic zeal of the reformers, at a time when the cathedral of St Andrews and many other churches were wrecked. This is followed by a complementary, better informed description of the cathedral, by Andrew Aird, in a more industrial age than that of Gibson.

The cathedral was under construction during the English Wars, and Gibson portrayed Bruce and Archbishop Wishart as twin heroes of the Scots nation. Curiously, in view of the Glasgow connection, he failed to mention Wallace at all – perhaps proof that the cult of Wallace was not always as prevalent as it is in our day. Certainly, Scotland's currently best-known national hero did have a link with Glasgow, because in 1305, when engaged in guerilla warfare ever since his reversal at Falkirk in 1298, he was seized at the farm of Robroyston (within the modern city area). Wallace was then taken to London and tried at Westminster Hall before execution. The absence of reliable contemporary records means that we need to use Blind Harry's account from the time of James IV. The obscurity of the language is such that our extract will be brief.

The story of the Wars of Independence, as told by Gibson, made a much more emphatic Glasgow connection with the heroic priestly figure of Archbishop Wishart. Wishart is shown as a resolute figure who dared to show an independence of spirit, a defiance that led to his imprisonment by the English:

> When the contest between Bruce and Baliol happened, and king Edward, as umpire, had ordered the competitors to meet him at Norham, bishop Wishart also attended; and the king of England, after making a long and premeditated speech, in which he told the prelates and nobels present, that although he might justly claim the superiority of the kingdom of Scotland, as belonging to him by right, yet, as a friend and an arbiter, elected by themselves, he would labour to compose the present controversy in the best manner he could; for the right, said he, although there are different pretenders, belongeth only to one, and, for myself, I determine to wrong no

> man, but to do that which is just, assuring myself you will all acquiesce, and take him for king who shall be pronounced so to be. The king having finished, Robert bishop of Glasgow arose, and gave him hearty thanks, in the name of the rest, for the good affection he bore to their country, and the pains he had taken to come and remove their debates; assuring him, at the same time, that it was from the good opinion they entertained of his wisdom and equity, that they had submitted to him, as sole arbiter, the judgement and decision of this weighty affair; but where it had pleased him to speak of a right of superiority over the kingdom, it was sufficiently known that Scotland from the foundation of the state, had been a free and independent kingdom, and not subject to any other power whatsoever: that their ancestors had valiantly defended themselves against the Romans, Picts, Britons, Saxons and Danes, and all others who sought to usurp upon them; and . . . all true-hearted Scotsmen will stand for the liberty of their country to their deaths; for they esteem their liberty to be more precious than their lives, and in that quarrel will neither separate nor divide.

Gibson doesn't make his sources clear and he may simply be talking up the Glasgow man's involvement, but the speech he puts into Wishart's mouth seems to anticipate some of the best lines from the Declaration of Arbroath by thirty odd years. Wishart died in 1326.

The next extract dealing with Glasgow's cathedral is a poem Sir Launcelot Bogle, by W.E. Aytoun, an amusing tale of a crusading Knight buried outside the cathedral walls, in which mock medieval language is mixed with Glasgow place-names like 'the deep Cowcaddens wood'. This section about the earlier centuries and the cathedral concludes with the aforementioned piece from Rob Roy, Walter Scott's great novel about Highlands and Lowlands in the early eighteenth century. The links (and tensions) between Glasgow and the North and West Highlands are a recurring theme in literature but never better expressed than in characters like Rob Roy and the Bailie Nicol Jarvie, of whom you will hear more in a later chapter.

'The Life of St Kentigern'

JOCELINUS OF FURNESS

Glasgow's coat of arms is familiar to all. The four symbols: the bird, the tree, the bell and the fish with a ring in its mouth, are the subject of a rhyme once known by every Glasgow child. They are combined with the motto 'Let Glasgow Flourish', which, as Bailie Nicol Jarvie in Walter Scott's Rob Roy *said, 'is judiciously and elegantly putten round the town's arms, by way of a by-word', to form the full coat of arms of the city. They link the city with its earliest years and foundation legend.*

The bird, the tree, the bell and the fish are all associated with the sixth-/seventh-century figure of St Kentigern or St Mungo. Kentigern was a missionary among the Britons of Wales and Strathclyde and the supposed founder of the church in Glasgow. The saint's life was written, probably in the twelfth century, by Jocelinus or Joceline, a monk of Furness. This writer should be distinguished from Jocelin, the twelfth-century Bishop of Glasgow who rebuilt the Cathedral dedicated to Mungo after fire had destroyed the old building.

Kentigern, as befits a saint, had a miraculous birth. His mother, Thenew (from whom by linguistic contortion comes the name of Glasgow's St Enoch Square), was the unmarried daughter of a pagan King of Lothian, who, being found to be pregnant, was cast adrift in a small boat. She was miraculously preserved and landed safely at Culross in Fife where she gave birth to Kentigern. He was raised there by St Servanus or Serf and grew up blessed with every gift of mind and body and 'beyond all his companions he was precious and amiable in the eyes of the holy old man.' From this loveable nature of the body came his alternative name of Mungo – 'dear friend'.

Our first extract from Jocelinus' Life tells the story of Kentigern restoring life to a robin, killed by his fellow pupils at Culross. The miraculous tree, another story of the Saint's childhood, is featured in the second extract. The other elements of the coat of arms come from later in the Saint's life. The third extract recounts the visits the Saint paid to Rome and the gifts he came home with '. . . ornaments of the Church, and whatever lends grace to the house of the Lord', and the sanctified bell doubtless featured among these Papal gifts. The final extract tells of the mature Kentigern and King Rederech and Queen Languoreth. The unfaithful Queen has given away her wedding ring to her lover. It is found on his finger by the King and thrown in the Clyde, and the Queen is condemned for adultery but rescued by Kentigern having the ring miraculously recovered from the belly of a fish swimming in the Clyde.

Our text is translated from the original Latin by Bishop Alexander Forbes of Brechin and was published in the series The Historians of Scotland *in 1874.*

OF THE LITTLE BIRD THAT WAS KILLED, AND THEN RESTORED TO LIFE BY KENTIGERN

The fellow-pupils of S. Kentigern, seeing that he was loved beyond the rest by their master and spiritual father, hated him, and were unable either in public or private to say anything peaceable to him. Hence in many ways they intrigued against, abused, envied, and backbit him. But the Lord's boy ever had the eye of his heart fixed upon the Lord; and mourning more for them than for himself, cared little for all the unjust machinations of men. Now a little bird, which, on account of the colour of his body, is called the redbreast, by the will of the Heavenly Father, without whose permission not even a sparrow falleth to the ground, was accustomed to receive its daily food from the hand of the servant of God, Servanus, and by such a custom being established it showed itself tame and domesticated unto him. Sometimes even it perched upon his head, or face, or shoulder, or bosom; sometimes it was with him when he read or prayed, and by the flapping of its wings, or by the sound of its inarticulate voice, or by some little gesture, it showed the love it had for him. So that sometimes the face of the man of God, shadowed forth in the motion of the bird, was clothed in joy, as he wondered at the great power of God in the little creature, to Whom the dumb speak, and the irrational things are known to have reason. And because that bird often approached and departed at the command and will of the man of God, it excited incredulity and hardness of heart in his disciples, and convicted them of disobedience. And this will not seem strange to any one, seeing that the Lord by the voice of a mute animal under the yoke reproved the madness of the prophet, and Solomon, the wisest of men, sent the sluggard to the ant, that by considering her labour and industry, he might cast away his torpor and sloth. Moreover, a certain saint and sage invited his religious to consider the work of bees, that in their little bodies they might learn the beautiful discipline of service. And perhaps it will seem wonderful to some that a man so holy and perfect should take delight in the play and gesture of a little bird. But such should know that perfect men ought sometimes to have their rigours mitigated by something of this kind, that they who mentally approach to God should sometimes descend to our level; just as the bow ought occasionally to be unbent, lest it be found, from too long tension, nerveless and useless, at the needful time, in the disgrace of the arrow. Even birds, in passing through the air, sometimes are able to rise with extended wings, and sometimes closing them, to descend towards earth.

Therefore on a certain day, when the saint entered his oratory to offer up to God the frankincense of prayer, the boys, availing themselves of the absence of the master, began to indulge in play with the aforesaid little bird, and while they handled it among them, and sought to snatch it from each other, it got destroyed in their hands, and its head was torn from the body. On this play became sorrow, and they already in imagination saw the blows of the rods, which are wont to be the greatest torment of boys. Having taken counsel among themselves, they laid the blame on the boy Kentigern, who had kept himself entirely apart from the affair, and they showed him the dead bird, and threw it away from themselves before the old man arrived. But he took very ill the death of the bird, and threatened an extremely severe vengeance on its destroyer. The boys therefore rejoiced, thinking that they had escaped, and had turned on Kentigern the punishment due to them, and diminished the grace of friendship which Servanus had hitherto entertained for him.

When Kentigern, the most pure child, learnt this, taking the bird in his hands, and putting the head upon the body, he signed it with the sign of the cross, and lifting up holy hands in prayer to the Lord, he said, 'Lord Jesus Christ, in Whose hands is the breath of every rational and irrational creature, give back to this bird the breath of life, that Thy blessed name may be glorified for ever.' These words spake the saint in prayer, and straightway the bird revived, and not only with untrammelled flight rose in the air in safety, but also in its usual way it flew forth with joy to meet the holy old man as he returned from the church. On seeing this prodigy the heart of the old man rejoiced in the Lord, and his soul did magnify the Lord's boy in the Lord, and the Lord, Who alone doeth marvellous things, and was working in the boy. By this remarkable sign, therefore, did the Lord mark out, nay, in a way, presignify, as his own, Kentigern, and announced him beforehand, whom in after times, in manifold ways, He made still more distinguished by wonders.

OF THE FIRE EXTINGUISHED THROUGH ENVY BY THE COMPANIONS OF KENTIGERN, AND BY HIS BREATH BROUGHT DOWN FROM HEAVEN UPON A LITTLE BRANCH OF HAZEL

It was the rule of S. Servanus, that each of the boys whom he trained and instructed should, during the lapse of a week, carefully attend to arrange the lamps in the church, while the Divine office was being celebrated there by day and by night; and for this purpose, when the others had gone to sleep, should attend to the fire, lest any neglect from default of light should happen to the Divine service. It happened that S. Kentigern, in the order of his course, was appointed to this service, and, while he was doing it diligently and in order, his rivals (inflamed with the torches of envy, nay, blinded, as it is the peculiarity of perverse men to envy the advance of their betters, to persecute, to pervert, and to diminish the good which in themselves they have not, nor will to have, nor can have), on a certain solemn night secretly extinguished all the fire within the habitations of the monastery and the places in its neighbourhood. Then, as if ignorant and innocent, they sought their beds, and when about cockcrow, as was his custom, at the sacred vigils, S. Kentigern arose, as custom required that he should attend to the lights, he sought for fire everywhere round about and did not find it.

At length, having found out the wickedness of his rivals, he determined in his mind to give place to envy, and began to leave the monastery. But when he had come to the hedge which surrounded that habitation, returning to himself, he stood still, and armed his soul to endure perils from false brethren, and to bear the persecution of the froward. Then going back to the house, he laid hold of and drew out a bough of a growing hazel which had come up beside the hedge, and, enkindled by faith, he besought the Father of Lights to lighten his darkness by the pouring in of new light, and in a new way to prepare for himself a lantern by which he might clothe with healthful confusion those his enemies who persecuted him. Lifting therefore a pure hand, he sighed the bough with the sign of the cross, and blessing it in the name of the holy and undivided Trinity breathed upon it. A wonderful and remarkable thing followed! Straightway fire coming forth from heaven, seizing the bough, as if the boy had exhaled flame for breath, sent forth fire, vomiting rays, and banished all the surrounding darkness, and so in His light seeing light, he walked into the House of God. God therefore sent forth His light, and led him and brought him unto the monastery, even unto His holy hill and unto His dwelling. And so he went unto the altar of God, who gave joy to his youth by so clear a sign, and kindled the lamps of the church, that the Divine office might be celebrated and finished in due season. Therefore was the Lord his light and his salvation, that he might no longer fear any of his rivals, because He gave sentence for him, and defended his cause against those unjust, envious, and deceitful youths, so that their malice might no more prevail against him.

All were astonished, beholding this great vision, when that torch burnt without injury to itself, as when in olden time the bush which appeared to Moses seemed to be burnt, and yet was not consumed. For it was one and the same Lord who wrought the self-same wonder in the bush and in the twig of hazel; for the Same who destined Moses as a lawgiver for the people of the Hebrews, that he might lead them out of the bondage of Egypt, deigned to destine Kentigern as a preacher of the Christian law, to many nations, that he might rescue them from the power of the devil. In the end that torch was extinguished from heaven, when the lamps of the church had been lighted, and every one more and more wondered, beholding these great things of God. For that hazel from which the little branch was taken, received a blessing from S. Kentigern, and afterwards began to grow into a wood. If from that grove of hazel, as the country folks say, even the greenest branch is taken, even at the present day, it catches fire like the driest material at the touch of fire, which in a manner laps it up, and, influenced by a little breath by the merit of the saint, sheds abroad from itself a fiery haze. And verily it was right that a miracle of this nature should continue, yea, perpetuate itself in his case, who, although in the verdure of the spring-time of life, the delight of the flesh was vigorous, yet inwardly was strong, and all the glory of the world, like the grass of the field, entirely withered because the Spirit of the Lord blew upon it, and the Word of God for ever abiding, by His enlightening consecrated to Himself that hallowed soul and undefiled body, and the fire of the Holy Spirit burnt him up as a whole burnt-offering, accepted as an odour of a sweet savour.

HOW ST KENTIGERN WENT SEVEN TIMES TO ROME, AND CONSULTED THE BLESSED GREGORY ABOUT HIS CONDITION

The blessed Kentigern, knowing that Britain in many provinces was smitten with many stripes by the Gentiles, and that the Church of God established therein was by idolaters in many ways reft and torn from the faith of Christ; discovering moreover that it was frequently assaulted by heretics, and that there were therein many things contrary to sound doctrine, and alien from the integrity of the faith of our holy mother the Catholic Church, set himself for a long time to deliberate within himself what cure he ought to apply to all these evils. In the end, he determined in his mind to visit the seat of Peter founded on a rock; and to prevent the tares growing up in the good wheat, he resolved by the wholesome teaching of the Holy Roman Church, and by acknowledging the oracles of the faith, to cast out every scruple of doubt from his mind, so as to be able to arrive by certain guidings at the light of the truth. For Britain, during the reign of the most holy king Lucius, in the papacy of Eleutherius by the preaching of the most excellent teachers Faganus and Divianus and others, whom Gildas the wise, the historian of the Britons, commemorateth, received the faith of Christ. It preserved that Christianity thus received whole and undefiled till the time of the Emperor Diocletian. Then the moon was turned into blood, and the flame of persecution against the Christians burnt brightly through the whole world. Then that scourge, inundating Britain, vehemently oppressed it, and pagan hands, mowing the first-fruits of the island, namely, Alban, took him out of the midst to be recorded in the Book of the Eternal King; and an innumerable company of others shortly after, voluntarily, and in ignorance, it offered to heaven.

From that time the worship of idols began to spring up and increase in that island, bringing in rejection and forgetfulness of the Divine law. But Christianity after this somehow revived and flourished; however, time went on, and first the Pelagian heresy prevailing, and then the Arian creeping in, defiled the face of the Catholic faith. This, however, sprang up again and flourished when these heresies were cast down and conquered by Saint Germanus, Bishop of Auxerre, a man truly apostolic, and made glorious by many miracles. Yet forthwith the invasion of the neighbouring Picts and Scots, hostile to the recognition of the name of Christ, drove away entirely both the faith and the faithful from the northern part of Britannia. Finally, Britannia was conquered by the Angles, still pagans, from whom it was called Anglia. The natives being driven out, it was given over to idols and idolaters. The indigenous inhabitants of the island, however, fled either across the sea into Little Britain, or into Wales, and though banished from their own land, all of them did not entirely abandon their faith. But the Picts, first mainly by S. Ninian, and then latterly by SS. Kentigern and Columba, received the faith. Then lapsing into apostasy a second time, by the preaching of S. Kentigern, not only the Picts, but also the Scots, and innumerable people gathered from the different parts of Britain, were, as we have said already, and shall say more at length hereafter, either turned to the faith or were confirmed therein.

However, holy Augustine, noted for his monastic life and habit, and other servants of God, religious, were sent commissioned to England by the most holy Pope Gregory, who, rich in the showers of sacred preaching, and glittering in the lightning power of miracles, either by themselves or by their disciples converting the whole island to Christ, and fully instructing them in the rules of faith and the institutes of the holy fathers, filled the whole land of Anglia with the sweet savour of Christ.

On account therefore of Britain being crushed by so many misfortunes, Christianity so often obscured, and even cast down, at different times diverse rites were found in her contrary to the form of the holy Roman Church and to the decrees of the holy fathers. In order, therefore, that he might learn and be able to meet and to remedy all these evils, blessed Kentigern, going forth from the monastery of which we have made mention, betook himself seven times to Rome, and brought home what he learnt there, in so far as the correction of Britain required it; but as he was returning for the seventh time he was attacked by a most grievous malady, and got home with the greatest difficulty.

One of his visits was made to Rome during the time that blessed Gregory presided on the apostolic seat, a man truly apostolic in office, authority, life, and doctrine, and the special apostle of England, for the English are the sign of his apostleship. He was as a vessel of solid gold adorned with every manner of precious stone, and was called Golden Mouth, because in expounding great parts of the Scripture he made it clear by the most lucid and polished style. His memory is as the work of the apothecary in making up the unguent, and as music in a banquet of wine, because by his honeyed writings, by his hymns composed according to the laws of music, he gladdened, and by his canonical institutions he strengthened and adorned, the house of God, the holy Catholic Church, diffused throughout the world. To this most holy Roman Pontiff he laid bare and declared in order his whole life, his election to the episcopate, his consecration, and all the events that had happened to him. But the saintly Pope, inasmuch as he was strong in the spirit of counsel and discretion, filled with the Holy Ghost, and knowing him for a man of God, and full of the grace of the blessed Spirit, confirmed his election and consecration, because he knew that both had come from God. And on the bishop on many occasions seeing it, and with difficulty obtaining it, he supplied what was wanting to his consecration, and destined him to the work of the ministry enjoined on him by the Spirit of God. Holy Bishop Kentigern, having received the apostolic absolution and benediction, returned home, bearing with him the codes of canons, many other books of Holy Scriptures, as well as privileges, and many relics of the saints, and ornaments of the Church, and whatever lends grace to the house of the Lord. And he gladdened his own by his return, as well as by many presents and religious gifts. He dwelt there for some time in great peace and (godly) conversation, and ruled holily and firmly both his see and his monastery with great care.

HOW THE SAINT MIRACULOUSLY RESTORED TO THE QUEEN THE RING WHICH SHE HAD IMPROPERLY GIVEN AWAY, AND WHICH WAS THROWN BY THE KING HIMSELF INTO THE RIVER CLUD

So S. Kentigern having, as we have told, returned home, and disposing himself to dwell by himself in mental solitude far from the throngs of men, willed not to be freely seen in public or to go abroad except in cases of great urgency. Nevertheless he ceased not, though against his will, to shine forth abroad in wondrous signs. Queen Languoreth, who has been mentioned above, living in plenty and delights, was not faithful to the royal chamber or the marital bed, as she ought to have been: for the heap of her treasures, the exuberance of her means of sensuality, and the elevation of power, were wont to minister incentives and fuel to the will of the flesh. She cast her eyes on a certain youth, a soldier, who, according to the perishing beauty of this perishing flesh, seemed to her to be beautiful and fair of aspect beyond many that were with him at court. And he, who without external temptation was himself ready enough for such a service as this, was easily induced to sin with her.

So as time passed, and the forbidden pleasures, frequently repeated, became more and more delightful to both of them – for bread eaten in secret, and stolen waters, according to Solomon, seemed to them to be sweeter; so from a rash act they proceeded to a blind love, and a royal ring of gold, set with a precious gem, which her lawful husband had intrusted to her as a special mark of his conjugal love, she very impudently and imprudently bestowed upon her lover, and he, more impudently and more imprudently placing it upon his finger, opened the door of suspicion to all who were conversant in the matter. A faithful servant of the king, finding this out, took care to instil the secret of the queen and the soldier into the ears of the husband, who did not willingly lend his ear or his mind to her disgrace, as the unworthiness of his wife was brought to him. It is an old and true proverb: it is difficult for a cuckold to put faith in one that reveals the failings of a beloved wife; and the odium is apt to fall rather upon the informer than upon the accused. But the detector of the adultery, in proof of the matter, showed the ring on the finger of the soldier; and by this proof persuading the king to believe him, he succeeded in kindling the spirit of jealousy within him.

So the king, being secretly assured of this, veiled under a calm demeanour the wrath of his soul against the queen and the soldier, and appeared more than usually cheerful and kind. But when a bright day occurred, he went out hunting, and summoning the soldier to accompany him, sought the woods and forests with a great company of beaters and dogs. Having uncoupled the dogs and stationed his friends at different places, the king with the soldier came down to the banks of the river Clud, and they, in a shady place on the green turf, thought it would be pleasant for both to sleep for a little. The soldier, worn out, and suspecting no danger, resting his head, stretching out his arm, and extending his hand, straightway slumbered; but the spirit of jealousy exciting the king, who simulated sleep, suffered him neither to slumber nor to take any rest. Seeing the ring on the finger of the sleeper, his wrath was kindled, and he with difficulty restrained his hand from his sword and from shedding of blood; but he controlled his rage, at least in part, and after drawing the ring off the finger threw it into the neighbouring river, and then, waking him up, ordered him to return to his companions and go home. The soldier waking up from sleep, and thinking nothing about the ring, obeyed the king's order, and never discovered what he had lost till he entered his house.

But when, on the return of the king, the queen in the usual manner came forth from her chamber and saluted him, from the mouth of him who was thus saluted there proceeded continuously threats, contempt, and reproach, while with flashing eyes and menacing countenance he demanded where the ring was which he had intrusted to her keeping. When she declared that she had it laid up in a casket, the king, in the presence of all his courtiers, commanded her to bring it to him with all haste; but she, still full of hope, entered the inner chamber as if to seek the ring, but straightway sent a messenger to the soldier, telling him of the anger of the king in demanding the ring, and ordering him to send it quickly. The soldier sent back to the queen to say that he had lost the ring and could not tell where. Then, fearing the face of the king, for the sake of concealment, he absented himself from court. In the meantime, as she sought further delays, and was slow in producing what, of course, she could not find, uselessly seeking here and there, the king in fury frequently calling her an adulteress, broke forth in curses saying, 'God do to me, and more also, if I judge thee not according to the law of adulterers, and condemn thee to a most disgraceful death. Thou, clinging to a young adulterer, hast neglected the king thy spouse; yet I would have made thee the sharer of my bed and the mistress of my kingdom: thou hast done it in secret; I will do it in public, and the sun shall manifest thine ignominy and reveal thy more shameful things before thy face.'

And when he had said much after this sort, all the courtiers praying for some delay, he with difficulty conceded three days, and ordered her to be imprisoned. Cast into a dungeon, she now contemplated death as imminent; but not the less did her guilty conscience torment her. O weighty and intolerable punishment, the damning testimony of a guilty conscience! Although one condemned to punishment may have external peace, yet he is acknowledged to be wretched and disturbed whom a gnawing conscience ceaselessly persecuteth. The spirit, therefore, of the guilty woman was vexed within her, and with contrite and lowly heart, with tearful prayer, she besought God not to enter into judgment with His handmaiden, but according to His great mercy, as formerly He had pity on the woman taken in adultery and placed in the midst before Him, so in a like case He would have mercy upon her. By the inspiration of the Lord, the woman in her great strait found out a wise device, and, sending a most faithful messenger to S. Kentigern, told him her whole misfortune, and from him, as her only deliverer, she urgently requested help. She also begged that at least he would use his influence with the king and beseech pardon for her, for there was nothing so great which he would, or could, or ought to deny him.

The saintly bishop, instructed by the Holy Ghost and by virtue from on high, knowing the whole story in order before the arrival of the messenger, ordered him to go with a hook to the bank of the river Clud aforesaid, to cast the hook into the stream, and to bring back to him straightway the first fish that was caught upon it and taken out of the water. The man did what the saint commanded, and exhibited in the presence of the man of God a large fish which is commonly called a salmon; and on his ordering it to be cut open and gutted in his presence, he found in it the ring in question, which he straightway sent by the same messenger to the queen. And when she saw it and received it, her heart was filled with joy, her mouth with praise and thanksgiving; her grief was turned into joy; the expectation of death into the dance of exultation and safety. Therefore the queen rushed into the midst and returned to the king the ring he had required, in the sight of all. Wherefore the king and all his court were sorry for the injuries done to the queen; and humbly on his knees he sought her pardon, and swore that he would inflict a very severe punishment, even death or exile if she willed, upon her slanderers. But she, wisely judging that mercy rather than the award of judgment was what she had to do with, was desirous that he should shew mercy, as a servant ought to have on his fellow-servant. She said, 'Far be it, my lord, O King, that any one should suffer on my account; but if thou willest that from my heart I should forgive thee for what injury thou hast done me, I will that thou put away all angry feeling from thy heart and mind, as I do against mine accuser.' And all, when they heard this, wondered and were glad. And so the king, and the queen, and the accuser are recalled to the grace of peace and mutual love. The queen, as soon as she could, betook herself to the man of God, and confessing her guilt, and making satisfaction by his advice, carefully corrected her life for the future and kept her feet from a similar fall. During her husband's lifetime she never revealed to any one the sign whereby the Lord had shown forth His mercy toward her, but after his death she told it to all who wished to know it.

Behold the Lord sitting in heaven willed to do by His servant Kentigern that which, clothed in our flesh, He condescended to do when conversing with men on earth. At His order Peter, casting a hook into the sea, drew out the great fish in whose mouth he found the piece of money, which he gave in tribute for the Lord and for himself. So by the command of S. Kentigern, in the Name of the Lord Jesus Christ, the queen's messenger, casting a hook into the river, took a fish, and bringing it thus to the saint found in it, when taken and opened, a ring which saved the queen from a double death. In both these cases, as it seemeth to me, there was rendered to Cæsar that which belongeth unto Cæsar, and unto God that which is God's. For in the piece of money the image of Cæsar was restored to him, and in the ring restored the flesh was redeemed from destruction, and the soul made in the image of God was cleansed from sin and restored to Him.

'Glasgow's Cathedral'

from A History of Glasgow

JOHN GIBSON, MERCHANT IN GLASGOW

Little is known of the author and the History of Glasgow *itself is a curious work, written very obviously from the perspective of a merchant and largely consisting of bare lists of facts and happenings in chronological form. These are punctuated by longer descriptions, such as those giving statistics about imports and exports into the city – invaluable information about the tobacco trade, for example, comes from this source.*

The following extract describes some of the prominent buildings of the city, followed by an account of the saving of Glasgow's cathedral from destruction when reforming frenzy was rife in the land.

GLASGOW'S CATHEDRAL

The public buildings in Glasgow are not unworthy of the attention of a stranger. The first and most ancient is the Cathedral or High Church, which is a magnificent building, and its situation greatly to its advantage, as it stands higher than any part of the city.

It has been intended to form a cross, though the traverse part has never been finished. The great tower is founded upon four large massive pillars, at the east end of the choir, as you go in to the nave of the church, which are each of them about thirty feet in circumference; the tower, which is twenty five and a half feet square within, is surrounded by a ballustrade, within which rises an octangular spire, terminated by a fane: the tower, upon the west end, is upon the same level, but appears not to have been finished, though it is covered over with lead, and in it a very large bell, eleven feet four inches diameter; the consistorial house stands upon the south side of the west entry, and is a very mean building. The principal entry was from the west, the gate eleven feet broad at base, and seventeen feet high; the west end of the choir is now appropriated for a place of worship, and is divided from the remaining part by a stone partition, and that is inclosed by another stone wall, parting it from the nave; this west entry being now shut up, it is impossible to form an adequate idea of the awful solemnity of the place, occasioned by the loftiness of the roof and the range of pillars by which the whole building is supported.

At the east end of the choir, and between the pillars supporting the tower, are two very large opposite windows, each of them forty feet high, and twenty-two feet wide at base; the one upon the north side consists of five pillars or bars, which divide it into six parallel windows, and over them a circular one, about ten feet diameter; the one upon the south side is divided by four pillars, but consists of two series, and over the upper row a circular one, the same as the other, and two smaller ones at each side. The nave of the church rises four steps higher than the choir; and on the west end stood the organ-loft, ornamented by a variety of figures, now defaced; the pillars here are done in a better taste than those in the choir, and their capitals are ornamented with fruits; on the arches of the pillars are galleries covering the side ailes, over which is an upper range of windows; by these, and the under range, together with the three capital ones facing the north, east, and south, the whole building was enlightened. The arched roof of the altar is supported by five pillars, over which was a fine terrace-walk, and above it a large window of curious workmanship, but now shut up; on the north side of the altar is the vestry, being a cube of twenty-eight feet, the roof arched, and vaulted at top, and supported by one pillar in the centre of the house; arched pillars, from every angle, terminate in the grand pillar, which is nineteen feet high. The chapter-house appears to have been in the north cross, which communicated with the nave by a vaulted entry. The lower part of the south cross is made use of as a burying place for the clergy of the city, and is, by much, the finest piece of workmanship in the whole building; it is fifty-five feet long, twenty-eight feet broad, and fifteen feet high, arched and vaulted at top, and supported by a middle range of pillars, with their capitals highly ornamented; corresponding to which are columns adjoining to the walls, which, as they rise, spring into semi-arches, and are everywhere met at acute angles by their opposites, and are ornamented with carvings, at the closing and crossing of the lines; at the east end of the choir, you descend by flights of steps, upon each side, into passages, which, in former times, were the principal entries to the burying vault, which is immediately under the nave; it is now made use of as a parish church for the Barony of Glasgow, and is full of pillars, some of them very massive, which support the arched roof; it is but a very uncomfortable place for devotion. The space under the altar and vestry, though now made use of as a burying place by the heretors of the Barony, was, in days of old, if we may credit tradition, appropriated to the keeping of the relics; and, indeed, by the beautiful manner in which this place is finished, one would imagine that it had not been destined for common use: here is shown St Kentigern or Mungo's monument, with his figure lying in a cumbent posture.

The whole length of the cathedral within is 284 feet, its breadth sixty-five feet, the height of the choir, from the floor to the canopy, ninety feet, and the height of the nave eighty-five feet, the height of the middle tower 220 feet. There are several winding staircases in the building, which lead to passages round the whole church.

No tombs, no monuments, worthy of being made mention of, are here to be met with; whatsoever works of art, that were either beautiful or magnificent, which the piety of our ancestors had reared to protect the ashes of the dead, and to hand down their names to posterity, fell a sacrifice to, and were destroyed by, the rude hands of a set of furious reformers.

This fabric was begun by John Achaius, bishop of Glasgow, in 1123, and was continued, by succeeding bishops, until such time as it was finished in the manner in which it stands at present. Great as the wealth of the See of Glasgow was, we find it insufficient for rearing and compleating so large a building; they had, therefore, recourse to all the churches in Scotland for assistance, as will appear from the following passage, contained in the forty-eighth canon of the provincial councils of the church of Scotland, held at Perth, in 1242 and 1269.

> *Ad haec statuimus firmiter observandum, quod a principio Quadragesimae usque ad octavas Paschae, negotium fabricae ecclesiae Glasguensis, omnibus diebus Dominicis et festivis, fideliter et diligenter, in singulis ecclesiis, post evangelium missae, parochianis exponatur, et indulgentia eidem fabricae subvenientibus concessa, quam in qualibet ecclesia scriptam esse praecipimus, aperte et distincte eisdem parochianis, vulgariter dicatur, et eleemosynae eorundem, ac bona decedentium ab intestato, ac etiam pie legata, secundum consuetudinem hactenus approbatam, fideliter colligantur; et decanis locorum in proximis capitulis, sine diminutione, assignentur; et infra dictum terminum nullus quaestionem pro negotiis aliis in ecclesiis parochialilbus admittat.*
>
> Moreover, we strictly enact, that the business of the building of the church of Glasgow be, upon all Lord's days and festivals, faithfully and diligently explained in all churches, after saying of the mass, from the beginning of Lent to the eight day after Easter; and that the indulgencies granted to those assisting at the said building, which we have ordered to be written in every church, may be

distinctly explained in the vulgar language to the parishioners; and that their alms, the effects of persons dying interstate, and pious legacies, may be faithfully collected, according to usage hitherto approved, and delivered to the deacons of places in the nearest chapter, without any deduction; and that, during the said space of time, no sermon, or any other business, be admitted in the parochial churches.

The famous school of masonry at Antwerp, which sent out so great a number of excellent architects, during the eleventh, twelfth, and thirteenth centuries, in all probability supplied the bishop of Glasgow with one, who, I suppose, gave the design of this church, or at least, assisted in the building of it. From an inscription on the abbey of Melrose, which was consecrated in 1146, we learn that the name of this man was John Murdo. It is as follows:

John Murdo sum tym callit was I,
And born in Parysse certainly,
And had in kepying all masom werk,
Of Sanctandroys, the hye kyrk
Of Glasgu, Melros, and Paslay,
Of Nyddyfsdayl, and of Galway.
Pray to God, and Mari baith,
And sweet St John, keep this haly kyrk frae skaith.

HOW THE CATHEDRAL WAS SAVED FROM DESTRUCTION

1579. An act having been passed by the estates, at the desire of the assembly, for demolishing whatsoever churches had been left undestroyed, the effects of which Mr Spotiswood says were, that

Thereupon ensued a pitiful vastation of churches and church-buildings, throughout all the parts of the realm; for every one made bold to put to their hands, the meaner sort imitating the example of the greater, and those who were in authority; no difference was made, but all the churches either defaced, or pulled to the ground; the holy vessels, and whatsoever else men could make gain of, as timber, lead and bells, were put to sale; the very sepulchres of the dead were not spared; the registers of the church, and bibliothecs cast into the fire; in a word, all was ruined; and what had escaped in the time of the first tumult, did now undergo the common calamity; and the preachers animated the people to follow these barbarous proceedings, by carrying out, that the places where idols had been worshipped ought, by the law of God, to be destroyed, and that the sparing of them was the reserving of things execrable.

The execution of this act for the west, was committed to the earls of Arran, Argyle, and Glencairn; and they, at the intercession of the inhabitants of Glasgow, had spared the cathedral; but in this year Mr Melvil, principal of the college, having, for a great while, solicited the magistrates to have it pulled down, that at last granted him liberty to do so; but when he, by beat of drum, was assembling the workmen for that purpose, the crafts (who justly looked upon the cathedral as one of the greatest ornaments of their town) ran immediately to arms, and informed Mr Melvil, that if any person presumed to pull down a single stone of the church, he should, that moment, be buried under it; and so much were they incensed at this attempt to destroy this ancient building, that if the magistrates had not come and appeased them, they would have put to death Melvil, with all his adherents. A complaint was hereupon made by the ministers, and the leaders of the insurrection were summoned to appear before the council at Edinburgh; where the king, at that time not thirteen years of age, approved of what the crafts had done, and commanded the ministers to proceed no farther in that affair; saying, that too many churches had been already destroyed, and that he would not tolerate any more abuses of that kind.

'Cathedral and College'

from Glimpses of Old Glasgow

ANDREW AIRD (1819–1899)

Andrew Aird published two volumes of reminiscences related to his own professional life, Letterpress Printing in Glasgow During the Last Fifty Years *(1882) and* Reminiscences of Editors, Reporters and Printers During the Last Sixty Years *(1890) as well as the more general* Glimpses of Old Glasgow (1894) *from which our extracts on two of the city's architectural treasures are taken.*

Glasgow Cathedral does deserve to be noticed in this section – if only because it has, against all the odds, survived as what the Penguin Buildings of Scotland *calls a 'strikingly complete and homogeneous building of the mid- and later thirteenth century.' Time, reformers and occasional bouts of institutional vandalism notwithstanding it is indeed the best preserved of the mainland Scottish cathedrals.*

Aird's enthusiastic praise of the stained-glass representation of Old Testament scenes – 'exquisite skill and brilliant effect' – has not been shared by later generations, who found the work, executed between 1859 and 1864 by Bavarian glass painters, to be less to their taste and, after the First World War, compromised in its source. Much of the Munich glass was replaced from the 1930s onwards.

Aird concludes his description of the Cathedral with an account of a visit in 1843 which serves as a valuable reminder of exactly how dirty and smoky the industry of nineteenth-century Glasgow made the 'dear green place'.

THE CATHEDRAL

This venerable edifice is perhaps the most splendid specimen of old-English ecclesiastical architecture in a comparatively entire state which is to be found in Scotland. Mr William Rodger, in his sketch, *Ancient Buildings of Glasgow*, says: 'On approaching this edifice we are struck with its elaborate masonry and its majestic proportions.'

Historians do not agree as to the time when the See of Glasgow was founded. That it is next to St Andrews in point of antiquity is beyond all doubt. With regard to the founders, Kennet in his *Parochial Antiquities* says it was founded by Kentigern or St Mungo in 560. Dr Helyn, speaking of the See of Asaph, in Wales, observes that the See was founded by Kentigern, a Scot, in 583, and that St Kentigern was then Bishop of Glasgow. The See was refounded in 1115, by David, Prince of Cumberland.

Prior to this period the Cathedral was a mean building, constructed with timber, and had got into a state of great decay. It was about this time that John Achaius, chaplain to Prince David, began to build a cathedral church at Glasgow, which required the effort of many years. It was at length consecrated to St Kentigern on 7th July, 1136. Joceline, who was Bishop of Glasgow from 1174 to 1199, finding the Cathedral too small rebuilt it of a much larger size, and in a more magnificent manner. After many years of skilful labour this edifice was solemnly consecrated in 1197. The Cathedral, which was thus rebuilt by Joceline, received, during many years, various additions and numerous embellishments by succeeding prelates of this See, as low down as the epoch of the Reformation. And this is one feature particularly deserving of notice as a boundary line between different epochs in ecclesiastical architecture, viz. the points where the labours of successive bishops ended and commenced.

Externally, the whole fabric on both sides is divided into compartments, by buttresses of equal dimensions, between which are placed windows in the pointed style, all somewhat dissimilar in their ornamentation. This succession of windows is interrupted by the transepts directly under the great tower in the centre of the church. The north and south windows in the transepts are each forty by twenty-two feet, divided with mullions and tracery. Above the first range of windows the wall terminates in a battlement, within which springs the lowest roof, till it meets the second or inner wall, which rises from thence for a number of feet. This, in like manner, is divided into compartments, by small square projections, between each of which are placed three narrow windows, in the pointed style, directly above each of these in the first storey; it then terminates in the same manner as the lower wall, and is capped with a leaden roof.

The chapter house was in the north cross of the Cathedral, and had a communication with the nave by a vaulted entry. The south cross was never completed, and was used in my younger days as a burial place for the clergy of the city. It was founded by Bishop Blackadder, who was appointed to the See in 1484. The architecture of it appears to have been finer than the rest of the building, and is supposed to be of no older date than the year 1500. It is still called Bishop Blackadder's Aisle. Its arched roof is supported by columns adjoining the outer walls. There is also a row of pillars in the centre, and the capitals of the whole are highly ornamented with figures and flowers. The area of its top was at one time formed into an ornamental piece of garden ground.

The consistorial house, in which the bishops held their ecclesiastical courts, projects from the south-west corner of the Cathedral. Between this and the tower, now removed, was the ancient entrance, by a large magnificent door, now shut up. This tower stood at the north-western extremity of the building, and was of a square form; it contained a clock, and was a plain structure, and not at all in keeping with the other parts of the building. It was removed at the renovation of the Cathedral a number of years ago. It was 126 feet high, and had a high leaden roof. The usual entry at present is on the south, which leads immediately into the choir. The appearance of the choir is very grand and impressive; it is 138 feet long, supported by eight pillars, four of which support the steeple, and are very large, being eighty-eight feet high, and thirty feet in circumference; the other four are twenty-seven feet high, and thirteen feet four inches in circumference.

The steeple is of a square form till it rises above the roof, when it terminates in a battlement, from within which springs the spire, of an octagonal form, with two battlements round it, the one above the other, and which rises to the height of 230 feet above the base of the building, terminating in a large gilded weather-cock. The columns are decorated with monumental tablets of marble, and other memorials of the dead, giving to the whole interior a very solemn and imposing effect.

The crypt, or vaulted cemetery, is situated immediately beneath the nave; it is 108 feet long by seventy-two feet wide, and is supported by sixty-five clustered pillars, some of which are eighteen feet in circumference. The height from the floor to the roof is about eighteen feet. It is lighted with forty-one windows, but from their smallness, and the position of the pillars, the interior is rendered dark and gloomy. Prior to the Reformation the crypt was used as a burial place, in which it is said St Mungo, the founder, is buried. Soon after the Reformation it was used as a place of worship for the heritors of the Barony Parish, and it continued to be so till 1798, when the congregation was removed to their new church in the immediate vicinity. The worshippers in this splendid abode of the dead might well say, in the words of the poet –

> The pillar'd arches are over our head,
> And beneath our feet are the bones of the dead.

It was entered, prior to the Reformation, by broad stairs at the east end of the nave, as at present, but when used as a place of worship, the entry was by the churchyard. When the crypt was vacated as a place of worship, the heritors of the Barony Parish, assuming it to be their property, covered the surface with earth about three feet deep, and sold it for burying places, permitting the purchasers to enclose their respective places with iron rails, which greatly injured the architectural effect. In 1835 the officers of the Crown not only claimed the property, but demanded a repetition of the price, and prevented the further use of it as a cemetery. This crypt is an uncommonly rich specimen of early English: the piers and groins are of the most intricate character, the most beautiful designs, and excellent execution. The groins have rich bosses, and the doors are greatly enriched with foliage and other ornaments; the piers have very fine flowered capitals.

Sir Walter Scott has made this the scene of a striking incident in *Rob Roy*.

In ascending from the crypt to the nave the change brings a pleasing relief to the mind. On the windows all around, Old Testament scenes are depicted with exquisite skill and brilliant effect, appealing to the heart and spirit with all the tenderness of that human sympathy, and all the sacred awe of that Divine element, which makes the history of the chosen people so touching and sublime. The drawing and colouring in these pictures are beyond all praise, giving a bold relief to the objects which is uncommon in glass painting. In all the windows this is remarkable, and it imparts a strength and distinctness to the figures that seem to startle every beholder.

How graphically the poet depicts such a building when he says:

> How reverend is the face of this tall pile,
> Whose ancient pillars rear their marble head
> To bear aloft its arch'd and ponderous roof,
> By its own weight made steadfast and immovable,
> Looking tranquility!

The view from the top of the steeple is picturesque and interesting in a high degree. Beneath, and close at hand, is the Necropolis, a burying-ground, beautified both by nature and art, where the most prominent of the monuments with which it is studded is that of John Knox, 'the Reformer of a nation', to whom our country is so much indebted for the purity of her religious creed and the excellence of her popular education: and at our feet lies the burial-ground of the Cathedral, which is of a striking and peculiar character; for though in reality extensive, it is small in proportion to the number of the inhabitants who are interred within it, and whose graves are almost all covered with tombstones. The broad, flat, monumental stones are placed so close to each other that the precincts appear to be flagged with them, and, though roofed only by the heavens, resembles more the floor of an old English church, where the pavement is covered with sepulchral inscriptions, than the surface of a Scottish graveyard.

There is a well-known Glasgow myth regarding an ill-fated piper and his dog, lost in the maze of the *subterranean way*, popularly believed to exist between the vaults of the Cathedral and those of the old kirk of Rutherglen, long ago demolished, where the false Menteith plotted for the delivery of Wallace to the English. This may probably be accounted for by a rude footpath having been formed by the masons engaged in the erection of that magnificent edifice, and who then lodged in the more important neighbouring town of Rutherglen, Glasgow being unable to accommodate so many stranger workmen! These ancient brethren of the mystic tie, therefore, formed a rude path over the Gallowmuir, in their daily journeys between the two little towns, crossing the Clyde at one of the fords. To this circumstance, aided by the superstitious fancies of a rude age, impressed with awe at the mystic Masonic ceremonies and processions attendant on the great work going on in Glasgow, may be ascribed the above myth; just as another myth, probably from the same cause, associates the builders of the 'Hie Kirk' with a race of pigmies.

We have to thank the craftsmen of Glasgow for the preservation of our venerable Cathedral, as in 1578, when the Reformed ministers of Glasgow with Andrew Melville at their head, persuaded the magistrates to pull it down and build two or three churches with the materials, and had all in readiness to commence operations, they rose in arms in a body, and threatened death to the first man that should touch a stone of the building, and to bury under the ruins all those who would raise their hands for such a purpose. The matter was reported to the King and Council, when James the sixth, to whose memory be all honour, decided in favour of the Trades of Glasgow, and sharply reproved the magistrates.

Fully fifty years ago – on a beautiful day in the month of June, 1843 – I remember taking two friends to visit the Cathedral. They were impressed with what they saw, and, with the desire of better showing them St Mungo and its surroundings, we asked permission to go to the top of the spire. The stairs were dark and dusty, so we felt thankful when the top was reached. We were doomed to disappointment, however. A change of wind had brought clouds of mist and smoke, which obscured everything. Our stay was brief, and when we reached *terra firma* we could hardly recognise each other. We were like a trio of chimney sweepers; with the hot day and perspiration we had adhibited a liberal share of the 'stour' which had accumulated on the stair for many decades. Truly we were fit subjects for a thorough cleansing.

'Captured in Glasgow'

from The Wallace

BLIND HARRY (fl. 1470–1492)

(The description of the capture of Wallace at Robroyston at times resembles a movie fight-scene. Even today, the landscape round about the present-day monument to these events is strangely empty and evocative.)

Robroyston was near the place beside
And but one house where Wallace used to bide . . .
After midnight in hands they have him tane,
Slumbered on sleep, no man with him but ane.
Keirly they took and led him frae that place.
Did him to death withoutten longer space.
They thought to bind Wallace with strengths strong,
On foot he got these . . . among:
He gripped about, but no weapons he fand,
Yet with a stool that did beside him stand
The back of one he bursted in the thrang,
And of another the harns out he dang,
And als many as hands could on him lay,
By force him hint, for to have him away:
But that power on foot might not him lead
Out of that house while they or he were dead.
Sir John (*'False' Monteith*) saw wel by force it might not be,
Ere he were tane, rather he thought to die:
Menteith bade cease, and then spake to Wallace.
And showed him forth and ful right subtil case.

[And under promise of giving safe conduct Menteith seizes the brave Wallace and leads him to trial and execution.]

'The Rhyme of Sir Launcelot Bogle'

W.E. AYTOUN (1818–1865)

(WILLIAM EDMONDSTOUNE)

There's a pleasant place of rest, near a City of the West,
Where its bravest and its best find their grave.
Below the willows weep, and their hoary branches steep.
In the waters still and deep,
Not a wave!

And the old Cathedral Wall, so scathed and grey and tall,
Like a priest surveying all, stands beyond,
And the ringing of its bell, when the ringers ring it well,
Makes a kind of tidal swell
On the pond.

And there it was I lay, on a beauteous summer's day,
With the odour of the hay floating by;
And I heard the blackbirds sing, and the bells demurely ring,
Chime by chime, ting by ting,
Droppingly.

Then my thoughts went wandering back, on a very beaten track,
To the confine deep and black of the tomb,
And I wonder'd who he was, that is laid beneath the grass,
Where the dandelion has
Such a bloom.

Then I straightway did espy, with my slantly sloping eye,
And carved stone hard by, somewhat worn;
And I read in letters cold – Here . lyes . Launcelot . ye . bolde,
Off . ye . race . off . Bogile . old,
Glasgow . borne.

He . wals . ane . valyaunt . knychte . maist . terrible . in . fychte.
Here the letters fail'd outright, but I knew
That a stout crusading lord, who had cross'd the Jordan's ford,
Lay there beneath the sward,
Wet with dew.

Time and tide they pass'd away, on that pleasant summer's day,
And around me, as I lay, all grew old:
Sank the chimneys from the town, and the clouds of vapour brown
No longer, like a crown,
O'er it roll'd.

Sank the great Saint Rollox stalk, like a pile of dingy chalk;
Disappear'd the cypress walk, and the flowers.
And a donjon keep arose, that might baffle any foes,
With its men-at-arms in rows,
On the towers.

And the flag that flaunted there, show'd the gim and grizzly bear,
Which the Bogles always wear for their crest.
And I heard the warder call, as he stood upon the wall,
'Wake ye up! my comrades all,
From your rest!

'For, by the blessed rood, there's a glimpse of armour good
In the deep Cowcaddens' wood, o'er the stream;
And I hear the stifled hum, of a multitude that come,
Though they have not beat the drum,
It would seem!

'Go tell it to my Lord, lest he wish to man the ford
With partisan and sword, just beneath;
Ho, Gilkison and Nares! Ho, Provan of Cowlairs!
We'll back the bonny bears
To the death!'

To the tower above the moat, like one who heedeth not,
Came the bold Sir Launcelot, half undress'd;
On the outer rim he stood, and peer'd into the wood,
With his arms across him glued
On his breast.

And he mutter'd, 'Foe accurst! has thou dared to seek me first?
George of Gorbals, do thy worst – for I swear,
O'er thy gory corpse to ride, ere thy sister and my bride,
From my undissever'd side
Thou shalt tear!

'Ho herald mine, Brownlee; ride forth, I pray, and see,
Who, what, and whence is he, foe or friend!
Sir Roderick Dalgleish, and my foster-brother Neish
With his bloodhounds in the leash,
Shall attend.'

Forth went the herald stout, o'er the drawbridge and without,
Then a wild and savage shout rose amain,
Six arrows sped their force, and a pale and bleeding corse,
He sank from off his horse
On the plain!

Back drew the bold Dalgleish, back started stalwart Neish,
With his bloodhounds in the leash, from Brownlee.
'Now shame be to the sword that made thee knight and lord,
Thou caitiff thrice abhorr'd,
Shame on thee!

'Ho, bowmen, bend your bows! Discharge upon the foes,
Forthwith no end of those heavy bolts.
Three angels to the brave who finds the foe a grave,
And a gallows for the slave
Who revolts!'

The days the combat lasted; but the bold defenders fasted,
While the foemen, better pastied, fed their host;
You might hear the savage cheers of the hungry Gorbaliers,
As at night they dress'd the steers
For the roast.

And Sir Launcelot grew thin, and Provan's double chin
Show'd sundry folds of skin down beneath;
In silence and in grief found Gilkison relief,
Nor did Neish the spell-word, beef,
Dare to breathe.

To the ramparts Edith came, that fair and youthful dame,
With the rosy evening flame on her face.
She sigh'd, and look'd around on the soldiers on the ground,
Who but little penance found,
Saying grace!

And she said unto her lord, as he lean'd upon his sword,
'One short and little word may I speak?
I cannot bear to view those eyes so ghastly blue,
Or mark the sallow hue
Of thy cheek!

'I know the rage and wrath that my furious brother hath
Is less against us both than at me.
Then, dearest, let me go to find among the foe
An arrow from the bow,
Like Brownlee.'

'I would soil my father's name, I would lose my treasured fame,
Ladye mine, should such a shame on me light:
While I wear a belted brand, together still we stand,
Heart to heart, hand to hand!'
Said the knight.

'All our changes are not lost, as your brother and his host
Shall discover to their cost rather hard!
Ho, Provan! take this key – hoist up the Malvoisie,
And heap it, d'ye see,
In the yard.

'Of usquebaugh and rum, you will find, I reckon, some,
Besides the beer and mum, extra stout;
Go straightway to your tasks, and roll me all the casks,
As also range the flasks,
Just without.

'If I know the Gorbaliers, they are sure to dip their ears
In the very inmost tiers of the drink.
Let them win the outer-court, and hold it for their sport,
Since their time is rather short,
I should think!'

With a loud triumphant yell, as the heavy drawbridge fell,
Rush'd the Gorbaliers pell-mell, wild as Druids;
Mad with thirst for human gore, how they threaten'd and they swore,
Till they stumbled on the floor,
O'er the fluids!

Dumb as death stood Launcelot, as though he heard him not,
But his bosom Provan smote, and he swore:
And Sir Roderick Dalgleish remark'd aside to Neish,
'Never sure did thirsty fish
Swallow more!

'Thirty casks are nearly done, yet the revel's scarce begun,
It were knightly sport and fun to strike in!'
'Nay, tarry till they come,' quoth Neish, 'unto the rum –
They are working at the mum,
And the gin!'

Then straight there did appear to each gallant Gorbalier
Twenty castles dancing near, all around,
The solid earth did shake, and the stones beneath them quake,
And sinuous as a snake
Moved the ground.

Why and wherefore they had come, seem'd intricate to some,
But all agreed the rum was divine.
And they look'd with bitter scorn on their leader highly born,
Who preferr'd to fill his horn
Up with wine!

Then said Launcelot the tall, 'Bring the chargers from their stall;
Lead them straight unto the hall, down below:
Draw your weapons from your side, fling the gates asunder wide,
And together we shall ride
On the foe!'

Then Provan knew full well as he leap'd into his selle,
That few would 'scape to tell how they fared,
And Gilkison and Nares, both mounted on their mares,
Look'd terrible as bears,
All prepared.

With his bloodhounds in the leash, stood the iron-sinew'd Neish,
  And the falchion of Dalgeish glitter'd bright –
'Now, wake the trumpet's blast; and, comrades, follow fast;
  Smite them down unto the last!'
  Cried the knight.

In the cumber'd yard without, there was shriek, and yell, and shout,
  As the warriors wheel'd about, all in mail.
On the miserable kerne, fell the death-strokes stiff and stern,
  As the deer treads down the fern,
  In the vale!

Saint Mungo be my guide! It was goodly in that tide
  To see the Bogle ride in his haste;
He accompanied each blow, with a cry of 'Ha!' or 'Ho!'
  And always cleft the foe
  To the waist.

'George of Gorbals – craven lord! thou didst threat me with the cord,
  Come forth and brave my sword, if you dare!'
But he met with no reply, and never could descry
  The glitter of his eye
  Anywhere.

Ere the dawn of morning shone, all the Gorbaliers were down,
  Like a field of barley mown in the ear;
It had done a soldier good, to see how Provan stood,
  With Neish all bathed in blood,
  Panting near.

'Now ply ye to your tasks – go carry down those casks,
  And place the empty flasks on the floor.
George of Gorbals scarce will come, with trumpet and with drum,
  To taste our beer and rum
  Any more!'

So they plied them to their tasks, and they carried down the casks,
  And replaced the empty flasks on the floor;
But pallid for a week was the cellar-master's cheek,
  For he swore he heard a shriek
  Through the door.

When the merry Christmas came, and the Yule-log lent its flame
To the face of squire and dame in the hall,
The cellarer went down to tap October brown,
Which was rather of renown
'Mongst them all.

He placed the spigot low, and gave the cask a blow,
But his liquor would not flow through the pin.
'Sure, 'tis sweet as honeysuckles!' so he rapp'd it with his knuckles,
But a sound, as if of buckles,
Clash'd within.

'Bring a hatchet, varlets, here!' and they cleft the cask of beer:
What a spectacle of fear met their sight!
There George of Gorbals lay, skull and bones all blanch'd and grey,
In the arms he bore the day
Of the fight!

I have sung this ancient tale, not, I trust, without avail,
Though the moral ye may fail to perceive;
Sir Launcelot is dust, and his gallant sword is rust,
And now, I think, I must
Take my leave!

'In the Laigh-Kirk'

from Rob Roy

WALTER SCOTT (1771–1832)

The action takes place in 1715 just before the Jacobite Rebellion. Our narrator is the young English hero, Francis or Frank Osbaldistone, who has become embroiled in Jacobite intrigues and has come north to look for the outlaw Rob Roy MacGregor. Arriving in Glasgow accompanied by the rascally and garrulous Andrew Fairservice, Frank goes to the Barony or Laigh Kirk of the Cathedral, i.e., the lower level of the magnificent thirteenth-century structure. Scott paints a superbly imagined picture of Glasgow in the aftermath of the 1707 Union and on the eve of its rise to prosperity. Rob Roy *was published in 1817, much of it being written on the edge of MacGregor country at Ross Priory on Loch Lomondside, and to some extent it has echoes of Scott's first great novel* Waverley *– an outsider comes into an alien Highland setting and is strangely drawn to Romantic Jacobitism.*

Scott is often credited with being the inventor of the historical novel and certainly most of the characteristics of that genre – accuracy, credibility and historical awareness – are to be found here. So too is a sense of the dramatic possibilities of evocative location, as in the scene described in our extract, when Osbaldistone encounters a mysterious stranger who issues a warning about his presence in Glasgow. This stranger is shown in due course to be Rob Roy himself.

This episode comes after a good proportion of the novel has elapsed, but there is no doubt that the Glasgow and the Highland passages are virtually unmatched in all of historical fiction. At times Scott even seems to anticipate the cinema with his sense of the dramatic possibilities. It can be no accident that the nineteenth-century stage adaptation attained a popularity greater than almost any play in Scottish theatrical history. As to the structure of the plot, this extract skilfully introduces the themes of old and new and of Highland and Lowland character, and subtly prepares the reader for the revelation of Rob and of the novel's other great character, the Glasgow merchant, Bailie Nicol Jarvie.

IN THE LAIGH-KIRK

We now pursued our journey to the north-westward, at a rate much slower than that at which we had achieved our nocturnal retreat from England. One chain of barren and uninteresting hills succeeded another, until the more fertile vale of Clyde opened upon us; and with such dispatch as we might we gained the town, or, as my guide pertinaciously termed it, the city, of Glasgow. Of late years, I understand, it has fully deserved the name, which, by a sort of political second-sight, my guide assigned to it. An extensive and increasing trade with the West Indies and American colonies, has, if I am rightly informed, laid the foundation of wealth and prosperity, which, if carefully strengthened and built upon, may one day support an immense fabric of commercial prosperity, but, in the earlier time of which I speak, the dawn of this splendour had not arisen. The Union had, indeed, opened to Scotland the trade of the English colonies; but, betwixt want of capital, and the national jealousy of the English, the merchants of Scotland were as yet excluded, in a great measure, from the exercise of the privileges which that memorable treaty conferred on them. Glasgow lay on the wrong side of the island for participating in the east country or continental trade, by which the trifling commerce as yet possessed by Scotland chiefly supported itself. Yet, though she then gave small promise of the commercial eminence to which, I am informed, she seems now likely one day to attain, Glasgow, as the principal central town of the western district of Scotland, was a place of considerable rank and importance. The broad and brimming Clyde, which flows so near its walls, gave the means of an inland navigation of some importance. Not only the fertile plains in its immediate neighbourhood, but the districts of Ayr and Dumfries, regarded Glasgow as their capital, to which they transmitted their produce, and received in return such necessaries and luxuries as their consumption required.

The dusky mountains of the Western Highlands often sent forth wilder tribes to frequent the marts of St Mungo's favourite city. Hordes of wild, shaggy, dwarfish cattle and ponies, conducted by Highlanders, as wild, as shaggy, and sometimes as dwarfish, as the animals they had in charge, often traversed the streets of Glasgow. Strangers gazed with surprise on the antique and fantastic dress, and listened to the unknown and dissonant sounds of their language, while the mountaineers, armed even while engaged in this peaceful occupation with musket and pistol, sword, dagger, and target, stared with astonishment on the articles of luxury of which they knew not the use, and with an avidity which seemed somewhat alarming on the articles which they knew and valued. It is always with unwillingness that the Highlander quits his deserts, and at this early period it was like tearing a pine from its rock, to plant him elsewhere. Yet even then the mountain glens were overpeopled, although thinned occasionally by famine or by the sword, and many of their inhabitants strayed down to Glasgow – there formed settlements – there sought and found employment, although different, indeed, from that of their native hills. This supply of a hardy and useful population was of consequence to the prosperity of the place, furnished the means of carrying on the few manufactures which the town already boasted, and laid the foundation of its future prosperity.

The exterior of the city corresponded with these promising circumstances. The principal street was broad and important, decorated with public buildings, of an architecture rather striking than correct in point of taste, and running between rows of tall houses, built of stone, the fronts of which were occasionally richly ornamented with mason-work; a circumstance which gave the street an imposing air of dignity and grandeur, of which most English towns are in some measure deprived, by the slight, unsubstantial, and perishable quality and appearance of the bricks with which they are constructed.

In the western metropolis of Scotland, my guide and I arrived on a Saturday evening, too late to entertain thoughts of business of any kind. We alighted at the door of a jolly hostler-wife, as Andrew called her, the Ostelere of old father Chaucer, by whom we were civilly received.

On the following morning the bells pealed from every steeple, announcing the sanctity of the day. Notwithstanding, however, what I had heard of the severity with which the Sabbath is observed in Scotland, my first impulse, not unnaturally, was to seek out Owen; but on enquiry I found that my attempt would be in vain, 'until kirk-time was ower'. Not only did my landlady and guide jointly assure me that 'there wadna be a living soul either in the counting-house or dwelling-house of Messrs. MacVittie, MacFin, and Company,' to which Owen's letter referred me, but, moreover, 'far less would I find any of the partners there. They were serious men, and wad be where a' gude Christians ought to be at sic a time, and that was in the Barony Laigh Kirk.'

Andrew Fairservice, whose disgust at the law of his country had fortunately not extended itself to the other learned professions of his native land, now sung forth the praises of the preacher who was to perform the duty, to which my hostess replied with many loud amens. The result was, that I determined to go to this popular place of worship, as much with the purpose of learning, if possible, whether Owen had arrived in Glasgow, as with any great expectation of edification. My hopes were exalted by the assurance, that, if Mr Ephraim MacVittie (worthy man) were in the land of life, he would surely honour the Barony Kirk that day with his presence; and if he chanced to have a stranger within his gates, doubtless he would bring him to the duty along with him. This probability determined my motions, and, under the escort of my faithful Andrew, I set forth for the Barony Kirk.

On this occasion, however, I had little need of his guidance; for the crowd, which forced its way up a steep and rough-paved street, to hear the most popular preacher in the west of Scotland, would of itself have swept me along with it. On attaining the summit of the hill, we turned to the left, and a pair of folding doors admitted us, amongst others, into the open and extensive burying-place which surrounds the Minster, or Cathedral Church of Glasgow. The pile is of a gloomy and massive, rather than of an elegant, style of Gothic architecture; but its peculiar character is so strongly preserved, and so well suited with the accompaniments that surround it, that the impression of the first view was awful and solemn in the extreme. I was indeed so much struck, that I resisted for a few minutes all Andrew's efforts to drag me into the interior of the building, so deeply was I engaged in surveying its outward character.

Situated in a populous and considerable town, this ancient and massive pile has the appearance of the most sequestered solitude. High walls divide it from the buildings of the city on one side; on the other, it is bounded by a ravine, at the bottom of which, and invisible to the eye, murmurs a wandering rivulet, adding, by its gentle noise, to the imposing solemnity of the scene. On the opposite side of the ravine rises a steep bank, covered with fir-trees closely planted, whose dusky shade extends itself over the cemetery with an appropriate and gloomy effect. The churchyard itself had a peculiar character; for though in reality extensive, it is small in proportion to the number of respectable inhabitants who are interred within it, and whose graves are almost all covered with tombstones. There is therefore no room for the long rank grass, which, in most cases, partially clothes the surface of those retreats, where the wicked cease from troubling, and the weary are at rest. The broad flat monumental stones are placed so close to each other, that the precincts appear to be flagged with them, and, though roofed only by the heavens, resemble the floor of one of our old English churches, where the pavement is covered with sepulchral inscriptions. The contents of these sad records of mortality, the vain sorrows which they preserve, the stern lesson which they teach of the nothingness of humanity, the extent of ground which they so closely cover, and their uniform and melancholy tenor, reminded me of the roll of the prophet, which was 'written within and without, and there was written therein lamentations and mourning and woe.'

The Cathedral itself corresponds in impressive majesty with these accompaniments. We feel that its appearance is heavy, yet that the effect produced would be destroyed were it lighter or more ornamental. It is the only metropolitan church in Scotland, excepting, as I am informed, the cathedral of Kirkwall, in the Orkneys, which remained uninjured at the Reformation; and Andrew Fairservice, who saw with great pride the effect which it produced upon my mind, thus accounted for its preservation. 'Ah! it's a brave kirk – nane o' yere whigmaleeries and curliewurlies and open-steek hems about it – a' solid, weel-jointed mason-wark, that will stand as lang as the warld, keep hands and gunpowther aff it. It had amaist a douncome lang syne at the Reformation, when they pu'd doun the kirks of St Andrews and Perth, and thereawa', to cleanse them o' Papery, and idolatry, and image worship, and surplices, and sic like rags o' the muckle hure that sitteth on seven hills, as if ane wasna braid eneugh for her auld hinder end. Sae the commons o' Renfrew, and o' the Barony, and the Gorbals, and a' about, they behoved to come into Glasgow ae fair morning, to try their hand on purging the High Kirk o' Popish nick-nackets. But the townsmen o' Glasgow, they were feared their auld edifice might slip the girths in gaun through siccan rough physic, sae they rang the common bell, and assembled the train-bands wi' took o' drum. By good luck, the worthy James Rabat was Dean o' Guild that year – (and a gude mason he was himsell, made him the keener to keep up the auld bigging,) and the trades assembled, and offered downright battle to the commons, rather than their kirk should coup the crans, as others had done elsewhere. It wasna for luve o' Paperie – na, na! – nane could ever say that o' the trades o' Glasgow – Sae they sune came to an agreement to take a' the idolatrous statues of sants (sorrow be on them) out o' their neuks – And sae the bits o' stane idols were broken in pieces by Scripture warrant, and flung into the Molendinar burn, and the auld kirk stood as crouse as a cat when the flaes are kaimed aff her, and a'body was alike pleased. And I hae heard wise folk sae, that if the same had been done in ilka kirk in Scotland, the Reform wad just hae been as pure as it is e'en now, and we wad hae mair Christian-like kirks; for I hae been sae lang in England, that naething will drived out o' my head, that the dog-kennel at Osbaldistone Hall is better than mony a house o' God in Scotland.'

Thus saying, Andrew led the way into the place of worship.

Notwithstanding the impatience of my conductor, I could not forbear to pause and gaze for some minutes on the exterior of the building, rendered more impressively dignified by the solitude which ensued when its hitherto open gates were closed, after having, as it were, devoured the multitudes which had lately crowded the churchyard, but now, enclosed within the building, were engaged, as the choral swell of voices from within announced to us, in the solemn exercises of devotion. The sound of so many voices, united by the distance into one harmony, and freed from those harsh discordances which jar the ear when heard more near, combining with the murmuring brook, and the wind which sung among the old firs, affected me with a sense of sublimity. All nature, as invoked by the Psalmist whose verses they chanted, seemed united in offering that solemn praise in which trembling is mixed with joy as she addresses her Maker. I had heard the service of high mass in France, celebrated with all the éclat which the choicest music, the richest dresses, the most imposing ceremonies, could confer on it; yet it fell short in effect of the simplicity of the Presbyterian worship. The devotion, in which every one took a share, seemed so superior to that which was recited by musicians, as a lesson which they had learned by rote, that it gave the Scottish worship all the advantage of reality over acting.

As I lingered to catch more of the solemn sound, Andrew, whose impatience became ungovernable, pulled me by the sleeve – 'Come awa,' sir – Come awa', we maunna be late o' gaun in to disturb the worship; if we bide here, the searchers will be on us, and carry us to the guard-house for being idlers in kirk-time.'

Thus admonished, I followed my guide, but not, as I had supposed, into the body of the cathedral. 'This gate – this gate, sir!' he exclaimed, dragging me off as I made towards the main entrance of the building, – 'There's but cauldrife law-wark gaun on yonder – carnal morality, as dow'd and as fusionless as rue leaves at Yule – Here's the real savour of doctrine.'

So saying, we entered a small low-arched door, secured by a wicket, which a grave-looking person seemed on the point of closing, and descended several steps as if into the funeral vaults beneath the church. It was even so; for in these subterranean precincts, why chosen for such a purpose I knew not, was established a very singular place of worship.

Conceive, Tresham, an extensive range of low-browed, dark, and twilight vaults, such as are used for sepulchres in other countries, and had long been dedicated to the same purpose in this, a portion of which was seated with pews, and used as a church. The part of the vaults thus occupied, though capable of containing a congregation of many hundreds, bore a small proportion to the darker and more extensive caverns which yawned around what may be termed the inhabited space. In those waste regions of oblivion, dusty banners and tattered escutcheons, indicated the graves of those who were once, doubtless, 'princes in Israel'. Inscriptions, which could only be read by the painful antiquary, in language as obsolete as the act of devotional charity which they implored, invited the passengers to pray for the souls of those whose bodies rested beneath. Surrounded by these receptacles of the last remains of mortality, I found a numerous congregation engaged in the act of prayer. The Scotch perform this duty in a standing, instead of a kneeling posture, more, perhaps, to take as broad a distinction as possible from the ritual of Rome than for any better reason, since I have observed that in their family worship, as doubtless in their private devotions, they adopt, in their immediate address to the Deity, that posture which other Christians use as the humblest and most reverential. Standing, therefore, the men being uncovered, a crowd of several hundreds of both sexes, and all ages, listened with great reverence and attention to the extempore, at least the unwritten, prayer of an aged clergyman,* who was very popular in the city. Educated in the same religious persuasion, I seriously bent my mind to join in the devotion of the day, and it was not till the congregation resumed their seats that my attention was diverted to the consideration of the appearance of all around me.

At the conclusion of the prayer, most of the men put on their hats or bonnets, and all who had the happiness to have seats sate down. Andrew and I were not of this number, having been too late of entering the church to secure such accommodation. We stood among a number of other persons in the same situation, forming a sort of ring around the seated part of the congregation. Behind and around us were the vaults I have already described; before us the devout audience, dimly shown by the light which streamed on the faces through one or two low Gothic windows, such as give air and light to charnel-houses. By this were seen the usual variety of countenances, which are generally turned towards a Scotch pastor on such occasions, almost all composed to attention, unless where a father or mother here and there recalls the wandering eyes of a lively child, or disturbs the slumbers of a dull one. The high-boned and harsh countenance of the nation, with the expression of intelligence and

* I have in vain laboured to discover this gentleman's name, and the period of his incumbency. I do not, however, despair to see these points, with some others which may elude my sagacity, satisfactorily elucidated by one or other of the periodical publications which have devoted their pages to explanatory commentaries on my former volumes; and whose research and ingenuity claim my peculiar gratitude, for having discovered many persons and circumstances connected with my narratives, of which I myself never so much as dreamed.

shrewdness which it frequently exhibits, is seen to more advantage in the act of devotion, or in the ranks of war, than on lighter and more cheerful occasions of assemblage. The discourse of the preacher was well qualified to call forth the various feelings and faculties of his audience.

Age and infirmities had impaired the powers of a voice originally strong and sonorous. He read his text with a pronunciation somewhat inarticulate; but when he closed the Bible, and commenced his sermon, his tones gradually strengthened, as he entered with vehemence into the arguments which he maintained. They related chiefly to the abstract points of the Christian faith, subjects grave, deep, and fathomless by mere human reason, but for which, with equal ingenuity and propriety, he sought a key in liberal quotations from the inspired writings. My mind was unprepared to coincide in all his reasoning, nor was I sure that in some instances I rightly comprehended his positions. But nothing could be more impressive than the eager enthusiastic manner of the good old man, and nothing more ingenious than his mode of reasoning. The Scotch, it is well known, are more remarkable for their exercise of their intellectual powers, than for the keenness of their feelings; they are, therefore, more moved by logic than by rhetoric, and more attracted by acute and argumentative reasoning on doctrinal points, than influenced by the enthusiastic appeals to the heart and to the passions, by which popular preachers in other countries win the favour of their hearers.

Among the attentive group which I now saw, might be distinguished various expressions similar to those of the audience in the famous cartoon of Paul preaching at Athens. Here sat a zealous and intelligent Calvinist, with brows bent just as much as to indicate profound attention; lips slightly compressed; eyes fixed on the minister, with an expression of decent pride, as if sharing the triumph of his argument; the forefinger of the right hand touching successively those of the left, as the preacher, from argument to argument, ascended towards his conclusion. Another, with fiercer and sterner look, intimated at once his contempt of all who doubted the creed of his pastor, and his joy at the appropriate punishment denounced against them. A third, perhaps belonging to a different congregation, and present only by accident or curiosity, had the appearance of internally impeaching some link of the reasoning; and you might plainly read, in the slight motion of his head, his doubts as to the soundness of the preacher's argument. The greater part listened with a calm satisfied countenance, expressive of a conscious merit in being present and in listening to such an ingenious discourse, although, perhaps, unable entirely to comprehend it. The women in general belonged to this last division of the audience; the old, however, seeming more grimly intent upon the abstract doctrines laid before them; while the younger females permitted their eyes occasionally to make a modest circuit around the congregation; and some of them, Tresham, (if my vanity did not greatly deceive me,) contrived to distinguish your friend and servant, as a handsome young stranger, and an Englishman. As to the rest of the congregation, the stupid gaped, yawned, or slept, till awakened by the application of their more zealous neighbour's heels to their shins; and the idle indicated their inattention by the wandering of their eyes, but dared give no more decided token of weariness. Amid the Lowland costume of coat and cloak, I could here and there discern a Highland plaid, the wearer of which, resting on his basket-hilt, sent his eyes among the audience with unrestrained curiosity of savage wonder; and who, in all probability, was inattentive to the sermon, for a very pardonable reason – because he did not understand the language in which it was delivered. The martial and wild look, however, of these stragglers, added a kind of character which the congregation could not have exhibited without them. They were more numerous, Andrew afterwards observed, owing to some cattle-fair in the neighbourhood.

Such was the group of countenances rising tier on tier, discovered to my critical inspection by such sunbeams as forced their way through the narrow Gothic lattices of the Laigh Kirk of Glasgow; and, having illuminated the attentive congregation, lost themselves in the vacuity of the vaults behind, giving to the nearer part of their labyrinth a sort of imperfect twilight, and leaving their recesses in an utter darkness, which gave them the appearance of being interminable.

I have already said that I stood with others in the exterior circle, with my face to the preacher, and my back to those vaults which I have so often mentioned. My position rendered me particularly obnoxious to any interruption which arose from any slight noise amongst these retiring arches, where the least sound was multiplied by a thousand echoes. The occasional sound of rain-drops, which, admitted through some cranny in the ruined roof, fell successively, and splashed upon the pavement beneath, caused me to turn my head more than once to the place from whence it seemed to proceed; and when my eyes took that direction, I found it difficult to withdraw them; such is the pleasure our imagination receives from the attempt to penetrate as far as possible into an intricate labyrinth, imperfectly lighted, and exhibiting objects which irritate our curiosity, only because they acquire a mysterious interest from being undefined and dubious. My eyes became habituated to the gloomy atmosphere to which I directed them, and insensibly my mind became more interested in their discoveries than in the metaphysical subtleties which the preacher was enforcing.

My father had often checked me for this wandering mood of mind, arising perhaps from an excitability of imagination to which he was a stranger; and the finding myself at present solicited by these temptations to innattention, recalled the time when I used to walk, led by his hand, to Mr Shower's chapel, and the earnest injunctions which he then laid on me to redeem the time, because the days were evil. At present, the picture which my thoughts suggested, far from fixing my attention, destroyed the portion I had yet left, by conjuring up to my recollection the peril in which his affairs now stood. I endeavoured, in the lowest whisper I could frame, to request Andrew to obtain information, whether any of the gentlemen of the firm of MacVittie & Co. were at present in the congregation. But Andrew, wrapped in profound attention to the sermon, only replied to my suggestion by hard punches with his elbow, as signals to me to remain silent. I next strained my eyes, with equally bad success, to see if, among the sea of upturned faces which bent their eyes on the pulpit as a common centre, I could discover the sober and business-like physiognomy of Owen. But not among the broad beavers of the Glasgow citizens, or the yet broader brimmed Lowland bonnets of the peasants of Lanarkshire, could I see any thing resembling the decent periwig, starched ruffles, or the uniform suit of light brown garments, appertaining to the head clerk of the establishment of Osbaldistone and Tresham. My anxiety now returned on me with such violence, as to overpower not only the novelty of the scene around me, by which it had hitherto been diverted, but moreover my sense of decorum. I pulled Andrew hard by the sleeve, and intimated my wish to leave the church, and pursue my investigation as I could. Andrew, obdurate in the Laigh Kirk of Glasgow as on the mountains of Cheviot, for some time deigned me no answer; and it was only when he found I could not otherwise be kept quiet that he condescended to inform me, that, being once in the church, we could not leave it till service was over, because the doors were locked so soon as the prayers began. Having thus spoken in a brief and peevish whisper, Andrew again assumed the air of intelligent and critical importance, and attention to the preacher's discourse.

While I endeavoured to make a virtue of necessity, and recall my attention to the sermon, I was again disturbed by a singular interruption. A voice from behind whispered distinctly in my ear, 'You are in danger in this city.' I turned round as if mechanically.

One or two starched and ordinary-looking mechanics stood beside and behind me, stragglers, who, like ourselves, had been too late in obtaining entrance. But a glance at their faces satisfied me, though I could hardly say why, that none of these was the person who had spoken to me. Their countenances seemed all composed to attention to the sermon, and not one of them returned any glance of intelligence to the inquisitive and startled look with which I surveyed them. A massive round pillar, which was close behind us, might have concealed the speaker the instant he uttered his mysterious caution; but wherefore it was given in such a place, or to what species of danger it directed my attention, or by whom the warning was uttered, were points on which my imagination lost itself in conjecture. It would, however, I concluded, be repeated, and I resolved to keep my countenance turned towards the clergyman, that the whisperer might be tempted to renew his communication under the idea that the first had passed unobserved.

My plan succeeded. I had not resumed the appearance of attention to the preacher for five minutes, when the same voice whispered, 'Listen – but do not look back.' I kept my face in the same direction. 'You are in danger in this place,' the voice proceeded; 'so am I – Meet me to-night on the Brigg, at twelve preceesely – keep at home till the gloaming, and avoid observation.'

Here the voice ceased, and I instantly turned my head. But the speaker had, with still greater promptitude, glided behind the pillar, and escaped my observation. I was determined to catch a sight of him, if possible, and, extricating myself from the outer circle of hearers, I also stepped behind the column. All there was empty; and I could only see a figure wrapped in a mantle, whether a Lowland cloak, or Highland plaid, I could not distinguish, which traversed, like a phantom, the dreary vacuity of vaults which I have described.

I made a mechanical attempt to pursue the mysterious form, which glided away, and vanished in the vaulted cemetery, like the spectre of one of the numerous dead who rested within its precincts. I had little chance of arresting the course of one obviously determined not to be spoken with; but that little chance was lost by my stumbling and falling before I had made three steps from the column. The obscurity which occasioned my misfortune covered my disgrace; which I accounted rather lucky, for the preacher, with that stern authority which the Scottish ministers assume for the purpose of keeping order in their congregations, interrupted his discourse, to desire the 'proper officer' to take into custody the causer of this disturbance in the place of worship. As the noise, however, was not repeated, the beadle, or whatever else he was called, did not think it necessary to be rigorous in searching out the offender; so that I was enabled, without attracting farther observation, to place myself by Andrew's side in my original position. The service proceeded, and closed without the occurrence of anything else worthy of notice.

As the congregation departed and dispersed, my friend Andrew exclaimed, 'See yonder is worthy Mr MacVittie and Mrs MacVittie, and Miss Alison MacVittie, and Mr Thamas MacFin, that they say is to marry Miss Alison, if a' bowls row right – she'll hae a hantle siller, if she's no that bonny.'

My eyes took the direction he pointed out. Mr MacVittie was a tall, thin, elderly man, with hard features, thick grey eyebrows, light eyes, and, as I imagined, a sinister expression of countenance, from which my heart recoiled. I remembered the warning I had received in the church, and hesitated to address this person, though I could not allege to myself any rational ground of dislike or suspicion.

I was yet in suspense, when Andrew, who mistook my hesitation for bashfulness, proceeded to exhort me to lay it aside. 'Speak till him – speak till him, Mr Francis – he's no provost yet, though they say he'll be my lord neist year. Speak till him, then, – he'll gie ye a decent answer for as rich as he is, unless ye were wanting siller frae him – they say he's dour to draw his purse.'

It immediately occurred to me, that if this merchant were really of the churlish and avaricious disposition which Andrew intimated, there might be some caution necessary in making myself known, as I could not tell how accounts might stand between my father and him. This consideration came in aid of the mysterious hint which I had received, and the dislike which I had conceived at the man's countenance. Instead of addressing myself directly to him, as I had designed to have done, I contented myself with desiring Andrew to enquire at Mr MacVittie's house the address of Mr Owen, an English gentleman; and I charged him not to mention the person from whom he received the commission, but to bring me the result to the small inn where we lodged. This Andrew promised to do. He said something of the duty of my attending the evening service; but added, with a causticity natural to him, that 'in troth, if folk couldna keep their legs still, but wad needs be couping the creels ower throughstanes, as if they wad raise the very dead folk wi' the clatter, a kirk wi' a chimley in't was fittest for them.'

4
THE MERCHANT CITY
Introduction

For all the commerce and industry with which we now associate Glasgow, and the by-products of industrialisation – slums, pollution, dirt and noise – earlier travellers united in praising the city for its beauty and neatness. Edmund Burt wrote in the late 1720s:

> Glasgow is, to outward appearance, the prettiest and most uniform town that I ever saw; and I believe that there is nothing like it in Britain.
>
> It has a spacious carrifour, where stands the cross; and going round it, you have, by turns, the view of four streets, that in regular angles proceed from thence. The houses of these streets are faced with ashler stone, they are well sashed, all of one model, and piazzas run through them on either side, which give a good air to the buildings.

Glasgow commerce was evidently sufficiently prosperous to ensure that the city's civic buildings were remarkable for their quality. Richard Franck travelled in Scotland in 1656 and compiled his *Northern Memoirs*, in which he wrote:

> Now, let us descend to describe the splendour and gaiety of the city of Glasgow, which surpasseth most, if not all the corporations in Scotland. Here it is you may observe four large fair streets, modell'd, as it were, into a spacious quadrant; in the centre whereof their market-place is fix'd; near unto which stands a stately tolbooth, a very sumptuous, regulated, uniform fabrick, large and lofty, most industriously and artificially carved from the very foundation to the superstructure, to the great admiration of strangers and travellers. But this state-house, or tolbooth, is their western prodigy, infinitely excelling the model and usual build of town-halls; and is, without exception, the paragon of beauty in the west; whose compeer is no where to be found in the north, should you rally the rarities of all the corporations in Scotland . . .

> In the next place, we are to consider the merchants and traders in this eminent Glasgow, whose store-houses and ware-houses are stuft with merchandize, as their shops swell big with foreign commodities, and returns from France, and other remote parts, where they have agents and factors to correspond, and inrich their maritime ports, whose charter exceeds all the charters in Scotland; which is a considerable advantage to the city-inhabitants, because blest with privileges as large, nay, larger than any other corporation. Moreover, they dwell in the face of France, and a free trade, as I formerly told you. Nor is this all, for the staple of their country consists of linens, friezes, furs, tartans, pelts, hides, tallows, skins, and various other small manufacturers and commodities, not comprehended in this breviat.

This picture of a thriving trading community is reinforced by our extract from Daniel Defoe's *Tour through the Whole Island of Great Britain*. Defoe was writing in the immediate aftermath of the 1707 Treaty of Union – a measure which had been very unpopular in Glasgow. Walter Scott has Bailie Nicol Jarvie observe in *Rob Roy*:

> There's naething sae gude on this side o' time but it might hae been better, and that may be said o' the Union. Nane were keener against it than the Glasgow folk, wi' their rabblings and their risings and their mobs, as they ca' them now-a-days.

However, as the Bailie points out, Glasgow flourished from the access to the wider colonial markets that the Union brought and the rise of the Tobacco Lords was a significant feature of eighteenth-century Glasgow. John Strang's account of this colourful and influential group comes from *Glasgow and its Clubs* – a work of far wider interest than the title would suggest.

The rise of manufacturing industry, with the textile industry, in the vanguard, transformed Glasgow from the pretty cathedral town and university city depicted by Franck and Burt into a more recognisably industrial community. Glasgow's industrial growth drew in workers from beyond its boundaries, and a letter about the desire of a group of these workers, Catholic Highlanders, to enlist in the army in 1794, is a reminder of the varied sources of the city's workforce. In later generations more and more Highlanders were attracted to the city's industry, commerce and public services; Irish immigration (particularly after the Potato Famine of 1848), Jewish settlement, and in our own day immigration from Asia and the Caribbean have all added to the city's ethnic mix.

At the height of the Victorian period Glasgow was seen as the 'workshop of the world', 'the second city of the Empire', and its vast range of manufacturing industries were recorded in Francis H. Groome's epic *Ordnance Gazetteer of Scotland*.

Glasgow was, however, more than just a manufacturing centre. It was also a centre of banking, of commerce and of every conceivable form of retail trade. In 1871 a twenty-one-year-old of Irish extraction opened a grocer's shop in Glasgow's Stobcross Street. By dint of hard work, exploitation of modern transport and communications and a quite remarkable talent for publicity, the young man, Thomas Lipton, built up a world-wide trading company. By the age of thirty he was a millionaire; by 1898 he had been knighted; by 1902 he was a baronet. He died in 1931, leaving his fortune to charitable causes. Lipton was an exceptional case, but the city was full of merchants and businessmen in a smaller and more modest line of business, and building their villas in Bridge of Weir or Helensburgh.

John Buchan, who knew his Glasgow from his school and university days spent in the city, portrayed such a one in his romantic retired Glasgow grocer, Dickson McCunn, whose banker observed of him:

> The strength of this city . . . does not lie in its dozen very rich men, but in the hundred or two homely folk who make no parade of wealth. Men like Dickson McCunn, for example, who live all their life in a semi-detached villa and die worth half a million.

Not least of these businesses were the great Glasgow drapery warehouses such as the one which Frederick Niven describes in The Staff at Simson's. Campbell, Stewart & MacDonald's and its host of rivals provided not only Glasgow but, through their commercial travellers, the whole of Scotland, with fabrics and clothing, disseminating the latest fashions to the small towns and villages.

Buchan, as we said, knew Glasgow and Glaswegians, and the enterprise of the Glaswegian and his capacity to thrive in the most unlikely circumstances is demonstrated by his tale of 'Divus' Johnston. Buchan's contemporary, J.M. Barrie, said that there were 'few more impressive sights in the world than a Scotsman on the make' – but even Barrie had never seen a Glaswegian transformed into a god.

'A City of Business'

from A Tour Through the Whole Island of Great Britain

DANIEL DEFOE (1660–1731)

The author of Robinson Crusoe *and* Moll Flanders *had a life as varied and adventurous as that of any of his fictional characters, being in succession a hosiery merchant, soldier, secret agent, government propagandist and the father of the English novel.*

Defoe's knowledge of Scotland was first gained when he served as a secret agent for the English government in the tense years before the passing of the Act of Union. He obviously travelled fairly extensively in Scotland, penetrating as far as John o' Groats, while gathering information for his Tour, *which was published in three volumes in 1724–1726.*

Defoe's enthusiastic account of Glasgow: '. . . the cleanest and beautifullest, and best built city in Britain, London excepted' portrays what is almost a pre-industrial city. Defoe notes some muslin and linen manufacturing and the processing of sugar, but he concludes that it is 'a city of business' and describes the impact of the post-Union opening of the American colonial trade and the changing attitude to the Union which this produced – an attitude which we have already noted in the words of Scott's Bailie Nicol Jarvie.

Defoe also notes that once-famous Glasgow product the salted herring. So significant at one time was the Clydeside herring curing industry that a salt herring used to be known as a 'Glasgow Magistrate'.

It is interesting to see that even in the early eighteenth century the great Scottish diaspora was well underway. Defoe observes that Scots were volunteering to go out to the American colonies as indentured servants with the long-term aim of setting up as planters in their own right: '. . . if it goes on for many years more, Virginia may rather be called a Scots than an English plantation.'

A CITY OF BUSINESS

With the division of Cunningham I quitted the shire of Ayre, and the pleasantest country in Scotland, without exception. Joining to it north, and bordering on the Clyde itself, I mean the river, lies the little shire of Renfrew, or rather a barony, or a sherriffdom, call it as you will. It is a pleasant, rich, and populous, though small country, lying on the south bank of the Clyde; the soil is not thought to be so good as in Cunningham. But that is abundantly supplied by the many good towns, the neighbourhood of Glasgow, and of the Clyde, and great commerce of both. We kept our route as near along the coast as we could, from Irwin; so that we saw all the coast of the Firth of Clyde, and the very opening of the Clyde itself. The first town of note is called Greenock; 'tis not an ancient place, but seems to be grown up in later years, only by being a good road for ships, and where the ships ride that come into, and go out from Glasgow, just as the ships for London do in the downs. It has a castle to command the road and the town is well built, and has many rich trading families in it. It is the chief town on the west of Scotland for the herring fishing; and the merchants of Glasgow, who are concerned in the fishery, employ the Greenock vessels for the catching and curing the fish, and for several parts of their other trades, as well as carrying them afterwards abroad to market.

Their being ready on all hands to go to sea, makes the Glasgow merchants often leave their ships to the care of those Greenock men; and why not? for they are sensible they are their best seamen; they are also excellent pilots for those difficult seas.

The country between Pasely and Glasgow, on the bank of Clyde, I take to be one of the most agreeable places in Scotland, take its situation, its fertility, healthiness, the nearness of Glasgow, the neighbourhood of the sea, and altogether, at least, I may say, I saw none like it.

I am now come to the bank of Clyde: the Clyde and the Tweed may be said to cross Scotland in the south, their sources being not many miles asunder; and the two firths, from the Firth of Clyde to the Firth of Forth, have not an interval of above twelve or fourteen miles, which, if they were joined, as might easily be done, they might cross Scotland, as I might say, in the very centre.

Nor can I refrain mentioning how easy a work it would be to form a navigation, I mean a navigation of art from the Forth to the Clyde, and so join the two seas, as the King of France has done in a place five times as far, and five hundred times as difficult, namely from Thouloze to Narbonne. What an advantage in commerce would this be, opening the Irish trade to the merchants of Glasgow, making a communication between the west coat of Scotland, and the east coast of England, and even to London itself; nay, several ports of England, on the Irish Sea, from Liverpool northward, would all trade with London by such a canal, it would take up a volume by itself, to lay down the several advantages of Scotland, that would immediately occur by such a navigation, and then to give a true survey of the ground, the easiness of its being performed, and the probable charge of it, all which might be done. But it is too much to undertake here, it must lie till posterity, by the rising greatness of their commerce, shall not only feel the want of it, but find themselves able for the performance.

I am now crossed the Clyde to Glasgow, and I went over dry-footed without the bridge on which occasion I cannot but observe how differing a face the river presented itself in, at those two several times when only I was there; at the first, being in the month of June, the river was so low, that not the horses and carts only passed it just above the bridge, but the children and boys playing about, went everywhere, as if there was no river, only some little spreading brook, or wash, like such as we have at Enfield-Wash, or Chelston-Wash in Middlesex; and, as I told you, we crossed it dry-foot, that is, the water was scarce over the horses' hoofs.

But my next journey satisfied me, when coming into Glasgow from the east side, I found the river not only had filled up all the arches of the bridge, but, running about the end of it, had filled the streets of all that part of the city next the bridge, to the infinite damage of the inhabitants, besides putting them in to the greatest consternation imaginable, for fear of their houses being driven away by the violence of the water, and the whole city was not without apprehensions that their bridge would have given way too, which would have been a terrible loss to them for 'tis as fine a bridge as most in Scotland.

Glasgow is, indeed, a very fine city; the four principal streets are the fairest for breadth, and the finest built that I have ever seen in one city together. The houses are all of stone, and generally equal and uniform in height, as well as in front; the lower story generally stands on vast square Doric columns, not round pillars, and arches between give passage into the shops, adding to the strength as well as beauty of the building; in a word, 'tis the cleanest and beautifullest, and best built city in Britain, London excepted.

It stands on the side of a hill, sloping to the river, with this exception, that the part next the river is flat, as is said above, for near one third part of the city, and that exposed it to the water, upon the extraordinary flood mentioned just now. Where the streets meet, the crossing makes a spacious market-place by the nature of the thing, because the streets are so large of themselves. As you come down the hill, from the north gate to the said cross, the Tolbooth, with the Stadhouse, or Guild-Hall, make the north-east angle, or, in English, the right-hand corner of the street, the building very noble and very strong, ascending by large stone steps, with an iron balustrade. Here the town-council sit, and the magistrates try causes, such as come within their cognizance, and do all their public business.

On the left-hand of the same street is the university, the building is the best of any in Scotland of the kind; it was founded by Bishop Turnbull, *Ann.* 1454, but has been much enlarged since, and the fabric almost all new built. It is a very spacious building, contains two large squares, or courts, and the lodgings for the scholars, and for the professors, are very handsome; the whole building is of frestone, very high and very august.

The cathedral is an ancient building, and has a square tower in the middle of the cross, with a very handsome spire upon it, the highest that I saw in Scotland, and, indeed, the only one that is to be called high. This, like St Giles's at Edinburgh, is divided now, and makes three churches, and, I suppose, there is four or five more in the city, besides a meeting or two. But there are very few of the episcopal dissenters here; and the mob fell upon one of their meeting so often, that they were obliged to lay it down, or, if they do meet, 'tis very privately.

Glasgow is a city of business; here is the face of trade, as well foreign as home trade; and, I may say, 'tis the only city in Scotland, at this time, that apparently increases and improves in both. The Union has answered its end to them more than to any other part of Scotland, for their trade is new formed by it; and, as the Union opened the door to the Scots in our American colonies, the Glasgow merchants presently fell in with the opportunity; and though, when the Union was making, the rabble of Glasgow made the most formidable attempt to prevent it, yet, now they know better, for they have the greatest addition to their trade by it imaginable; and I am assured that they send near fifty sail of ships every year to Virginia, New England, and other English colonies in America, and are every year increasing.

The share they have in the herring-fishery is very considerable, and they cure their herrings so well, and so much better than is done in any other part of Great Britain; that a Glasgow herring is esteemed as good as a Dutch herring, which in England they cannot come up to.

As Scotland never enjoyed a trade to the English plantations till since the Union, so no town in Scotland has yet done any thing considerable in it but Glasgow: the merchants of Edinburgh have attempted it; but they lie so out of the way, and the voyage is not only so much the longer, but so much more hazardous, that the Glasgow men are always sure to outdo them, and must consequently carry away that part of trade from them, as likewise the trade to the south, and to the Mediterranean, whither the ships from Glasgow go and come again with great advantage in the risk, so that even in the insuring there is one per cent difference, which is a great article in the business of a merchant.

The Glasgow merchants have of late suffered some scandal in this branch of trade, as if they were addicted to the sin of smuggling; as to that, if others, for want of opportunity, are not in capacity to do the same, let those who are not guilty, or would not, if they had room for it, throw the first stone at them; for my part I accuse none of them.

I have not time here to enlarge upon the home trade of this city, which is very considerable in many things, I shall only touch at some parts of them (viz.)

1. Here is one or two very handsome sugar-baking houses, carried on by skilful persons, with large stocks, and to a very great degree. I had the curiosity to view one of the houses, and I think it equal to, if not exceeding most in London. Also there is a large distillery for distilling spirits from the molasses drawn from the sugars, and which they called Glasgow brandy, and in which they enjoyed a vast advantage for a time, by a reserved article in the Union, freeing them from the English duties, I say for a time.

2. Here is a manufacture of plaiding, a stuff cross-striped with yellow and red, and other mixtures for the plaids or veils, which the ladies in Scotland wear, and which is a habit peculiar to the country.

3. Here is a manufacture of muslins, and, perhaps the only manufacture of its kind in Britain, if not in Europe; and they make them so good and so fine, that great quantities of them are sent into England, and sold there at a good price; they are generally striped, and are very much used for aprons by the ladies, and sometimes in head-clothes by the English women of a meaner sort, and many of them are sent to the British plantations.

4. Here is also a linen manufacture; but as that is in common with all parts of Scotland, I do not insist so much upon it here, though they make a very great quantity of it, and send it to the plantations also as a principal merchandise.

Nor are the Scots without a supply of goods for sorting their cargoes to the English colonies, even without sending to England for them, or at least not for many of them; and 'tis needful to mention it here, because it has been objected by some that understood trade too, that the Scots could not send a sortable cargo to America without buying from England; which goods, so bought from, must come through many hands, and by long carriage, and consequently be dear bought, and so the English merchants might undersell them.

But to answer this in the language of merchants, as it is a merchant-like objection. It may be true, that some things cannot be had here so well as from England, so as to make out a sortable cargo, such as the Virginia merchants in London ship off, whose entries at the Custom-house consist sometimes of 200 particulars; and they are at last fain to sum them up thus: certain tin, turnery, millinery, upholstery, cutlery, and Crooked-Lane wares; that is to say, that they buy something of every thing, either for wearing, or kitchen, or house-furniture, building houses or ships (with every thing else in short) that can be thought of, except eating.

But though the Scots cannot do this, we may reckon up what they can furnish, and what is sufficient, and some of which they can go beyond England in.

1. They have several woollen manufacturers which they send of their own making; such as the Sterling serges, Musclebrow stuffs, Aberdeen stockings, Edinburgh shalloons, blankets, &c. So that they are not quite destitute in the woollen manufacture, though that is the principal thing in which England can outdo them.

2. The trade with England being open, they have now, all the Manchester wares, Sheffield wares, and Newcastle hard wares; as also the cloths, kerseys, half-thicks, duffels, stockings, and coarse manufactures of the north of England, as cheap brought to them by horse-packs as they can be carried to London; nor is the carriage farther, and, in some articles, nor so far by much.

3. They have linens of most kinds, especially diapers and table-linen, damasks, and many other sorts not known in England, cheaper than England, because made at their own doors.

4. What linens they want from Holland, or Hamburgh, they import from thence as cheap as can be done in England; and for muslins, their own are very acceptable, and cheaper than in England.

5. Gloves they make better and cheaper than in England, for they send great quantities thither.

6. Another article, which is very considerable here, is servants, and these they have in greater plenty, and upon better terms than the English; without the scandalous art of kidnapping, making drunk, wheedling, betraying, and the like; the poor people offering themselves fast enough, and thinking it their advantage to go; as indeed it is, to those who go with sober resolutions, namely, to serve out their times, and then become diligent planters for themselves; and this would be a much wiser course in England than to turn thieves, and worse, and then be sent over by force, and as a pretence of mercy to save them from the gallows.

This may be given as a reason, and, I believe, is the only reason why so many more of the Scots servants, which go over to Virginia, settle and thrive there, than of the English, which is so certainly true, that if it goes on for many years more, Virginia may be rather called a Scots than an English plantation.

I might go on to many other particulars, but this is sufficient to show that the Scots merchants are at no loss how to make up sortable cargoes to send with their ships to the plantations, and that if we can outdo them in some things, they are able to outdo us in others; if they are under any disadvantages in the trade I am speaking of, it is that they may perhaps, not have so easy a vent and consumption for the goods they bring back, as the English have, at London, or Bristol, or Liverpool; and that is the reason why they are now, as they say, setting up a wharf and conveniences at Alloway in the Forth, in order to send their tobaccos and sugars thither by land-carriage, and ship them off there for Holland, or Hamburgh, or London, as the market presents.

Now, though this may be some advantage (viz.) carrying the tobacco from fourteen to fifteen miles over land; yet, if on the other hand it calculated how much sooner the voyage is made from Glasgow to the capes of Virginia, than from London, take it one time with another, the difference will be found in the freight, and in the expense of the ships, and especially in time of war, when the channel is thronged with privateers, and when ships wait to go in fleets for fear of enemies; whereas the Glasgow men are no sooner out of the Firth of Clyde, but they stretch away to the north west, are out of the wake of the privateers immediately, and are often times at the capes of Virginia before the London ships get clear of the channel. Nay, even in times of peace, and take the weather to happen in its usual manner, there must always be allowed, one time with another, at least fourteen to twenty days difference in the voyage, either out or home; which, take it together, is a month to six weeks in the whole voyage, and for wear and tear, victuals and wages, is very considerable in the whole trade.

'The Tobacco Lords'

from Glasgow and its Clubs

JOHN STRANG (1795–1863)

The tobacco lords who formed the Hodge Podge Club, Strang's account of which is the source for our extract, were the rich merchants who dominated the city's enormously profitable trade with the British colonies in America and the West Indies from the 1720s through to the outbreak of the American Revolution in 1775. The access to the American colonies which came with the Union of the Parliaments in 1707, and the geographical advantage which the Glasgow merchants had with their easy access to the Atlantic soon meant that a rich trade was developed between Scotland and the colonies. At first the Scottish merchants had used English ships and traded from English ports like Whitehaven, but, as Strang tells us, by 1735 the Glasgow Virginia merchants had fifteen ships registered in Clyde ports engaged in the Western Ocean trade.

Some indication of the scale of this trade can be gleaned from the Customs returns for the Clyde ports for 1771/72. Almost 34 million pounds weight of tobacco entered from Virginia alone, with another 12 million pounds coming from Maryland and North Carolina. This total, over 20,000 tons, was obviously not all smoked in Scottish pipes, over 20 million pounds was exported to France and 15 million pounds went to Holland. The Glasgow merchants also managed to find room in their vessels for 179,544 gallons of rum as well as vast quantities of sugar from the West Indies, timber from the forests of New England and such minor cargoes as 25 otter skins from Virginia and 1101 deer skins from North Carolina. The wealth that this brought into Glasgow could be seen both in the haughty behaviour of the tobacco lords, so well described by Strang, and in the houses in and around Glasgow built by these merchants. Glasgow's Museum of Modern Art, formerly Stirling's Library, in Royal Exchange Square, was originally built in 1778 for one of the greatest of these tobacco lords, William Cunninghame of Lainshaw, on what was then farmland on the far western edge of the city.

Apart from the prosperity this trade brought to Glasgow and the Clyde it also had the effect of moving the economic centre of Scotland westwards. Traditionally the bulk of Scottish export trade had been from the east coast ports to Scandinavia, the Baltic, Germany and Holland. From the middle ages Scottish trade to the Continent had passed through a Staple Port – initially Middleburg, then Bruges and finally at Campveere on the Dutch island of Walcheren. While there had been west coast trade – to Ireland and France, for example – this had not been on anything like the scale of the North Sea trade. The growth of the Western Ocean trade, even after the disruption caused by the loss of the American colonies, and the linked development of the Clyde were instrumental in ensuring the rapid growth of Glasgow from a small provincial city to the economic dynamo of Scotland. Glasgow increased in population from around 31,000 in the 1750s to 147,000 in 1821, by which time it had, for the first time, overtaken Edinburgh as Scotland's largest city. The influences of the twin forces of manufacturing and trade are hard to disentangle in this process, but the effects of trade were undoubtedly profound: the phenomenal population growth of the Clyde port of Greenock from around 2000 in 1700 to 27,500 in 1831 shows more distinctly the influence of maritime trade.

THE TOBACCO LORDS

If the world has had its ages of iron, silver, and gold, Glasgow also assuredly had, during even the last century and a half, its peculiar and distinctive mercantile ages. It had, for example, its salmon and herring, its tobacco, its sugar, its cotton, its iron, and its steam-boat building ages in regular progressive succession – one peculiar business or handicraft generally holding for a season its paramount sway, and then calmly yielding the supremacy to another.

Previous to the union of Scotland and England, the fish trade with foreign countries, carried on as it was particularly by Walter Gibson, who at one time was Provost of Glasgow, must be regarded as one of first-rate importance, when we consider the size and situation of the town – bringing the City, as it then did, into active commercial intercourse with France and Holland, and exchanging thereby the products of the Clyde for the luxuries of the Continent. After the happy compact – or *unhappy* as it was regarded by many in Scotland at the time – was signed and sealed, which certainly linked more closely two otherwise rival commercial communities of the same isle, an immediate impetus was given to the commerce of Glasgow. The American Colonies, hitherto the exclusive field for English enterprise, were opened to the merchants of the West of Scotland; and partnerships were at once formed, and vessels charted and thereafter built, for carrying on at first an extensive barter trade, and at length a regular commercial intercourse with Virginia, Maryland, and Carolina.

Perhaps among the changeful peculiarities connected with the commercial chronology of Glasgow, there is none more extraordinary than the rise, progress, and decay of the Tobacco Trade, or of the lofty position in the social scale which the limited class of citizens engaged in that lucrative traffic so speedily attained and so soon lost. This trade seems to have originated about the year 1707, and was conducted on principles which could not fail to prove lucrative. The method for a considerable time of carrying on this business was to despatch with every vessel a supercargo, who, on arrival, bartered his goods for tobacco, and remained until he had either sold all his goods, or at least got sufficient tobacco with which to load his vessel, when he returned home with his cargo and any goods that were unsold. Each adventure in this way was at once closed, and the profit on the transaction was known and realised. The first vessel belonging to Glasgow which crossed the Atlantic was in 1718; and soon after the imports of tobacco became so considerable in the Clyde, as seriously to diminish the imports of the same article at the ports of Bristol, Liverpool, and Whitehaven. Frugality on the part of those who were early engaged in this traffic has been assigned for the success of the Glasgow tobacco merchants; while, on the part of others, it has also been insinuated that not a little was due to the fact of the whole trade being cunningly conducted *in partnership with the Crown*, by which more was to be gained than can now possibly be done, in these days of stringent Excise and Customhouse *surveillance*. Be this as it may, it is at least certain that the English, when they found themselves smarting under the competition, brought forward this allegation of fraud on the part of the Glasgow importers of tobacco, to crush the trade in West of Scotland; for we find that in the year 1721 the whole individuals engaged in this trade throughout England banded themselves together to effect this object, through the Government of the day; but, for the honour of Glasgow, it is consolatory to know that all their evil endeavours proved ineffectual, and instead of being able to put down, as they hoped they would, the commerce so energetically maintained between America and Glasgow, their envious efforts only tended to increase and enlarge its power. In the year 1735 the Virginia merchants in Glasgow could boast of having fifteen large vessels, belonging to the ports of the Clyde, engaged in the tobacco trade, besides many others which they had chartered from other ports; and, by the year 1750, they had a still greater number. The twenty following years may indeed be considered as the very hey-day or culminating point of the tobacco trade in Glasgow. During that period an unexampled extent of business in the intoxicating weed passed through the Glasgow merchants' books; and having there paid toll in the shape of profit, it was sent to all parts of the Continent of Europe, and to not a few of the leading ports of England and Ireland. The fact is, that between the year 1760 and 1775, Glasgow became the great emporium for tobacco in the empire; for, while the whole import into Great Britain in 1772 was 90,000 hogsheads, Glasgow alone imported 49,000!

From the large extent to which this particular branch of business was carried on in Glasgow, it seems almost miraculous how a sufficient capital could at that period be found for it, either in the East or West of Scotland. In those days, however, the Virginia merchants, in making their export purchases, did not go, as foreign traders now do, with cash in hand or with an acceptance to pay for them at a certain limited date; the only understanding between buyer and seller being, that on the return of the vessel which carried out the goods payment would be made; and if any poor manufacturer or tradesman had the hardihood to ask for payment before the tobacco lord ordered it, he could never again expect to be favoured with the great man's custom. By adopting this very knowing plan of purchase and payment, it is quite plain that these tobacco merchants traded chiefly on the capital of those from whom they bought their goods; but, as the sellers were numerous and the purchasers few, the disadvantages to the one class from such a system were less felt than were the advantages to the other. For the goods purchased in the English market such facilities could not be asked, nor, if they had been, would they have been granted. But to meet any want of capital then, the new banks, established in the City by several of the leading tobacco lords themselves, were found ready to do the needful.

During the period when this trade was in the ascendant, it is perhaps scarcely necessary to repeat what all the old historians of the City have told us, that the persons engaged in it ruled with a very high hand. With a hauteur and bearing, indeed, since altogether unparalleled, they kept themselves separate from the other classes of the town; assuming the air and deportment of persons immeasurably superior to all around them; and treating those on whom they looked down, but on whom they depended, with no little superciliousnes. For one of the *shopocracy* or *corkocracy* to speak to a tobacco-aristocrat on the street, without some sign of recognition from the great man, would have been regarded as an insult. They were princes on the *Plainstanes*, and strutted about there every day as the rulers of the destinies of Glasgow. Like the princely merchants, too, who formerly paced the Piazetta in Venice, or occupied the gorgeous palaces in the Strada Balbi of Genoa, the tobacco lords distinguished themselves by a particular garb, being attired, like their Venetian and Genovese predecessors, in scarlet cloaks, curled wigs, cocked hats, and bearing gold-headed canes. How long this state of matters would have continued, had not the outbreak of the American war interposed to arrest this tobacco traffic, and to compel the traders to seek for employment and wealth in other channels, it is impossible to say. All we know is, that very soon after that event, the tobacco aristocracy ceased to lead, and the scarlet cloaks gradually disappeared from the pavement.

Although the period during which this trade flourished in Glasgow was by no means long, yet how many monuments of its success and greatness have been left, either in the princely estates purchased from its gains, or in the magnificent city mansions reared for the accommodation and comfort of the merchant princes who then conducted it! Of the few of the latter which still stand intact within the precincts of the City, there are enough remaining to illustrate the wealth of the parties who could rear such structures, and who could maintain within their walls, as their possessors were wont to do, the style and hospitality of princes; while with those still mightier mansions which the wants of recent times have either sadly altered or entirely swept away, there were associated, but a few years ago, even more palpable evidences of bygone wealth and wassail. The wealth realised during the existence of the tobacco trade in Glasgow must have been very great; and what is more, it gave a stimulus to the future commerce of the City, which has materially aided in bringing it to its present condition. Supercilious though the possessors of such wealth as a class certainly were towards their less opulent fellow-citizens, they were nevertheless individually a gay and joyous set, on the most familiar and friendly footing with each other, and with those also who, in other walks of life, were justly looked upon as the notables of the City. No doubt, the circle in which these tobacco lords moved was more narrow and limited than any that has since succeeded it; but, at the same time, the parties of which it was composed were men possessed of that education, activity, energy, and talent, that almost justified them in assuming the position which they did. The pride of the tobacco prince, like the tobacco palace, has, however, long passed away; leaving, we suspect, to us, in these latter days, but an indistinct idea of the height to which, in point of extravagance, it was actually carried.

HIGHLAND TEXTILE WORKERS

Glasgow 10th March 1794

Sir

This will be delivered to you by the Rev. Mr Alexr. McDonell, Pastor of the Roman Catholic Congregation in this place. A considerable part of that Congregation consists of the poor people from the Highlands and Islands of Scotland who were induced to settle in this City and the neighbourhood from the prospect of finding employment, by means of an Association of Gentlemen some time ago formed here for preventing emigration to foreign parts, and by whose means employment was accordingly found for them, till lately that stagnation in the Manufactures of the place has thrown many of them idle and in want of bread. Understanding that the Gentlemen of the Roman Catholic persuasion in Scotland have addressed his Majesty with an offer to raise a Regiment for his Majesty's service, Mr McDonell thinks that if the offer be accepted a considerable number of his Congregation may be disposed to serve their King and Country, and in justice to all concerned, we as Managers appointed by the Association think it our duty to declare that under Mr McDonell's prudent and exemplary tuition, his Congregation have always demeaned themselves as loyal subjects and orderly peaceable members of Society.

We have the honour to be with great respect

Sir

Your most obedient humble servants

George McIntosh

Arch. Grahame

David Dale

'Let Glasgow Flourish'

ANDREW PARK (1807–1863)

Air – *Cauld Kail*

Some sing of love, some sing of war,
And some their tales of pity,
But here's a wiser strain by far,
'Tis Clutha's noble city!
That place of commerce, wealth, and power
Which wit and genius nourish,
May still her Tree majestic tower –
Huzza! let Glasgow flourish!

For Clutha's famous city stands
In all-increasing splendour,
And daily do new-peopled lands
Their varied treasures send her!
She grows in science, wealth, and arts,
In beauty quite enchanting; –
In starry eyes, and glowing hearts,
And all that once was wanting.

And here's to you ye maidens fair;
Ye maidens chaste and pretty! –
Where'er ye are may ye declare
Love for your native city.
Then, sing with me her growing power,
Which wit and genius nourish –
May still her Tree majestic tower;
Huzza! let Glasgow flourish!

'Manufactures and Industries'

from Ordnance Gazetteer of Scotland, 1883

EDITED BY FRANCIS H. GROOME

Even today, in an era when the city's traditional heavy industries have markedly declined, the popular image of Glasgow's manufactures and industries centres on shipbuilding, locomotives and other heavy engineering activities. However, as the following extract from the Ordnance Gazetteer of Scotland *demonstrates, for much of the eighteenth and nineteenth century Glasgow was renowned as a centre of textile production. Spinning, weaving, dyeing and printing linen, cotton and, to a lesser extent, wool occupied a large proportion of the city's work force and contributed greatly to the growth of the city.*

Some indication of the significance of the textile industries can still be seen in the city in, for example, the polychrome splendour of the Templeton's Carpet Factory overlooking Glasgow Green. The façade, designed by William Leiper in 1888, and inspired by the Doge's Palace in Venice, is a eloquent reminder of the wealth and confidence of Glasgow industrialists in the high-Victorian era.

The Gazetteer *goes on to give an account of Glasgow's chemical industries, glass and pottery manufacturers – all of which were of considerable significance at various periods in the city's history. The chemical industry certainly gave Glasgow's skyline one of its most famous features – 'Tennant's Stalk' – the 455-foot-high chimney erected at Tennant's St Rollox Chemical Works at Townhead on the north side of the city. Groome describes it as a 'monster chimney for the purpose of carrying off and preventing any injury from the noxious gases that might arise' in the manufacture of soda, sulphuric acid, and bleaching powder, at what was in the 1830s and 1840s Europe's largest chemical works. The chimney may have carried away the noxious gases from the city centre (though their effect on the communities downwind was less certain and less considered) but the industry was one which was both dangerous to the health of its workers and produced a vast amount of toxic waste. The 'Stalk' was demolished in 1922. The soda waste spoil heaps are now the site of the Sighthill tower blocks, erected in the 1960s.*

MANUFACTURES AND INDUSTRIES

The manufactures and industries of Glasgow present a most wonderful combination. So singularly varied and extensive are they, that the city 'combines several of the special characteristics of other cities. It has the docks and ports of Liverpool, the tall chimneys and manufactories of Manchester, with the shops of Regent Street, and the best squares of Belgravia.' 'Glasgow,' says Dr Strang, 'unites within itself a portion of the cotton-spinning and weaving manufactures of Manchester, the printed calicoes of Lancashire, the stuffs of Norwich, the shawls and mousselines of France, the silk-throwing of Macclesfield, the flax-spinning of Ireland, the carpets of Kidderminster, the iron and engineering works of Wolverhampton and Birmingham, the pottery and glass-making of Staffordshire and Newcastle, the shipbuilding of London, the coal trade of the Tyne and Wear, and all the handicrafts connected with, or dependent on, the full development of these. Glasgow has also its distilleries, breweries, chemical works, tan-works, dye works, bleachfields, and paper manufactories, besides a vast number of staple and fancy handloom fabrics which may be strictly said to belong to that locality.' The textile factories lie to the east, while engineering shops and foundries lie to the north, north-east and south, and the ship-building yards are to the west.

We have already seen that there are some traces of early manufacture of cloth in Glasgow, but in all probability it was very small. When the letter of Guildry was granted in 1605, we have evidence in it that silk, linen, and hardware, etc., from France, Flanders, and England, were dealt in, and that there were manufactures of wool and linen cloth. The first manufactory the city possessed was a weaving establishment started by Robert Fleyming in 1638, who obtained from the magistrates a lease of some premises in the Drygate. It was not till after the Union, however, that any of them attained prominence, when linen and cotton cloth and plaidings were tried. The manufacture of plaiding indeed, as we have already seen from Mr Commissioner Tucker's report, seems to have made some progress in the middle of the seventeenth century, but it must have greatly advanced, for in the close of the century Glasgow plaids had attained some celebrity in Edinburgh, then the aristocratic centre of the kingdom. The inhabitants were proud of their handiwork, for we find that in 1715 the magistrates presented to the Princess of Wales, afterwards the Queen of George II, 'a swatch of plaids as the manufactory peculiar only to this place for keeping the place in Her Highness' remembrance, and which might contribute to the advantage thereof, and to the advancement of the credit of that manufactory' – a gift which her royal highness graciously received, and returned her 'hearty thanks to the magistrates of Glasgow for their fyne present.' The commerce with America seems to have first suggested and encouraged the introduction of manufactures into the city on a more extended plan that the home trade which had previously existed. Defoe, in the first edition of his *Journey*, in 1723, makes no mention of any industry, excepting tobacco and sugar; but in a subsequent edition, 1727, he mentions, besides two sugar-baking houses and a distillery, that 'Here there is a manufacture of plaiding, a stuff crossed-striped with yellow, red, and other mixtures, for the plaids or veils worn by the women in Scotland,' and also 'a manufacture of muslins, which they make so good and fine that great quantities of them are sent into England and to the British plantations, where they sell at a good price. They are generally striped, and are very much used for aprons by the ladies, and sometimes in head-cloths by the meaner sort of English women.' He says there also was 'a linen manufacture, but as that is in common with all parts of Scotland which improve in it daily, I will not insist upon it as a peculiar here, though they make a very great quantity of it and send it to the plantations as their principal merchandise.' The importance of the linen weaving in Glasgow is said to date from 1700, and to be somewhat peculiar. Ure, in his *History of Rutherglen and East Kilbride*, tells of a William Wilson, a native of East Kilbride, who took the name of William Flakefield from the place at which he had lived. Along with his father and brother he went to Glasgow near the close of the seventeenth century, but ere he had been there long he joined the Scottish Guards and went to the Continent, where his attention was attracted by a German handkerchief woven in blue and white chequers. So much was he struck by it that, having been brought up as a weaver, he determined to weave one like it whenever he had an opportunity. When he at length returned to Glasgow in 1700 he brought his handkerchief with him, and after many patient trials and failures he succeeded in making a number like it – the first of the kind ever woven in Great Britain. They were at once successful and met with a ready sale, looms multiplied, and in a few years Glasgow had become famous for this new branch of the linen trade. Everyone who engaged in it made money except the unfortunate who introduced it, and who, whether from want of capital or from some return to his early roving habits, died in poverty, with the appointment of town drummer.

The legislature granted great encouragement to the making of linen in Scotland, and by this the trade in Glasgow was so fostered that the city began to assume importance as a manufacturing town. An Act of

Parliament passed in 1748 – prohibiting the importing or wearing of French cambrics under severe penalties – and another passed in 1751 – allowing weavers in flax or hemp to settle and exercise their trades in any part of Scotland, free from all corporation dues – conjoined with the bounty of 1½d. per yard on all linens exported at or under 1s. 6d. per yard, contributed largely at the outset to the success of the linen trade. Between 1730 and 1745 many new industries were introduced into the city. Glasgow was the first place in Great Britain in which inkle wares were manufactured. In 1732 a Glasgow citizen named Harvey brought away from Haarlem, at the risk of his life, two inkle looms and a workman, and by this means fairly succeeded in establishing the manufacture in Glasgow, and breaking the Dutch monopoly in the article. The Dutch workman he had brought with him afterwards took offence and went to Manchester, and introduced the inkle manufacture there. Gibson, in his *History of Glasgow*, gives an account of the manufactures and industries in 1771, and it is worth noticing, as he seems to have taken great pains to make it exact. He mentions different kinds of linen, checkered handkerchiefs, diaper, damask, cambric, lawn, muslin handkerchiefs, 'Glasgows' or lawn mixed with cotton, and carolines which are the chief things. Besides these there were industries in brushes, combs, horn and ivory; copper, tin, and white iron; delf and stonewares; gloves, handkerchiefs, silk, and linen; men's hats, jewellery, inkles, iron, tanned leather, printed lines, ropes, saddlery, shoes, stockings, and thread; and Spencer, in his *English Traveller* (1771), mentions as the industries the herring trade, the tobacco trade, the manufacture of woollen cloth, stockings, shalloons, and cottons; muslins, the sugar trade, distilling, the manufacture of boots and shoes, and other leather goods, including saddles; and the manufacture of house furniture.

The vast improvements which were effected in the production of cotton yarn by the inventions of Hargreaves and Sir Richard Arkwright gave still a fresh impulse to the manufactures affected, and capital, seeking new outlets after the failure of the tobacco trade, was invested largely in cotton manufacture. Through the subsequent improvements effected on the steam engine by James Watt, it became no longer necessary for mills to be erected only where a large water supply was available, and it was possible to raise them in the midst of a rich coal field, and alongside of a navigable river with a port. The first steam engine used in Glasgow for spinning cotton was erected in Jan. 1792. It was put up at Springfield, on the south side of the Clyde, opposite the lower steamboat quay. This work, which at that time belonged to Mr Todd, and later to Todd and Higginbotham, was removed at immense expense, in virtue of the Clyde Trustees Act of 1840 to afford space for the extension of the harbour. The works of Messrs S. Higginbotham, Sons & Gray are now to the east, opposite Glasgow Green, and at them spinning, weaving, dyeing, and printing are carried on very extensively. A power-loom had, however, been introduced previously. According to Pagan 'the power-loom was introduced to Glasgow in 1773 by Mr James Louis Robertson of Dunblane, who set up two of them in Argyle Street, which were set in motion by a large Newfoundland dog performing the part of a gin horse.' This statement has since, however, in 1871, in letters to the *Glasgow Herald*, been disputed by Mr John Robertson, a Pollokshaws power-loom tenter, who asserts that a man named Adam Kinloch, whom he met in 1845, and who was then eighty-five years of age, 'made the first two power-looms that ever were made in the world, and drove them with the use of a crank by his own hand in a court off the Gallowgate' in 1793. About 1794 there were forty looms fitted up at Milton, and in 1801 Mr John Monteith had 200 looms at work at Pollokshaws near Glasgow, and the extension of power-loom factories and of the cotton trade generally became so rapid as almost to exceed belief. In 1818 there were within the city 'eighteen steam weaving factories, containing 2,800 looms, and producing 8,400 pieces of cloth weekly.' There were altogether fifty-two cotton mills in the city, with 511,200 spindles, the total length being over 100,000,000 yards, and the value upwards of £5,000,000. Including the, at that time, outlying districts now in 'natural Glasgow,' and all the looms in the surrounding districts usually kept at work by Glasgow merchants, there were nearly 32,000 steam and hand looms at work. There were also in the city eighteen calico printing works and seventeen calendering houses. In 1854 the number of cotton spinning factories was 39, of cotton weaving factories thirty-seven, of cotton spinning and weaving factories sixteen, the number of spindles was 1,014,972, the number of power-looms 22,335, and the number of persons employed 24,414. In 1875 the number of spindles was 1,500,000, the number of power-looms 27,500, and the number of persons employed 33,276. Besides the works of Messrs Higginbotham already mentioned, two of the largest cotton factories in Scotland are those of Messrs Galbraith at Oakbank and St Rollox. They employ about 1800 persons, and produce nearly 400,000 yards of cotton per week.

The woollen manufactures in most of their departments are much less prominent in Glasgow and its neighbourhood than in many other parts of Scotland. The manufacture of carpets, introduced first in 1757, is, however, carried on to a considerable extent, and employs a number of hands. In 1854 there were seven worsted, spinning, and weaving factories, with 14,392 spindles, 120 power-looms, and 800 hands. In 1861 there were

11,748 spindles, fourteen power-looms, and 1,422 hands; 'and though since then considerable fluctuations have been caused by the disturbed condition of trade arising from the state of the coal and iron industries in 1873–1874, and subsequently from the failure of the City of Glasgow Bank in 1878, there has been on the whole a proportional increase.' One work alone at Greenhead now employs upwards of 500 hands, and the annual value of the trade is nearly £200,000. There are also a number of silk and rope, flax and jute factories, which, in 1854, had 74,705 spindles and 2,050 hands. In 1861 they had 44,224 spindles, 231 power-looms, and 2,206 hands; and here again a fitting increase has taken place.

Altogether about one-eighth of the population of Glasgow, between the ages of ten and forty, are employed in connection with these factories with their accompanying processes of bleaching, dyeing, and printing. An establishment for the manufacture of bandanas was started at Barrowfield in 1802 by Messrs Monteith, Bogle, & Co., and the superior manufacture of the article itself and the successful application of the Turkey-red dye have given to Glasgow bandanas a fame and a preference in almost every commercial mart in the world, and rendered this one of the staple industries in the city, for the manufacture, now shared in by other companies, is carried on upon a scale of great magnitude. Independently of this the manufacturing operations of various other parts in Scotland are kept in motion by Glasgow capital, and even in the North of Ireland vast numbers of the muslin weavers are in the direct and constant employment of Glasgow houses. The manufacture of sewed muslin is carried on by over fifty firms in Glasgow, and employs more than 10,000 women. The Messrs Macdonald, who, in 1856, erected the large block of warehouses already mentioned, close to the post office, had, for some time prior to their retirement during the commercial crisis of 1857, 1,500 men and 500 women on their establishment, and gave besides employment to between 20,000 and 30,000 needle-women in the west of Scotland and the north of Ireland. They sent into the market annually a quantity of sewed muslin valued at half a million.

The soft goods trade is, as might be expected, largely developed in Glasgow, and the retail and wholesale trades are often united, the merchants importing goods largely from England and abroad, and sending them out wholesale to smaller traders situated in almost every village and town in Scotland, and not a few in Ireland, and, notwithstanding the magnitude of such transactions, the poorest customer is supplied as readily and courteously with a yard of tape as the richest with an order of a very much more extensive nature. Of the two gentlemen, brothers, who originated this mixed wholesale and retail soft goods trade, one filled the office of chief magistrate of the city, and was knighted. For the purposes of their business they, in 1858, erected in Ingram Street a very large block of buildings in the fine picturesque old Scottish style. Another firm who started in the same line of business about 1850 at first occupied premises with a rental of £1,300, and ultimately purchased them.

Chemical manufactures were commenced in Glasgow in 1786, when Mr Charles Macintosh, so well-known for some of his discoveries in applied chemistry, introduced into Glasgow from Holland the manufacture of sugar of lead. This article had been previously imported from the latter country, but in a very short time the tables were turned, and instead of importing it Glasgow sent considerable quantities to Rotterdam. About the same time the firm established the manufacture of cudbear, an article of great importance in the manufacture of dyeing. In 1799 Mr Macintosh also made the first preparation of chloride of lime in a dry state, which has since been so extensively prized and used as a bleaching powder, and still later he established the well-known manufacture of waterproof cloths, which has, however, latterly been transferred to Manchester. In 1800 the chemical manufactures of Glasgow received a fresh great impulse from the erection by Messrs Tennant, Knox & Co., of a chemical work at St Rollox in the northern suburbs of Glasgow for the manufacture of sulphuric acid, chloride of lime, soda, soap, etc. This is now the most extensive chemical work in the world, covering upwards of thirteen acres, containing between 100 and 200 furnaces, employing about 1,200 hands, and annually transforming 80,000 tons of raw material into soda, bleaching powder, sulphuric acid, etc. The firm have connections and agencies in every considerable mart both at home and abroad. In 1843 the company erected a 'monster chimney' for the purpose of carrying off and preventing injury from any noxious gases that might arise in the process of their manufacture. It is still counted one of the sights of the city. It was erected at a cost of about £12,000, and measures forty feet in diameter at the base, and 455 feet in height.

The manufacture of bottles and bottle glass was commenced at Glasgow in 1730, the first bottle-house being about where the south end of Jamaica Street now is, and probably near the site of the custom house. At first the trade does not seem to have been very brisk, for the workmen were only employed for four months in the year, but now the manufacture is carried on very extensively in Anderston and Port Dundas. The manufacture of flint glass was begun in 1777 by Messrs Cookson & Co. of Newcastle, and under other firms is still carried on with great vigour. The earthenware manufacture was commenced at Delftfield, near the Broomielaw, in 1748. This was the first pottery in

Scotland, but for a long period the quality was decidedly inferior to the English make, and the goods produced only of the lowest quality, and the consumption in consequence mostly local. Since, however, about 1829, and more especially since 1842, the manufacture has been greatly increased and improved. New establishments have been erected, and the productions have attained a beauty of design and a delicacy of finish which now enable them to compete successfully in all departments, and in both the home and foreign markets, with the well-known Staffordshire ware. There are now (1882) about twenty potteries within the city, the largest being at Garngad Hill, where about 1,000 hands are employed. The manufactures include every kind of product from the coarsest earthenware to the finest porcelain, and the exports, both coastwise and foreign, amount to over 12,000 tons a year. The rope manufacture, which dates from 1696, is considerable, and so is the brush trade, which was first introduced in 1755. The tanning of leather on a considerable scale began soon after the Union, and a shoe trade that followed it had attained in 1773 such importance that there were two firms in that year each employing over 300 hands. The trade is now of large extent for both home and foreign supply. The brewing business is very old, and Glasgow was in the seventeenth century noted for the excellence of its ale. It has greatly increased in latter times, and Messrs Tennent, of the Wellpark Brewery in Duke Street, are among the largest exporters of porter and bitter ale in the kingdom, their produce bearing the highest character in the foreign markets. There are twelve breweries. The first distillery was established in Kirk Street, Gorbals, in 1786, by William Menzies, his license being the fourth granted in Scotland. At that period the duty little exceeded one penny per gallon, and the best malt spirits sold at about 3s per gallon. The trade both by distilleries and agencies for houses situated elsewhere has now become a very extensive one, the premises of the distillery at Port Dundas being almost the largest in the world. There are many other industries, too numerous to be particularly noticed, and, in short, Glasgow may be set down as the workshop of Scotland, there being, with a very few exceptions, hardly an article useful to mankind that is not made in the city of St Mungo.

All the iron trade of Scotland, with small exception, belongs directly or indirectly to Glasgow, concentrating here its business, commercially and financially, and drawing hence almost all the articles of consumpt connected with its works and workers. The iron industry, now of such importance to the city, seems to have been introduced in 1732 by the Smithfield Company, for the manufacture for export of all sorts of hard ware. M'Ure describes their warehouse as 'built on an eminency near the north side of the great key or harbour at the Breamielaw,' and says that it contained 'all sorts of iron work, from a lock and key to an anchor of the greatest size.' The trade went on in a fair way, for in 1772 there were imported into the Clyde 836 tons of bar iron and 896 tons of pig iron, while the exports of manufactured iron were 671 ⅓ tons, of which a little over 489 tons went to Virginia. The trade had not increased to a very great extent, though it was growing, but about 1839, or perhaps a little earlier, it began to show signs of greater development, which rapidly took place in consequence of the introduction of the hot-air blast, devised by Mr James B. Neilson, manager of the Glasgow gas-works, and of the greater demand for iron of all sorts, following on the introduction of the railway system. A great deal of the iron reaches Glasgow in the form of pig iron, and at different works within the city it is rolled and manufactured. The six furnaces of the Govan Iron-Works – popularly known as 'Dixon's Blazes', from Mr Dixon who erected them about 1837 – in Gorbals, form a curious feature in the city, and throw against the sky a lurid reflection which is seen all over the city. Besides the Govan works, some of the other large premises are the Glasgow Iron-Works at Garngad Road, the Blochhairn Steel Works near the Alexandra Park, the Parkhead Forge at Parkhead, and the Govan Forge and Steel Company, who manufacture the heaviest class of forgings for ships, marine and ordinary engines, and mild steel castings and forgings of all description. For castings of various sanitary and architectural appliances, the very large Saracen (at Possil) and Sun Foundries (near St Rollox) have a wide and well-earned reputation. The increase of the iron trade in Glasgow corresponds with that for the whole of Scotland. In 1778 over the whole country there were only eight furnaces at work, and their produce was only one-sixth of what it would be now for the same number, such has been the improvement that has taken place in the methods of operation.

The following table shows the increase since:

Year.	No. of Furnaces	Tons Produced
1806	18	22,840
1823	22	30,500
1833	31	44,000
1843	62	248,000
1851	114	740,000
1861	122	1,040,000
1870		1,206,000
1879	97	932,000

The prosperity of the trade between 1833 and 1851 is well shown by the great increase in the number of the furnaces and the improvements in manufacture by the increased output that these furnaces could produce. From an average output of nearly 1,400 tons per furnace in 1833, the quantity rose, in 1843, after the introduction of the hot blast, to 4,000, and this has since again more than doubled. In place of the 489 tons that had been sent to Virginia in 1772, there were sent in 1860, to America alone, no less than 78,000 tons, and though this in 1861 fell in consequence of the war to 35,000 tons, France increased its consumption by 14,000 tons, and Spain increased hers by the same amount. In 1880 the total shipments of iron from Glasgow amounted to 259,425 tons. In 1881 this was much exceeded, as the shipments amounted to 339,407 tons, and for the present year (1882), up to the end of September, the shipments are 44,709 tons over those for the corresponding period last year, while at the same date the stock stored in Glasgow amounts to 626,766 tons.

Another of the great sources of Glasgow's prosperity and success has been the abundance of coal in the surrounding district, which has not only provided fuel for iron-works, the factories, and the steamships, but has also formed in itself an importance article of export. When the coal in the neighbourhood began to be worked is not exactly known, but we know that in Scotland in the fourteenth century coal was a common article of merchandise, and was exported and sometimes taken as ballast for ships. The first notice we find of the Glasgow coalfield is in 1578, when the Archbishop let the 'coilheuchtis and colis within the baronie of glasgw' for the space of three years at the yearly rent of £40 Scots (equal to about £5 sterling at the time), and 270 'laids' of coal (the 'laid' being, according to Mr Macgeorge, about 320 pounds). These coal pits were probably in Gorbals. In 1655 the town council let these pits, or others, probably in the same quarter in 'the muir heughe,' at a rent of £33, 4s., the tenants to employ eight hewers, and not to charge more than 4d. for nine gallons. In 1760 the price per cart of about half a ton was 1s. 3d., but they came after this rapidly dearer, for in 1778 they were 3s. for about the same quantity. In the latter year the whole quantity taken to Glasgow, including what was used for Glasgow, Greenock, and Port Glasgow, as well as what was exported elsewhere, was only 181,800 carts, or about 82,000 tons. In 1836 there were thirty-seven pits in the neighbourhood, from which 561,049 tons of coal were brought to Glasgow, of which 124 were exported, and 437,047 tons were used in the city. In 1852 the exports were 200,560 tons, and the whole quantity brought into the city was probably about 1,074,558. In 1858 the quantity of coal, cinders, and culm exported coastwise was 76,744 tons, and abroad 56,696, or a total of

133,440 tons. The following table shows a the later growth of the trade:

Year	Coastwise	Foreign	Total
1860	104,931	55,058	159,989
1871	187,159	153,256	340,415
1878	271,178	295,542	566,720
1881		129,038	

'The Warehouse'

from The Staff at Simson's

FREDERICK NIVEN (1878–1944)

In our section on 'The City of Culture' we met Neil Munro's character, Jimmy Swan, sales representative for a Glasgow drapery warehouse. Frederick Niven's 1937 novel, The Staff at Simson's, *gives us another look at one of these important and typically Glaswegian institutions.*

Niven, born in Chile of Scottish parents, returned to Glasgow with his parents in time to receive his education at Hutcheson's Grammar School. When he left school a compromise was struck between his parents' anxiety that he enjoy a safe career and his own love of the arts. He was apprenticed to a soft goods warehouse, while attending evening classes at the Glasgow School of Art. His novel is based on his recollections of the 1890s and his life in the shirtings, flannelette and wincey departments of a company that would have seemed very familiar to Jimmy Swan.

Our extract, the first two chapters from the novel, introduces the cast of well-observed and individualistic characters who make up 'The Staff at Simson's' and also shows us, with an artist's eye for detail, round the warehouse itself.

Simson's stands, in some respects, on the very verge of the modern world. As the story starts a telephone is being installed, but letters are still copied in a letter-press – the typewriter has evidently not yet made its way into the 'wareus' – nor have female staff.

Niven became a journalist and a prolific novelist. He emigrated to Canada after the First World War and many of his novels have Canadian themes, but he continued, as in The Staff at Simson's *to draw on Glasgow for other books. In* The Staff at Simson's, *as in his other work drawing on his warehouse apprenticeship,* Justice of the Peace, *Niven records and celebrates the mercantile Glasgow of his younger days.*

INTRODUCING THE STAFF

In the last decade of the XIXth century the roll-call at Simson's was thus:

John Simson, son of the founder of the firm, more like a bearded farmer from the shires than a townsman, then in his fiftieth year, father of three – one girl, two boys – and devoted to his buxom, amiable wife in a manifest but nonuxorious fashion; Robert Simson, his bachelor brother, ten years his junior – as large of design as John, but with more urbanity. A pattern-designer of the city, skilful with his pencil in more than the applied art which provided him and his family with their daily bread, once drew a caricature of Robert for the menu-card of a Dinner of Soft-Goods Manufacturers in which that junior partner of the Simson house was represented as a big, smooth cupid with eyes of innocence.

In the warehouse, head of the Fancy Goods department, and sort of general manager or adviser for all the others, was Alexander Maxwell, close upon fifty then, but wearing his years well. He was a dapper man. His shock of silver hair and his bearing, his carriage, made him seem like a stage ambassador to young Laurie of the Dress Goods. Once or twice in his life he had been taken for a doctor, or medical specialist, perhaps because of his care of his hands, and by reason of the precise way he used them. His moustache was cropped, in a period when many men affected hirsute tusks. His wife, he often thought, was the most elegant lady he had ever seen. Both he and she admired Mrs Maxwell tremendously. Women (especially as exemplified in herself) and dress were her idolatries. Their family – in the order of its coming – was boy, girl, girl, boy. Mr Maxwell had placed the elder boy, his school-days over, in a chartered accountant's office, loath to condemn him to what he called the dog's life of manufacturing.

Alexander Maxwell had two assistants in his department: Jack Corbett, discontented – not with the warehouse, but by reason of badgering at home – and always pondering, while travelling towards his suburb in the evenings, coloured pamphlets on South Africa, New Zealand, Australia, Canada; and Johnny Leng, bandy-legged, of dark hue and Semitic cast of countenance, who strove to cheer the obviously sad Corbett with the latest bawdy story.

Head of the Shirtings department was Tom Huntley, a widower, a few years older than the junior partner, a loose-jointed man, his gait that of one tolerant, uncensorious, jack-easy. He had often a little laugh of acceptance or dismissal when some others might question or reprove. His chief assistant was Dan Huntley, not related (Tom had no relatives anywhere to his knowledge), a youth fond of vivid checks, white Ascot ties held with a gold horse-shoe pin, whose home was a two-room and kitchen flat in the transpontine district of Gorbals, where father, mother, brother, sister and he crowded together in hilarious amity, all sharing the same delight in loud attire and music-hall songs and, when they could, in going to the races. Danny of the Shirtings had a secret – an ambition that had nothing to do with the warehouse. He hoped, some day, to be on the music-hall stage. Clog-dancing was his speciality. Without loss of breath he could clog-dance and at the same time solemnly produce mirthful patter. On many a Saturday evening he gave exhibitions of his skill at the more obscure working-men's clubs. Others on the stages of the leading music-halls had begun so. Why not he? Tom Huntley's second assistant was Willie MacEwan, who always wore a hat of the latest style, shirts and ties of the moment's mode. He was as bandy-legged as Johnny Leng, his manner at one and the same time courteous and vulgar, and there was something, to most, engaging, charming about that squint, that cast, in his vivacious eyes.

Henry Braid, and he but thirty, was head of the Dress Goods, and he had just given an engagement ring to his girl. To his future father-in-law he had explained, 'I'm a pushing young man with the world before me,' for in those days one asked the girl's father for her hand (as they used to say), and he – having already discussed the matter with the observant mother – had an 'Aye' or a 'Nay' ready. Braid had two assistants, Arthur Laurie and Alisdair Lennox, called Alice for short because of his niminy utterance and feminine fancies. Laurie, who lived in a village southward from the city, was a tenor singer at parties there, devoted to amateur productions of light opera and to a different girl annually. Lennox was a long, lean young man who walked with a waver as of a willow in a breeze, spoke with a cultivated lisp and was ready to talk to the texture and shade of socks as his two sisters to discuss stockings and lingerie.

'They ought to ha' christened him Jenny Lennox,' said Sandy Bain (head of the Flannelettes) one day – Sandy, 'the card' of Simson's who always seemed to be in need of a shave, perhaps because, liking to lie in bed late in the mornings, he shaved when he got hame frae the wareus at nicht. By the date of this narrative, he was a staunch teetotaler. When chided for that he would explain, jabbing the bibulous bigot who objected in the midriff, or grabbing hold of him by lapel or coat-button to gain full attention, that it was purely a matter of finance. 'I hae four weans noo, twa lads and twa lassies. I ken naething better than to be hauf-drunk a' the time. It's the ideal state in this dissillusionin' world – but no' when ye hae weans. When the publican comes in at the door, poverty comes in at the windy. And noo ye ken – and to hell wi' ye!'

Sandy Bain of the Flannelettes was of the same age as Tom Huntley of the Shirtings. Little Watty Yule, one of his assistants, though also a teetotaler, was a tax on Sandy's patience. Watty's heaven was in the church-hall at social gatherings, conversazione, soirée ('cookie-shine' in the warehouse word); and to lend a hand at these functions and convivial gatherings, assisting at the tea-urn or the coffee-urn, was all he asked. How often he had winsomely inquired, 'May I press you to a jelly?' impossible to speculate. When anyone forgot his name he would say, 'Yule. Yule remember me.' There was an extraordinary scene in the Flannelette department one day, Sandy Bain violently swearing at Watty and telling him that some morning he would kill him. The staff at Simson's gave ear, and then they heard: 'Say good-morning to me, but dinna every morning say tae me, "*Good-morning, have you used Pear's Soap?*" If ye say it again, I'll kill ye, as sure as Daith! It's beyond human endurance.'

Sandy's other assistant at that time was one William Mackay, a son of a one-time wealthy West Indies' sugar broker who had known of it in his purse when the governments of France and Germany and Austria gave bounties to their sugar producers and Continental beet-sugar strove against the West Indian cane variety. There was to be a revival of sugar-refining in Glasgow later, but too late for William's father. He was in his final seventies when that day came, and his youngest son would have turned forty had he been alive. There were four others, two girls and two boys and never, perhaps, was there a family composed of such disparate individuals – but their motto, to judge by the behaviour of each other, might have been *Live and Let Live*. None took the part of censor. It is conceivable that William, the youngest, was somewhat the pet of the family, though unspoilt thereby. In his infancy the best he could make of his name was Wem, so Wem he was for good at home. Through somebody in the warehouse who knew one of his brothers, it was carried there. So Wem he was in Cochrane Street also.

Head of the Wincey department was Andrew Middleton – fifty-five – a tall, gnarled man of a hue suggestive of jaundice but spare and strong, who trod the Glasgow planestanes with long, lithe stride. He was troubled at times, the market for winceys being in a declining state, lest he might be discharged, but hopeful (considering that he had been with the firm in the days of the founder) that instead of being dismissed he might be pensioned. He was another dweller in Gorbals where, in two rooms and a kitchen with Mrs Middleton, he suffered – as she – uncomplaining, in fact encouraging, the violin-practice of their only issue, a lad, then, of twenty. *Vee-o-lon*, by the way, was what Andy always called the instrument of his son's devotion. In public, talking of the boy, he would say it was far better for him to be practising the 'vee-o-lon' than kicking his heels in the close in the evenings. In private, he dreamt that some day he would see his son on the platform of St Andrew's Halls, in evening dress, bowing after a last encore, to a wildly enthusiastic audience packed to the hot ceiling.

He had but one assistant, and at times it was difficult to find work for both apart from pulling down a stack of cloth and building it up again. Of that assistant, Norman Nairn, we shall hear anon how he was, with the best intention in the world, deplorably led astray by Danny Huntley of the Shirtings or (from another standpoint) restored to reason when it seemed he had *gone gite*.

George Laidlaw and Dick Robertson were, at that time, in the Production department, into which buyers never entered. There were the Loom Books, the Yarn Books, the P.C. (or Production Cost) Books. As for George Laidlaw: Here, as in most communities there was a tendency for the component parts to fall into categories. In office, warehouse, club, camp, regiment, where-not, there are generally the markedly jolly one, markedly silly one, comic one, sober one, king's fool, people's favourite, the one who listens to the troubles of others and wisely advises, the one who borrows, the one who outstandingly lends, the religious one who but gives example of holiness, and the religious one who is a missioner. George Laidlaw was the sullen one, the dour one, the bully all under the one hat. Tall, loutish, he went about with a twist to his nostrils, as though everywhere finding an objectionable odour, hectoring those whom he thought he could hector, twisting the office-boy's arm, if it seemed that youngster was not fittingly servile to him, and surly even to Maxwell, Middleton, and Sandy Bain, his seniors by many a year. His eyes had only two expressions – one might almost say two lacks of expression. When alone they were as those of a dulled cod; when any one spoke to him they seemed to be made of a hard blue stone.

Dick Robertson was the younger son of a leather merchant, known in the Glasgow of those days as Leather Robertson. To be in the leather business, Leather Robertson said, was a dog's life, and he would not condemn all his sons to it. The third boy, Richard, he indentured to the Simsons.

Also in the Production department was young Robert Simson ('Bob' to his family, and to the staff), second son of the senior partner. Ian, the elder boy (christened John, but so called to distinguish him from his father), was at university, a faculty for winning scholarships and bursaries having decided the father to send him there. Even if, eventually, he was to be a manufacturer, a university education, it was decided, was all to the good. As for Bob, John Simson considered that it would be throwing good money after bad to send him to college from high-school.

The brothers were excellent friends. Ian did not vaunt his capacity for study over Bob, and in games they had a common interest. Bob had only just started to learn the business, his careless school-days over, with

Laidlaw and Robertson in that other office to rear of the main warehouse. Ian found many an opportunity to look in at Cochrane Street. His mother's uncertain notion that he might become a professional man was not to his heart at all. The 'wareus' for him! He liked it. He liked the feeling of the place on his visits. The pillars that supported the roof, the pillars of wincey and flannelette, the stacks of fancy goods, dress goods, the young men at work with suggestion of exuberant spirits: place and people appealed to him. Their world belonged to him. Thus it was, however, Bob, the younger, was put into the business when his high-school days were over and Ian, the elder, was at university.

Below stairs was the calender-man, 'old Fenwick'. Looking down the well, through which he got his daylight from the upper warehouse, one could see his bald head glinting over his machines (hydraulically driven then), that were like the mangles de luxe. Of his private life, till the pathos and the tragedy of it had an end, none knew in the warehouse. The men there only felt that he was odd. Of that he was aware, and sometimes made attempts to be normal with them by aid of a droll story. But his droll stories were not of the normal sort. He might just as well not have troubled to try to establish easy and close relations. An account of a physical peculiarity of Lord Byron (the poet, ye ken), a story about Nell Gwynn (King Charles the Second's mistress, ye ken), an account of how a certain *grande dame*, who had met the Duke of Wellington, gave her subaltern godson a letter of introduction to him in which she asked the duke, as an old soldier, to give the lad what advice he could to one on the threshold of a military career – and the advice, that might have shocked and affronted the old lady had her godson dared to report it to her: stories of that sort were not the normal droll story for them. The jokes which he sometimes cracked (out of Elizabethan and Restoration plays, had they only known), though nearer to giving his success in his object, were not entirely of the right *genre*. So he remained odd, even in these amiable efforts.

Duncan Ramsay, wrapped in a leathern apron, like a farrier's, was the packer and chief porter, with headquarters down in the basement where, between the red-painted iron pillars supporting the ceiling, a huge packing-press stood and from nails in the walls hung stencils. Duncan Ramsay was a man unhappy in his married life as he had been in his boyhood. He came from a family the members of which almost all showed but one eyebrow, a black line across a beetling forehead with no gap atop the nose; and he had married a woman whose eyes (as was the way with most of her people) were so close-set as to give the impression that she could look through a peep-hole with both eyes at once. Nature refused to give them children, try as they would. They had been trying for ten years. He had married at twenty-five, and was thus thirty-five at the commencement of this narrative. Each wanted to have a baby, and each blamed the other for lack of success in their endeavours. Their case was one that would have been of intense interest to Sigmund Freud, alive then, but not taken seriously so far by any save himself.

Two assistants he had, one Peter Pringle, and the other, Willie Scott. Pringle lived alone in these days in a meagre room, hard by the old Gallowgate, an attic in one of the 'lands', torn down these years. His hollow cheeks made Andy Middleton suspect tuberculosis, but Peter could flip from the floor to his shoulder a bale of one hundred and fifty pounds, as if it were a feather. One of his social accomplishments was whispering-singing. Sometimes, down in the packing basement, one might see a circle of the staff round him, all silent, all more than gravely attentive, with heads close, bending towards him. They were listening to his whispered but charmingly modulated rendering of some song, perhaps:

My wee dug's deid,
My puir wee thing,
My bow-wow. . .

Dan Huntley was a great admirer of his gift and virtuosity in it, but had one definite adverse criticism; it would be of no use in the music-halls. Whispering-singing, he opined, like performing fleas, was only for a close circle. 'You couldna entertain a whole audience at the Gaiety wi' it frae the stage.' Other accomplishments Peter Pringle had, of which you shall hear in due course.

Willie Scott was stocky and heavy but, though seemingly more robust than Pringle, always required a helping hand to elevate loads to his shoulder. Duncan Ramsay thought he was lazy. Somewhere in the neighbourhood of the Bridgegate he lived in a room and kitchen 'house' with a mother who occasionally added to income by going out, in bonnet and dolman, to do needlework, and a sister who was employed in a boot factory in which, by the way, Leather Robertson (Dick Robertson's father) had shares – though, of that frail link between the second porter in the basement and the young man in the Production department, neither was aware. Willie was a youth of magnificent phrases, such as 'I wouldna allow even my faither to strike me,' or 'Yer mither is always yer mither.' The perky office-boy (Tommy Bruce), whose duties – and sometimes pretended duties or needs – carried him through all the warehouse and down into the basement frequently on hearing such remarks would strike an attitude and declaim: 'You can take from me me life, but you cannot take from me me Victoria Cross,' and go off, skip and jump, up the stairs, Willie glaring after him.

That office boy had two ways of balancing the petty-cash book, when it did not balance of its own accord. One of them was to pocket what was in the box beyond the amount expected by his calculations. The other, was to pay in the deficit when, after repeated calculations, it was miserably clear that deficit there was. He had been in the Simson counting-house some time before his quaint way of book-keeping was discovered by Maitland. Maitland was the clerk, son of a farmer whose farm was away out southward from the city, on the verge of the moors. (The elder Maitland was determined that all his sons would not be farmers – a dog's life he called farming.) When Maitland reported the matter of the office-boy's accountancy to John Gilmore, who was cashier, there was profound silence in the office for several tense seconds.

Mr Gilmore seemed to be stunned, but suddenly he recovered, and was taken with a fit of laughter that nearly choked him, troubled as he was with the chronic bronchial catarrh. He was a slender man, going bald even in those days, who had been clerk in the reign of John the First. He had bulbous, protruding eyeballs on which it seemed the retina had just been thinly painted in faint blue. The effect was as of constant amazement at the world; but he was skilled, even when actually instead of only apparently amazed, at keeping his own counsel.

One morning 'Alice' Lennox came into the counting-house on warehouse business and, seeing the private-room door open – sign that the bosses were both out – delayed a while to tell Mr Gilmore of a pair of socks he had seen, a pair of socks. He had been to a 'dawnce', he began, a 'vewy' swell affair.

'There was a guest there,' said he, 'wearing the most beautiful socks I evah saw.'

'Do you tell me so?' inquired Mr Gilmore, staring at him, eyes popping.

'Oh, vewy beautiful,' Alisdair expatiated. 'The textcha was perfect.'

'God sakes! Do you tell me so?' Gilmore huskily and politely asked.

There came the sound of the opening of the outer door, and then the step of Robert Simson in the corridor. Arranging his tie and shooting his cuffs, Alisdair daintily departed. The cashier remained rigid, frigid, tranced, gazing at the door into the warehouse, as it swung back on Alice's exit, slowed, and gently shut with a faint sigh from the silencer affixed to it to prevent slamming.

'O Lord!' Mr Gilmore pled to the ceiling. His head slowly turned towards Maitland. 'We'll hae to examine him some day,' he huskily declared, 'and see what we'll see.'

Maitland, for all reply, gave one little snort. The farmer's son who rose at six-thirty every morning – tramping six and a half miles to Thornliebank station that he might be in Cochrane Street by nine – and who reached home out among the pewits at eight every evening, had deep contempt for dudes.

The office door opened and Mr Robert trod past the counter to his room with a 'Morning!'

'Good-morning, sir' said Gilmore, Maitland, and the little ex-schoolboy hunched, worried, over the petty-cash book.

THE WAREHOUSE

The premises of John Simson were more or less of a common architectural standard. In that quarter were many kindred fronts, interiors, and rears. Facing the street was a row of wide, high windows, of opaque green glass half-way up and plain glass beyond. On the coloured portion of the most westerly window (which lit the bosses' private-room) was the name *John Simson*. On the next one (of the counting-house) was the word, *Manufacturer*. Then came the broad door that stood open, held so by a hook near the floor, when the summer was over Scotland and even in Cochrane Street, through the smoke-canopy of that industrial city, the sun shone, laying gold-leaf on the chimney-pots, spreading radiance on the dark stones fronts, thrusting bright shafts into doorways and illuminating in pale yellow curves the arches under which lorry-men backed their horses over the cobbles. In winter, when the door was shut, flush to the street was the rubric painted across it:

JOHN SIMSON.
SHIRTINGS, WINCEYS,
FANCY GOODS, FLANNELETTES,
DRESS GOODS.

Eastward, beyond the entrance, were four more windows, three of these devoid of any lettering and then, on the last one, again JOHN SIMSON. These were of the Shirtings department and behind the most easterly was the small office in which Tom Huntley wrote his letters to all the world, letters which the office-boy collected and carried away to copy in the old press, which was in direct descent, by its appearance, from the printing presses of Caxton and Guttenberg.

Entering Simson's one advanced along a corridor at end of which, to left, was a door labelled *Office*. Ahead was another, a swing door, reinforced at its base with a sheet of zinc, so that it could be kicked open by men carrying loads and with no free hand. Its upper part was of frosted glass, save for a disc left transparent in the centre, like a bull's eye, toward the avoidance of collisions there. Swinging that open, most of the warehouse was revealed in one comprehensive glance.

The Shirtings department, of course, was not visible. You had to turn to right, and to right again, to enter it, but otherwise the main warehouse was clear to view between stacks of cloth of many sorts, columns of winceys, flannelette and the rest, that seemed flimsily to aid the red-painted iron columns in sustaining the roof. Upon that floor stood a long counter (of the Fancy Goods department) with a gap for further progress at either end. At that counter, Mr Maxwell, Corbett, and Johnny Leng, over their pattern and order-books, would look up without raising their chins to see who came when the door was opened. Beyond them were more stacks of 'soft-goods'.

On each side of that columned interior was a gallery. Broad flights of steps on either side led up to these, with strong metal balusters on which porters, carrying great loads on their shoulders, could lay a hand to aid their balance. When Tommy Bruce first saw the galleries they reminded him of pictures he had seen of oriental bazaars. In the gallery-recesses to left and right (right: Wincey and Flannelettes – left: Dress Goods) were more columns of cloth among which one could see the warehousemen at work, and hear them, too – hear the voices antiphonally intoning words and numbers as in some strange rite.

The whole place was roofed with glass. In centre was what at first sight seemed like an enormous vat of polished wood but, on advancing towards it, it revealed itself as what, in warehouse parlance, was 'the well'. Looking down there, one had a glimpse of the calender-man's bald head in a haze of fluff rising from some bolt of cloth quaking through his mangle-like machine. To left was a door leading into the receiving and despatching chamber where was a hoist that rose and fell by hydraulic power between that floor and the basement. A flight of stairs, there, also gave access to the basement – the packers' quarters and old Fenwick's. At the far end of that chamber heavy broad doors opened into the cobbled court, where the lorry horses tossed their nose-bags and pigeons fluttered and pottered, pecking at the scattered dole, while loading or unloading was in progress.

In that rear court, into which the lorries backed with a great clash of iron-shod hoofs, when the bosses were out, employees 'dying for a smoke' would sometimes stand for five minutes having a whiff of tobacco – for the head-packer would permit no one to come to his basement for that. He was king down there, and in direct Doric, or in what Dunbar called 'our ancient Ingliss', if he smelt tobacco-smoke coming from the little room in the far corner, he would hammer on the door and tell whoever was inside what the place was for and that it was 'nae' smoking-room. In the packing basement were often little gatherings of the staff, especially of the juniors. Not by any means were these gatherings always in utter truancy; but when two or three happened to meet there while employed upon some rightful labour for which they were on the salary-list of John Simson, they might take a breathing-spell.

Such a breathing-spell was being taken on the day of this chapter by Dan Huntley, Bob Simson, and Arthur Laurie, to watch Duncan Ramsay at work. Over the base of the great press he had spread a length of sacking, and with Pringle and Scot handing him the bolts, or pieces, he had built a neat stack. All watched while he slipped the sacking-ends over the pile, drew it down, smoothed it with an occasional helping hand from his two assistants.

'That's fine. Now! An easy press!' he ordered.

Peter stepped to one side and began to turn the wheel, while all looked on anxiously or admiringly to see how the pile responded.

'Fine – not a sag anywhere,' Duncan announced, and plunged to his desk for the big needles and twine.

It was at that stage that a sudden emotion of levity possessed the watching juniors. They began to jiggle this way and that, joggle one against another, each shooting out a hip as though in practice for the scrums of a football match. Ramsay stitched on, heedless of them, but anon, aware of their play, felt the grudge of a labourer against idlers – or they just fussed him, bothered him.

'It's a pity some of you lads have nae work to do,' he growled.

Willie Scott, either in deference to his boss's mood, or to suggest that he was no idler, interjected an inquiry.

'What stencils do ye want?' he asked.

The young men became more ebullient, and plunged into one of the hilarious games of the 'wareus', each making passes at the waistcoat of another in attempts to flip it open, or inserting quick crooked finger under a necktie, and twitching it out.

'Look out! I had a tie-clip! You've sent it flying somewhere!'

The fun grew wilder. To keep one's own waistcoat buttoned while yanking open others was the object of the hurly-burly. Footsteps on the stairs caused a lull, but they were only of the office-boy, bringing his brush-container (part of the outfit, now obsolete or antique, for copying letters) to fill it with water. The lull was but momentary. Whoops of renewed laughter sounded and echoed dully from the ceiling of that packing basement in Cochrane Street.

'Hie, you young devils,' Duncan yelped, 'dinna get in my way or I'll gie ye a slap with my stencilling brush.'

Just then down came Maitland with quick clatter on the brass-edged steps.

'Hurry up, young fellow-my-lad,' he called to the office-boy, 'you're to go out. Mr Maxwell and Mr Gilmore both want you. It's urgent.'

Mr Maxwell and Mr Gilmore – both! The young warehousemen let their play go. They, too, might be wanted upstairs. Dan Huntley, Bob Simson, and Arthur Laurie, buttoning their waistcoats, fled to their departments by different routes, for there were two other stairways besides the one from the chamber directly above. There was a flight of steps that came down from the Shirting department and another from the far corner of the warehouse under the Flannelette gallery, both of these to the calendering basement, which was connected by a doorway with the packing-room.

Tommy Bruce, splashing water from the filled container, hurried across the cemented basement, upstairs, and smartly into the office where were Mr Maxwell and Mr Gilmore in close talk.

'See here, Tommy,' said the cashier, 'Mr Maxwell wants you to dash along to the Exchange and go in and ask for Mr Simson, and see him, himself. Tell him from Mr Maxwell that Mr Sinclair, the Canadian buyer, is coming along in a few minutes. Give me that – give me that brush and water-contraption – I'll hang it up for you.'

Only a day or two later that outing of Tommy's would not have been necessary. There were men then at work in the office installing that new-fangled thing, the telephone, their activities there making each member of the staff feel that he lived in progressive days of invention and discovery.

Tommy leapt for his cap. Just as he was going out into Cochrane Street, Wem Mackay was coming in. There seemed to be hilarity in the air that day. As they passed, Wem made a flick with right hand for Tommy's waistcoat, but Tommy, chuckling, held an arm across his breast and thus prevented the disturbance of his attire – unaware that the flick of the right hand had been just a feint to deflect his eyes from the flip of the other hand. The pinnacle of that fun had been achieved. His trousers had been snapped open in one deft movements, and away he went, unaware, to George Square and down Ingram Street, sartorially shocking, or amusing, according to the minds of those who observed. He wondered why two passing gamins yodelled at him. He wondered what a very old man meant by halting and pivotting to wave a stick at him and gibber some words.

'The old goat's mad,' he surmised.

It was a fine day in Glasgow. The pavements were dry. A little wind stirred the dropped packing-straw at warehouse entrances. The harness of passing dray-horses shone. From Miss Cranston's tea-rooms came odours of tea and coffee, crumpets and buttered scones. The plate-glass windows shone like upright slabs of glare ice and reflected, as in a quick shadow-show, the people going past – there and gone. Preparations were being made for an imminent royal visit to the city, a royal procession. Lintels were being decked with bunting, flagpoles were being affixed to doorways. Municipal carts went heavily by laden with gravel to be strewn on some of the streets toward prevention of the downfall of caracoling horses.

Running across Queen Street towards the Royal Exchange, Tommy raised a group of grain-pecking pigeons. They swept over his head with their little 'Ohs!' of alarm and flurry of wings, and flew, a pennant of blue, over the head of Marochetti's Wellington, dropping unconscious contempt on that warrior. Slowing abruptly from a run to a young man's business walk, as though subdued by the Corinthian dignity of the Royal Exchange, he entered its portals. Within a commissionaire with medalled breast challenged him.

'Yes, young fellow?'

'I want to see Mr Simson – personally.'

'Mr Simson. You'll find him in there – in the second room, I believe. Knock before you go in. He may be in conference with other gentlemen. And here, wait a minute. Button up your trousers before ye gang in.'

'O Lord!' gasped Tommy, and then, 'Thank you,' he said, and adjusted his dress, wondering how long he had been like that, and who was the culprit. Had it happened down in the basement? No, Mr Maxwell or Mr Gilmore would have noticed it in the office. Wem – that's who it was: Wem Mackay, when they met in the corridor.

There was something almost awe-inspiring about that interior. There was a cloistral quiet, a definite dignity. His footsteps, as he thrust open a door and passed into a tiled passageway, rang loud and he felt he would tiptoe. But he was in haste, for Mr Maxwell and Mr Gilmore had impressed upon him the need for haste. He came to the second door, knocked, and entered.

In the middle of a large and almost palatial room was a group of men – very old men they seemed to that stripling. They were city fathers. They were a yarn merchant (business acquaintance of his boss), a wine merchant (friend of his boss), a saltpetre merchant (another friend of his boss), men who came staidly and dignified into the counting-house to inquire, 'Mr Simson in?' and who, after conference in the private-room, went out as though with high seriousness to make Glasgow flourish.

They did not hear Tommy enter. John Simson was there too, but he did not hear. They were milling and whirling and whooping with merriment, each trying to protect his waistcoat while he assaulted other waistcoats. A hat was knocked off in the scrimmage – his boss's, John Simson's. Tommy saw Mr Mackenzie, the yarn merchant, flip at the neck-tie of Mr Renfield, the very venerable saltpetre merchant.

'Excuse me, sir,' he began, advancing on the mêlée.

They desisted. They looked at him in amazement, wondering where he came from, how he had sprung to life there. They buttoned their waistcoats, frowning severely at him. Mr Simson retrieved his hat from the floor.

'What?' he rumbled, just that: 'What?' violently.

'Excuse me, sir, but Mr Sinclair, the Canadian buyer, will be at the wareus in a few minutes, and Mr Maxwell and Mr Gilmore think you ought – should – I mean, would like to be there when he arrives.'

'All right,' growled John Simson, looking as if he hated his office-boy.

Tommy wheeled to the door and held it open – and lo, just as his great boss turned from the group to follow, one of the old gentlemen made a pass at Mr Simson's chest with one hand, a pass which was deflected with a hint of annoyance – the game being apparently finished – and with the other hand furtively achieved the pinnacle of that sport.

What was Tommy to do? Holding the door open, he wondered. No, he could not say, 'Sir, you are undone.' That, he felt, would be as much as his job would be worth, even though he was indentured for three years. The papers would be cancelled.

John Simson strode violently along the corridor and Tommy hurried alongside to open the next door for him, but the boss, forging ahead, opened it for himself, let it swing back against the boy and strode violently, like a colonel of foot leading a charge, past the commissionaire who came to attention and saluted, then looked at Tom in the rear and winked. That had been a curious and riotous conference!

Away along Ingram Street went John Simson on one side, and on the other his office-boy. Gamins yodelled at the great man, as he branged along, but he did not appear to observe them nor to hear them. He was annoyed that the office-boy had found out that the Royal Exchange was not always as serious a haunt as it looked. He hoped the confounded infant would not tell the news to the staff. Should he advise the boy not to say a word? No, let it go.

He was several laps ahead of Tommy at the door of the warehouse. Within, Mr Maxwell, shaking hands with Mr Sinclair, heard the masterful tread.

'Here's Mr Simson now,' he said. 'I know his walk. He'll be delighted to see you.'

The trend went into the office and halted there.

'Mr Sinclair arrived? 'John Simson asked.

'In the wareus, sir, in the wareus,' replied Gilmore.

Into the warehouse, with a wide sweep of the door, went Mr Simson and advanced on Mr Sinclair, breezy, bonhomous, holding out his hand.

'How do you do?' he bellowed. 'Delighted to see you again.'

'Look at your pants,' Mr Sinclair commanded, with a pointing finger.

While that quaint meeting was in progress, Tommy Bruce, as though upon important business, dived swiftly behind some columns of cloth in search of Wem Mackay to give him, if he had a chance, one smite between the ribs for what he had done.

‘ ‘Divus’ Johnston’

from The Runagates Club

JOHN BUCHAN (1875–1940)

As this chapter on ‘The Merchant City’ will have suggested, the Glaswegian has, over the years, proved to be an enterprising and entrepreneurial individual, quick to adapt to changing circumstances. Few, however, even in their most grandiose moments (and one thinks of the Tobacco Lords strutting on the Plainstanes) ever became Gods.

John Buchan’s story, told by Lord Lamancha at the Runagates Club, deals with ‘Divus’ Johnston who had ‘been an elder in a kirk in the Cowcaddens’ and now was worshipped as a God by South Sea islanders. The idea of two Scots meeting overseas in strange circumstances is a familiar one, fuelled by the truth and legend of the wandering Scot. There is, for example, the story of the frontier dispute in Bessarabia where a Russian General and a Turkish Pasha met to arbitrate the dispute. After concluding their negotiations in diplomatic French the Tsar’s general turned to the representative of the Ottoman Empire with the words: ‘Weel, Jock, and foo’s aa wi ye in Inverurie?’

‘Divus’ Johnston *first appeared in 1913 in a magazine and was republished in Buchan’s last short-story collection* The Runagates Club *in 1928. ‘Divus’ is Latin for god.*

‘DIVUS’ JOHNSTON

In deorum numerum relatus est non ore modo decernentium sed et persuasione vulgi.

SUETONIUS

We were discussing the vagaries of ambition, and decided that most of the old prizes that humanity contended for had had their gilt rubbed off. Kingdoms, for example, which younger sons used to set out to conquer. It was agreed that nowadays there was a great deal of drudgery and very little fun in being a king.

‘Besides, it can’t be done,’ Leithen put in. ‘The Sarawak case. Sovereignty over territory can only be acquired by a British subject on behalf of His Majesty.’

There was far more real power, someone argued, in the profession of prophet. Mass-persuasion was never such a force as today. Sandy Arbuthnot, who had known Gandhi and admired him, gave us a picture of that strange popular leader – ascetic, genius, dreamer, child. 'For a little,' he said, 'Gandhi had more absolute sway over a bigger lump of humanity than anybody except Lenin.'

'I once knew Lenin,' said Fulleylove, the traveller, and we all turned to him.

'It must have been more than twenty years ago,' he explained. 'I was working at the British Museum and lived in lodgings in Bloomsbury, and he had a room at the top of the house. Ilyitch was the name we knew him by. He was a little, beetle-browed chap, with a pale face and the most amazing sleepy black eyes, which would suddenly twinkle and blaze as some thought passed through his mind. He was very pleasant and good-humoured, and would spend hours playing with the landlady's children. I remember I once took him down with me for a day into the country, and he was the merriest little grig . . . Did I realise how big he was? No, I cannot say I did. He was the ordinary Marxist, and he wanted to resurrect Russia by hydraulics and electrification. He seemed to be a funny compound of visionary and *terre-à-terre* scientist. But I realised that he could lay a spell on his countrymen. I have been to Russian meetings with him – I talk Russian, you know – and it was astounding the way he could make his audience look at him like hungry sheep. He gave me the impression of utter courage and candour, and a kind of demoniac simplicity . . . No, I never met him again, but oddly enough I was in Moscow during his funeral. Russian geographers were interesting themselves in the line of the old silk-route to Cathay, and I was there by request to advise them. I had not a very comfortable time, but everybody was very civil to me. So I saw Lenin's funeral, and unless you saw that you can have no notion of his power. A great black bier like an altar, and hundreds and thousands of people weeping and worshipping – yes, worshipping.'

'The successful prophet becomes a kind of god,' said Lamancha. 'Have you ever known a god, Sandy? . . . No more have I. But there is one living today somewhere in Scotland. Johnston is his name. I once met a very particular friend of his. I will tell you the story, and you can believe it or not as you like.'

I had this narrative – he said – from my friend Mr Peter Thomson of 'Jessieville', Maxwell Avenue, Strathbungo, whom I believe to be a man incapable of mendacity, or, indeed, of imagination. He is a prosperous and retired ship's captain, dwelling in the suburbs of Glasgow, who plays two rounds of golf every day of the week, and goes twice every Sunday to a pink, new church. You may often see his ample figure, splendidly habited in broadcloth and finished off with one of those square felt hats which are the Scottish emblem of respectability, moving sedately by Mrs Thomson's side down the avenue of 'Balmorals' and 'Bellevues' where dwell the aristocracy of Strathbungo. It was not there that I met him, however, but in a Clyde steamboat going round the Mull, where I spent a comfortless night on my way to a Highland fishing. It was blowing what he called 'wee bit o' wind', and I could not face the odorous bunks which opened on the dining-room. Seated abaft the funnel, in an atmosphere of ham-and-eggs, bilge and fresh western breezes, he revealed his heart to me, and this I found in it.

'About the age of forty' – said Mr Thomson – 'I was captain of the steamer *Archibald McKelvie*, 1,700 tons burthen, belonging to Brock, Rattray, and Linklater of Greenock. We were principally engaged in the China trade, but made odd trips into the Malay Archipelago and once or twice to Australia. She was a handy bit boat, and I'll not deny that I had many mercies vouchsafed to me when I was her skipper. I raked in a bit of salvage now and then, and my trading commission, paid regularly into the British Linen Bank at Maryhill, was mounting up to a fairish sum. I had no objection to Eastern parts, for I had a good constitution and had outgrown the daftness of youth. The berth suited me well, I had a decent lot for ship's company, and I would gladly have looked forward to spending the rest of my days by the *Archibald McKelvie*.

'Providence, however, thought otherwise, for He was preparing a judgment against that ship like the kind you read about in books. We were five days out from Singapore, shaping our course for the Philippines, where the Americans were then fighting, when we ran into a queer lown sea. Not a breath of air came out of the sky; if you kindled a match the flame wouldna leap, but smouldered like touchwood; and every man's body ran with sweat like a mill-lade. I kenned fine we were in for the terrors of hell, but I hadna any kind of notion how terrible hell could be. First came a wind that whipped away my funnel, like a potato-peeling. We ran before it, and it was like the swee-gee we used to play at when we were laddies. One moment the muckle sea would get up on its hinder end and look at you, and the next you were looking at it as if you were on top of Ben Lomond looking down on Luss. Presently I saw land in a gap of the waters, a land with great blood-red mountains, and, thinks I to myself, if we keep up the pace this boat of mine will not be hindered from ending two or three miles inland in somebody's kail-yard. I was just wondering how we would get the *Archibald McKelvie* back to her native element when she saved me the trouble; for she ran dunt on some kind of a rock, and went straight to the bottom.

'I was the only man saved alive, and if you ask me how it happened I don't know. I felt myself choking in a whirlpool; then I was flung through the air and brought down with a smack into deep waters; then I was in the air again, and this time I landed amongst sand and tree-trunks and got a bash on the head which dozened my senses.

'When I came to it was morning, and the storm had abated. I was lying about half-way up a beach of fine white sand, for the wave that had carried me landwards in its flow had brought me some of the road back in its ebb. All round me was a sort of free-coup – trees knocked to matchwood, dead fish, and birds and beasts, and some boards which I jaloused came from the *Archibald McKelvie*. I had a big bump on my head, but otherwise I was well and clear in my wits, though empty in the stomach and very dowie in the heart. For I knew something about the islands, of which I supposed this to be one. They were either barren wastes, with neither food nor water, or else they were inhabited by the bloodiest cannibals of the archipelago. It looked as if my choice lay between having nothing to eat and being eaten myself.

'I got up, and, after returning thanks to my Maker, went for a walk in the woods. They were full of queer painted birds, and it was an awful job climbing in and out of the fallen trees. By and by I came into an open bit with a burn where I slockened my thirst. It cheered me up, and I was just beginning to think that this was not such a bad island, and looking to see if I could find anything in the nature of coconuts, when I heard a whistle like a steam-siren. It was some sort of signal, for the next I knew I was in the grip of a dozen savages, my arms and feet were lashed together, and I was being carried swiftly through the forest.

'It was a rough journey, and the discomfort of that heathen handling kept me from reflecting upon my desperate position. After nearly three hours we stopped, and I saw that we had come to a city. The streets were not much to look at, and the houses were mud and thatch, but on a hillock in the middle stood a muckle temple not unlike a Chinese pagoda. There was a man blowing a horn, and a lot of folk shouting, but I paid no attention, for I was sore troubled with the cramp in my left leg. They took me into one of the huts and made signs that I was to have it for my lodging. They brought me water to wash, and a very respectable dinner, which included a hen and a vegetable not unlike greens. Then they left me to myself, and I lay down and slept for a round of the clock.

I was three days in that hut. I had plenty to eat and the folk were very civil, but they wouldn't let me outbye and there was no window to look out of. I couldna make up my mind what they wanted with me. I was a prisoner, but they did not behave as if they bore any malice, and I might have thought I was an honoured guest, but for the guards at the door. Time hung heavy on my hands, for I had nothing to read and no light to read by. I said over all the chapters of the Bible and all the Scots songs I could remember, and I tried to make a poem about my adventures, but I stuck at the fifth line, for I couldna find a rhyme to McKelvie.

'On the fourth morning I was awakened by the most deafening din. I saw through the door that the streets were full of folk in holiday clothes, most of them with flowers in their hair and carrying palm branches in their hands. It was like something out of a Bible picture book. After I had my breakfast four lads in long white gowns arrived, and in spite of all my protests they made a bonny spectacle of me. They took off my clothes, me blushing with shame, and rubbed me with a kind of oil that smelt of cinnamon. Then they shaved my chin, and painted on my forehead a mark like a freemason's. Then they put on me a kind of white nightgown with a red sash round the middle, and they wouldna be hindered from clapping on my head a great wreath of hothouse flowers, as if I was a funeral.

'And then like a thunder-clap I realised my horrible position. *I was a funeral.* I was to be offered up as a sacrifice to some heathen god – an awful fate for a Free-kirk elder in the prime of life.

'I was so paralytic with terror I never tried to resist. Indeed, it would have done me little good, for outside there were, maybe, two hundred savages, armed and drilled like soldiers. I was put into a sort of palanquin, and my bearers started at a trot with me up the hill to the temple, the whole population of the city running alongside, and singing songs about their god. I was sick with fear, and I durstna look up, for I did not know what awesome sight awaited me.

'At last I got my courage back. "Peter," I says to myself, "be a man. Remember your sainted Covenanting forefathers. You have been chosen to testify for your religion, though it's no likely that yon savages will understand what you say." So I shut my jaw and resolved before I died to make a declaration of my religious principles, and to loosen some of the heathen's teeth with my fists.

'We stopped at the temple door and I was led through a court and into a muckle great place like a barn, with bats flying about the ceiling. Here there were nearly three thousand heathens sitting on their hunkers. They sang a hymn when they saw me, and I was just getting ready for action when my bearers carried me into another place, which I took to be the Holy of Holies. It was about half the size of the first, and at the end of it was a great curtain of leopards' skins hanging from roof to floor. My bearers set me in the middle of the room, and then rolled about on their stomachs in adoration before the curtain. After a bit they finished their prayers and crawled out backwards, and I was left alone in that fearsome place.

'It was the worst experience of my life. I believed that behind the skins there was a horrible idol, and that at any moment a priest with a knife would slip in to cut my throat. You may crack about courage, but I tell you that a man who can wait without a quiver on his murderers in the middle of a gloomy kirk is more than human. I am not ashamed to confess that the sweat ran over my brow, and my teeth were knocking in my head.

'But nothing happened. Nothing, except that as I sat there I began to notice a most remarkable smell. At first I thought the place was on fire. Then I thought it was the kind of stink called incense that they make in Popish kirks, for I once wandered into a cathedral in Santiago. But neither guess was right, and then I put my thumb on the proper description. It was nothing but the smell of the third-class carriages on the Coatbridge train on a Saturday night after a football match – the smell of plug tobacco smoked in clay pipes that were no just very clean. My eyes were getting accustomed to the light, and I found the place no that dark; and as I looked round to see what caused the smell, I spied something like smoke coming from beyond the top of the curtain.

'I noticed another thing. There was a hole in the curtain, about six feet from the floor, and at that hole as I watched I saw an eye. My heart stood still, for, thinks I, that'll be the priest of Baal who presently will stick a knife into me. It was long ere I could screw up courage to look again, but I did it. And then I saw that the eye was not that of a savage, which would be black and blood-shot. It was a blue eye, and, as I looked, it winked at me.

'And then a voice spoke out from behind the curtain, and this was what it said. It said, "God-sake, Peter, is that you? And how did ye leave them a' at Maryhill?"

'And from behind the curtain walked a muckle man, dressed in a pink blanket, a great red-headed man, with a clay pipe in his mouth. It was the god of the savages, and who do ye think it was? A man Johnston, who used to bide in the same close as me in Glasgow. . .'

Mr Thomson's emotion overcame him, and he accepted a stiff drink from my flask. Wiping away a tear, which may have been of sentiment or of mirth, he continued:

'You may imagine that I was joyful and surprised to see him, and he, so to speak, fell on my neck like the father of the Prodigal Son. He hadna seen a Scotch face for four years. He raked up one or two high priests and gave instructions, and soon I was comfortably lodged in a part of the temple close to his own rooms. Eh, man, it was a noble sight to see Johnston and the priests. He was a big, red-haired fellow, six feet four, and as strong as a stot, with a voice like a north-easter, and yon natives fair crawled like caterpillars in his presence. I never saw a man with such a natural talent for being a god. You would have thought he had been bred to the job all his days, and yet I minded him keeping a grocer's shop in the Dalmarnock Road.

'That night he told me his story. It seemed that he had got a post in Shanghai in a trading house, and was coming out to it in one of those God-forgotten German tramps that defile the China seas. Like me, he fell in with a hurricane, and, like me, his ship was doomed. He was a powerful swimmer, and managed to keep afloat until he found some drifting wreckage, and after the wind had gone down he paddled ashore. There he was captured by the savages, and taken, like me, to their city. They were going to sacrifice him, but one chief, wiser than the rest, called attention to his size and strength, and pointed out that they were at war with their neighbours, and that a big man would be of more use in the fighting line than on an altar in the temple.

'So off went Johnston to the wars. He was a bonny fighter, and very soon they made him captain of the royal bodyguard, and a fortnight later the general commanding-in-chief over the whole army. He said he had never enjoyed himself so much in his life, and when he got back from his battles the whole population of the city used to meet him with songs and flowers. Then an old priest found an ancient prophecy about a Red God who would come out of the sea and lead the people to victory. Very soon there was a strong party for making Johnston a god, and when, with the help of a few sticks of trade dynamite, he had blown up the capital of the other side and brought back his army in triumph with a prisoner apiece, popular feeling could not be restrained. Johnston was hailed as divine. He hadna much grip of the language, and couldna explain the situation, so he thought it best to submit.

' "Mind you," he said to me, "I've been a good god to these poor blind ignorant folk." He had stopped the worst of their habits and put down human sacrifices, and got a sort of town council appointed to keep the city clean, and he had made the army the most efficient thing ever heard of in the islands. And now he was preparing to leave. This was what they expected, for the prophecy had said that the Red God, after being the saviour of his people, would depart as he had come across the sea. So, under his directions, they had built him a kind of boat with which he hoped to reach Singapore. He had got together a considerable fortune, too, chiefly in rubies, for as a god he had plenty of opportunities for acquiring wealth honestly. He said there was a sort of greengrocer's and butcher's shop before his altar every morning, and he got one of the priests, who had some business notions, to sell off the goods for him.

'There was just one thing that bothered Mr Johnston. He was a good Christian man and had been an elder in a kirk in the Cowcaddens, and he was much in doubt whether he had not committed a mortal sin in accepting the worship of these heathen islanders. Often I argued it out with him, but I did not seem able to comfort him rightly. "Ye see," he used to say to me, "if I have broken anything, it's the spirit and no the letter of the commandment. I havena set up a graven image, for ye canna call me a graven image."

'I mind that I quoted to him the conduct of Naaman, who was allowed to bow in the house of Rimmon, but he would not have it. "No, no," he cried, "that has nothing to do with the point. It's no a question of my bowing in the house of Rimmon. I'm auld Rimmon himself." '

'That's a strange story, Mr Thomson,' I said. 'Is it true?'

'True as death. But you havena heard the end of it. We got away, and by-and-by we reached Singapore, and in course of time our native land. Johnston, he was a very rich man now, and I didna go without my portion; so the loss of the *Archibald McKelvie* turned out the best piece of luck in my life. I bought a share in Brock's Line, but nothing would content Johnston but that he must be a gentleman. He got a big estate in Annandale, where all the Johnstons came from long ago, and one way and another he has spent an awful siller on it. Land will swallow up money quicker than the sea.'

'And what about his conscience?' I asked.

'It's keeping quieter,' said Mr Thomson. 'He takes a great interest in Foreign Missions, to which he subscribes largely, and they tell me that he had given the funds to build several new kirks. Oh yes, and he's just been adopted as a prospective Liberal candidate. I had a letter from him no further back than yesterday. It's about his political career, as he calls it. He told me, what didna need telling, that I must never mention a word of his past. "If discretion was necessary before," he says, "it's far more necessary now, for how could the Party of Progress have any confidence in a man if they heard he had once been a god?" '

5
THE CLYDE MADE GLASGOW
Introduction

'Glasgow made the Clyde, and the Clyde made Glasgow', so runs the proverbial wisdom. It is indeed hard, even today when the significance of the river to the city has so markedly diminished from the high water mark of the Victorian or Edwardian era, to think of Glasgow without thinking of its river, its shipbuilding and engineering, and its trade.

Thanks to many years of expensive work and much ingenuity Glasgow turned the unpromising waters of the Clyde into a deep-sea port at the heart of the city, but for most of the city's history the Clyde at Glasgow was a shallow river of no commercial significance. In 1812, when Henry Bell started the first commercial steamer service on the river with the *Comet*, even though she only drew four feet, her times of sailing had to be adjusted for tidal conditions. Even so, on her first trip she managed to run aground at Erskine.

The City authorities had been under pressure from Glasgow merchants, anxious to develop their trade with the American and West Indian colonies, to enable them to bring their cargoes into the city. As the Western Ocean trade developed after the Union Glasgow merchants grew increasingly unhappy with having to use the city's Renfrewshire outport of Port Glasgow. Port Glasgow had been created in the 1600s at Newark and by 1710 the main Custom House for the Clyde was established there. Glasgow-owned ships would make their trading voyages to the plantations of the New World and return laden with tobacco and sugar to Port Glasgow. The Burgh of Port Glasgow's motto suggests this trading pattern: *Ter et quater anno revisens aequor Atlanticum impunens* (Three and four times a year revisiting the Atlantic with impunity).

Having sailed three or four thousand miles across the Atlantic they had to have their bulk cargoes broken into smaller consignments for the last fifteen miles to the Glasgow warehouses – an expensive and inconvenient expedient for what was a rapidly developing commerce, with the potential to bring great wealth to the city. As Bailie Nicol Jarvie, in Walter Scott's *Rob Roy* observed: 'Now, since St Mungo catched herrings in the

Clyde, what was ever like to gar us flourish like the sugar and tobacco-trade? Will ony body tell me that, and grumble at the treaty that opened us a road west-awa' yonder?'

A variety of schemes to deepen the Clyde and facilitate the 'road west-awa' yonder' were proposed, but matters began to make progress when the English engineer John Golborne was hired in 1768. His plan involved making the river deepen itself by erecting dykes at right angles to the river – increasing the scouring effect of the river by speeding the flow of water. This, together with a limited amount of dredging, was designed to produce a four or five feet deep channel into the heart of the city. Golborne's plan was successful, and by the 1770s coasting vessels were able to discharge Irish oatmeal at the Broomielaw; but still the river was too shallow to allow ocean-going vessels to reach the city.

Golborne's scheme was developed by Thomas Telford who advised joining up the ends of Golborne's projecting groynes: the river was in effect canalised and the scouring effect increased. By 1818 foreign-going ships were regularly sailing up to the Broomielaw and in the 1820s steam-powered dredgers were at work, widening and deepening the river.

If trade was restricted by the shallows of the Clyde, shipbuilding in the city also had to wait until the river was deep enough to permit the launching of sizeable vessels. It was not until the early decades of the nineteenth century, and with the work of engineers like David and Robert Napier and James Cook, that the marine industries became prominent in Glasgow. James Cleland's *Annals of Glasgow*, published in 1816, surveys the city's industries and commerce but does not record a single shipyard operating within the city's boundaries. An extract from the *Annals of Glasgow* written in the pioneering days of steam on the river illustrates the early years of development.

Like any other development, the coming of steamships to Glasgow aroused the interest of writers. The novelist John Galt was among the earliest of those to use these changes as the framework for his work. His episodic novel *The Steam-Boat,* published in 1822, relates the adventures of Thomas Duffle on the new Clyde steamers.

Of course this change in the river did not meet with universal approval. The Glasgow-born poet Thomas Campbell (the author of Ye Mariners of England) was one who saw the transformation of the Clyde from a sylvan salmon-rich stream to an industrial site in negative terms. His poem 'Lines on revisiting a Scottish River' is not the last nostalgic comment by an exiled Scot who returns home and regrets the changes. Campbell's poem was written in 1827, the year in which he was elected Rector of Glasgow University. A more positive reaction comes from the late-

Victorian Bass Kennedy and his Bridgeton weaver's poem to his wife, 'Doon the Watter at the Fair', which concludes that:

A twalmonth's toil in Glesca toun
Is lichtsome, I declare,
Wi' twa-three days' diversion doon
The watter at the Fair.

Bass Kennedy's lines serve as a useful reminder that the changes on the river were not simply of economic and commercial significance, but opened up new opportunities for pleasure and recreation for the city's inhabitants.

Iron shipbuilding can be said to have had its real start in Glasgow when in 1841 Robert Napier converted an old wooden shipbuilding yard at Govan to the new technology, starting Glasgow and the Clyde on the route to pre-eminence in iron, and later steel, shipbuilding. The pace of change was swift, even if in the 1850s travel writers could still speak of 'Govan, with its still half-rural aspect'. The peak of this pre-eminence was perhaps reached in the early years of the twentieth century, and our extracts from Neil Munro and 'James Hamilton Muir' paint vivid pictures of the river and its industries at that time. A poem by W.J.F. Hutcheson, somewhat reminiscent in style of Kipling's 'McAndrew's Hymn', celebrates the skill of the engine builder in the hey-day of the marine steam engine.

H.V. Morton gives an impression of the river in the troubled years of the 1920s and 1930s, and an extract from the opening of George Blake's fine novel *The Shipbuilders* further illustrates this difficult period.

After the Second World War the story of the Clyde is, sadly, one of progressive decline. The city-centre docks – Kingston, Queen's and Prince's – closed in the 1960s and 1970s, the city's shipyards closed one after another, until the Glasgow shipbuilding industry now consists of only one general shipyard with an uncertain future – Kvaerner Govan, and one specialist naval yard – Yarrow Shipbuilders.

'Steam Boats'

from Annals of Glasgow

JAMES CLELAND (1770–1840)

James Cleland was a Glasgow cabinetmaker with a flair for statistics and public service. He was appointed as Glasgow's Superintendent of Public Works in 1814, wrote the article on Glasgow for the Encyclopaedia Britannica *and published his* Annals *in 1816.*

Cleland's account of early steamers on the Clyde is an important contemporary source and was published just four years after the first Clyde steamer made its tentative way down river.

STEAM BOATS

By the application of steam, the velocity of vessels is considerably increased, the certainty of the passage in a given time ensured, and the rate of conveyance reduced. The application of this power to the propelling of boats has engaged the attention of the ingenious for a considerable time past.

In 1785, Mr Millar of Dalswinton built a vessel with two keels, between which he introduced propelling paddle-wheels. A number of difficulties having unexpectedly presented themselves, that ingenious mechanic felt it necessary to lay the experiment aside.

In 1794, the Earl of Stanhope constructed a vessel, to be moved by steam-paddles, placed under her quarters. The mechanism not having answered the expectation of his Lordship, the scheme was given up.

In 1801, Mr Symington, with the approbation and concurrence of Lord Dundas,* fitted up a steam-boat on the Forth and Clyde Navigation, which was never matured, on account of the injury it did to the banks of the Canal.

The steam-propelling system, as an article of trade, was destined to perpetuate the memory of Mr Robert Fulton, a native of North America, who, on 3rd October, 1807, launched a Steam-Boat, which plied between

* Lord Dundas was, at that time, Governor of the Forth and Clyde Navigation.

New York and Albany with very considerable success. Having at length completely succeeded in establishing steam-propelling boats, for conveying passengers and goods, the Government of the United States were induced to build a frigate, which they called Fulton the First, in honour of their countryman, who had first brought the steam-propelling system to public account.

It was not, however, till the beginning of 1812, that steam was successfully applied to vessels in Europe, as an article of trade. At that period, Mr Henry Bell, an ingenious, untutored engineer, and Citizen of Glasgow, fitted up, or it may be said, without the hazard of impropriety, that he invented the steam-propelling system, and applied it to his boat, the *Comet*, for as yet he knew nothing of the principles which had been so successfully followed out by Mr Fulton.

After various experiments,* the *Comet* was at length propelled on the Clyde by an engine of three horse power, which was subsequently increased to six. Mr Bell continued to encounter and overcome the various and indescribable difficulties incident to invention, till his ultimate success encouraged others to embark in similar undertakings, which has been done in a ratio only to be credited by the knowledge of the number of vessels which have been placed on the river. Owing to the novelty and supposed danger of the passage in the Frith below Dumbarton, in vessels which had so small a hold of the water, the number of passengers at the outset were but small. The public, however, having gained confidence by degrees, in a navigation, which became at once expeditious and pleasant, it was preferred to every other mode of conveyance; for the expedition of the voyage, and beauty of the scenery on the banks of the Clyde, are such as to attract alike the attention of the man of business and pleasure; and the watering-places all along the coast have been crowded with company beyond all former precedent, in consequence of steam conveyance. It has been calculated that, previous to the erection of Steam-boats, not more than fifty persons passed and repassed from Glasgow to Greenock in one day; whereas, it is now supposed that there are from four to five hundred passes and repasses in the same period. The passage between Glasgow and Greenock is about twenty-six miles, and is usually performed in three hours; and often, when the wind and tide are favourable, it is performed in less than two

* The boats on the Clyde have been hitherto propelled by two paddle-wheels, similarly constructed to undershot water mill-wheels, placed on each side of the vessel. In some boats, they are placed at right angles to their sides; in others, they are fitted in a circular direction; while a third, displays the oblique form. It is no easy matter, however, to say which of them produces the best effect, as the mould of the vessels, the size and situation of the engine, and a number of other circumstances, have all to be taken into the account.

hours and one-half. The cabin and steerage are fitted up with every suitable convenience; the former is provided with interesting books, and the various periodical publications. Breakfasts, dinners, &c. are provided for those who may require them. The cabin fare is four shillings, and the steerage two shillings and sixpence.

Since the *Comet* began to ply on the river, it is very common to make the voyage of Campbeltown, Iveraray, or the Kyles of Bute, and return to Glasgow on the following day. Steam-Boats have also been sent from the Clyde to Ireland, Liverpool, and London, some of whom weathered heavy gales of wind and encountered high surfs.

Steam-Boats are now plying on the Forth, the Tay, the Avon, the Severn, the Thames, the Yare, the Trent, the Tyne, the Mersey, the Ouse, the Humber, the Orwell, &c. &c.

On the 30th day of November, 1815, Mr James Cook, an eminent engineer in Tradestown, Glasgow, exhibited and explained the machinery, paddles, &c. of a Steam-Boat, to their Royal and Imperial Highnesses, John and Louis, Arch-Dukes of Austria, with a view of placing stream-vessels on some of the rivers of Germany. Mr Cook has since furnished the Austrian Government with plans and models, illustrative of the latest improvements on the steam-paddle apparatus. Since the period alluded to, a steam-boat has been built at St Petersburgh, in Russia.

'Clyde Cruising'

from The Steam-Boat

JOHN GALT (1779–1839)

First published in 1822, The Steam-Boat *is one of a group of Galt's novels which he called 'Tales of the West', which take their setting and their characters from the part of Scotland where Galt was born (Irvine) and grew up (Greenock.)*

The Steam-Boat, *perhaps the least well-known of the 'Tales of the West', is one of the earliest works of fiction to be inspired by the new opportunities for mass travel opened up by the advent of steam power at sea. As Cleland noted in the previous extract there had been a huge increase in river traffic brought about by the coming of the early steamships, which, while they might not have been significantly faster than sailing ships, were certainly more reliable.*

Galt's protagonist, a Glasgow shopkeeper called Thomas Duffle, takes up the habit of cruising on Clyde steamers to enjoy the benefits of sea-air and keep off what his landlady describes as 'the hyperchonders'. The early years of the nineteenth century saw a rising interest in sea-air and sea-bathing as a cure for a variety of diseases and Thomas Duffle's first journey, in June 1819, takes him down-river on the Waterloo *steamer to Greenock and then on to Helensburgh, where steamer pioneer Henry Bell's Baths Inn provided 'hot and cold baths for invalid persons, and others afflicted with the rheumatics, and suchlike incomes'.*

Galt's novel is in reality a collection of unrelated tales narrated by the people Mr Duffle meets on his voyages. Galt is entertaining in, for example, contrasting Duffle's anxieties about his Clyde adventures with tales of West Indian hurricanes, but these interpolated stories are hardly relevant to the theme of this anthology. We have therefore selected the opening of the novel and some extracts from the linking narrative which give a feel of this period when the ordinary Glaswegian first discovered the joys of going 'doon the watter'.

CLYDE CRUISING

Having been for several years in what Mrs MacLecket, my worthy landlady, calls a complaining way, I was persuaded by her advice to try the benefit of the sea air in the steam-boat to Greenock; and I found myself greatly advantaged by the same. I am not, however, sure that the benefit which my strength and appetite received in those sea voyages was so much owing to the change of air, and the wholesome fume of the salt-water that I breathed, as from the conversible and talkative company which I found among the other passengers; by which my spirits were maintained in a state of jocund temperance, and my thoughts so lifted out of the cares of business, that I was, for the time, a new creature, bringing back with me to behind the counter a sort of youthiness that lasted sometimes more than a fortnight; keeping off what Mrs MacLecket called the hypochonders, till I again fell out of order, by that constant constipation to the shop, which I now understand was the original cause of all my complaints.

I have often since reflected on my jaunts and travels, and the many things that I saw, as well as the extraordinary narrations of which I was participant in the hearing; and it seemed to me, that I could not better employ my time and talent, during the long winter nights, than in putting down some account of the most remarkable of the stories which medicated so veritably towards the gradual restoration of that brisk and circling state of my blood, that has made me, in a manner, as Mrs MacLecket judiciously says, a very satisfactory man.

When I had tried my hand at two or three of the stories, I read them over to Mr Thomas Sweeties, my neighbour, the grocer, and he thought them so vastly entertaining, that, by his encouragement, together with the pleasure which Mrs Maclecket seemed to take in the bits she now and then heard, when she could spare time from her householdry to listen, I was led to proceed further and further, until I compiled this book; which I hope will reward the courteous reader who may vouchsafe to favour it with an attentive perusal, as much as it did to me in the inditing, and no author can wish his reader a more delectable benefaction. For I was so taken up, not only with the matter, but the manner of the different narrations, while I brought them back to mind, that I was transported, as it were, out of my own natural body, and put into the minds of the narrators, so as to think with their thoughts and to speak with their words, by which, as Mr Sweeties observed, an instinct for learning has been manifested on my part, such as he had never met with, and is altogether wonderful in a man who has lived in the Saltmarket since the eighty-three, in which year I gave up travelling the country with the pack, having at that time two hundred pounds gathered in the Ship Bank, besides a character for sobriety and cannyness among the merchants, which was worth more than double that sum in the way of credit. Thank God, through all the changes that have happened since, I have kept aye my feet, and can afford to take my pleasure may be another year, although I should have no occasion for the sake of health, and that without wronging anybody. I don't, however, say this of my means as a brag; but only as I am now venturing to come before the public in the book-making line, it may be known that I am not led thereto in the way of bread, but to solace myself; with a reasonable probability, at the same time, of bringing forth something that may contribute to the pastime of other folk of a sedentary habitude. I shall not, therefore, expatiate in this place at any greater length; for having thus heard the origin and occasion of my writing and sending out a book, the reader will naturally now be anxious to know of what it consists; on which account I will stop my prefactory pen, and open with the substantiality of the matters of which I design to treat.

It was, I think, on the 16th day of June, in the year of our Lord, A.D. 1819, that I embarked at the Broomielaw, on board the *Waterloo* steam-boat, bound to her head port, the town of Greenock, with an understanding that passengers were to be landed at any place in the course of the voyage, wheresoever their needs and affairs might require. As my adventure was for health and pleasure, I resolved to go with her to all the different places which she might be obligated to visit, and return home with her in the evening, Mrs MacLecket telling me, that there might be a risk, at my time of life, in changing my bed. Embarking then, as I have said, we got under way at eight o'clock, and shortly after, the passengers that had not breakfasted before they came out in the morning, retired to the steward's room, where they were very comfortably entertained at an easy rate – in so much, that for the ploy of the thing, I wished I had not taken mine with Mrs MacLecket; but I was over persuaded by her of the danger of going upon the water with an empty stomach. However, I had not much cause to repine at this; for while the rest were busy with the eatables, I entered into some discourse with a decent elderly gentleman, concerning foreign parts, and such matters as were material to a man like me, in going upon his first voyage. This stranger I found of great solidity of mind that was surely past the common: he had seen much of the world, and had read the book of man through and through.

We had therefore leisure, as we sailed along, to observe the beauties of Port-Glasgow, which is a town of some note in the shipping trade, but more famous on account of its crooked steeple with a painted bell, the like, as I was told, not being in all the west of Scotland. However, in this matter, as Mr Sweeties argued with me, I had a plain proof of the advantages of travelling, and of the exaggerations in which travellers sometimes deal, for, upon a very careful inspection of the steeple, I could see neither crook nor flaw in it; and as for the bell, I can speak on the veracity of my own ears, that be it painted or be it gilded, it is a very fine sounding bell – as good every bit as the one in the Brig-gate steeple of our own city, than which no better bell need be. At the same time, it behoves me to observe, that I do not undertake to avouch that the steeple of Port-Glasgow has not got any thraw; for considering, as was pointed out to me by a jocose gentleman from Greenock, who was also a passenger, that both the townhouse and steeple are erected on forced ground, it was very probable it might have declined from the perpendicular, and that the story of its twist may, therefore, have arisen from the probability or likelihood of the accident taking place. I have heard, however, since, that the Greenock gentlemen are not altogether to be trusted in the repetition of any story derogatory to the exploits and ornaments of Port-Glasgow, for that, from an ancient date, there has been feud and hostility between the two towns, insomuch that 'the Port' has been apprehensive of a design on the part of Greenock to stop the navigation of the river, and utterly to effect their ruin, by undoing their harbour, which is one of the best and safest in the Clyde, a *caput mortuum* of emptiness, as much as it often is in the spring of the year, when the vessels that trade therein are all out seeking employment in foreign countries. Indeed, I have myself some reason to think, that the aforesaid Greenockian was not altogether without a spice of malice in his remarks; for he made me observe how very few of the Port-Glasgow lums were reeking, which, he said, was a proof of the inhospitable character of the inhabitants, showing, that neither roast nor boil was preparing in the houses, beyond what was requisite for the frugal wants of the inmates. But although there was truth over all controversy in the observe, Mr Sweeties has told me that, on some occasions, he has seen not only plenty, but both punch and kindness, in houses in Port-Glasgow, highly creditable to the owners; and, I think, there must be surely some foundation for the notion, although I cannot speak from my own personal experience, for the soldier's mother having a friend from Ayrshire in the town, left us there, and, by her absence, obligated me to look out for another companion to entertain me in the remainder of the voyage. But this was not a matter of such facility as might be thought, for the major number of the passengers being for Greenock, they were all taken up with counting by their watches how long time they would be of reaching the customhouse stairs, and telling one another of the funny deeds and sayings of some of their townsfolk, who, by all accounts, are the cleverest people in the whole world and not only the cleverest, but the drollest, having a capacity by common, and a manner, when they are inclined for sport, that is most surprising. I shall, however, have something more to say about them by and by; meanwhile, let it be enough for the present, that, in the whole course of the voyage from Port-Glasgow to Greenock, I got no satisfaction. They turned their backs to my enquiries as if I had been nobody, little reflecting that the time would come, (as may now be seen here) when I would depict them in their true colours, and teach them that there is truth in the proverb, which says, 'It's not the cloak that makes the friar'; for I perceived they thought me but an auld-fashioned man, little knowing that there was the means in my shop of getting as fashionable a coat as the sprucest of the saucy sparks had on, to say nothing of the lining I could put in the pouches.

When we came to the town of Greenock, I was much surprised to see it a place of great extent and traffic, of which I had no notion; more especially was I struck with wonder at the customhouse, that is a most stately erection, bearing a similitude to our jail; and I was grieved that I had paid my passage to Helensburgh, because it prevented me from viewing the vast of shipping and curiosities of this emporium; but as I have, through life, resigned myself at all times, and on all occasions, to the will, as it were, of the things I could not control, I submitted, for the present, to the disappointment, resolving, at some future period, to make a voyage from the Broomielaw on purpose to take a survey of Greenock, and to note at leisure, as it behoves a traveller to do, the manners and customs of the inhabitants, together with the religious ceremonies and antiquities of the place. Accordingly, having pacified my mind in this manner, I stayed in the steam-boat with the passengers that were bound for Helensburgh, until the Greenockians, with their bag and baggage, were put on the shore, which took place at the stairs forenent the customhouse. And here let me pause and make a remark for the benefit of persons intending to see foreign parts, to the effect that they should both read and enquire anent the places they purpose to see, before they depart, by which they will be enabled to regulate their course in a more satisfactory manner, than if they go away on such light hearsays, as I did on my first voyage.

After landing, as I have noticed, our cargo of Greenockians, the steam was again set to work, and the vessel, with all that orderliness and activity which belongs to the enginery, moved round, and, turning her latter end to Greenock, walked over the waters straight to Helensburgh. This is not a long voyage naturally, being no more than four miles, if so much; but it is not without dangers; and we had a lively taste and type of the perils of shipwreck in crossing the bank – a great shoal that lies midway in the sea; for it happened that we were later for the tide than the captain had thought, so that, when we were in what the jack-tars call the mid-channel, the gallant *Waterloo*, that had come all the way from Glasgow like a swan before the wind, stuck fast in the mud. Never shall I forget the dunt that dirled on my heart when she stopped, and the engines would go no further. Fortunately, as I was told, this came to pass just at the turn of the tide, or otherwise there is no saying what the consequences might have been; it being certain, that if the accident had happened an hour before, we should have been obligated to wait more than two hours, instead of half an hour; and if, in the course of that time, a tempest had arisen, it is morally certain, the vessel lying high and dry, that the waves would have beaten over her, and, in all human probability, dashed her to pieces, by which every soul on board would to a certainty have perished; for we were so far from land, both on the Greenock and the Helensburgh coast, that no help by boat or tackle could have been afforded. It was a dreadful situation, indeed, that we were in; and when I reflected on the fickleness of the winds, and the treachery of the seas, my anxieties found but a small comfort in the calm that was then in the air, and the glassy face of the sunny waters around us. However, I kept up my spirits, and waited for the flowing of the tide with as much composure as could reasonably be called for, from a man who had never been a venture at sea before, but had spent his days in a shop in the Saltmarket, as quietly as an hour-glass ebbing its sands in a corner.

While we were in this state, I fell into discourse with a sailor lad who had come home from Jamaica in the West Indies, and was going over from Greenock to see his friends, who lived at the Rue, on the Gairloch side; and falling into discourse, we naturally conversed about what might be the consequence of our lying on the bank, and if the vessel should chance to spring a leak, and such other concerns as, from less to more, led us on to talk of ships sinking in the great ocean, or taking fire thousands of miles from any land, and all those other storms and perils among which the lot of the mariner is cast.

Just as the sailor had got to this crisis of his story, the steam-boat began to move, and in the course of a minute or two she was paddling her way towards Helensburgh; and her motion made everybody again so jocose and lively, that I could not but marvel at the depths of the mysteries of the heart of man. As we drew near to the shore, the sailor had forgotten all the earnest solemnity of his tale, and was the blithest in the boat. Fain would I have questioned him about the particulars of what ensued when he found himself in the plantation; but he was no longer in a humour to attend to me, his heart being taken up with the thought of getting to his friends – just like a young dog that has broken loose from a confinement; so that I was left in a kind of unsatisfied state, with the image of the broken ship in my mind, with her riven planks and timbers, grinning like the jaws of death amidst the raging waters; the which haunted me till I got a chack of dinner at the hotel, and a comfortable tumbler of excellent old double-rum toddy. But I should mention, that till the dinner was gotten ready, I had a pleasant walk along the shore, as far as the Cairn-dhue, and saw on the right hand, among its verdant plantations, the lordly castle of Ardincaple, and on the left, ayont the loch, the modern mansion which the Duke of Argyle is building there among the groves of Roseneath; with which, it's my opinion, no situation in this countryside can compare, for hill and dale, and wood and water, and other comely and romantic incidents of Highland mountains, all rocky and fantastical, like a painted picture by some famous o'er-sea limner.

When I had ate my dinner and drunk my toddy at the pleasant hotel of Helensburgh, in which there are both hot and cold baths for invalid persons, and others afflicted with the rheumatics, and suchlike incomes, I went out again to take another walk, for I had plenty of time on my hands, as the steam-boat was not to sail for Glasgow till six o'clock. At first, it was my intent to take a survey of the country and agriculture, and to see what promise there was on the ground of a harvest; but in sauntering along the road towards the hill of Ardmore, I fore-gathered with Mr and Mrs M'Waft, and four of their childer. They had been for some time at Helensburgh for the salt water, the gudeman having been troubled with some inward complaint that sat upon his spirits, and turned all to sour that he ate or drank.

Nobody could be more glad to see an old acquaintance than they were to see me, and Mrs M'Waft was just in a perplexity to think that I could ever have ventured to leave my shop so long, and come such a voyage by myself; but I told her that I had been constrained by the want of health, and that maybe before the summer was done she might see me again; for that I had got a vast of entertainment, and was, moreover, appetized to such a degree, that I had made a better dinner that day, and with a relish, than I had done for years past; which she was very happy to hear, hoping the like in time would be the lot of her gudeman, who was still in a declining way, though he took the salt water inwardly every morning, and the warm bath outwardly every other day. Thus, as we were standing in the road, holding a free-and-easy talking about our ails and concerns, and the childer were diverting themselves pu'ing the gowans and chasing the bees and butterflies, Mr M'Waft said that I could do no less than go back with them and take a glass of wine, and, insisting kindly thereon, I found myself obligated to do so; accordingly, I turned with them, and went into the house where they had their salt-water quarters.

It was one of the thackit houses near the burn – a very sweet place, to be sure, of its kind; but I could not help wondering to hear how Mr M'Waft ever expected to grow better in it, which, compared with his own bein house on the second flat of Paterson's lan', was both damp and vastly inconvenient. The floor of the best room was clay, and to cover the naked walls they had brought carpets from home, which they hung round them like curtains, behind which carpets all sorts of foul clothes, shoes, and things to be kept out of sight, I could observe, were huddled.

Meanwhile, Mrs M'Waft had got out the wine and the glasses, and a loaf of bread that was blue moulded from the damp of the house; and I said to her, 'that surely the cause which had such an effect on the bread, must be of some consequence to the body.' 'But the sea and country air,' replied Mr M'Waft, 'makes up for more than all such sort of inconveniences.' So we drank our wine and conversed on divers subjects, rehearsing, in the way of a sketch, the stories related in my foregoing pages, which both the mistress and gudeman declared were as full of the extraordinaries as any thing they had ever heard of.

'Lines on Revisiting a Scottish River'

THOMAS CAMPBELL (1777–1844)

And call they this Improvement? – to have changed,
My native Clyde, thy once romantic shore,
Where Nature's face is banish'd and estranged,
And heaven reflected in thy wave no more;
Whose banks, that sweeten'd May-day's breath before,
Lie sere and leafless now in summer's beam,
With sooty exhalations cover'd o'er;
And for the daisied green-sward, down they stream
Unsightly brick-lanes smoke, and clanking engines gleam.

Speak not to me of swarms the scene sustains;
One heart free tasting Nature's breath and bloom
Is worth a thousand slaves to Mammon's gains.
But wither goest that wealth, and gladdening whom?
See, left but life enough and breathing-room
The hunger and the hope of life to feel,
Yon pale Mechanic bending o'er his loom,
And Childhood's self as at Ixion's wheel,
From morn till midnight task'd to earn its little meal.

Is this Improvement? – where the human breed
Degenerate as they swarm and overflow,
Till Toil grows cheaper than the trodden weed,
And man competes with man, like foe with foe,
Till Death, that thins them, scarce seems public woe?
Improvement! – smiles it in the poor man's eyes,
Or blooms it on the cheek of Labour? – No –
To gorge a few with Trade's precarious prize,
We banish rural life, and breathe unwholesome skies.

Nor call that evil slight; God has not given
This passion to the heart of man in vain,
For Earth's green face, th' untainted air of Heaven,
And all the bliss of Nature's rustic reign.
For not alone our frame imbibes a stain
From foetid skies; the spirit's healthy pride
Fades in their gloom – And therefore I complain,
That thou no more through pastoral scenes shouldst glide,
My Wallace's own stream, and once romantic Clyde.

'Doon the Watter at the Fair'

BASS KENNEDY (c. 1888)

Come listen tae me, Nannie dear,
  My cantie, tosh aul' wife,
We've stood for five an' thirty year
  The tussel an' the strife.
An' yearly as the time cam' roun',
  We never missed, I'm shair,
Tae spen' oor sair-won pastime doon
  The watter at the Fair.

Ye min' yon July morn langsyne,
  A rosy morn like this,
You pledged tae be for ever mine,
  An' sealed it wi' a kiss.
On board the *Petrel*, near Dunoon,
  Ye yielded tae my prayer,
An' aye sin' syne we've managed doon
  The watter at the Fair.

When you a snod mill lass, an' I
  A Brigton weaver chiel,
Then lad an' lass on deck did vie
  At rantin' jig or reel.
Aye tae the fiddler tint the tune,
  We danced the hin'maist pair,
An' took the brag frae a' gaun doon
  The watter at the Fair.

Sae haste an' bind yer siller hair,
  An' don your Paisley shawl,
We're still a cantie, couthie pair,
  The mair we're growin' aul'.
Though grey my locks an' bare my croon,
  An' you my frailties shair,
We'll taste again life's morn gaun doon
  The watter at the Fair.

The witchin' woodlan's waving green,
  An' bosky banks and braes
That fringe the bonnie Clyde, hae been
  Oor playgrun' a' oor days.
An' while the Maker hale an' soun',
  Is pleased oor lives tae spare,
We'll blithely trip thegither doon
  The watter at the Fair.

Sae haste ye, Nannie, come awa',
  An' dinna langsome be,
For thrangin' tae the Broomielaw,
  The focks gaun by wi' glee.
A twalmonth's toil in Glesca toun
  Is lichtsome, I declare,
Wi' twa-three days' diversion doon
  The watter at the Fair.

'Harbour Life'

from The Clyde, River and Firth

NEIL MUNRO (1863–1930)

Neil Munro was many things: journalist, literary critic, short story writer, historical novelist, and the creator of wonderfully enduring comic characters like Para Handy and Erchie. His personal and professional life, however varied, was lived out (apart from a brief journalistic exile in Falkirk) around the waters of the Clyde – from his birth in Inveraray on Loch Fyne, through journalism in Greenock and Glasgow, to retirement in Helensburgh. Glasgow's river played a large part in his life and the essential interconnectedness of Munro's writings is nowhere better illustrated than in the depiction of the harbour of Glasgow given in his 1907 book The Clyde, River and Firth.

Quite apart from expecting to find the Vital Spark *sailing into Munro's colourful prose, any lover of the tales of Para Handy, the early episodes of which were written at the same time as* The Clyde, *will remember the trial of Para Handy, recounted in* The Vital Spark's Collision, *and smile at the reference to the 'loyal lies of witnesses' or wonder if the origins of the melodeon-playing Sunny Jim are to be found in Munro's reference to 'an unseen concertina playing some sailor's jog for canticle'.*

Munro laments the passing of the Clutha steamers, the small up-and-down river passenger ferries operated by the Clyde Navigation Trust. The service began in 1884, and although it only lasted nineteen years it won its way into the hearts of the Glaswegians and into local folklore. Not for nothing did Munro make Sunny Jim a former hand on the Clutha: The favourite Clutha on the Clyde, when the Clutha's was rinnin', was the yin I was on; hunners o' trips used to come wi' her on the Setturdays on the aff-chance that I wad maybe gie them a baur.

The Clutha ferries sailed from Victoria Bridge in the heart of the city, calling at all the main shipbuilding and engineering centres and docks down as far as Whiteinch. The profitability of the service was undermined by the coming of Glasgow's subway system in 1896 and by the completion of the electrification of the tramway system in 1901.

The suggestion that the harbour, 'whose name is known to the uttermost ends of the earth', should be wholly unfamiliar to Glasgow citizens, may seem strange and paradoxical, but was in fact largely accurate. The great dock areas of Queen's Dock and Prince's Dock were shut off from the passer-by, and the view down-river from the Victoria and Glasgow (or Jamaica Street) Bridges was and is blocked by the railway bridge taking the lines into Central Station. The bridge which, in more recent times, afforded the best view of shipping at the Broomielaw (on the north bank), and at Bridge Wharf (on the south bank), George V Bridge, was not built until 1927.

Munro's interest in, indeed his love for the river, is confirmed not only by the charming pages of The Clyde, River and Firth, *but by his comic short fiction and the many articles he wrote for his long-running column 'The Looker-On' in the* Glasgow Evening News.

HARBOUR LIFE

Like Melrose, Glasgow Harbour should perhaps be seen at night, or at the end of an Autumn afternoon, when a swollen sun, setting behind thickets of masts, gilding the stream, glorifying smoky cloud, transfiguring dingy store and tenement, closes a vista that captivates the eye and spurs the imagination as might some vision of a Venice stained and fallen from virtue, an abandoned mistress of the sea. In such an hour and season we forget the cost of mercantile supremacy, and see in that wide fissure through the close-packed town a golden pathway to romance, or the highway home to our native hills and isles. The other aspect – that of dark bewildering hours, is only known most poignantly to native sailors who carry about the world with them a not unpleasing thought of a familiar Avernus full of phantom fleets whereof one special ship must be discovered ere the dawn; an Avernus intricate, and ill to traverse, with a head bemused by farewell rum; with dancing lights on the foul high tide, roaring Lucigen flares, sheds gulping a ghostly radiance; with sounds of chains, cranes, capstans; the panting of sleepless engines, the cries of spectre stevedores and lumpers; with odours of spice and tar, wine, fruit, oil, hides, and a thousand other pungent sweet or acrid things unknown. The ship (with luck) is found, her Blue Peter high at the truck, though unseen in the darkness; the Old Man swears at the lubberly late-comer, who awkwardly bears his dunnage over the gang-plank; friends on the quay cry after him, 'Ye didna shake hands, Jack,' to which he retorts: 'Lord! neither I did; ach! it doesna maitter; I'll be back in a year or twa.' And so, carelessly, goes forth to the mercy of sea and storm another fearless spirit with a vast deal more of sentiment in his soul than you might think to hear that last good-bye.

Come to the harbours by day, and then I grant there is little glamour to be found; come on a wet November day especially, to look for some not particularly distinguishable shipping-box at the far end of some not very distinctive mile-long quay, and before you have found it the melancholy of things will have bitten to your very heart. I do not wonder that to all but those whose business takes them there, the harbour, whose name is known to the uttermost ends of the earth, should be wholly unfamiliar to Glasgow citizens. They may see the upper end of it from the train as they cross on the railway bridges morning and afternoon from and to suburban villas or the coast; they may once or twice have ventured down to the channel in a 'Clutha', to feel some vague emotion in a scene so strange, but as a rule the harbour, with its vast activities, its 'earnest of romance', lies wholly beyond their interest or curiosity. They would as soon think of going to St Joceline's Crypt. Streets noisy and unbeautiful lead down to it from either side; its waters do not invite aquatic recreation. Itinerant bagpipers (invariably playing 'The Cock o' the North') discourage the sensitive intruder from the most feasible entrance to it at the side of the Jamaica Bridge, and all the other less obvious portals are apt to be encumbered by an intoxicated mercantile marine, or by mighty waggons laden with boiler plates that traverse the granite setts with a din infernal.

It is a pity the up-and-down river service of little 'Clutha' steamers is no more, for if it was not profitable to the coffers of the Clyde Trustees who owned the vessels, it kept the city in touch with what has really made its fortunes and made more manifest the Trust's importance. Yet it is still possible to pass the harbour in review by going on one of the many steamers that daily sail from the Broomielaw for the towns upon the Firth. The Broomielaw is really Glasgow's heart, though some folk think it is George Square. The name to-day seems quite ironic, for neither Broom or Law is obvious there, where Glasgow Bridge divides the harbour proper from the upper stream that flows by less busy, more neglected banks past the Green; but once the yellow flowers of *planta genista* flourished there, when our grandfathers could ford the river with their kilts tucked up. There is here no spacious channel like the Mersey, but only a fairway of 620 feet at its widest and 362 at its narrowest point; nor closely hemming warehouses such as on the Thames appear to court disaster for their windows from the yards of ships. The clean, gay, holiday-looking steamers for the coast seem half intruders, and out of harmony with the squat long lines of cargo sheds, and the piles of offices and dwelling-houses in their rear; you can fancy that they gladly steam away each morning to a 'cleaner, greener land'. Going with them you pass wharves lined at first by packets that ply to English and Irish ports; then by berths where greatly favoured big Atlantic, Mediterranean and Indian liners – Allan and Anchor – safely warp among countless hazards from puffing tugs and unwieldy hopper dredgers; then by the jaws of docks, and past ferries, and into the far-extending region where the shipbuilding yards have gathered, and so on to the meadows, and finally to the welcome sea.

There are innumerable tales of what the passenger has said on such a harbour voyage, and how the captain – witty fellow! – made reply; they are in all the other books about the Clyde, and need not be repeated. The raconteur, in truth, is an impertinent intrusion on the sentiment of this Titanic scene, wherein etcher and painter have discovered aspects arresting and sublime, for all the dullness and even ugliness of the details. More patently obtrusive to the voyagers I must confess will seem the odour of which the cleansing operations of the city have not yet wholly rid the oily water we traverse. If the city fathers, however, have been slow to find conviction of the sin it is to pollute their river, they have entered on the process of regeneration in no niggard spirit, and the result of their great new sewage operations is apparent already. A pleasing tag for municipal banquet speeches and for the humorists of the local press has reference to the imminent restoration of the salmon at the Broomielaw. We can scarcely hope for angling at Stobcross or Pointhouse Ferry, Highland Lane or Linthouse, but even now, bewildered trout and surely foolish grilse, inheriting some instinct for the linns where their forebears spawned among the hills, are found curiously forcing their way through the wake of steamers in the harbour or struggling in the basins, to be captured and stuffed for some riverside parlour and furnish forth another airy paragraph.

And yet it is not on a steamer one can get at the veritable heart of the harbour; for that takes days and nights and seasons. One must haunt the ferries, whose low-hulled craft traverse the stream incessantly, bearing the workers to and from their toil; one must linger on the quays and listen to the jabber of Gaelic and Irish 'hands', pilots, and ferrymen; of Lascars shivering in thin dongarees, bent – poor misguided souls! – on imposing shells upon a 'sea-born' city; of Spanish onion-sellers, fezzed Greeks with sample rugs and gold embroidery; truculent Dago rogues with ugly knives; Dutch nondescripts looking askance at frowzy women from the slums, sometimes a slit-eyed Chinese, or Barbadian – 'true Badian born, neither crab nor Creole'; furtive native crimps, silk-capped coal-trimmers, fussy super-cargoes, brass-bound mates, German, Galician, Doukhabor, and Scandinavian emigrants. One must see the ships disgorge themselves under mighty derricks, of ore from New Caledonia, timber from Oregon, nitrates from Iquique; crates of odorous fruit from Spain, tuns of wine from France and Portugal; palm oil and ivory from South Africa, cotton, tea, spice, and jute from India; tea from China; cattle, corn, flour, beef, scantling and doors and windows ready-made from the United States; wheat from Canada, Egypt and Russia; sugar, teak and mahogany from the West Indies, tinned food and gold from Australasia.

Nor even then can one rightly comprehend the harbour who has not brooded beside sheer-leg and crane-jib that are mightily moving enormous weights as if they had been toys; swallowed the coal-dust of the docks, dodged traction engines, eaten Irish stew for breakfast in the Sailors' Home, watched Geordie Geddes trawl for corpses, sat in the fo'c'sles of 'tramps', stood in a fog by the pilot on the bridge, heard the sorrows of a Shore Superintendent and the loyal lies of witnesses in a Board of Trade examination, who feel bound to 'stick by the owners' and swear their engines backed ten minutes before the accident; or sat on a cask in the Prince's Dock on peaceful Sabbath mornings when the shipping seemed asleep, or an unseen concertina played some sailor's jig for canticle.

As for the types of vessels you shall meet there, I cannot do better than quote from the talented authors of *Glasgow in 1901*, who deal with our harbour lovingly.

> The liner de luxe, as Liverpool people understand her in the *Oceanic* or the *Campania* or the *St Louis*, is not to be seen on the narrow Clyde, and the Cardiff man, accustomed to his miles of coal traders, will find disappointment here; still, if you were to spend a diligent morning in the docks, you will find few types of the British mercantile marine amissing. The Transatlantic passenger steamers of the Allan and Anchor firms; the strange East-Coastish lines of the Donaldson carriers ('lines like a hat-box', as an old shipper had it), the queer shaped turret ships of the Clan Company, which look as though they had swallowed more cargo than they could digest, the big bright-funnelled South American traders, bristling with derricks and samson-posts; the China Mutual steamers, with their names in the script of Far Cathay on their bows; the Loch Line sailing ships, which clip Australian records every season as keen as any 'grey-hound of the Atlantic'; the four-masted Frenchmen from New Caledonia, the teak-carrier from Rangoon, the auxiliary screw laden

with seal oil and skins from Harbour Grace, the nitrite barque from Chili, the City steamers from India and the Persian Gulf – you can find them all. Then there are the squadrons of tramps that thrash from Bilbao to the Clyde with ore and back again with coal; the Italian fruit boats, the stout cross-channel packets, the Highland steamers, and top-sail schooners which congregate in the Kingston Dock.

The harbour life slops over its actual precincts, and the neighbouring streets, as in other ports, bear a marine impress. Their tall 'lands' of flat fed from a common stair are the homes of folk whose men are 'on the quays' or 'sailing foreign' or 'stoking on the old *Furnessia*'; there is no seaman so black or poor that he cannot get some kind of lodging there. Ship-chandlers' shops, slop shops, shops where binnacle lights, patent logs, and sextants, marlin and nautical almanacks fill the windows, others that delight the eye of youth with visions of sheath-knives and revolvers, and the coin and paper currency of every imaginable foreign state, are there, and licensed shops innumerable that seek the suffrages of the sailorman by making a speciality of the 'schooner' or beer at twopence. High over all is the tower of the Sailors' Home at the Broomielaw, nowadays a good deal too far east of the busy docks for Jack's convenience.

'Shipbuilding'

from Glasgow in 1901

JAMES HAMILTON MUIR

We have already introduced 'James Hamilton Muir', the pseudonym adopted by three young Glasgow men, Muirhead Bone (1876–1953) his older brother James (1872–1962) and Archibald Hamilton Charteris (1874–1940), for their survey of Glasgow at the start of the twentieth century.

Glasgow in 1901 *divides its treatment of the city into three parts: 'Glasgow of the Imagination', 'Glasgow of Fact – The Place' and 'Glasgow of Fiction – The Man and his Haunts'. The treatment of the Clyde and the city's shipbuilding tradition obviously falls into the 'Glasgow of Fact' section but for a modern reader the description of the scale and variety of the city's shipyard output in 1901 could equally well be categorised as 'Glasgow of the Imagination' or 'Glasgow of Fiction'.*

The shipyard and the docks 'James Hamilton Muir' records have obviously gone, replaced by Conference and Exhibition Centres, housing, and projected Science Centres. Still surviving at Govan are the derelict graving docks, which, even in their decay evoke something of the scale and impact of the river in its heyday.

Neil Munro, himself no stranger to writing about Glasgow and the Clyde, paid tribute to the 'quite unusual knowledge and literary talents' of the 'James Hamilton Muir' collective and, as we shall see, quotes from them in his own evocation of the river. Munro suggests that James Bone was 'especially erudite in all concerning the life of the river'. This taste for the nautical ran in the Bone family; Muirhead's etchings have already been mentioned, and a third brother, David, became Commodore of the Anchor Line and also wrote a number of novels of the sea, most famously The Brassbounder.

SHIPBUILDING

Our modern university may not impress you, the cathedral you may never see (for lack of a native to lead you to it); but our shipbuilding yards are a different matter. Before you are two days in the city you are aware of their existence; and if their importance is a matter beyond you, at least you must be impressed by our belief in it. We believe, every Glasgow man of us, that our shipbuilding is a thing to be talked of, and a most honourable and dignified business to have for the chief industry of a city. Sheffield is known to the world for cutlery, Birmingham for pedlars' wares and nails and bullets, and Manchester for 'Manchester goods'. But Glasgow is the maker of ships, and her sons are proud of their seemly product. The Clyde builder may pride himself, too, on his achievement. Following no man, he hewed out a path for himself; borrowed no capital, but, his own door dug coal and iron and wrought up these into that modern wonder, the steamship. And through a century he counts his tale of triumphs from the *Comet* to the *Campania*. Now and then, it is true, he had the wit to use the ideas of other men, to weld their inventions to his own purpose and to profit by their errors. But take him for all in all, he is the figure which dominates modern shipbuilding, the inspirer and pioneer to whom all other builders must bow, and without whom the glorious company of ships had shrunken to a half. The teachers of youth are very right; of more moment to Glasgow than her other industries, her college, her cathedral, is the building of her ships.

If you glance at the history of the industry you find the Clyde's name writ on every page. Sailing ships may be left out of the account; they are part of an older scheme of things, and their building is now no man's special business. Still, if you insist on it, the Clyde can produce you whole sheaves of laurels gathered by her clippers, which have even sailed into the pages of literature, for was not the *Narcissus* herself 'born in the thundering peal of hammer beating upon iron in black eddies of smoke under a grey sky on the banks of the Clyde?' We may say, without any straining of facts, that steam navigation was born on our river. For the first vessel constructed for the purpose of steaming in open water was that designed by Henry Bell, built by John Wood, of Port-Glasgow, launched into the Clyde in 1812, and christened the *Comet* because she flashed through the water at a rate of nearly six miles an hour. No doubt there were earlier vessels of the kind – the small pleasure boat which, with Robert Burns on board, appeared to the wonder of beholders on Dalswinton Loch; Symington's other venture, the *Charlotte Dundas*, which ran for a perilous season on the Forth and Clyde Canal, and (as American cousins would perhaps remind us) Fulton's *Clermont* of the Hudson. But if these are to be counted, we may shift our ground and aver that but for the discoveries of a lank Greenock youth who came to Glasgow at the age of eighteen, not one of them had ever cleft water.

When steam propulsion had been shown to be practicable, the next step was to make it cheap enough for alliance with commerce, and in solving this problem in economics the Clyde again played chief part. Of first importance was the invention of the marine compound engine, a discovery which, by doubling the motive power of ships, began a new epoch in steam navigation, so much did it expand its possibilities and open the way for further development. For stationary engines the compound principle had been employed for several years. John Elder, of Fairfield, was the first to adapt it to marine purposes. Using it in conjunction with the surface condenser (originally introduced by David Napier in 1822, but little applied till his own time) he increased the pressure of steam from about thirty to eighty pounds to the square inch and reduced the coal consumption by almost one-half. Another benefit we owe to Elder's ingenuity was the modification of the compound principle to screw-propelled vessels with inverted engines, and it was this contrivance which led to the screw supplanting the paddles for ocean steaming. Compound engines permitted the steam to be used twice; triple-expansion, which came into force a few years later, forced it to do duty a third time. This invention was introduced by Mr Alexander Taylor, of Newcastle, in 1882, but Dr Kirk, who was one of the partner of John Elder & Company, had been experimenting on a similar contrivance at the same time, and it was his model which was applied to the Admiralty ships. A further compounding was planned by Mr Walter Brock, of Denny & Company, in the form of quadruple-expansion engines, which demanded as basis an initial pressure of 180 pounds to the square inch when the steam is first used as it comes from the boiler. In the days of Henry Bell a five pound pressure was considered something uncanny. Thus, the Clyde engineer, bit by bit, tightened his hold upon steam, and by his instant embodiment in his work of these and other inventions increased the prestige which Napier and Denny had brought to his river.

While these important changes were made in the engine room, the structure of the vessel itself had altered greatly. The material changed from wood to iron, then from iron to steel, and in both cases our district has its claim ready as innovator. A small vessel constructed on the Monkland Canal about 1822 is generally set down as the first vessel built of iron, and before the paddle steamer *Windsor Castle*, an eighteen-knot racer of the sixties, was constructed by Caird, of Greenock, there was no steel steamer afloat. The case for the Clyde, as regards many important structural improvements, need not, perhaps, be pushed too far. From France came mild steel as a material, and from England the longitudinal and cellular bottom system and its application to water-ballast; still, it was here that these inventions were developed and turned to their greatest use, and it was here that owners came in the heyday of shipping when the best in the market was wanted.

If you select the route in which fine workmanship and great speed are first necessities, the Clyde's prestige is most clearly demonstrated.

The North Atlantic, it is agreed, is the royal racecourse of maritime nations. Here the reward in mail subsidies, big rates, and quickest of returns awaits the successful, and here is Fame in a pilot cutter with her loudest trumpet blowing. And to serve the transatlantic service are engaged in their highest form the art and practice of shipbuilding and marine engineering. The engines of the *Sirius,* first vessel to cross the Atlantic under steam, were constructed by Thomas Wingate, of Whiteinch. From 1840 to 1851, 1864 to 1872, 1880 to 1891, and 1892 to 1899 the Clyde-built steamers held the supremacy of the Atlantic. It was the four famous pioneer steamers of the Cunard line – *Britannia*, *Arcadia*, *Caledonia*, and *Columba* – built on the river in 1840, and all engined by Robert Napier, that by the speed of their paddles first brought America within fourteen days' distance of Europe. In 1863 the *Scotia*, constructed by Napier, made the first passage of nine days; Tod & Macgregor's *City of Rome* the first of eight days; Elder's *Alaska* the first of seven; Thompson's *City of Paris* the first of six; and although that old Clyde decoration, 'the blue ribbon of the Atlantic', now adorns the log of a liner made in Germany, the five days' passage is yet to make. If the Clyde builder is resting on his oars for the moment, it is not that his skill has failed, but that he has not been bidden to beat the newest Germans. The brains and the hammers are still on the Clyde, but as long as British shipowners reckon small coal consumpts far above records he must bide his time. When the day comes the five days' passage will, without doubt, be added to his other laurels.

If for the fleeting moment, of course, the Clyde is somewhat overshadowed in certain respects, if her record for building the fastest ship has gone one airt, and for building the biggest ship another, she still stands unapproached and alone in the magnitude and catholicity of her undertakings.

It is the distinction of the Clyde shipyards that they can build any kind of vessel from a trawler to a battleship. The builders have the skill and experience, and the yards have the appliances which are required for any type of war vessel, trading vessel, or pleasure craft. Elsewhere you may find – but not often – that in a given year more ships of a certain class were built than on the Clyde. Belfast and Stettin, for instance, are at the moment undoubtedly ahead of the Clyde in building great passenger steamers; but it is only here that you see every kind and manner of ship on the stocks. In the philosophy of Mr Squeers, when you have spelt the name of any kind of craft from d-r-e-d-g-e-r to b-a-t-t-l-e-s-h-i-p you may go to Glasgow and see it a-building.

Thus if you would establish a service of weekly steamers, say, to the sea-coast of Bohemia, your fleet, with their twin-screws and six-decks, may be laid down and delivered within the year; or if you are a millionaire seeking an 8000-ton yacht that will float on a six-foot draught, 'so that if it was ordainit to be stickit, it would be stickit in shallow water'; or if you are a romantic syndicate, desiring a boat to dredge the Spanish Main for treasure; or the simple inventor of a perpetual motion gearing which (in a suitable ship) will let a British owner sail nearer the wind than ever, why, then, the Clyde has, in one or other of its yards, the builder you need; and for a price you may have your heart's desire. If you come it will be in good company, for all the world comes here to buy; and if cost is not the cheapest, at any rate all the world profits sufficiently by the purchase to come again a-shopping. So that 'Clyde-built', you may say, is engraved on the nameplate of every type (well, nearly every type) of craft that rides water, salt or fresh. Peace and war alike bring grist to our river's mill; for peace brings orders for merchantmen, and war (or the fear of war) orders for ships to protect them. And so the two kinds of craft may be seen sitting cheek by jowl in the Govan shipyards.

The honour of presenting the first Clyde-built steamer to the British Navy on the open sea belongs to Dumbarton. The Dennys had built a boat named the *Marjory*, and had sent her under her own steam to her purchaser on the Thames. On her voyage, it is related, she fell in with a British fleet on the Downs, and vastly amazed the officers and men of His Britannic Majesty. Many of them – like the Kirkintilloch saddler – recording his impression of the *Charlotte Dundas* – 'Thocht frae hell she had cam hither – A-privateering.' Others thought her a fire-ship from France despatched before her time. But to solve all doubts she was hailed and her port demanded. 'Dumbarton, on the Clyde,' came the proud reply, and in this manner Clyde shipbuilding and the Royal Navy made the first bow of their long and honourable acquaintance.

Some time elapsed before the importance of the new power laid to their hand came home to the Lords Commissioners of the Admiralty, but since Robert Napier astounded the drowsy dockyard mandarins by constructing an iron floating battery for the Crimea in the space of three months, the Clyde has no reason to complain of its share in the making of the British Navy, nor the British Navy of the Clyde's contributions. Old shipbuilding hands, who squabble o' nights in riverside taverns over bygone days and piece together ancient Atlantic records, will tell you that it is now forty years since they can remember a time when there was no British warship on our stocks or in our fitting-out basins. The tardy supply of armoured plate, and the generous views held by the Clyde workmen on the subject of holidays and Admiralty 'ways of doin'', rob the river of many a bonnie order that, without doubt, should be hers; but even when, *pour encourager les autres*, an eminent firm was suspended from the contract list, the Clyde figured highest in the Naval Estimates, and more particularly in the Supplementary Estimates. Without her aid the First Lord would be hard pressed to execute a presentable naval programme, for our river is always counted on for two-fifths of the contract work. Last year the Admiralty paid over two millions to the Clyde builder, this being an amount larger by some hundred thousand pounds than that which came the way of the Thames and Barrow establishments put together. In the present year it is proposed to lay out nearly five and a half millions, and of that sum about half goes to the Clyde. The purchases have included every type of vessel that figures in the Navy list – first-class cruisers of the three grades, such as the 14,000-ton *Good Hope* and *Leviathan* now in the river, the 12,000-ton *Bacchante*, and the 9,800-ton *Bedford* and *Monmouth* that you may see on the Govan and Fairfield stocks; second-class cruisers, the last to be handed over being the *Hyacinthe* in 1900; gunboats, torpedo boat destroyers, Admiralty tugs, and all the other mailed gauntlets that are required for hands that rule the waves. And the Clyde war vessels, like her merchantmen, sail under many flags; a very considerable squadron could be organised from the units she has contributed to other navies. Considering only those in commission, there is the Japanese battleship *Asahi* 15,200 tons, built at Clydebank last year, which, but for the fact that she has a sister-ship, would be the largest war vessel in the world; and the *Chizoda*, a cruiser of 2,452 tons. America has the *Scipio,* 3,385 tons, built by Denny; the *Mayflower*, 2,690 tons, built by Thompson; and the *Sterling*, 5,663 tons, built by Duncan; Russia the *Moskoa* and *Opit*, of 3050 tons and 3,920 tons, both built at Fairfield; Portugal the *Africa*, 2,990 tons, and *India*, 1,200 tons, built by Denny; Holland the *Havik* and the *Zeemeuw*, 350 tons each, all built at Fairfield; Turkey the *Azizah*, *Orkanuh*, and *Osmaneh*, each of 6,400 tons, built at Fairfield; France and Spain, and Italy have at one time or another purchased war craft of varying power from our builders, while most of the little South American republics have a Clyde gunboat.

The prestige of the Clyde merchantman is, perhaps, not so all-apparent as it was in the days when the Nordeutscher Lloyd started their great enterprise with seven Fairfield vessels, or when the Compagnie Générale Transatlantique purchased second-hand Clyde liners to establish a French service of the first class; but with all respect to Stettin and Belfast, it is not yet eclipsed. The Clyde yards, which have fought in the van of shipbuilding progress since the conquest of steam began, have records to inspire and traditions to uphold, and despite pneumatic tools and trade unions, there still lingers a kind of *esprit de corps* among the builders and their men, a belief in the yard and its destinies. The practical outcome of this is the famed 'Clyde finish', which means the final touch of craftsmanship applied to its most scientific end, and although some allege it to be a fetish, it yet weighs with shipowners, and the shipowner is not a man of sentiment. It is said to mean the perfect articulation of parts making for durability and smoothness in working, and all this spells economy. At any rate the half-dozen Clyde foremen who first crossed the North Sea to teach the German operatives their business, say they did not leave their secret at Stettin; and the Clyde builder will prove to you that the building of the world's great steam yachts – which demands the highest excellence of workmanship – is not done at Belfast.

The elite of the great liners, you will find, first smelt water on the dingy Clyde. Here were launched the famous Cunarders, from the *Britannia* to the *Lucania,* the best pick of the Orient liners (including the *Ophir*, which it would be now high treason to dispute, is the most resplendent merchantman afloat), of the Castle, the Union, the Pacific, British India, P. & O., Royal Mail, Hamburg-American – in fact of every company of note, if you except the White Star – a corporation which grieves the Clyde man to the heart by launching elsewhere the biggest vessels on earth every other year.

But apart from Clyde 'finish' in the liners, it exists indisputably in the other branches of the industry. The Calais-Dover service, which has the most fastidious clientele on earth; the Queenborough and Flushing, Havre and Dieppe, Liverpool and Isle of Man, Tilbury and Boulogne (where plies with her six thousand passengers the Fairfield-built *La Marguerite*, the biggest paddle steamer afloat), and the Isle of Wight and Bristol Channel routes, all depend almost exclusively on boats from Fairfield, Clydebank, and Dumbarton. Thus the traveller is not surprised to find that the fleet of passenger steamers on the Clyde is the fastest and best in existence, or to learn that when it is considered advisable to withdraw a boat from Clyde she finds a respectful welcome on the Thames. As early as the sixties we had an eighteen-knot steamer on these waters, and when the American Civil War broke out, and Europe was searched for fast vessels to 'run the blockade' of the Federal fleet into the ports of the South, the Clyde, in the *Rothesay Castle, Kelpie*, *Falcon* and *Flamingo*, supplied the most famous. Nowadays you can travel from Ardrossan to Arran at the rate of twenty-one miles an hour in the *Glen Sannox*. As showing at once the exploitation of Clyde shipbuilding and the importance of the Glasgow man's time – even on holiday – it may be mentioned that this amazing steamer, built purely for a thirty-mile passage, has the dimensions of an early Cunarder. And it is not only Europe that the Clyde provides with river steamers. Every year the alligators on the Amazon are startled by a new wonder in twin-screw awning-deckers. When the Rajah of Sarawak puts along the shore it is in his Clyde-built paddle boat; and after toiling through the swamps and forests of Africa the traveller to the great lakes will find the Clyde steamer and Broomielaw accent of her engineer borne over their mysterious depths.

Coming to the cargo boat proper, and her near relation, the 'composite liner', we find they can be produced in every class from the 14,000-ton *Saxonia*, of Clydebank, to the little east coast trawlers which a Govan firm is said to be able to knock together while the buyer takes a fairly long stroll round the yard. That useful, hard-working class of ship which Mr Kipling has likened to a 'shuttle', but which the plain, unassuming man calls 'tramp', provides the bulk of the Clyde's output, but, as one trader resembles another most mathematically, there is little to be said on that head save that the Clyde builder has yet failed to unite carrying capacity with supreme ugliness of line in the way that will move your stevedore to tears of joy as he sights a new East Coaster drawing nigh his sheds.

There remain 'specialities' and the greatest of these is the dredger. Every type of these pioneers of shipping commerce can be purchased in either of our two yards which are concerned wholly in their making and perfecting. It was Simons & Company, of Renfrew, who set the first steam dredger a-working in 1824, and this alert old firm last year in *La Puissante*, a stern-well construction of 4,000 tons, built for the Suez Canal, put into the water the largest and most powerful of its class in the world. Were space permitted for eulogies on stern-wheel steamers, vehicular ferries, pontoons, and barges, the picture of the Clyde output would be near completion. A few types, it is true, we have still to add – vessels for Arctic exploration and submarine warfare – before the Clyde can claim to be the encyclopedia of modern shipbuilding, but the first will come in time if the North Pole holds out, and when the second is no longer caviare to the Admiralty, it shall find a place in our menu. To show that the Clyde shipbuilder keeps in the front of his times, the latest trick in marine engineering and river turbine-motor passenger steamer that is to run at least twenty-three miles an hour, and could, but for the danger to passengers' hats, add another ten, was launched at Dumbarton this year. And it is not only such old-fashioned problems as sailing the waters that are confronted here. The Clyde has an eye on the future, and in the same workshop is building an airship for a Spanish gentleman, which, we are assured, will fulfil a more practical purpose than flying from one *chateau d'Espagne* to another.

The construction of steam yachts has been associated with the river from the infancy of steam propulsion. To old Robert Napier came all men of his time with advanced notions in navel architecture, and to this great builder, in 1829, came a notable English yachtsman, Thomas Hopeton Smith, of Tednorth, with a desire to possess a pleasure yacht driven by steam. Napier reduced the squire's plans to practice, and built for him a 400-ton boat, the first vessel of its kind ever put in the water. During the succeeding twenty years he built eight yachts for the adventurous Englishman, who, it is said, lost the confidence of his wife and the Royal Yacht Squadron's membership in return for the honour of pioneering the steam yacht. The largest of his fleet, a vessel of 700 tons and thirty horse-power, named the *Fire King II*, he offered to race from Dover round the Eddystone Lighthouse and back against anything afloat for a wager of five thousand guineas, but no one could be found to take up his challenge. The *Fire King II* cut a great figure in her day, and as the steam yacht grew in favour among the restricted class concerned, the Clyde was installed as builder in ordinary and in extraordinary to the great ones of the earth. British royalty, it is true, have not yet come north for the State barge, and thus you must be prepared to find on the Clydeside something apart from sympathy when the mishaps of the new *Victoria and Albert* are mentioned; but, on the other hand, it was here the Czar of All the Russias ordered his celebrated *Livadia*, the most autocratic and expensive pleasure vessel – always excepting the said *Victoria and Albert* – ever constructed. This remarkable boat was built by John Elder & Company, of Fairfield, to the designs of Admiral Popoff of the Russian Navy. Her distinguished designer, who is stated to have invented a battleship to rotate on its own axis, intended the vessel to remain perfectly steady in all weathers, and the *Livadia* was planned with a construction underneath, which was to act as a breakwater to the hull proper. One expert has called her turbot-shaped, another held that her lines were those of a cup placed on an inverted saucer, and another that the mock turtle originally suggested her shape, but in any case she was the only vessel which made billiards at sea seem at all feasible. She was 235 feet long, 153 feet broad, and had a draught of six feet six inches; her gross tonnage measured 7,700, and her yacht measurement, according to Thames Club rules, showed an aggregate of 11,600 tons. For construction the Czar had to foot a bill of nearly £300,000. The launch was a great affair, and is still remembered on the Clyde as a red-letter event. Nor will it be forgotten soon that on that day Glasgow was publicly referred to, and by a Grand Duke of Russia, as 'the centre of the intelligence of England'.

The revolution in naval architecture that the *Livadia* was expected to forerun, however, has not yet become prominent, but this we must put down to the fact that she still remains ahead of any practical use we can make of her lesson. The Clyde's recent contributions to steam yachting have taken more the form of ideal liners than experiments in hydrodynamics. The American millionaire, to be sure, has shown a few idiosyncrasies in ideas of what is what in a floating hotel. Mr Gordon Bennett's *Lysistrata*, for instance, dispenses with masts, and has a cycling track on deck, while at her bow electric eyes (after the Chinese theory, 'if ship no got eyes, no can see; if no can see, no can go') glare balefully on mere work-a-day craft. But compared with Czar Alexander's revolutionary ideas, these are mild novelties indeed. Particularly impressed by the Clyde article, the American dollar lord for the last ten years has gone nowhere else when he would outdo the sovereigns of the earth in maritime grandeur and dignity. Clydebank has built the *Mayflower* and the *Wahma*, each a vessel of 1,800 tons; Inglis, the *Varuna*, 1564 tons; and Scott, of Greenock, the *Tuscarova*, 580 tons. Two others, the *Lysistrata* and the *Marguerita*, which lay in the river together at the beginning of the year, commanding universal respect, if only by the mere fact that they cost a quarter of a million between them, gave to the Clyde the last words on the subject of steam-yacht construction.

In conclusion one may add that the Clyde produced for the world's shipping last year 296 vessels, representing an aggregate tonnage of about 487,000 tons, and of these fifty-four vessels were for Dutch, Austrian, Spanish, German, South American, Japanese, United States, French, Russian, Norwegian, and Colonial owners. Included in the list are a first-class cruiser, a nineteen-knot troopship, torpedo boat destroyers, whose contract speed is thirty knots, two 12,000-ton 'composite' liners, Red Star, P. & O., Allan, and Anchor liners, fast paddle steamers for cross-channel service, tramps, sailing ships, dredgers, and the two yachts for millionaires.

'Twin-Screw Set – 1902'

WILLIAM J. F. HUTCHESON (1883–1951)

Week after week I watched the darlings growing
Like two strange children in an orphan home,
Aft from the thrust block to the stop-valve throw-in,
Up from the bedplate to the L.P. dome.
One afternoon we swept the pit logs cleanly,
Set down a line of wedges, steel on wood,
Then laid the bedplate as you would a pin lay,
And saw the thing was good.

We squared it up and lined the eight great bearings;
Bedded the crankshaft down, and set up well
The eight box columns, and with plumbline fairings
Brought crosshead slides dead true and parallel.
We dropped connecting rods into their places
And bedded down the great big bottom ends;
Chipped oil grooves in the smooth whitemetal faces,
And felt they were our friends.

We faired the cylinders central and level,
Marked in the fitted bolts and screwed them tight;
Set the condenser, faced-up by 'The Devil',
One inch cast iron, and considered light.
We lined the pumps behind the L.P. columns,
And steam reverser, a new patent stunt;
Set starting gear and other what-d'ye-call-'ems
Upon the engine front.

The piston rods to pistons were adjusted,
The thrust shoes on their collars brought to bear;
Fixed lubricators with their dripper worsted,
Put balanced valves on the eccentric gear;
Connected pumps and tubed the big condenser,
Packed well its ferrules; and later the exhaust
Pipe pattern tried to place, so its ends were
Cast true and nothing lost.

We set the valves; the bearing leads were taken,
The cleading fixed, and platforms laid in place;
Handrails and footplates put, and not a shake in
The whole arrangement from the top to base.
Survey them there, each one of them a beauty,
Five thousand H.P. on point six cut-off;
Designed for honest cross-Atlantic duty,
And each one looks a toff.

Take note of them; the crankshaft fourteen inches,
The L.P. cylinders are sixty-seven;
Stroke forty-eight; high-bred like all the princes,
An inspiration from the hosts of heaven.
The thrust is seven, all valve travels ditto,
The crosshead pin's diameter's the same;
Connecting rods at middle are a bit o'
That figure's sacred name.

The great propellers, shining like a sovereign,
Are seventeen feet diameter, three blades;
Seventy square feet of bronze on each shaft hovering
To push her through the currents and the trades.
They take their steam full bore about two-twenty,
The furnaces one hundred feet below
The funnel tops; and, fed with coal aplenty,
What care they if it blow!

‘The Launch’ and ‘The Board Room’

from *In Search of Scotland* and *In Scotland Again*

BY H. V. MORTON (1892–1979)

Henry Vollam Morton was one of the most popular travel writers of the period before and immediately after the Second World War. His popular and easy style made his books commercially successful: In Search of Scotland, *for example, passed through six impressions in six months.*

In Search of Scotland, *from which our description of a launch comes, was published in 1929, at a time when Clyde shipbuilding was in an acute depression. There is little suggestion of this in Morton’s description, except perhaps for his reference to an old workman saluting the new ship and lifting ‘... his greasy cap to eight months wages’. Indeed, in the commercial conditions of 1929, the probability would have been that the launch would have meant a layoff for many of the black squad of riveters and welders whose labour formed the ship from the beams and plates of steel.*

Morton’s description of a shipyard waiting-room, with its boardroom table and the glass-cased models of completed contracts, appears in his 1933 book In Scotland Again. *In this extract Morton acknowledges the ‘tragically silent’ state of the Clyde’s once great industry.*

When ‘James Hamilton Muir’ wrote their book in 1901 the Clyde was building over half a million tons of shipping a year, albeit with the help of a substantial warship building programme. When Morton visited the Clyde for his 1933 book the river was at the bottom of the Depression and the rusting skeleton of contract number 534 was lying in a silent John Brown’s shipyard at Clydebank. Work would not recommence on what became the Queen Mary *until April 1934.*

THE LAUNCH

If you have never seen the launching of a ship there is still a thrill in life for you...

You go through the shipyard gates. Every one is smiling. They will not admit that they are excited. They will, in fact, tell you that it is all in the day's work, that they are so used to it that it is just a matter of routine, but – don't believe them! No man with a heart in his body could be unmoved by the birth of a ship; and when you have been hammering at her for eight months; when you have been sitting up in a bos'n's cradle playing hell with a pneumatic riveter; when you have been standing in the remote intellect of an electric crane swinging the proud body, plate by plate, into position – not excited? I refuse to believe it.

She lies, marvellously naked, high and dry on the slipway. She has no funnels, no masts, and no engines. Her bridge is there, unpainted and innocent of glass. High on her decks men run, shouting and peering over the edge of the steel cliff to the distant shipyard. Everything is ready, waiting for the Clyde.

Her stern, with its innocent propellers, is lifted high as a house above the water; five minutes' walk back along her hull, in the shadow of her forecastle head, is a little railed-in platform covered in scarlet cloth.

It is charming to see men who have riveted her flanks performing a last service by delicately knocking tacks into half a yard of red bunting!

The tide oozes on. Men look at their watches. Pretty girls arrive in motor-cars and stand in the shadow of workshops, gazing up at the ship, reading her name – *Empress of the East*, shall we say? – printed in big bronze letters high on the sharp prow. Groups of men in dungarees, who for eight months have worked on the ship, gather and gaze up too, laugh and joke and smoke cigarettes and admire the beauty chorus.

In the shadow of the hull men, creeping about in the mud like rats, loosen great blocks of timber until at the moment when the tide is high a few swift hammer blows along the length of her keel will send her downward to the water.

Every minute is now important. There is a laugh from the workmen as a fellow, high on the forecastle head, flings down a rope which dangles above the scarlet platform. But it ceases to be a common rope as it nears the platform: its last few yards are coloured red, white, and blue. An official of the shipyard, very important, mounts the steps of the platform bearing a bottle of champagne disguised in a tight overcoat of red, white, and blue ribbons. This he attaches to the hanging rope, and he stands there steadying the dangling bottle.

The time has come! The guests move out from the work-sheds and mount the scarlet platform. The woman who is to launch the ship stands nervously fingering the hanging bottle.

'What do I do?' she whispers to the helpful official.

'Well, ye see, tak' the bottle like this and fling it har-r-rd as if ye'd break the ship and – try and hit this bolt-head!'

He walks forward and puts his finger on the steel plates.

The Clyde is high . . .

A woman's hand in a brown suéde glove, trembling a little, holds the champagne bottle. The shipyard becomes silent! Work stops! Cranes become still! You can hear the hammering of other yards across the Clyde. The tug that is waiting out on the flood tide for the new ship sounds her siren three times in salute: 'Come along, come along, come along!' A piercing whistle rings out from somewhere, there is a great shout, the sound of hammers on wood beneath the ship, a tremendous air of frantic but invisible effort and the vast monster seems suddenly to fill with life! She does not move; but you know that in one second she will move! In the tremendous suspension of that second the brown suéde glove tightens on the champagne bottle and a woman's voice says:

'Good luck to the *Empress of the East!*'

Crash! The champagne bottle hits the steel plates fair and square with a smothered tinkle of splintered glass, and great bursts of white foam fly left and right to fall like snow and to fizz a second and vanish on the scarlet platform; and now – off she goes! She moves! Hurrah! Good luck to her!

We see a wonderful thing! We see the great ship sliding backwards to the water! She makes no noise. The enormous thing just fades smoothly Clydewards, leaving behind her two broad wooden tracks of yellow grease. Silent as a phantom she is! Her stern takes the water, dips, dips, deep down. (Will she ever rise?) You watch her breathless as she dives into the Clyde to the distant sound of spray: and then her movement slows up as she meets the resistance of the water. She is almost afloat! She lies almost at the end of the two parallel grease tracks. She floats! She bounces gracefully and goes on bouncing, very high and light in the water, bouncing her great steel body as if enjoying the first taste of her buoyancy.,

'Hurrah! Good luck to the *Empress of the East!*'

We lift our hats. Among a group of workmen an old man lifts his cap for a second as his eyes follow her out to the Clyde – lifts his greasy cap to eight months' wages:

'Good-bye and – good luck!'

But it is not yet over. As she floats we hear for the first time an unforgettable sound: it is the crack and creak of breaking wood, the falling asunder of the great timbers beneath her as she crushes them and drags them with her until the river all round her is alive with heavy spars, which leap up in the water beneath her hull.

Then suddenly gigantic iron chains, whose links are the thickness of a man's arm, begin to move. Until now they lay on either side of the slipway in twelve-foot heaps. They move slowly at first, but gather amazing speed. The mighty things roll over and over in clouds of dust and rust, and go bounding down to the riverside as if to pull the ship back to her birthplace, thundering after her, leaping through the mud until they take the strain, tighten out and hold her steady in the narrow stream. . .

I stand there with the feeling that I have seen the coming to life of a giant, the breaking-away of all the shackles that held it from its element, and the glad acceptance of its fate.

I look down through the stark skeleton of poles which cradled her from the beginning, and I see her framed in the vista, still bouncing a little as if amused by the water – the symbol of Glasgow and the Clyde!

She will go to many places in her busy life carrying the name of Glasgow across the oceans of the world. Men may love her as men love ships. On her bridge, so bare and inexperienced now, men will stand guiding her through storms to various harbours. She will become wise with the experience of the seas.

But no shareholder will ever share her intimacy as we who saw her so marvellously naked and so young slip smoothly from the hands that made her into the dark welcome of the Clyde.

THE BOARD ROOM

I went to the offices of a Clyde shipyard to meet a friend, and I was shown into the waiting-room. It was a dignified, solid, polished mahogany room from which all knowledge of world chaos had been carefully concealed. The room was living in the bright prosperity of the Edwardian Age when a man in a silk hat might drop in on the spur of the moment to order a couple of liners. At least that is how it impressed me. It impressed me also as a fragment of a world that has vanished. Nothing in our world is quite so solid and assured as the waiting-room of a Clyde shipyard. Even the clubs of Pall Mall, to which this room bears a distinct resemblance, have subtly changed with the times, but here beside the Clyde, now so tragically silent, this rich, confident room lingers on in a condition of suspended animation.

Vast glass cases occupy one side of the room, and in them stand six-foot models of liners and warships. The compelling atmosphere of the room insists that the visitor should walk round inspecting them, admiring them and behaving as though the act of ordering a ship is an ordinary everyday affair – as indeed it was in the good old days.

In the middle of the room is a great polished table with gigantic padded chairs set round it. Pots that hold about half a pint of ink stand on the shining expanse, and one feels that round the table have gathered members of foreign governments writing cheques for millions of pounds.

What a stupendous age it was, the age before the War. This room, built for the reception of Admiralty officials and the directors of shipping companies, reflected the grandeur of it, turning the mind to a day when Britain's confidence and pride were supreme. I felt that it should be preserved in some museum: models, table, chairs and everything. Figures in silk hats and frock coats might be set round the table in attitudes of earnest discussion, so that our impoverished descendants may know what it looked like when Britannia ruled the waves.

On the walls were framed photographs which pictured the distinguished children of the shipyard forging ahead on the high seas, looking rather new and innocent but supremely competent and adequate. Who, I wondered, names destroyers? Somewhere in the Admiralty is an unknown poet. Their names are as right and apt as the names of hounds: *Spindrift*, *Sardonyx*, *Morning Star*, *Paragon*, *Unity*, *Swift*, *Mischief*, *Mindful* ... wonderful, perfect names.

The door of the waiting-room opened and my friend came in:

'How are you?'

'Oh, not too bad. No work.'

'Will things ever get better?'

'Ask me something else.'

Then I took him by the arm and led him out into the silent place where the empty slipways go down to the Clyde, in order that the magnificent room might hear nothing of our troubles, and go on dreaming of the old ships and the old times and – the old cheques.

'A Ship is Launched'

from The Shipbuilders

GEORGE BLAKE (1893–1961)

Born in Greenock on the Firth of Clyde, George Blake studied law at Glasgow University, but, like many young men of his generation his studies were interrupted by war service. He was wounded at Gallipoli, and after the war, entered on a career in journalism on the Glasgow Evening News *under the editorship of Neil Munro. He later worked on London literary magazines and became a director of the Porpoise Press, a pioneering, if ultimately unsuccessful, attempt to create a publishing house to serve the writers of the Scottish literary renaissance of the 1920s and 1930s. Blake wrote extensively on Scottish literary matters and was much concerned with what he saw as the 'kailyard' school's concentration on rural Scotland. To remedy this defect he set about the creation of a body of work dealing with working- and middle-class life in industrial Scotland.*

The Shipbuilders, *published in 1935, focuses on the very different but interwoven lives of Leslie Pagan, the director of a long-established family shipbuilding concern which is faced with closure in the face of the industrial depression of the 1930s and of Danny Shields, a riveter in Pagan's yard, Blake portrays Pagan and Shields enjoying closer links than simply employer and employee – Danny had served as Leslie Pagan's batman in the war and something of that comradeship carries over, perhaps slightly implausibly, into their working relationship.*

The novel opens with the launch of the Estramadura, *the last contract on the yard's books and with the post-launch reception, held in a boardroom very similar to that depicted by H.V. Morton in an earlier extract in this section.*

Apart from this fiction dealing with the Clyde, its ships and shipbuilders, Blake's interest in the subject-matter spilled over into a company history of the British India shipping line and two attractive works on the history and topography of the Clyde – Down to the Sea *and* The Firth of Clyde.

A SHIP IS LAUNCHED

It was all over. The ship *Estramadura*, taking the water like a swan, was safely launched. And here was the party at cake and wine in the boardroom, garrulous in reaction from the strain.

Leslie Pagan knew that he ought to have been particularly pleased, but he felt empty and lost; and that worried and puzzled him. He was not, he reflected, a chap given to thinking much about his states of mind, and to be thus aware of detachment from the people about him was like feeling the first symptoms of an oncoming cold. Odd, indeed, to be standing thus before the big fireplace, ostensibly chatting to little Mrs Moles, the Consul's wife, and yet to feel remote from it all, a mere spectator of the ceremony that succeeds the launching of a new vessel. Had the woman suddenly broken off her chatter and challenged him to repeat her last remark, he could not for the life of him have done it.

Perhaps it was natural that his mind should be on the ship. (A glance through the window across the tangled derricks and litter of the yard assured him that they were getting her safely to the fitting-out berth, the tugs nosing like animals at her bow and flanks.) She was a beauty; to the making of her he had brought a passionate concern. Then, God knew, that last anxious business of her launching had been a trial for him, as it always is for every builder of ships. (Remember the *Daphne* that went over from the stocks at Linthouse and carried scores of good men to death in the Clyde.) For the man with the responsibility, the pretty ceremony of breaking wine on steel plates had been an irritating irrelevance.

But it had gone well. The *Estramadura* was safely launched. Little Mrs Moles, after much giggling and a display of girlish ignorance, had raised the bottle in her gloved hand, cried the brave name aloud, and let the silken ribbons swing. A thin metallic sound of splintered glass, a small spurt of foam, a wet smear on the sheer bows of the ship – and then the awful moment when the hammers thudded on the chocks and drag-chains rattled, and it seemed that she would never move; then moved ever so slowly, then seemed to stop, and at last slipped away, roaring and at a speed that brought the heart to the mouth, to take the water with a rush, plunge wildly once, shiver a little, then come to rest – safely launched and water-borne. Now they had her snug in the fitting-out basin, and Leslie Pagan saw with his mind's eye a flickering film of her progress towards completion, saw her steam out at length, all white paint and yellow funnels, for her trials over the measured mile at Skelmorlie.

And little Mrs Moles, kittenish on this great day of her life, was still talking, while he said 'Yes' and 'No' and 'Oh, indeed!' mechanically.

Distraction came at last.

'Excuse me moment,' he said hurriedly. 'My father. . .'

The old man had stood up and was rapping at the polished mahogany for attention.

'Ladies and gentlemen, will you see to it that your glasses are charged?'

A lovely figure of an old gentleman, Leslie reflected, the recognition coming on a wave of emotion. Seventy-eight, but tall and straight as a soldier; clean-shaven, with only a hint of the old-fashioned in his double-breasted buff waistcoat, his stock, and a suspicion of whisker, still ruddy like his thick strong hair, before his ears. A gentleman of the old school, indeed – though his grandfather had been a ploughman and his father had spoken nothing else but the broad Scots tongue.

Son watched father with the detachment that had so strangely come upon him. He saw him immobilise the hurrying waiters with a glance, marked the familiar grasp of the lean hand at the left lapel, heard the small preliminary cough. And he knew what the speech would be.

It was well-delivered this day of the *Estramadura*'s launching, but it had a new power to depress Leslie Pagan. Lord, how the old man lived in the warm security of the past, in the greatness of glories departed! Clyde built . . . the grand old theme, but a bitter one in a year of doubtful grace.

Yes, they had built beautifully in Pagan's – clippers in the day of such beauties, swift steamers for coastal routes (for they left the bigger stuff to others), destroyers of grace and speed, yachts of moving loveliness. There were the half-models of them on the walls, as the old man's white hand indicated: a fine flotilla, created by men who had the art of the thing in their blood, mighty craftsmen before the Lord. It was a fine story to tell, and no one could tell it better or more lovingly than his father, who had lived through the most splendid chapters of it – but was it not near an end?

There was not a single order on the books.

That was what he could not get out of his mind. That accounted for his uneasiness and for the detachment of which he was so unusually aware. Not a single order on the books; the fine, long story of Pagan's come to an end after all these years. And the old man drivelling away – he used the word in his mind – drivelling away as if everything was as it used to be.

The devil of it was that he had tried more than once to get his father to understand, and failed. He had gone through the obvious arguments – the fantastic shrinkage of world trade; the development of building abroad; state subsidies to foreign builders and owners; the ghastly mess of currencies. But the old man would just not see it, as if his wonted clarity of mind were befogged by the assumptions of age. A passing phase, my boy. Lived through half a dozen slumps in my day, and none the worse of it. It will all come right. No patience, you young fellows. Plenty of reserves. . .

Yes, plenty of reserves. It was a thought that, to his vague surprise, frightened Leslie Pagan. If he were to chuck it all up to-morrow, he would still have plenty to live on, quite apart from the large sum of money he would get from his father in due course. Why, after all, carry on in the face of those economic facts he could not elude? Why?

For relief from the problems that so instantly and awkwardly beset him he made his eyes focus on the scene about him. His father stood, tall and distinguished, beyond the mahogany table, talking. It was a fine fire that blazed behind him. (One at each end of the room! It was the first time he had thought of the wastefulness of it.) Faces of men and women round the table, smiling a little vacantly, nodding to the old man's periods, glasses in their hands. The half-models glistened on the walls, taking the firelight as the October dusk closed in. A waiter, absurdly holding a bottle by its neck in a napkin, stood under the portrait (by Sir John Watson Gordon, P.R.S.A.) of grandfather John Pagan. Through the window he could see the gantries against the evening sky that was darkling over the holms of Renfrewshire.

His eyes came to rest on the hat of little Mrs Moles before him. In his aloofness from life he saw it as preposterous that a human being should cover her hair with such decorative absurdities. A shell of felt with a band of silk round it, and gee-gaws embroidered on the silk – good God! And he knew that it was a cheap hat. Poor little soul, acting the Consul's wife and launching ships on her husband's six hundred a year!

The train of thought brought his eyes to rest at length on his own wife – Blanche, standing there near the old man and smiling encouragement and possession at once into his face. That was Blanche: not often to be discovered in public in an attitude quite perfectly natural. She was not an actress, not a fool in her poses, but inveterately it was a studied and composed façade she presented to the Scottish world about her. He hated the thought which invaded his mind in that moment of aloofness, but all his senses were too alert to permit of a conventional self-deceit. How could this Blanche, this Englishwoman he had taken for a wife, understand what the old man said of the tradition of the Clyde and the Scots artisan? And he knew that she cared little. He knew that the end of Pagan's, or the end of his connection with Pagan's; would naturally and inevitably delight her. Farewell to dirty Clydeside, to drab, unpolished Glasgow!

He was afraid, and more afraid of her power over him than exasperated by the intrusion of the feminine into his man's life. He loved her. He remembered the girl she had been. A thousand sweet intimacies could not be forgotten. She had taken his body to hers, craving to receive and nurture his seed. She was the mother of John.

Dear, difficult Blanche, for whom his love was at once a warmth and an uneasiness! Out of the windows of his detachment he was seeing her that day afresh. Middle-age, that comes early to her blond type, was still at bay before her spirit and watchfulness. Her hair and complexion were as bright and fresh as ever, her eyes as blue and quick. Was there a shade of heaviness showing under her jaws and about her throat? And for all the slimness of her ankles in their silk, for all the slender suavity of her waist, was there not a tell-tale spreading of the hips?

To admit these things to himself was to be all the prouder of her smartness. She was still eager in life, still gay in exile, with her neat and severe brown costume and her little hat snugged down over her left eye at that adorably girlish angle. Why, at this particular moment, must he see her as a sweet enemy?

He was checking himself for disloyalty in thought when a shuffling among the company told him that his father was nearing the end of his speech. There was a flutter of mild applause, then:

'And now that your glasses are charged, ladies and gentlemen, I ask you to drink good luck to the *Estramadura* and her owners.'

Good luck! Good luck! Good luck! The phrase sounded round the table, polite and automatic for the most part. 'The *Estramadura* and her owners!' Old, deaf Mr Maciver of the Lighthouse Trust was a little late with his bellow of 'Good luck to *Estramadura* – and to Pagan's!' and some ladies had to check their sniggers.

Leslie Pagan started to move through the press towards his wife, murmuring apologies. Señor Martinez, for the owners, was speaking, but he knew what the man would say. They had built ships for the South Americans before and heard scores of flowery Latin insincerities. 'The repootacion of the Clyde – we know it well in Araguay. . . The name of Pagan, it is what you say 'ouse'old werd among ar peple. . .' Dammed little Dago, nosing for months past into other peoples business, always exasperatingly polite and warily mean. The thing was to see that the ship was secure in the basin and to know how Blanche proposed to spend the evening.

He reached her side when the last toast was being drunk. 'Pagan's. . .' Well, his father had said all he wanted to say and would be brief in reply. 'Pagan's. . .' The people were stirring to get away even as the old man spoke. He whispered into her ear.

'Going home now, Bee? I've got the Riley outside, and I won't be a minute at the basin.'

'Oh, good evening, Mrs Graham! So nice of you to come. . .'

That was Blanche playing the hostess with perfect grace and complete insincerity. It had to be done, he supposed; and Mrs Graham and a dozen others deserved no more. What worried him was that the triviality should have so curiously affected him.

She turned to him, the conventional smile fading from her lips.

'My dear, I must go to the Club for an hour at least,' she confided to him. 'Whyte's waiting for me in the Daimler. I'll be back about seven. You'll remember that Sir Archie's coming in this evening.'

'Oh, I see. Right you are, dear.'

His answer sounded a little empty. He had so much wanted to be alone with her after the fuss and boredom of the ceremony. Vaguely he resented that pull of the Club – that passion for Contract that was to him almost incomprehensible; and he was quite definitely dismayed by the thought of an evening with Sir Archie, to him the empty and garrulous second holder of a Lord Provost's conventional baronetcy. It was a pity they could not have a cosy and intimate evening alone together.

Blanche stood up, smoothing her gloves over her shapely hands.

'About seven, then, darling?' she said.

'Yes, about seven. I've got some things to do here first,' he answered.

He spent more time with the yard manager and the foreman rigger than he needed to do. Though he knew that they were anxious now, the ship safely moored, to get back to their Corporation bungalows up in Queenshill, something moved him to hang about where the tall vessel overshadowed the quay.

'Moorings all right now, Tosh?' he asked.

'Safe as houses, Mr Leslie,' answered the foreman rigger.

'It's not likely to blow tonight, is it?'

'I'm not sure it's not, sir. Besides, I've got a squad standing by.'

'Good!'

But still he could not go, and the other two waited while he walked the length of the ship and back again. He knew she was safe as she could be. But he did not want to go. Young John would be alone in his nursery at home. But would Blanche be gone in the Daimler that he had seen standing behind the main gates?

He hailed the yard manager in a low voice.

'Any word from the boiler-shop, Mr Crawford?'

'They're ready as soon as we are.'

'Good!'

It was all very silly. There was nothing he could do. He was keeping two decent men from their tea. He felt their uneasiness rolling towards him out of the shadow in which they stood.

'Well, I suppose it's all right,' he said at length, his voice echoing back from the high cliff that was the newly launched *Estramadura*. 'She's a nice job, when you look at her.'

'A topper!' said the foreman rigger gravely.

'As nice a job as we've ever done,' added Mr Crawford.

As nice a job as Pagan's had ever done. And there was not a single order on the books to follow her.

Leslie strove to order his mind.

'Well, there's nothing more, I suppose?' he asked a little emptily.

'Nothing, Mr Leslie. She's fine now.'

'Righto! I'll get along. Good night, boys.'

'Good night, sir.'

He walked up towards the gate, threading his way almost unconsciously through the piles of timber and angle-iron and over the rails and ropes that would have been the undoing of a stranger. Not a single order on the books – it was incredible. Yet he had to grasp and master it. 'Pagan's closing down' – he saw the bills of the Glasgow evening papers. Or they would be more likely to make it 'Clyde Shipyard Sensation'; and he would read it as he passed for the last time along the mean little main street of Dalpatrick, seeing it blaze from the boards before every grubby little newsagent's shop.

He came up to the Riley, standing by the timekeeper's office. Old Donald Macrae, superannuated from rigging these fifteen years, hirpled out to greet him.

'Hullo, Donald! My wife gone?'

'She's awa' in the big caur wi' the man.'

'Right. I'll get along too. A nice launch to-day.'

'It was that, sir,' replied the old man, closing the door of the car. 'As clean a job as ever I seen. Good night, sir.'

Good night! Good night! He was hearing too many good nights with the note of finality in them, thought Leslie as he turned into the street. And now there was nothing to do but go home and await Blanche's return. She was off to her Club, to her inveterate Bridge. (Again he had to try to resist the feeling of being deserted, and could not.) John would be at home in his nursery; dear, precious John, at the thought of whom his heart beat faster. But he could not spend two hours, three hours, with John, waiting for Blanche to come home and complete the circle that seemed to have been so strangely and ominously broken.

He swung the car into the Dumbarton Road, with so much of the life of Glasgow pulsing along its sidewalks and in swaying, coloured trams and juggernaut buses, with the pavements aglow in reflections from lighted shop windows: all lively after the grey drabness of the streets by the riverside; and in the very act of turning he knew what he would do – stop at O'Glinchey's public house and find some of the old hands at the bar there and, as he loved to do now and again, stand them a drink. Danny Shields would be among them, and long Jock Macgrory out of the paint store, and Jimmy Affleck the cranesman. To-night it seemed imperative he should see them, those rough innocents whose destinies were so strangely in his hands.

He was still seeing himself and his actions as from a distance. For the first time he fully realized the oddness, in the world's eyes, of master drinking with man. It would have troubled his father, who was just, but saw industry as a stern battlefield, with Capital and Labour as implacable and natural enemies. And it would have horrified Blanche, this rough drinking in such a place with such men.

Parking the Riley in the side-street, he pushed open a swing-door to be met by a gust of hot, exhausted air, heavy with the mingled smells of sawdust, strong tobacco, oily clothes and beer. The house was busy, burly men in working clothes and dirty cloth caps two deep along the counter. The ugly tongue of Clydeside assailed his ears, every sixth word a fierce and futile obscenity; they spat much as they seemed to breathe. He saw the scene as one of degradation, and yet, understanding, he neither recoiled or condemned. They were the men he knew – passionate, strong and true to the core.

His quick glance took in many a familiar face that smiled an uneasy greeting, but he saw the group of older hands he sought, deep in argument in a corner by the fire. They greeted him with a respectful forthrightness.

'Evenin', boss!' said they all.

'Evening, boys! What about the usual drink to the ship? Yours, Jock?'

They all said the same – 'Haulf and haulf-pint, if you please' – that strange and powerful solace of the Scots working-man: a half-glass of whisky taken neat and washed down by a glass of the heavy Scotch ale. Leslie ordered glasses and pints for them, as he knew they expected, a whisky and soda for himself.

'Best respects, boss,' the murmur went round the circle, and the whisky disappeared. They would linger over the beer to talk.

He was never uneasy with those old hands, who had taught him so much of their trades in his apprenticeship. Nor could talk flag long where Danny Shields was: Danny Shields, bow-legged, broad-shouldered riveter whom a hard life and four years of Gallipoli and Sinai and Palestine and Flanders had left with the heart and mind of a boy. Now, however, there was gravity on the odd, birdlike face with the strong clean-shaven lips and jaw.

'Some of them are sayin' doon in the yard, boss,' he began at once, 'that there'll mebbe be a big pay-off.'

Leslie's heart sank. How did these things get around? How could he tell them the cold truth?

'Things are not looking too good,' he admitted gravely. Then he shook fear from him. 'But there are enquiries – some enquiries coming in. We're not done yet.'

'Aye, trade's gey bad all the same.' This was long Jock Macgrory, a grave man with a thin, drooping moustache of grey and a nasal impediment in his speech. 'Dalmuir closed for good. Fairfield empty. Caird's doon bye at Greenock closed for good. Thon wee place at old Kilpatrick . . . Christ! Govan looks like a bloody cemetery. It's hard times right enough for the Clyde.'

'Well, we've been gey lucky at Pagan's,' broke in Jimmy Affleck – desperately as it seemed to Leslie.

And Danny Shields's strong spirit rose to meet the challenge of pessimism, to refuse it existence.

'Aye, and our luck's going to stay wi' us!' he cried. 'Good health and respects again, boss!'

He plunged at his tankard and drained it vehemently.

'Yes,' said Leslie, putting down his empty glass also, 'we're not going to worry yet. And now I must get along. Can I give anybody a lift?'

'If you could drop me at Scotstoun, sir —' suggested Danny modestly.

'Come along then. Good night, boys.'

Good night! Good night! Always that sombre phrase. He hardly spoke to the man in the seat beside him as they sped up the busy road towards Glasgow. This new awareness of his responsibility could not leave him. The best part of a thousand men, with their women and children, depended on him. It was easy enough at most times to see them, in his father's way, as a mass, impersonally, but with eyes sharpened by the imminence of danger he saw them as individuals capable of suffering – decent able workmen like Danny Shields and long Jock Macgrory and Jimmy Affleck to be put out on the dole, to hang about street corners, to be denied their right to work, to know emptiness indescribable!

The voice of Danny roused him from his brooding.

'This'll do me, sir.'

'Right you are, Danny.'

He steered the car into the kerb and the little man clambered out onto the pavement.

'I'm very much obliged to you, sir –'

And must he, too, say that fatal good night – Danny Shields, who had been his batsman from the beginning of the war to its end and was his friend, bound to him by ties innumerable and strong? They had shared danger, degradation, and folly. Above the relationships of master and man, officer and private, they had lived together every emergency of the masculine world; Danny Shields ever with the desperate humour of the western Scot on his lips, the grin of inexhaustible mischief in his face, and courage and steadfastness in his simple heart – a man.

Leslie had almost let him go, when something moved him to a confidence,

'Danny!' he said sharply.

'Sir.'

'I say, Danny, if – if there have to be changes at the yard, you're not to worry. I'll see that you have a job. That all right?'

The habit of the old soldier asserted itself in Danny Shields then. Squaring his body, he clicked his heels and swung his hand in salute to the stained cap of cheap tweed.

'Yes, sir', he replied.

6
JOCK TAMSON'S BAIRNS
Introduction

This section deals with the life of the people of Glasgow, their living conditions, their housing, their social life. For a century or more now it has been this aspect of Glasgow which, more than any other, has determined the world's view of it, its image. The form of building which symbolised this was, and to a large extent still is, the tenement; examples of that particular type of working-class housing (though not exclusively working-class) are still with us as we reach the end of the twentieth century. This section includes a number of extracts reflecting different views of Glasgow tenement life and comparable and contrasting housing types in the last hundred years.

First, an excerpt from a novel which may have contributed more than most to our image of living conditions in Glasgow at the beginning of the twentieth century. It is *The Rat-Pit* by Patrick MacGill. MacGill came to Scotland from Donegal; his experiences at that time ensured that his novel had strong autobiographical features. *The Rat-Pit* introduces an important new element into the story of Glasgow's people – Irish immigration. None of the buildings from the Cowcaddens brought to skin-crawling life by MacGill has survived, mercifully, but the drive to housing and social reform was to be reinforced by interest in The Rat-Pit and its companion novel, *Children of the Dead End.* The desperate campaign for improvements in the slums of Glasgow began in the nineteenth century and to an extent was not complete even into our own day. However, a considerable boost in the struggle against urban squalor came in 1859 with the provision for the city of fifty million gallons of clean water every day, thanks to the energetic Glasgow blend of civic socialism. This came about as a result of the Loch Katrine Water Supply Scheme. Opening this magnificent example of civil engineering, which piped water from the Trossachs some thirty-five miles into the city, Queen Victoria said: 'Such a work is worthy of the enterprise and philanthropy of Glasgow, and I trust it will be blessed with complete success.' James Nicholson the poet also gave *A Welcome to the Waters of Loch Katrine*.

As a complete contrast we include a chapter from *Aunt Bel* by Guy McCrone, set around the same time in 1892, but offering a wildly different slice of society – one which lives somewhere in the vicinity of Great Western Road. The thing to note here is that Aunt Bel, as in the case of McCrone's better-known *Wax Fruit* sequence of three novels, is a historical novel, written in 1949.

The epitome of a lighter, more humorous view of Glasgow folk can be found in J.J. Bell's Wee Macgreegor stories, which have certain resemblances to those of the versatile Neil Munro. The juvenile adventures of Wee MacGreegor, or MacGregor Robinson (the Christian name hints that here we have yet another Glaswegian of Highland descent), were followed by a loyal readership in the *Glasgow Evening Times* and in book form in the early years of this century. The story included here, however, *Hullo, Glesca Hielanders!* has him on the Western Front with his pal Wullie.

Next we have Munro's Erchie MacPherson, part-time waiter and kirk beadle at the emblematic St Kentigern's Church, and a wonderful surveyor of the Glasgow scene. For whatever reason, whether as a result of 'tapping' his friend the coal-merchant Duffy, or by limiting his visits to the 'Mull o' Kintyre Vaults', Erchie could afford at one time to live in one of the 'better types' of tenement. This was in Buccleuch Street in the Garnethill area of the city, near to the splendid National Trust Tenement House we know today. Such an area was not quite what Erchie had in mind, no doubt, when he spoke with some irony of the 'auld-established and justly popular slum hoose' – or, in other words, decrepit and overcrowded.

So what is there about this Glasgow tenement that so shapes and fixes social living in people's minds? Obviously it is mainly to do with the communal life engendered by the common stair, the closemouth, the back court and so on. Such experiences were bound to remain in the memory, especially with the subsequent uprooting and resettlement in peripheral estates or 'schemes'. This anthology could have included any number of reminiscences of tenement life, some of them of the 'Semmits Were For Ne'erday' variety; instead we have turned to a poet's view – a modern poet, born in Glasgow but usually associated with more northerly places. Iain Crichton Smith's novel, The Tenement, isn't set in the city, rather in some nameless town in the west, but the building's anonymity seems to make it stand for all tenements everywhere.

One of the themes of Smith's book is the repression and violence which hide within buildings like the tenement, and in the Glasgow context some of the most vivid stories of repression and violence are found in the city's criminal archives. The next piece, a poem by Janet Hamilton called Heaven Knows, tells one of these stories. This gives a clearly partial view of the celebrated trial of Madeleine Smith in 1857 – partial because the poet makes it pretty clear that she believes Madeleine to be guilty of the murder of her lover, as charged. The verdict, as the world knows, was the uniquely Scots one of 'Not Proven'. The home of Madeleine where she met her lover Emile – strange the preponderance of Continental names – in the Blythswood estate of the West End scarcely comes under the heading of a tenement building. Still there today, it is more of a terraced townhouse, but retains something of the tenement's aura of a confined and claustrophobic psychological milieu. An except from a journal gives some of the public reaction:

> What a putrefying layer of debasement, lust and hypocrisy, festering under the smooth skinned surface of society in moral-living, church-going, theatre-hating, Sabbath-keeping Glasgow do the occurrences present out of which arose the trial of Madeleine Smith!

Another piece we include in this chapter, which has crime as a driving force, is taken from *No Mean City* by McArthur and Kingsley Long. This was like *The Rat-Pit* in that it attracted a great deal of notoriety and it also caused establishment figures to react adversely to the negative publicity. It certainly will not be the last book about Glasgow to produce that kind of response.

The final piece in this section is an extract from a novel by and about one of the later groups of immigrants. Chaim Bermant's *The Patriarch* gives a compelling fictional account of the Jewish community in Glasgow on the south side of the city, where many of their real counterparts live even today. The novel tells the story of the Rabinowitz family, who take the name of Raeburn when they come to Scotland, from the 1890s until the late 1960s. A key district for the Jewish population is Pollokshields, which at the novel's close is being populated by further ethnic groups, this time from the Indian sub-continent. Will this population in turn, one wonders, one day be the source and inspiration of a similar novelistic saga?

'Norah and Sheila'

from The Rat-Pit

PATRICK MACGILL (1891–1963)

Patrick MacGill made his mark on the world of books in 1914 with his first novel, Children of the Dead End. *This told the story of Dermod Flynn, a poor Irish youth from Donegal who came to Scotland with a potato-picking gang, fell into bad ways, was forced into living as a tramp before becoming a navvy on the Kinlochleven hydroelectric scheme and working as a railway labourer. The impact of the story, quite apart from its intrinsic merits, was enormously heightened by it being autobiographical – Dermod Flynn was Patrick MacGill.*

MacGill, despite a lack of anything other than a primary school education, discovered or developed in himself a genuine talent for writing. Even while navvying he had contributed items to newspapers, and, while working at Greenock on the Caledonian Railway's permanent-way gang, published a collection of his poetry. This got him noticed in both the Scottish and the English press and he was invited to Fleet Street to take up a staff post on the Daily Express. *From this appointment he was, even more improbably, recruited by John Dalton, Canon and Treasurer of St George's Chapel, to work at Windsor Castle as a secretary and librarian.*

While working there he wrote his second novel, The Rat-Pit. *The two novels are interwoven, but the first focuses on Dermod Flynn, the second on Dermod's tragic sweetheart Norah Ryan. Dermod and Norah come from the same village, attend the same school but lose touch when Dermod is hired out as a child farm hand. Later, they find themselves on the same potato-picking squad in Scotland but again are separated when Norah goes back to Donegal at the end of the season while Dermod is ashamed to return because he has lost all his money gambling. Norah returns to Scotland and the tattie-howking but is seduced by a rich farmer's son and becomes pregnant. The farmer's son refuses to acknowledge any responsibility for Norah and she seeks refuge in Glasgow with her countrywoman, Sheila Carol. Sheila, the* beansho, *'that woman', as the censorious Donegal villagers had called her, had sunk into the underclass of Glasgow when she, too, had given birth to an illegitimate child.*

The 'rat-pit' of the title was the lodging house for destitute women where Norah sought shelter on her arrival in Glasgow while searching for Sheila. MacGill's novels powerfully evoke the world of lodging houses, of life lived on the edge of destitution, and the grey grinding poverty not far below the surface of the city. Children of the Dead End *and* The Rat-Pit *are not the first or the last novels about poverty in Glasgow; what makes them significant is that they are by a writer who actually lived in the world he describes. MacGill's knowledge of the life of the underclass is revealed through telling touches like the tramp sleeping on a dung pit for warmth and the blankets in Sheila's rented room stamped with the landlord's mark 'Stolen from James Moffat'.*

MacGill's anger at the social conditions he experienced in Ireland and in Scotland burns in every page. In the earlier, Irish, chapters of both books he attacks oppressive priests, landlords and merchants. In the scenes set in Glasgow the hypocrisy of slum landlords and sweatshop owners and the contrast between the prosperous city, symbolised by the ornate magnificence of the Municipal Buildings 'where the rich folk meet and talk', and the rat-infested slums is brought home to readers through Norah and Sheila's experiences.

NORAH AND SHEILA

The address on the letter which Norah received from Sheila Carrol was '47 Ann Street, Cowcaddens', but shortly after the letter had been written the Glasgow Corporation decided that 47 was unfit for human habitation, and those who lived there were turned out to the streets.

It was late in the evening of the day on which she left Jean and Donal that Norah came to No. 47, to find the place in total darkness. She groped her way up a narrow alley to the foot of a stair and there suddenly stepped on a warm human body lying on the ground.

'What the devil' – Ah, ye're choking me, an old person that never done no one no harm,' croaked a wheezy voice, apparently a woman's under Norah's feet. 'I only came in oot of the cauld, lookin' for a night's shelter. Hadn't a bawbee for the Rat-pit. Beg pardon! I'm sorry; I'll go away at once; I'll go now. For the love of heaven don't gie me up to the cops. I'm only a old body and I hadn't a bawbee of my own. I couldn't keep walkin' on all night. Beg pardon, I'm only a old body and I hadn't a kirk siller piece for the Rat-pit!'

'I'm sorry, but I didn't know that there was anyone here,' said Norah, peering through the darkness. 'I'm a stranger, good woman.'

'Ye're goin' to doss here too,' croaked the voice from the ground.

'I'm lookin' for a friend,' said Norah. 'Maybe ye'll know her – Sheila Carrol. She lives here.'

'Nobody lives here,' said the woman, shuffling to her feet. 'Nobody but the likes of me and ones like me. No human being is supposed to live here. I had at one time a room on the top of the landin', the cheapest room in Glasgow it was. Can't get another one like it now and must sleep out in the snow. Out under the scabby sky and the wind and the rain. It wasn't healthy for people to sleep here, so someone said, and we were put out. Think of that, and me havin' the cheapest room in the Cowcaddens. If the cops find me here, it's quod. Wha be ye lookin' for?'

'A friend, Sheila Carrol.'

'Never heard of her.' The voice, almost toneless, seemed to be forcing its way through some thick fluid in the speaker's throat. The darkness of the alley was intense and the women were hidden from one another.

'Everybody that stayed here has gone, and I don't know where they are,' the old woman continued. 'Don't know at all. Ye dinna belong to Glesga?' she croaked.

'No, decent woman.'

'By yer tongue ye'll be a young girl.'

'I am.'

'Mind ye, I'm a cute one and I ken everything. It's not every one that could tell what ye are by yer tongue. Are ye a stranger?'

'I am,' answered Norah. 'I was never in Glasgow before.'

'I knew that too,' said the old woman. 'And ye want lodgin's for the night? Then the Rat-pit's the place; a good decent place it is – threepence a night for a bunk. Beg pardon, but maybe ye'll have a kid's eye (threepence) extra to spare for an old body. Come along with me and I'll show the way. I'm a cute one and I know everything. Ye couldn't ha'e got into better hands than mine if ye're a stranger in Glasgow.'

They went out into a dimly-lighted lane and Norah took stock of her new friend. The woman was almost bent double with age; a few rags covered her body, she wore no shoes, and a dusty, grimy clout was tied round one of her feet. As if conscious of Norah's scrutiny she turned to the girl.

'Ah! Ye wouldn't think, would ye, that I had once the finest room in the Cowcaddens, the finest – at its price:'

'The Rat-pit's a lodgin' place for women,' the old creature croaked after an interval. 'There are good beds there: threepence a night ye pay for them. Beg pardon, but maybe ye'll pay for my bunk for the night. That's just how I live; it's only one night after another in my life. Beg pardon, but that's how it is.' She seemed to be apologising for the crime of existing. 'But ye'll maybe have a kid's eye to spare for my bunk?' she asked.

'All right, decent woman,' said Norah.

'What do they cry ye?'

'Norah Ryan.'

'A pretty name, and my name's Maudie Stiddart,' said the old woman.

Ten minutes later the two women were seated in the kitchen of the Rat-pit, frying a chop which Norah had bought on their way to the lodging-house.

The place was crowded with women of all ages, some young, children almost, their hair hanging down their backs, and the blouses that their pinched breasts could not fill sagging loose at the bosom. There were six or seven of these girls, queer weedy things that smoked cigarettes and used foul words whenever they spoke. The face of one was pitted with small-pox; another had both eyes blackened, the result of a fight; a third, clean of face and limb, was telling how she had just served two months in prison for importuning men on the streets. Several of the elder females were drunk; two fought in the kitchen, pulling handfuls of hair from one another's heads. Nobody interfered; when the struggle came to an end the combatants sat down together and warmed their hands at the stove. At this juncture a bare-footed woman, with clay caked brown behind her ankles and a hairy wart on her chin, came up to Norah.

'Ye're a stranger here,' she said.

'I am, decent woman.'

'Ye're Irish, too, for I ken by yer talk,' said the female. 'And ye've got into trouble.'

She pointed at the girl with a long, crooked finger, and Norah blushed.

'Dinna be ashamed of it,' said the woman; then turning to Maudie Stiddart she enquired: 'And ye're here too, are ye? I thought ye were dead long ago? Jesus! but some people can stick it out. There's no killin' of 'em!'

'Oh, ye're a blether, Mary Martin,' said Maudie, turning the chop over on the stove. 'Where are ye workin' now?'

'On the free coup outside Glesga.'

'The free coup?' asked the young girl who had just left prison, lighting a cigarette. 'What's that at all?'

'The place to where the dung and dust and dirt of a town is carried away and throwed down,' Mary Martin explained. 'Sometimes lumps of coal and pieces of metal are flung down there. These I pick up and sell to people and that's how I make my livin'.'

'Is that how you do?' asked the girl with a shrug of her shoulders.

'Everyone isn't young like you,' said Mary, sitting down on a bench near the stove. The girl laughed vacantly, tried to make a ring of the cigarette smoke, was unable to do so, and walked away. Mary Martin turned to Maudie and whispered something to her.

'Ah, puir lass!' exclaimed Maudie.

'And the one to blame was a toff, too!' said Mary. 'They're all alike, and the good dress often hides a dirty hide.'

'Beg pardon, but have ye got anything to ate?' asked Maudie.

'Nothin' the night,' answered Mary. 'Only made the price of my bed for my whole day's work.'

'Will ye ate something with us?' asked Norah.

'Thank ye,' said Mary Martin, and the three women drew closer to the chop that was roasting on the stove.

The beds in the Rat-pit, forty in all, were in a large chamber upstairs, and each woman had a bed to herself. The lodgers undressed openly, shoved their clothes under the mattresses and slid into bed. One sat down to unlace her boots and fell asleep where she sat; another, a young girl of seventeen or eighteen, fell against the leg of the bed and sank into slumber, her face turned to the roof and her mouth wide open. The girl who had been in prison became suddenly unwell and burst into tears; nobody knew what she was weeping about and nobody enquired.

Maudie, Mary, and Norah slept in three adjoining beds, the Irish girl in the centre. The two older women dropped off to sleep the moment their heads touched the pillows; Norah lay awake gazing at the flickering shadows cast by the solitary gas-jet on the roof of the room. The heat was oppressive, suffocating almost, and not a window in the place was open. Women were still coming in, and only half the bunks in the room were yet occupied. Most of the newcomers were drunk; some sat down or fell on the floor and slept where they had fallen, others threw themselves in on top of the bed and lay there with their clothes on. An old woman whose eye had been blackened in a fight downstairs started to sing 'Annie Laurie', but forgetting what followed the first verse, relapsed into silence.

Norah began to pray under her breath to the Virgin, but had only got half through with her prayer when a shriek from the bed on her left startled her. Maudie was sitting upright, yelling at the top of her voice. 'Cannot ye let an old body be?' she cried. 'I'm only wantin' a night's doss at the foot of the stairs. That's not much for an old un to ask, is it? Holy Jesus! I cannot be let alone for a minute. Beg pardon; I'm goin' away, but ye might let me stay here, and me only an old woman!'

Maudie opened her watery eyes and stared round. Beads of sweat stood out on her forehead, and her face – red as a crab – looked terrifying in the half-light of the room.

'Beg pardon,' she croaked, and her voice had a sound like the breaking of bones. 'Beg pardon. I'm only an old woman and I never did nobody no harm!'

She sank down again, pulled the blankets over her shoulders and fell asleep.

Fresh arrivals came in every minute, staggered wearily to their bunks and threw themselves down without undressing. About midnight a female attendant, a young, neat girl with a pleasing face, entered, surveyed the room, helped those who lay on the floor into a bed, turned down the gas and went away.

Slumber would not come to Norah. All night she lay awake, listening to the noise of the dust-carts on the pavement outside, the chiming of church clocks, the deep breathing of the sleepers all around her, and the sudden yells from Maudie's bunk as the woman started in her sleep protesting against some grievance or voicing some ancient wrong.

The daylight was stealing through the grimy window when Norah got up and proceeded to dress. A deep quietness, broken only by the heavy breathing of the women, lay over the whole place. The feeble light of daybreak shone on the ashen faces of the sleepers, on the naked body of a well-made girl who had flung off all her clothing in a troubled slumber, on Mary Martin's clay-caked legs that stuck out from beneath the blankets, on Maudie Stiddart's wrinkled, narrow brow beaded with sweat; on the faces of all the sleepers, the wiry and weakly, the fit and feeble, the light of new-born day rested. Suddenly old Mary turned in her sleep, then sat up.

'Where are ye goin' now?' she called to Norah.

'To look for a friend,' came the answer.

'A man?'

'A woman called Sheila Carrol is the one I'm lookin' for,' said Norah. 'I went to 47 Ann Street last night, for I had a letter from her there. But the place was closed up.'

'Sheila Carrol, they cry her, ye say?' said the old woman, getting out of bed. 'Maybe it's her that I ken. She came from Ireland with a little boy and she used to work with me at one time. A comely strong-boned wench she was. Came from Frosses, she once told me.'

'That's Sheila!'

'And she's left 47?'

'So I hear.'

'Then take my advice and try No. 46 and No. 48,' said Mary Martin; 'and also every close in the street. The people that lived in 47 will not gang far awa' from it. They'll be in the next close or thereabouts. What do they cry you, lass?' asked the old woman, slipping into her rags.

'Norah Ryan.'

'A pretty name it is indeed. And have ye threepence to spare for my breakfast, Norah Ryan? I haven't a penny piece in all the wide world.'

Norah gave threepence of her hard-earned money to Mary, sorted her dress and stole out into the streets to search for Sheila Carrol.

Norah travelled through the streets all day, looking for her friend and fearing that every eye was fixed on her, that everybody knew the secret which she tried to conceal. Her feet were sore, her breath came in short, sudden gasps as she took her way into dark closes and climbed creaking stairs; and never were her efforts rewarded by success. Here in the poorer parts of the city, in the crooked lanes and straggling alleys, were dirt, darkness and drunkenness. A thousand smells greeted the nostrils, a thousand noises grated on the ears; lights flared brightly in the beershops; fights started at the corners; ballad singers croaked out their songs; intoxicated men fell in the gutters; policemen stood at every turning, their helmets glistening, their faces calm, their eyes watchful. The evening had come and all was noise, hurry, and excitement.

'Isaac Levison, Pawnbroker; 2 Up,' Norah read on a plate outside the entrance of a close and went in.

'I wonder if Sheila will be here?' she asked herself, and smiled sadly as she called to mind the number of closes she had crawled into during the whole long trying day.

Dragging her feet after her, she made her way up the crooked stairs and rapped with her knuckles at a door on which the words 'Caretaker's office' were painted in black letters. A woman, with a string for a neck and wisps of red hair hanging over her face, poked out her head.

'Up yet,' was the answer when Norah asked if anybody named Sheila Carrol dwelt on the stairs.

'After all my searchin' she's here at last,' said the young woman. 'It's Sheila Carrol herself that's in the place.'

The beansho opened the door when she heard a rapping outside. She knew her visitor at once.

'Come in, Norah Ryan,' she said, catching the girl's hands and squeezing them tightly. 'It's good of ye to come. No one from Frosses, only Oiney Dinchy's gasair, have I seen here for a long while. But ye'll be tired, child?'

'It's in an ill way that I come to see ye, Sheila Carrol,' said Norah. 'It's an ill way, indeed it is,' and then, sitting down, she told her story quietly as if that which she spoke of did not interest her in any way.

'Poor child!' said Sheila, when the pitiful tale came to an end. 'Why has God put that burden on yer little shoulders? But there's no use in pining, Norah. Mind that, child!'

'I would like to die, Sheila Carrol,' said Norah, looking round the bare room, but not feeling in the least interested in what she saw. One chair, a bed, a holy water stoup, a little black crucifix from which the arms of the Christ had fallen away, an orange box on which lay a pair of scissors and a pile of cloth: that was all the room contained. A feeble fire burned in the grate and a battered oil-lamp threw a dim light over the compartment.

'I once had thoughts that were like that, meself,' said Sheila. She placed a little tin pannikin on the fire and fanned the flame with her apron. 'People face a terrible lot in body and in soul before they face death. That's the way God made us, child. We do be like grains of corn under a mill-stone, and everything but the breath of our bodies squeezed out of us. Sometimes I do be thinkin' that the word "hope" is blotted from me soul; but then after a wee while I do be happy in my own way again.'

'But did ye not find yer own burden hard to bear, Sheila?'

'Hard indeed, child, but it's trouble that makes us wise,' said the beansho, pouring tea into the pannikin that was now bubbling merrily. 'The father of me boy died on the sea and me goin' to be married to him when the season of Lent was by. The cold grey morning when the boat came in keel up on Dooey Strand was a hard and black one for me. Ah! the cold break of day; sorrow take it! The child came and I was not sorry at all, as the people thought I should be. He was like the man I loved, and if the bitin' tongues of the Frosses people was quiet I would be very happy, I would indeed, Norah! But over here in this country it was sore and bitter to me. I mind the first night that I stopped in Glasgow with the little boy. He was between my arms and I was lookin' out through the window of 47 at the big clock with the light inside of it. It was a lazy clock that night and I thought that the light of day would never put a colour on the sky. But the mornin' did come and many mornin's since then, and stone-cold they were too!'

Then Sheila told the story of her life in Scotland, and Norah, hardly realising what was spoken, listened almost dumbly, feeling at intervals the child within her moving restlessly, stretching out as if with a hand and pressing against her side, causing a quivering motion to run through her body.

Sheila's story was a pitiful one. When first she came to Glasgow she took an attic room at the top of a four-storeyed building and for this she paid a weekly rent of three shillings and sixpence.

''Twas the dirty place to live in, Norah, for all the smells and stinks of the houses down under came up to me,' said the woman. 'And three white shillin's and sixpence a week for that place that one wouldn't put pigs into! The houses away at home may be bad, but there's always the fresh air and no drunk men or bad women lyin' across yer door every time ye go outside. 47 was a rotten place; worse even than this, and this is bad. Look at the sheets and blankets on the bed behind ye, Norah, look at the colour of them and the writin' on them.'

Norah gazed at the bed and saw on every article of clothing, stamped in large blue letters, the words: 'STOLEN FROM JAMES MOFFAT'.

'That's because someone may steal the rags,' said Sheila. 'This room is furnished by the landlord, God forgive him for the furnishin' of it! And he's afraid that his tenants will run away and try to pawn the bedclothes. Lyin' under the blankets all night with STOLEN FROM JAMES MOFFAT writ on them is a quare way of sleepin'. But what can a woman like me do? And 47 was worse nor this; and the work! 'Twas beyond speakin' about!

'The first job I got was the finishin' of dongaree jackets, sewin' buttons on them, and things like that. I was up in the mornin' at six and went to bed the next mornin' at one, and hard at it all the time I wasn't sleepin'. Sunday was the same as any other day; always work, always the needle. I used to make seven shillin's a week; half of that went in rent and the other half kept meself and my boy. Talk about teeth growin' long with hunger at times when the work was none too plentiful! Sometimes, Norah–'

Sheila paused. Norah was listening intently, her lips a little apart, like a child's.

'Sometimes, Norah, I went out beggin' on the streets – me, a Frosses woman too,' Sheila resumed with a sigh. 'Then one night when I asked a gentleman for a few pence to buy bread he handed me over to the police. Said I was accostin' him. I didn't even know what it meant at the time; now – But I hope ye never know what it means... Anyway I was sent to jail for three weeks.'

'To jail, Sheila!' Norah exclaimed.

'True as God, child, and my boy left alone in that dirty attic. There was I not knowin' what was happenin' to him, and when I came out of prison I heard that the police had caught him wanderin' out in the streets and put him in a home. But I didn't see him; I was slapped into jail again.'

'What for, Sheila?'

'Child neglect, girsha,' said the woman, lifting her scissors and cutting fiercely at a strip of cloth as she spoke. 'I don't know how they made it out again' me, but the law is far beyond simple people like us. I was put in for three months that time and when I came out–'

A tear dropped from Sheila's eyes and fell on the cloth which lay on her lap.

'The little fellow, God rest his soul! was dead,' said the woman. 'Then I hadn't much to live for and I was like to die. But people can stand a lot one way and another, a terrible lot entirely. After that I thought of making shirts and I got a sewin' machine from a big firm on the instalment system. A shillin' a week I had to pay for the machine. I could have done well at the shirt-makin', but things seemed somehow to be again' me. On the sixth week I couldn't pay the shillin'. It was due on a Friday and Saturday was my own pay day. I prayed to the traveller to wait for the morrow, but he wouldn't, and took the machine away. 'Twas the big firm of — too, that did that. Think of it! them with their mills and their riches and me only a poor woman. Nor it wasn't as if I wasn't wantin' to pay neither. But that's the way of the world, girsha; the bad, black world, cold as the rocks on Dooey Strand it is, aye, and colder.

'Sometimes after the sewin' machine went I used to go out on the streets and sing songs, and at that sort of work, not at all becomin' for a Frosses woman, I could always make the price of a bunk in the Rat-pit, the place where ye were last night, Norah. Ah! how often have I had my night's sleep there! Then again I would come back to 47 and start some decent work that wasn't half as easy or half as well paid as the singin' of songs. So I went from one thing to another and here I am at this very minute.'

Sheila paused in her talk but not in the work which she had just started.

'Not much of a room, this one, neither,' she remarked, casting her eye on the bed, but not missing a stitch in her sewing as she spoke. 'Four shillin's I pay for it a week and it's supposed to hold two people. Outside the door you can see that ticketed up, "To hold two adults", like the price marked on a pair of secondhand trousers. I'm all alone here; only the woman, old Meg, that stops in the room behind this one, passes through here on her way to work. But ye'll stay here with me now, two Frosses people in the one room, so to speak.'

'What kind of work are ye doin' here?' asked Norah, pointing to the cloth which Sheila was sewing.

'Shirt-finishin', Sheila replied. 'For every shirt there's two rows of feather-stitchin', eight buttonholes and seven buttons sewed on, four seams and eight fasteners. It takes me over an hour to do each shirt and the pay is a penny farthing. I can make about fifteen pence a day, but out of that I have to buy my own thread. But ye'll be tired, child, listenin' to me clatterin' here all night.'

'I'm not tired listenin' to ye at all, but it's sorrow that's with me because life was so hard on ye,' said Norah. 'Everything was black again' ye.'

'One gets used to it all,' said Sheila with the air of resignation which sits on the shoulders of those to whom the keys of that delicious mystery known as happiness are forever lost. 'One gets used to things, no matter how hard they be, and one doesn't like to die.'

But now Norah listened almost heedlessly. Thoughts dropped into her mind and vanished with the frightful rapidity of things falling into empty space; and memories of still more remote things, faint, far away and almost undefined, were wafted against her soul.

The girl fell into a heavy slumber.

In the morning she awoke to find herself lying in bed, the blankets on which the blue letters STOLEN FROM JAMES MOFFAT were stamped wrapped tightly around her, and Sheila Carrol lying by her side. For a moment she wondered vaguely how she had got into the bunk, then raising herself on her elbow, she looked round the room.

The apartment was a very small one, with one four-paned window and two doors, one of which led, as Norah knew, out to the landing, and one, as she guessed, into the room belonging to old Meg, the woman whom Sheila had spoken of the night before. The window was cracked and crooked, the floor and doors creaked at every move, a musty odour of decay and death filled the whole place. A heap of white shirts was piled on the orange box that stood in the middle of the floor, one shirt, the 'finishing' of which had not been completed, lay on an old newspaper beside the fireplace. It looked as if Sheila had become suddenly tired in the midst of her feather-stitching and had slipped into bed. She was now awake and almost as soon as she had opened her eyes was out of the blankets, had wrapped a few rags round her bony frame and was busy at work with her needle. Sleep for the woman was only a slight interruption of her eternal routine.

'Have a wee wink more,' she cried to Norah,'and I'll just make a good warm cup of tay for ye when I get this row finished. Little rogue of all the world! ye're tired out and worn!'

Norah smiled sadly, got up, dressed herself, and going down on her knees by the bedside, said her prayers.

'It's like Frosses again,' said Sheila, when the girl's prayers came to an end. 'Even seein' ye there on yer knees takes back old times. But often I do be thinkin' that prayin' isn't much good. There was old Doalty Farrel;

ye mind him talkin' about politics the night yer father, God rest him! was underboard. Well, Doalty was a very holy man, as ye know yerself, and he used to go down on his knees when out in the very fields and pray and pray. Well and good; he went down one day on his knees in the snow and when he got home he had a pain in one of his legs. That night it was in his side, in the mornin' Doalty was dead. Gasair Oiney Dinchy was tellin' me all about it.'

'But they say in Frosses that God was so pleased with Doalty that He took him up to heaven before his time,' said Norah.

'But it's not many that like to go to heaven before their time,' Sheila remarked as she rose from her seat and set about to kindle the fire. At the same moment the door leading in from the compartment opened, and an old woman, very ugly, her teeth worn to the gums, the stumps unhealthily yellow, her eyes squinting and a hairy wart growing on her right cheek, entered the room.

'Good morra, Meg,' said Sheila, who was fanning the fire into flame with her apron. 'Are ye goin' to yer work?'

'Goin' to my work,' replied Meg and turned her eyes to Norah. 'A friend, I see,' she remarked.

'A countrywoman of my own,' said Sheila.

'Are ye new to Glesga?' Meg asked Norah, who was gazing absently out of the window.

'I have only just come here,' said the girl.

'Admirin' the view!' remarked Meg with a wheezy laugh as she took her place beside the girl at the window. 'A fine sight to look at, that. Dirty washin' hung out to dry; dirty houses; everything dirty. Look down at the yard!'

A four-square block of buildings with outhouses, slaty grey and ugly, scabbed on to the walls, enclosed a paved courtyard, at one corner of which stood a pump, at another a stable with a heap of manure piled high outside the door. Two grey long-bodied rats could be seen running across from the pump to the stable, a ragged tramp who had slept all night on the warm dunghill shuffled up to his feet, rubbed the sleep and dirt from his eyes, then slunk away from the place as if conscious of having done something very wrong.

'That man has slept here for many a night,' said Meg; then pointing her finger upwards over the roofs of many houses to a spire that pierced high through the smoke-laden air, she said: 'That's the Municipal Buildin's; that's where the rich people meet and talk about the best thing to be done with houses like these. It's easy to talk over yonder; that house cost five hunner and fifty thousand pounds to build. A gey guid hoose, surely, isn't it, Sheila Carrol?'

'It's comin' half-past five, Meg, and it's time ye were settin' out for yer work,' was Sheila's answer. 'Ye'd spend half yer life bletherin'.'

'A good, kindly and decent woman she is,' Sheila told Norah when Meg took her departure. 'Works very hard and, God forgive her! drinks very hard too. Nearly every penny that doesn't go in rent does in the crathur, and she's happy enough in her own way although a black Prodesan . . . Ah! there's some quare people here on this stair when ye come to know them all!'

Over a tin of tea and a crust Sheila made plans for the future. 'I can earn about one and three a day at the finishin',' she said. 'I have to buy my own thread out of that, three bobbins a week at twopence ha'penny a bobbin.'

'Ye used to be a fine knitter, Norah,' Sheila continued. 'D'ye mind the night long ago on Dooey Strand? God knows it was hardships enough for the strong women like us to sleep out in the snow, not to mention a young girsha like yerself. But ye were the great knitter then and ye'll be nimble with yer fingers yet, I'll go bail. Sewing ye might be able to take a turn at.'

'I used to be good with needle, Sheila,' said the girl.

'Then that'll be what we'll do. We'll work together, me and yerself, and we'll get on together well and cheaper. It'll be only the one fire and the one light; and now, if ye don't mind, we'll begin work and I'll show ye what's to be done.'

'A Welcome to the Waters of Loch Katrine'

JAMES NICHOLSON (1822–1897)

Thou comest to a city where men untimely die,
Where hearts in grief are swelling, and cheeks are seldom dry –
A city where merchant princes to Mammon basely kneel,
While those that drag the idol's car are crushed beneath the wheel.

Throughout her mighty system of tunnel and tube and main,
Thy healthful current is pulsing, pulsing through every vein;
In the fever den, in the attic, in cellars under the street,
The poor have long been waiting to quaff thy waters sweet.

Thou comest in thy beauty, like Godiva, long ago,
To save our sin-curst city from a tax of death and woe –
To cool the fire of the fever, and quench the fever of lust –
To moisten the lips of the dying, and moisten the poor man's crust.

O that from his inner vision thou could'st wash the scales of sin,
That thro' the darkened window heaven's glory might come in;
Restore to the cheeks of childhood the roses shed too soon,
And their infant lips will bless thee, for health is a precious boon!

O quench the fiery spirit that maddens the workman's brain,
That drags down reason from her throne, and riots in every vein,
Ere the stream becomes a river, and the river an ocean broad,
A dreary separating gulf betwixt his soul and God!

O would thy gushing waters might quench for ever and aye
Those fountains of fiery ruin that lead men's souls astray;
That drunkeries all were abolished, and, planted in their stead,
The reading-room and the school-room, and shops for the sale of bread!

'The West End'

from Aunt Bel

GUY McCRONE (1898–1977)

Guy McCrone was the cousin of James Bridie (O.H. Mavor), and was associated with Bridie in the founding of the Citizen's Theatre. He was also a respected musician and producer, who had studied music in Vienna. For a while in the 1940s and 1950s, though, he was a successful novelist, with the Wax Fruit *trilogy (*Antimacassar City, The Philistines *and* The Puritans*) proving especially popular. These novels were somewhat in the manner of Galsworthy's* The Forsyte Saga, *although with considerably more sentimentality and with somewhat superficial characterisation. They were actually historical novels, being, like* Aunt Bel, *set in the Glasgow of the 1890s.* Aunt Bel *is about probably the most interesting of his characters, Mrs Bel Moorhouse, who is by way of being a manipulator of a large family and all of their complex relationships.*

In this episode we meet her son Tom, daughter Isabel and Bel's own mother, the redoubtable Mrs Barrowfield, who represents an older Glasgow and who still lives in 'Monteith Row overlooking Glasgow Green', unaware that that district has gone down and is now 'a decaying locality'. McCrone cleverly interweaves the signs and symbols of social class and status – the excitement in this episode revolves around Bel's and Isabel's anticipation of a grand ball to be held in the wonderful new Municipal Buildings in George Square. Sometimes McCrone's historical researches show a little too clearly, as in the unconvincing detail about Tom cutting his head on the tram rail. Tom attends Kelvinside Academy, which may be a little private joke of McCrone's, who was an old boy of the rival Glasgow Academy.

The excerpt demonstrates a nice little comedy of manners, as in Bel's quite open desire to see 'their names in tomorrow's papers' and to try every subtle wile she knows to go to the ball with her husband – one who, we learn later in the novel, helps to give 'a backbone of complacent dependability to this great commercial city'.

THE WEST END

The age of twenty-one might be just the right age to set the bloom upon a son's charm, but now Bel was not so sure that nineteen did the same for a daughter.

It was shortly after two. Home only ten minutes ago, and standing on the first-floor landing, Bel cast eyes of exasperation, of frustration, of real anxiety about her, as Isabel, coming down from above, passed by glumly, carrying a hot-water can on her way to the kitchen in the basement.

'How is Tom now?' Bel asked, daring the blackness of Isabel's mood.

'If he had to cut his head open, he might at least have cut it open some other time.'

'Isabel!'

'Well, what about to-night?'

'How can you even think about to-night now?'

But Isabel merely continued on her way downstairs in quest of yet more hot water. Bel stared at her daughter's descending and indignant back. How callous young girls were becoming! How intent upon their own pleasures!

But this was serious. Her second son, Tom, had had an accident. He was for ever falling about, of course. But this time there might be concussion. Or perhaps blood-poisoning. Or a permanent and disfiguring scar.

Impotently, Bel looked about her. She turned automatically to close the door of her bedroom, from which, some minutes ago, she had hurried so abruptly, preparations for her afternoon rest interrupted. Now the March sun, bursting for a moment through gathering rain-clouds, was flooding the room with cold shafts of light. A carafe of water on her table had caught its beams, and, forming a prism, was making a little dazzle of rainbow colours. In the bedroom fireplace the flames flickered lazily in the sunshine. Over an easy-chair her husband's tail-coat had been spread out, that it should be creaseless for the evening. On a sofa her own dress of fine lace and black satin, costly, elegant, and new-made for to-night's function, was spread out to the same purpose.

The sight of it was too much for Bel. She closed the door quickly, turned, and went upstairs to the bedside of her son.

There was little of the natural nurse about her. She shrank from the sight of blood, even when, as now, it belonged to her own son. It should, she felt, be running tidily in Tom's veins and arteries. But in poor Tom's room it seemed to be everywhere.

He was now in bed. Sarah had stripped him of his dusty clothes, cleaned down his seventeen-year-old body as best she could, and got him into a nightshirt with the same firm purpose and as little embarrassment as when Tom had been a baby of three.

Sarah tyrannised over the household, as devoted servants will. There had been moments in the last years when Bel could almost have wished her away. But this afternoon she was thankful for her. Had there been no Sarah, she would have been forced to do all these unpleasant things herself. Now, Sarah being as she was, merely to offer to help would be to give offence.

Bel stood looking down upon her son. 'How do you feel now, darling?' she asked weakly.

'I don't think the cut can be very deep.'

'I wish they wid get a haud o' the doctor.' In moments of crisis Sarah was inclined to revert to the speech of working Glasgow.

'He's here.' Isabel, coming in with additional hot water, was followed by the man they were seeking. She explained how, quite providentially, Cook had recognized his brougham standing outside another house in the terrace.

The doctor was flushed and without breath from climbing two flights of stairs. He gave Mrs Moorhouse a friendly and deferential hand, speech being impossible for the moment, and shook a chubby and elderly fist with reassuring and professional playfulness at the boy on the bed. Thereafter he crossed over, sat down and took the patient's wrist in one hand, while he stroked his beard with the other.

'Pulse all right,' he said presently. Then he bent over Thomas Moorhouse and asked: 'And what do you think you've been doing to yourself, young man?'

Bel explained for him. Tom *would* ride his bicycle to school. This was quite unnecessary, with Kelvinside Academy so near. But there it was. Tom was always in a hurry. And Tom had a trick of using only one hand, while the other grasped his schoolbooks and what not. He had set out thus after the midday meal. So far as his mother could gather, he had swerved to avoid a flying hansom, got his wheels stuck in the groove of a tram-rail, and come down, cutting his head on the metal rail itself.

The doctor, who had been examining him, sat back, and said thoughtfully: 'Yes. Now I see what's what.' Adding: 'Good thing the trams are not electrified yet, or you might have been electrocuted into the bargain, Tommy.' He stood up. 'I'll have to do a bit of sewing. I think I'll take off my coat to it. So perhaps Mrs Moorhouse – I'll look in and tell you how he is when it's finished. In the drawing-room?'

Only too glad to take the hint, Bel and her daughter withdrew, leaving Tom with the doctor and Sarah.

Bel was not alarmed any more. The doctor had reassured her. She had begun to share her daughter's annoyance at Tom's very inconvenient, irresponsible behaviour. To-day of all days! Aimlessly she now followed Isabel into her bedroom. Like her mother's, Isabel's ball dress lay waiting, virgin white and new. On her dressing-table were a mother-of-pearl fan given her for the occasion by her father, one or two trinkets and long white gloves. In tissue paper, white and unsullied, were a pair of satin slippers.

Bel stroked the dress disconsolately. No. It was too bad of Tom. They had looked forward to the Lord Provost's Ball for weeks now. Although there had already been two such balls given in the new Municipal Buildings, this was to be by far the most brilliant; in celebration of the extension of the City of Glasgow's boundaries. Everybody was going. She had read that the Lord Mayor of every English and Irish city of consequence had been invited – beginning with the Lord Mayor of London. And, of course, the Lord Provost of every other Scottish city that was important enough to possess one. And, in addition, many of the real aristocracy were to be present.

Just after Christmas she had asked her husband, Arthur, to make certain that he, she and their elder children should receive cards. They would be nobodies, she had insisted, if their names did not appear in the published lists of those present.

Then, in the middle of January, a blow had fallen. The Prince of Wales's elder son, the Duke of Clarence, had died of the influenza that was then sweeping the country. The Court was in mourning. National and municipal functions throughout the land were cancelled.

But suddenly the ball had been reannounced for the middle of March. Bel and Isabel breathed once more. Now they could order their dresses. Black for Bel. White for Isabel. They must remain on the side of discretion this spring. Besides, what could be more becoming to a fair and comely dowager of forty-six than elegant black? Or virgin white to her nineteen-year-old counterpart?

And now Tom had appeared at the front door in a welter of dust and worse, on this the very afternoon of the great day! Just when his mother and sister had gone to rest themselves, that they might be in the best of looks for the evening.

'I think,' Bel said to Isabel, her voice full of exasperation, 'you might ask Cook to make a cup of tea.'

'It's only half-past two.'

'Never mind. I feel we need it. And perhaps the doctor, when he's finished with Tom –'

As Isabel descended the stairs yet again she became aware that her spirits were rising. She knew now, that if her mother could find a loophole, they would still go to-night.

In half an hour more the doctor was sitting in the drawing-room, drinking tea and telling Tom's mother and sister just what a nasty gash Tom had given himself, implying modestly that he, the doctor, was not quite unskilled, perhaps, in the sewing up of faces, and reassuring Bel that her younger son's handsomeness would, in the end, be none the worse for having had a difference with the tram-rails of Great Western Road.

'But what about poisoning, Doctor? Or concussion? What if he starts a temperature?'

'Well, Mrs Moorhouse, you could take his temperature – let me see – in the late afternoon; and again in the evening. My assistant would come round at once if anything was wrong.' And in answer to a look from Bel: 'You see, I'll be going with my wife to the Municipal Buildings to-night.'

'That's what *we* were hoping to do, Doctor!' The words burst from Isabel.

Bel was grateful to her. Now, without seeming unmaternal, she could smile at the child's impulsiveness, exchange knowing looks with the doctor and say: 'Isabel is going to be very disappointed. Do you think, Doctor–?'

The doctor put the tips of his fingers together, and sat gazing out into the Botanic Gardens opposite. 'Well, Mrs Moorhouse, I don't know really,' he said with maddening slowness. 'I wouldn't quite say–'

'Then we'll just give up the idea,' Bel said hurriedly, not because she had made up her mind to do any such thing, but because the doctor's pompous slowness had become unendurable. This produced the result she sought.

The doctor became alert. 'No, no, no! Go by all means, if your arrangements are made. The lad is fine. That's a grand woman that Sarah of yours. And it would be a pity for my young friend Isabel to miss–'

But all obstruction was not yet at an end.

At the proper tea-hour, Bel's mother, Mrs Barrowfield, descended from a cab. Mrs Barrowfield was vigorous, masculine-featured and very old. The Battle of Waterloo had been won when she was ten. She declared that she still remembered the bonfire and other celebrations on Glasgow Green. In so far as her clothes followed any fashions, they were those of the sixties. Even Bel was not now sure if the hard, grey side-curls were still her own. As old people will, Mrs Barrowfield doted on her grandchildren and bullied her daughter.

She found Bel in the drawing-room by herself. 'I just came up to see ye gettin' dressed,' she said, seizing her and giving her a vigorous kiss.

Bel received these advances coldly. 'How will you get home again, Mother?' she asked.

'I thought, maybe, you could leave here ten minutes early. That would give you time to drop me at the Row.' Mrs Barrowfield chose a comfortable chair and looked about her, beaming.

Bel was furious. The old lady had a flat in Monteith Row overlooking Glasgow Green – a decaying locality that Bel had wanted her to leave years ago. And now Mrs Barrowfield was suggesting that she, too, should squeeze into the family carriage on its way to the Municipal Buildings, crushing their finery, forcing Arthur, Senior, who would be cross enough already, to hurry his dressing, and causing them all to make a tiresome detour for nothing.

Besides, she hadn't wanted her mother to be here this evening, taking in every detail of her toilet. Bel had just discovered the virtues of tinted rice-powder. If she locked herself in the bathroom and applied it discreetly, it did wonders, Bel found, to a forty-six-year-old face. Her husband, Arthur, never really looked at her now, and she could count on the children noticing nothing. But it would not escape the old lady. Mrs Barrowfield's glasses were strong.

'Tom fell off his bicycle to-day and cut his head very badly,' Bel said maliciously, intent upon destroying her mother's smug cheerfulness.

'Tom? Have ye had the doctor?'

Already Bel regretted what she had said. She was beginning to glimpse the trouble she had loosed upon her own head. 'Oh yes, Mother. The doctor had to put in several stitches. But he says he'll be all right – that we needn't worry.'

'That's all very fine.'

'What do you mean, Mother?' Bel resented her tone. It implied that she, Bel, was taking Tom's mishap lightly.

'What happened?'

Dutifully, and at length, Bel told Tom's grandmother all that had occurred.

'Puir lamb!' Mrs Barrowfield took up her cup and stirred it thoughtfully.

'Yes; it's unfortunate,' Bel hazarded.

The old lady swallowed down her tea and held out her cup for more. 'Well,' she said with decision, 'that's the finish of your high jinks.'

'I don't understand, Mother.' But Bel understood perfectly; had, indeed, expected it. Her mother would, of course, now disapprove of her going to-night. But to have this entertainment given by the Lord Provost of Glasgow to the more important of his fellow-citizens, to the mayors and provosts of other towns, and to the aristocracy of the west of Scotland, called 'high jinks', jarred upon Bel's sense of propriety. Couldn't her mother see that their appearance, tonight, and the mention of their names in tomorrow's papers, would add cubits to the family stature?

'You canna go when the boy's had a serious accident.'

'But the doctor says it's not serious.'

Mrs Barrowfield merely drew herself up, looked at Bel coldly, and said: 'You can never be sure.'

'The young doctor's coming in to-night just to make certain he's all right.'

'Fancy'. Mrs Barrowfield had brought the baiting of her daughter to a fine art. Now she was implying that Bel was a heartless pleasure-seeker, quite unworthy of two fine sons and a pretty daughter.

'Hullo, Granny!'

As Isabel came into the room, Bel signalled to her with raised eyebrows and a look of desperation. She added the cue: 'Your granny says we are all to stay at home to-night and look after Tom.'

As Bel had intended, the Grosvenor Terrace ranks closed with a snap.

Isabel came forward, kissed her grandmother's glum face and sat kittenishly on the arm of her chair. 'You don't really, do you Granny?'

'It's yer duty.'

'Did you never want to go to balls, Granny?'

'Not if anybody's life was in danger.'

Isabel's voice took on a note of panic. 'Danger? Is Tom's life in danger? Oh, Granny, I didn't know!'

'Well, maybe not in danger, but–'

'Granny! You've no right to frighten me like that! I thought you had heard something I didn't know.' She grasped her grandmother's hand as though she sought its comfort.

The old lady's face relaxed. That was better. 'You're a silly wee thing,' she said, patting Isabel affectionately.

'And Mother and I have our new dresses,' Isabel added dejectedly.

Bel watched her daughter with amazement. If she herself had tried any such crude tactics at Isabel's age, Mrs Barrowfield would have reacted very differently.

'I tell you what I'll do,' the old lady said. 'If ye give me a bed here, I'll stay and see that the boy's all right. And ye can all go out and enjoy yerselves.'

'Oh, Granny! How kind!'

Isabel's mother was not, for the moment, sure that she did not want to smack Isabel for this. But an instant's reflection told her that the child had been right. It would save a stand-up battle and all the fuss about taking her mother home. The old lady would have the satisfaction of seeing them adorned in all their splendour, and the invalid would not now be overlooked. If, in the course of the evening, Mrs Barrowfield came to blows with an equally domineering Sarah, she, Bel, would not be there to see.

And thus it was that when the two Arthur Moorhouses – father and son – arrived home rather earlier than usual, they were received by a loving old lady, who kissed them both affectionately, told them that young Tom had had a little accident, but there was nothing whatever to be alarmed about, that it was really little more than a scratch; that she had consented to stay overnight, as anxiety must in no way be allowed to mix with their enjoyment; that Bel and Isabel were already gone to dress, and would look lovely in their new ball dresses. And were the Arthurs quite sure they wouldn't like a hurried cup of tea before they, too, went up to change?

'Hullo, Glesca Hielanders!'

from Courtin' Christina

J.J. (JOHN JOY) BELL (1871–1934)

Roughly contemporary with Neil Munro's Erchie and Para Handy, the Wee Macgreegor stories by J.J. Bell first appeared in the Glasgow Evening Times *in 1901. It is probable that there was an element of competition with Munro's characters, since they came out in the rival evening paper, the* Evening News. *At the same time, there is no doubt that, together, Erchie and Macgreegor established the idea that the life and manners of the Glasgow working class was an appropriate subject for literature. Both were taken to the hearts of Glasgow people, as can be judged by the fact that they enjoyed a wide membership when they reappeared in book form. This story comes from the second of the collections.*

Like Erchie, Macgreegor lives in that archetypal Glasgow dwelling – the tenement. He and his immediate family are firmly of the working class and when he grows up (most of the stories have Macgreegor as a wee boy), he takes a trade as a painter before joining his Uncle Robert in the grocery business. There is at the same time a feeling that the Robinsons are hard-working and well-doing enough to be able to find a penny to buy Macgreegor some toffee or take him to the Zoo for a treat.

This safe, ordered and perhaps just a bit cosy world, where the worst that can happen is breaking an aunt's teacup or being banned from the Sunday School soiree (the Robinsons are pretty evidently a part of the Glasgow version of the Protestant ascendancy), was suddenly shattered by the outbreak of the 1914–18 War. On his nineteenth birthday Macgreegor answered the patriotic call and enlisted along with many others from the city in the 9th Battalion Highland Light Infantry – the Glasgow Highlanders. The story included here describes how he is wounded in action in Flanders – unlike other writers of the period, Bell takes a realistic and, most surprisingly, an unsentimental approach to the Great War. The wounded Macgreegor is rescued by his pal from Glasgow, Willie Thomson, a weak and inadequate personality whom Bell shows as finding strength and a sense of purpose in his army service. Willie helps to keep his friend's spirits up by talking about life back in Glasgow. Wounded, Macgreegor is shipped home to Blighty and reunited with his Christina. So, all ends happily; but in this story many of the clouds of sentimentality characteristic of the period are blown away by a wind of realism, as can be seen from its opening sentence.

HULLO, GLESCA HIELANDERS!

Like a trodden, forgotten thing Private Macgregor Robinson lay on the Flanders mud, under the murk and rain. A very long time it seemed since that short, grim struggle amid the blackness and intermittent brightness. The night was still rent with noise and light, but the storm of battle had passed from the place where he had fallen. He could not tell whether his fellows had taken the enemy's trench or retired to their own. He had the vaguest ideas as to where he was. But he knew that there was pain in his left shoulder and right foot, that he was athirst, also that he had killed a man – a big stout man, old enough to have been his father. He tried not to think of the last, though he did not regret it: it had been a splendid moment.

He was not the only soldier lying there in the mud, but the others, friend or foe, were quite still. The sight of them in the flashes distressed him, yet always his gaze drifted back to them. His mind was a medley of thoughts, from the ugliest to the loveliest. At last, for he was greatly exhausted, his head drooped to his uninjured arm, his eyes closed. For a while he dozed. Then something disturbed him, and he raised himself and peered. In the flicker of a distant flare he saw a shape approaching him, crawling on hands and knees, very slowly, pausing for an instant at each still figure. It made Macgregor think of a big dog searching for its master – only it wore a helmet. Macgregor, setting his teeth, drew his rifle between his knees and unfixed the bayonet. . .

'Hist! Is that you, Macgreegor?'

'Wullie!'

'Whisht, ye – !'

'Oh, Wullie' – in a whisper – 'I'm gled to see ye!'

'I believe ye!' gasped Willie, and flattened out at his friend's side, breathing heavily. At the end of a minute or so – 'Ha'e ye got it bad, Macgreegor?' he inquired.

'So, so. Arm an' leg. I'm feelin' rotten, but I'm no finished yet. Ha'e ye ony water? Ma bottle's shot through.'

'Here ye are. . . Feelin' seeck-like?'

'I'm seeck at gettin' knocked oot at the vera beginnin.'

'Never heed. Did ye kill yer man?'

'Ay.'

'Same here. . . In the back. . . Ma Goad!'

'Ha'e we ta'en their trench?'

'Ay; but not enough o' us to haud it. We're back in the auld place. Better luck next time. No safe to strike a match here; could dae fine wi' a fag.'

There was a silence between them, broken at last by Macgregor.

'Hoo did ye find me, Wullie? What way are ye no back in the trench?'

'Wasna gaun back wi'oot ye – I seen ye drap – even if ye had been a corp. . . Been snokin aroun' seekin' ye for Guid kens hoo lang. I'm fair hingin' wi' glaur.'

'. . .I'm obleeged to ye, Wullie, but ye shouldna ha'e done it. Whauraboots are we?'

'I wisht I was sure. Lost ma bearin's. I doobt we're nearer the Germans nor oor ain lot. That's the reason I'm weerin' this dish-cover. But it's your turn to weer it. Ye've been wounded a'ready.'

'Na, na, Wullie!'

'Dae what I tell ye, ye – !' Willie made the exchange of headgear. . . 'I say, Macgreegor!'

'What?'

'This is Flanders. Ye mind oor bet? Weel, we're quits noo. I'm no owin' ye onything – eh?'

Macgregor grinned in spite of everything.

'Ay, we're quits noo, Wullie, sure enough.'

'If ever we get oot o' this, will ye len' us dew francs?'

' 'Deed, ay. . . Wullie, ye're riskin' yer life for me.'

'Awa' an chase yersel'! I wonder what that girl o' yours is thinkin'aboot the noo – if she's no sleepin'.'

There was a pause till Macgregor said awkwardly: 'Christina's finished wi' me.'

'Eh?'

'I couldna tell ye afore; but she had got wind o' Maggie.'

'Maggie! Oh, hell! But no frae me, Macgreegor, no frae me! Ye believe that?'

'Oh, ay.'

Willie let off sundry curses. 'But I suppose I'm to blame,' he said bitterly.

'Naebody to blame but masel'.'

'But did ye no explain to Christina? A' ye did was to canoodle wi' the wrang girl, pro tem. – a thing that happens daily. I couldna fancy a girl that naebody had ever wanted to cuddle; an' if I was a girl I couldna fancy a chap that –'

'Nae use talkin' aboot it, Wullie,' Macgregor said sadly, wearily.

'Aw, but her an' you'll mak' it up afore ye're done. If ye dinna, I'll want to kill masel' an' Maggie forbye. A' the same, I wisht fat Maggie was here the noo. I could dae fine wi' a bit squeeze.'

'My! ye're a fair treat!' said Macgregor, chuckling in his misery.

' '*Sh*! Keep still! Something comin'!'

The distant gun-fire had diminished. There were appreciable silences between the blasts. But during a flash Macgregor detected a helmeted crawling shape. Willie's hand stole out and grasped the bayonet.

'Number twa!' he muttered, with a stealthy movement. 'I maun get him!'

But Macgregor's ears caught a faint sound that caused him to grip the other's wrist. 'Wait,' he whispered.

The helmeted shape came on, looking neither to right nor left, and as it came it sobbed. And it passed within a few yards of them, and into the deeper gloom, sobbing, sobbing.

'Oh, Christ!' sighed Willie, shuddering. 'Put yer arm roun' me, Mac. I'm feart.'

Five minutes later he affected to jeer at himself. 'Weel, I'm rested noo,' he continued, 'an' it's time we was gettin' a move on. Mornin's comin', and' if we're spotted here, we're done for. Can ye creep?'

Macgregor tried and let out a little yelp.

'Na, ye canna. Ye'll jist ha'e to get on ma back.'

'Wullie, gang yersel' –'

'Obey yer corporal!'

'Ye're no a corp –'

'If they dinna mak' me a corporal for this, I'll quit the service! Onyway, I'm no gaun wi'oot ye. Same time, I canna guarantee no to tak' ye to the German lines. But we maun risk that. Ye'll ha'e to leave yer rifle, but keep on the dish-cover till I gi'e ye the word. . . Noo then! Nae hurry. I'll ha'e to creep the first part o' the journey. Are ye ready? Weel, here's luck to the twa o' us!'

There is no authentic description of that horrible journey save Willie's, which is unprintable.

It was performed literally by inches. More than once Willie collapsed, groaning, under his burden. Macgregor, racked as he was, shed tears for his friend's sake. Time had no significance except as a measure of suspense and torture. But Willie held on, directed by some instinct, it seemed, over that awful shell-fragment-studded mire, round the verges of shell-formed craters, past dead and wounded waiting for succour – on, on, till the very guns seemed to have grown weary, and the rain ceased, and the air grew chillier as with dread of what the dawn should disclose, and the blackness was diluted to grey.

'Drap the – dish-cover,' croaked Willie, and halted for a minute's rest.

Then on again. But at long last Willie muttered: 'I think it's oor trench. If I'm wrang, fareweel to Argyle Street! I'll ha'e to risk gi'ein' them a hail in case some silly blighter lets fly in this rotten licht. Slip doon, Mac – nae hurry – nae use hurtin' yersel' for naething. I'll maybe ha'e to hurt ye in a meenute... Noo for it!' He lifted up his voice. 'Hullo, Glesca Hielanders!'

It seemed an age until –

'Right oh!' came a cheerful response.

'Hurray!' yelled Willie, and rose stiffly to his feet.

Then with a final effort, he gave Macgregor the 'fireman's lift', and staggered and stumbled, amid shots from the other side, into safety.

‘The Building’

from The Tenement

IAIN CRICHTON SMITH (1928–1998)

The Tenement *is, like much of Smith's work in English at any rate, an extremely individualistic piece, difficult to define – probably a themed collection of short stories would be nearest. It has a series of short individual narratives set next to each other like residents in a tenement, or like flats opening off a common close and stair.*

Poet, novelist and dramatist, Smith came from Lewis and was educated at Nicolson Institute and Aberdeen University. He went on to teach English in Clydebank, Dumbarton and, closer to home, Oban High School. He was bilingual (and prolific) in Gaelic and English, with an unassailable reputation as a poet in both. In prose, his output was extremely varied, ranging from the much-loved Consider the Lilies *(with its marvellous picture of the old woman), a short novel showing a society in disintegration at the time of the Clearances, to the mischievously surreal* Murdo and Other Stories, *where at every turn of the page we seem to hear Iain Crichton Smith's own distinctively wheezy chuckle.*

This chapter from The Tenement *is pivotal to the book: in it Smith suggests the building itself has a kind of organic growth – just one of many metaphors for the peculiar form of communal life and at the same time alienation that is a tenement: ‘For some trivial reason one tenant might not talk to another one, for weeks, for months, for years: every one of us has his own dignity, his own honour.’ The chapter is really more like a prose poem than a story, with image succeeding image. Perhaps the metaphor which sticks in the mind is the tenement as ‘simply the stage on which things happen’. It seems clear that its actual location is unimportant, although there is mention of Helensburgh at one point in the book, and since the tenement is the type of building which is most characteristic of Glasgow (and since Smith was born there, moving to Stornoway at the age of two), its place in this anthology seems appropriate.*

THE BUILDING

The tenement was over a hundred years old. It faced the street with its grey granite stone, and its old windows which in order to be cleaned had to be manoeuvred on ropes like glassy sails, and its greenish door on which passing boys and men had scrawled graffiti. There were six flats in the tenement, some in good condition, some in bad: stone stairs led from floor to floor. Outside at the back was a maze of old pipes winding like rusty snakes: these usually suffered from bursts in the winter time, and there were arguments among the tenants about payment to the plumber.

The roof often needed repair, as water would come in on the tenants in the top flats. Four of the flats had been bought outright, two were rented. It was by no means the worst tenement in the street, for opposite it were worse ones, composed of cheap brick. In the latter, parties went on at weekends – there were rumours of prostitution – and on summer nights boys would sit on balconies shouting insults at the tourists or playing radios very loudly. Or they would emerge from the close on large black foreign bikes.

At night the tenants of the tenement would hear the shouts and songs of passing drunks, floating up from the street, as if magnified by the stone of the pavements or the walls. 'I'll cut you up, you bastard,' one voice would say, and another one, 'Pass the f. . .ing bottle!' Quarrels would break out suddenly between those who had minutes before been friends. Girls and women would scream as if they had been knifed and there would be the drumming of running feet. The women's language was as bad as that of the men and they would be heard encouraging two fighters. 'Put the f. . .ing boot in!' one would hear a girl scream in ecstasy. And the night was a time of preying, of quarrelling, of demented cries, as of shrill birds with bitter beaks.

The weather around the tenement changed. On spring days it was dry and clear, on summer days it was steamy and hot, on autumn days it was regretful and nostalgic, on winter days it was slushy and wet. And many different families over the years had seen that change in the weather, in the atmosphere, for there was considerable movement to and from the tenement. Wardrobes, sideboards and mirrors reflecting scarred whitewashed walls, were carried upstairs and downstairs. Chairs and sofas were abandoned momentarily on a landing. Wallpaper was stripped and pasted on, ceilings were painted, there was a flowering of hope and a fading of it. Old ranges were removed, new fireplaces installed. Ancient bells that had wires, and tinkled in the kitchen, were replaced by push-button ones. A whole world was born, a whole world ceased. In one flat there might be a din of modern music, in another the sentimental tones of John MacCormack, in yet another no music at all.

And everywhere there was a sense of the past as if while one was sitting in the living room the door might open and a woman or man dressed in Edwardian clothes might enter. When one was, for instance, stripping wallpaper one might find a message written by newly weds eighty years before – JOHN AND AGNES SIGNED THIS. Or it might say, WILLIAM STEEL, CARPENTER. What days, what nights, what suns, what moons, had circled that tenement: what beds had produced what children, who had perhaps played on the stairs, on the diminutive green at the back of the tenement where the washing was hung out on windy days, a gallery of mended shirts and vests and blouses.

Some tenants had kept cats against the law, some had not. Some had been working men, some had been professional men just starting, for in later, more successful years they would move from the tenement. And yet, perhaps it left its mark on all of them, so that, in their later private houses or in the windy council schemes, they would always remember the period, long or short, that they had spent there.

One could not say that the coming together into that tenement was anything other than a random action. The flats were like nests which happened to be beside each other, to which different birds came. It happened that two name-plates shone beside each other: there was nothing predestined about it. The inhabitants landed and left, and once they had left they might never see each other again. No roots were set down here as in villages, no stones echoed with remembered events, and the moon above it was not a local one. The curtains on the windows were of different colours, there were different coloured carpets on the floors, different ambitions inside the rooms. The flats existed differently in the minds of those who had left them and those who occupied them. Some remembered them with affection and some with loathing. Some could hardly believe that they had once lived there and, passing the building years later, in a car perhaps, would look up at the window of a room they had once occupied and feel an intense absence. Could they really have lived there? Surely not. Maybe they had inhabited different bodies then. They might even have an impulse to visit the flat again: where there had once been yellow armchairs there were now red ones, where once there had been an ancient bath as big as a stone grave, there was now a bathroom suite in warm colours.

The tenement survived all individuals who had inhabited it, the particulars which had been and gone. It survived the relentless blizzard of names, the ambitions, the despairs, the joys, the weddings, the funerals. It was like a soul which animates the body. Something of itself passed into the people who lived in it. Sweat leaked from the walls as if the tenement itself were perspiring. It sailed into the night and sailed back in the morning. With its eight windows facing the street it brooded over cars, pedestrians, the church opposite where the photographer knelt on a windy spring day as the bride's gown billowed outwards like a wave, as the shining black hearse moved slowly away with its crowns of flowers, as the minister stood meditatively near the gravestones in his black robe.

Beside it was a cafe that was open till eleven o'clock at night, in front of it was the church. Not far from it was the school, also built in grey granite. Its close was a mouth that swallowed, spat out. Its walls had graffiti on it almost as mysterious as Egyptian writing. Its bulging scarred green door had been painted years before. There was a window on the first landing which had white lacy curtains across it. The window on the second landing was uncurtained. The stairs were washed once a week. The landing lights were put on on alternate weeks by neighbouring tenants. For some trivial reason one tenant might not talk to another one, for weeks, for months, for years: every one of us has his own dignity, his own honour. It might be that one had used the other's bin without permission, or had forgotten his week for the light, or had heard the other talking behind his back. And these slights were burrs sticking in the heart, throbbing, feverish. For each one cries out, I am, I am, even in a tenement, perhaps especially in a tenement.

The building occupied space, occupied time. Around it other buildings had crumbled, risen, changed ownership. Its stone had been taken from a quarry that no longer existed. Its original masons, joiners, painters, were all dead. As Keats says that individual nightingales die though the generic nightingale doesn't, so each tenant would die but the tenement would seem to live for ever.

Sometimes the tenement could be imagined as a tree with transient nests in it, sometimes as composed of boxes that in turn held coffins, cradles, sometimes as a theatre where casts (actors and actresses) changed as they moved on to other plays. It might even be that the young ones were the old come back again in a different disguise or mask. The tenement in its transient solidity encouraged such speculations and baffled them by its enigmatic front. Windows too could be seen as eyes, fading, brightening. The door – what was it but the entrance to a fertile womb that bred incessantly? It was a prison door, it was a door for escaping through. It was a door which hid secrets, which released them to the world.

On spring days curtains, often white, fluttered at windows like ghosts trying to get in or trying to get out, with frantic motions, with fragile winds.

Any story that can be told about one tenant has at best only a frail relationship to the story of another tenant but there will be some connection, however passing, however faint. And sometimes the tenants can act together, each having his own idea of what is happening, each taking a colour from the others, each merging briefly with the others like a cloud fading into a second one. So that the tenement itself can be seen not as made of stone but like a cloud that changes shape, merciful, cruel, wandering.

At the time of which we are speaking, there were no children in the tenement, maybe because most of the flats weren't large. Old people, mostly widowed, stayed in them, or young couples as yet without children. Perhaps the tenement was too old to put up with children, perhaps it didn't like them. Perhaps the tenement itself was drawing to its end, and had had in its day its complement of children which had left and never returned. Perhaps it hated ingratitude, random brilliance, wanted to settle down in its old age. Who can tell about a tenement? Maybe it said to couples with children, This is not the place for you; Go somewhere else. I have had enough of young ones, I have grown philosophical, children have no history, I can't learn from them. I only want those who have lived, not those who are about to live. I am a listener to stories that have happened, not stories that might happen years from now. And in any case I know that the children will live their lives out elsewhere, far from here, even if they stay for a brief time. My face is a Greek one, flat and incurious, like one of these blind stone faces that one sees in a garden wall in Greece. I have neither love nor hate, I am simply the stage on which things happen. And nothing of importance happens to children. And in any case that is all that life is, a passing show. I am not so stupid or so proud as to think that I am anything other than a habitation: I do not confer a meaning. Perhaps there is no meaning. Perhaps I am the only meaning there is. Perhaps I am a hundred meanings, a thousand. Perhaps I am a dementia of my tenants, a chimera. I am changed, plastered anew, and to all that I submit. Yet there is in me something that is always recognizable, that exists through all alterations, all neglect. And perhaps that memory will persist somewhere even when my stone has crumbled to dust, and perhaps passing on a certain day in summer or autumn someone will be struck by a thought that is not his own but is wafted from me. Is there anyone who knows? Or is all, mystery?

‘Heaven Knows’

JANET HAMILTON (1795–1873)

Lines on the Trial of Madeleine Smith for the Murder of L’Angelier

Shade of the hapless stranger, lost L’Angelier,
   Whose life’s young light was quenched in guilt and shame,
Say, haunt’st thou still the lane, the fatal gate,
   Where to thy arms the fair, false syren came?

We seek not now thy ‘merits to disclose,
   Or draw thy frailties from their dread abode’;
We would not sit in judgment on the man
   Whose soul hath stood before the bar of God.

‘Not proven’ was thy thrice-repeated deed,
   Thou of the stony heart and dauntless eye:
Smile not; in Heaven’s high court thou yet shalt hear
   The unerring proven verdict of the sky.

A lovely isle lies cradled in the deep,
   Its flowery glades embowered in fruitful trees,
A weeping mother wanders on the beach
   And pours her sorrows on the seaward breeze.

Ah! to her widowed heart her only son
   She last had clasped upon that island shore;
He came, he saw, he loved, he sinned, he died –
   We wait till Heaven and time shall tell us more.

'The Like of Them'

from No Mean City

ALEXANDER MCARTHUR (1901–1947)
AND H. KINGSLEY LONG

This chapter comes from No Mean City, *a book which has been the subject of much controversy since its first publication in 1935. Critics such as Maurice Lindsay see this curious hybrid work as the cobbled together product of two different writers and an uneasy blend of fiction and journalism. Lindsay says of McArthur, 'the pathetic, unsuccessful journalist who dragged himself out of the slums to achieve, with the aid of a ghost-writer,* No Mean City, *and then, having lifted the lid off the fester of the notorious Gorbals, sank back into it again'. That apart, there is no doubt that the book immediately found an eager readership. In less than a year it went through six impressions and has continued to enjoy healthy sales right up to the present day.*

The setting, of course, is the Gorbals and adjacent areas of Glasgow – with places like Crown Street and Plantation often being mentioned. The cast is made up of the families or 'slummies' who live there, but most prominent of the players are the young warriors, simultaneously feared and admired, the 'razor-kings' as the authors call them. The main incident in this chapter is the confrontation between two brothers, one, Johnnie Stark, who is a 'razor king' and Peter, who is 'doing fairly well at his work' and is therefore labelled 'bourgeois'. Because of a certain amount of harping on about terms like 'bourgeois' and 'education,' the journalistic part of the book begins to pall at times. Its main strength, on the other hand, is the raw savagery of some of the speeches put into the mouths of the gang members like Johnnie. At times it is possible to see the macho appeal of such characters, who perhaps evoke memories of the 'gangster pictures' so much appreciated by cinema-loving Glasgow. Certainly, at the close of the chapter, there is a kind of Sicilian reverence about the way Mrs Stark (the brothers' mother) announces that a newly-born infant is 'a boy!' – in other words a male who can carry on the macho tradition of life in the Gorbals.

FROM *NO MEAN CITY*

'Publishers' Note'

In June 1934 Mr Alexander McArthur, writing from an address in the Gorbals, Glasgow, submitted to us two short novels.

Although neither of these was considered suitable for publication, we were greatly struck with their astonishing revelations concerning life in one section of the Empire's second city. Mr McArthur, we were told, had ben unemployed for the past five years and had fought the inevitable demoralisation of 'the idle years' (the title of one of his manuscripts) by writing novel after novel – without ever achieving publication – his scene being always the slums of Glasgow and his characters the men and women who shared with himself the tenement houses and the streets. He wrote with complete candour of the degradation, frustrated hopes and misery of the people, of the gangs and street battles in which young men found a vent for unused energy, and of the amazingly amoral acceptance of conditions which one could not call civilised. But unfortunately he could not present either his story or his characters in a manner that would secure the attention of the majority of readers.

Mr H. Kingsley Long, a London journalist, whom we had asked to read Mr McArthur's manuscript, visited Glasgow in September 1934, called on Mr McArthur there and told us, on his return to London, that he was much impressed by what he had seen and heard during that visit. Subsequently we invited Mr McArthur to London, and in the course of a number of interviews we satisfied ourselves as to the essential truth of his account of slum life in one section of Glasgow. Mr Kingsley Long also had many interviews with him, after which he and Mr McArthur decided to collaborate. This novel is the outcome of that collaboration.

'Authors' Preface'

The Authors wish to state that their novel deals only with one seam in the crowded life of the Empire's Second City. In their view unemployment and overcrowding are primarily responsible for conditions which may be paralleled in all great cities, but which are, perhaps, more conspicuous in Glasgow than in any other.

It is only fair to add that no other city is making a more determined effort to rehouse and to help its poorer citizens. Nor should it ever be forgotten that Glasgow, with less than a sixth of London's population, carries an equal burden of workless men and women.

A. McA.
H. K. L.

THE LIKE OF THEM

An understanding and reasoned contempt for one's neighbours, together with a fiercely *un*reasoning conviction of personal superiority, is not an uncommon phenomenon of the slum mind. Habit and custom may blind a man to squalor of his home, but they may not prevent him from sniffing disdainfully when he enters a friend's 'hoose' no more sordid, dirty and overcrowded than his own. Perhaps there is, all the time, a subconscious rebellion against conditions which are outwardly taken for granted. And, as there is no escape from these conditions except by imagination, many a tenement dweller, particularly before the years have withered his hopes, likes to think, and does, in fact, believe that he has something in him – some special gift of mind or body – to make him different from his fellows. He is always hoping, like Micawber, for something to turn up. In face of all evidence to the contrary, he is still confident that the day will come when his superiority will compel recognition.

It follows that society in the tenements is graded far more narrowly than in the outside world. One street may be definitely 'better class' than another and not such good class as a third. Families that have two rooms look down upon those that live in a 'single end'. Immense importance attaches to clothes, for, other things being equal, young people who are 'well put on' can always command the envious admiration of the poorly dressed. 'Education' also counts for a great deal, but the word is not given its proper meaning. In the Gorbals, for instance, the tendency is to look up to people who do not habitually speak the broad Glasgow dialect. Their 'education' consists in certain refinements of speech and avoidance of slang. Just as the uneducated Englishman is somewhat impressed by the superior 'Oxford accent' so, but in much greater degree, is the slum dweller impressed by the refined speech of a fellow slummie.

The advent of Bolshevism in distant Russia has had many diverse and unexpected effects in other countries. It has, for instance, crystallised in a single word the tenement-dweller's vague aspirations to social advancement. 'Bourgeois' is that word. In the Clyde valley and in South Wales and in the Durham coalfields and in all densely populated areas of extreme poverty, Communism has spread like a contagion or a Holy War. But in Glasgow at all events it has spread chiefly from mouth to mouth as a grand, but ill-comprehended word. It is a slogan and not a faith, for there is no faith among the masses in the slums. Any revolutionary preaching the class war, promising, that is to say, the overthrow of the 'haves' for the benefit of the 'have-nots', is assured of an approving audience. But most of them do not care a damn for his politics and have scant faith in his sincerity. They may vote 'Red', but that is because, whatever happens, *they* have nothing to lose. They may curse the 'bourgeoisie', but their personal dream of heaven upon earth is to be numbered in its ranks.

And so it happens that, except among the real 'politicians' and enthusiasts, the secret ambition of the slums is to present a 'bourgeois' front to the world.

Young Peter Stark, doing fairly well at his work and living now with the McGilverys, who were distinctly 'better class' than his own family, would have declared himself a Communist without hesitation and yet nothing pleased him more than to be taken for a 'bourgeois'. He wore a soft felt hat and twisted the brim jauntily in the 'bourgeois' manner. He was cultivating a small moustache chiefly because he thought it would give him the desired 'bourgeois' appearance. He never went out without collar and tie. And, though he was really better educated and more widely read than most of his companions, he was not truly interested in any possible reorganisation of society itself, but only in his own escape from the unsuccessful poverty-stricken masses of poor fools who constituted 'the proletariat'.

And he classed his elder brother among them although he knew that Johnnie was 'ambitious' like himself. It was certainly better to be a 'Razor King' than just one of the gang, but Peter felt sure that it wouldn't lead to anything worth while. It might, on the other hand, prejudice his own chances to have a brother who was too notorious and so Peter kept out of Johnnie's way and seldom looked in upon his own family in Crown Street.

Thus it happened that he learned of Johnnie's official engagement to Lizzie Ramsay, not from his mother or sisters, but from Martha Ramsay, who met him by chance one Saturday evening in Argyle Street. Peter, very smart in brown coat and soft felt hat, stood on the kerb near the Central Station Bridge with an evening newspaper under his arm. From time to time his fingers went to his upper lip to caress the budding moustache. He was thinking that people might easily mistake him for a good class office worker, even a bank clerk.

Martha Ramsay herself, who knew him only by sight, was immediately impressed as she came towards him by his complete difference from Razor King. She thought that Peter, at all events, would be a brother-in-law to be proud of. She stopped for a moment to pat her hair and smooth her blouse. Then she came up to him. He did not see her and she lightly touched his arm.

'Excuse me', she murmured, 'but I just wondered if you'd heard that your brother and our Lizzie are winchin' (courting)?'

Peter looked round in some surprise, straightened himself, and then raised the downward-curving brim of his hat the merest trifle. Martha was further impressed by this cultured acknowledgment of her greeting.

Peter had not taken in what she said, but he recognised Martha at once, said 'Hullo!' and smiled pleasantly.

'Ah was just asking you,' Martha repeated, 'whether you'd heard that your brother and our Lizzie are going with one another?'

He frowned and tried to hide his astonishment. For he was astonished. It had not occurred to him that Johnnie would ever fly so high, for, though he knew that he – Peter – was socially on a level with the Ramsays, he was equally well aware that Johnnie was not.

'No,' he said, after a moment's hesitation. 'I hadn't heard. Since I went to live in Rutherglen Road, I don't often go to see them in Crown Street.'

Martha searched his eyes and saw that he was telling the truth. She thought how well he spoke, and she didn't wonder in the least that he was inclined to keep away from his family.

'It's right enough all the same,' she went on. 'What's more, it looks as if they're going to get married soon and get a single apartment, somewhere in Govan Street, I think.'

Her own English was now carefully studied and her manner a little prim. In spite of himself, Peter flushed and felt nervously in his coat pocket for a cigarette.

'I don't suppose,' he said deliberately, 'your family'll care too much for the like of Johnnie, eh?'

'Oh, well–' Martha broke off and turned scarlet. He had completely spiked her guns by this frankness and now she was more embarrassed than he.

He lit his cigarette, broke the used match and threw it away. Then he looked at her and laughed sympathetically.

'Johnnie and I,' he said, 'don't see very much of each other, but he's well enough in his own way. You see, I'm not getting on so badly where I am now and I'll soon be married myself, likely, and living outside the Gorbals.'

Martha was pleased to hear that. Away from Razor King, Peter would not only make a most presentable brother-in-law, but she could already picture herself visiting him and his wife with her own young man.

'I like to hear of people getting on,' she said with warm friendliness, 'for I'm one of the lucky ones, too, that doesn't know what idle set (unemployment) is.'

Peter was interested. He asked her where she was working, and she told him volubly of her work in the big cigarette factory, of the bonus system there and of what some of the girls did with their few pounds in March and September of each year, leaving it to be understood that she didn't waste her money in the same way.

'I'm only getting thirty-five shillings a week in the meantime,' said Peter, giving confidence for confidence, 'but that's *only* for the meantime, believe me! Soon I'll be doing better than that.'

He was doing better already. He was earning two pounds five, not one pound fifteen, but it was characteristic of him at that time to say he earned less than he did, where other young men of the working-class would usually boast of a few shillings more than their pay envelopes actually contained. For one thing, Peter didn't want anybody but his sweetheart, Isobel McGilvery, to know his private affairs. And, for another, he liked to feel he had something in reserve. Before they parted, Martha was much more reconciled to the prospect of her sister's marriage to Johnnie.

As Peter climbed the stairs to the McGilverys' room-and-kitchen flat his mind was busy, not with his brother's approaching marriage, but rather with the possibility of his own early marriage to Isobel. Without realising it, he was jealous of Johnnie. It vexed him to think that his elder brother, living cheerfully on the rates and not hiding his opinion that most people who worked were fools for their pains, should be able to set up house with *his* girl just when he wanted to, while he, Peter, who was toiling and saving, had to wait to marry Isobel. But did they have to wait? Peter was resentfully saying 'no' to his own question as he opened the door on the landing with the check key he was now entitled to use.

Isobel was in the kitchen with her father and mother, and Peter, just as pleased as any other 'slummie' to be the bearer of tidings, good or ill, paused in the doorway to make his announcement effective.

'I heard from Martha Ramsay,' he informed them all with an air of calm unconcern, 'that that brother of mine is going to marry her sister, Lizzie – the one that works in the bakery.'

There was a gasp of astonishment followed by an excited and gratifying buzz of questions. Peter retailed all that he had heard, offering no comment.

At length, Mr John McGilvery, a slim man of medium height, whose baldness was emphasised by his black moustache, put down the newspaper he had been reading and looked over the top of his spectacles at his daughter's young man.

'Well,' he said deliberately, 'I hope it'll be for the good of yon brother of yours if he does get married. In any case it canny do him much harm.'

Isobel's father considered himself a politician and a staunch member of the Labour Party. Actually he took far more interest in football than in politics and knew vastly more about it, but he liked to talk about 'improving the status' of the working man because that contributed to his own sense of superiority. Now he insisted on reading extracts from a speech by J.H. Thomas, declaring, moreover, that the railwaymen had never had an abler leader.

'Maist of the working men, Peter,' he observed sententiously, 'are no good for themselves withoot a good man tae speak for them an' get them the best conditions, an' aw that. If you ever get into a good poseeshion, Peter, you'll find out that unless men are organised they're the lowest creatures on God's earth. You'll mebbe know that as it is?'

Now John McGilvery was no more than a working man himself and of working-class stock, but he was entirely without affectation in this contempt of his fellow-workers and of their mentality. He saw nothing odd about his attitude and neither did Peter. But the younger man was a little bored.

'Speaking for myself,' he replied, stifling a yawn, 'I'm going to be my own leader. I'm no' goin' to wait for any man to help *me*: I'm goin' to help myself.'

The brothers Stark did not meet until shortly before the wedding and then only by chance. Peter was paying one of his rare visits home, chiefly to see his mother. He did not expect to find any of the others indoors at three o'clock in the afternoon, and it was merely a business errand that had given him the opportunity to visit Crown Street at such an hour of the working day.

It happened, however, that Mrs Stark was away at a neighbour's house, called there urgently to lend a hand until the arrival of a midwife. And Peter found his brother in sole possession.

Johnnie, his waistcoat undone and his hair rumpled, was sprawling on the shake-down by the window. He had been drinking heavily that forenoon and now, after his sleep, he was surly-sober. Peter was oddly and suddenly embarrassed to know how to greet him, but he was spared the trouble of finding a conversational opening. His brother got up, scowled and nodded, and then walked without a word into the kitchen there to sluice his head beneath the tap. He came back, towel in hand, and with something like a grin on his lips.

'So you're here, Pete,' he began. 'It's a pure treat for the like of us to see ye these days. And how is it you're no' toilin'? You'll be takin' a day off likely, or mebbe they've made you general manager by now and you c'n just please yourself?'

It was hard to tell, either from voice or manner, whether Johnnie was merely jesting or whether there was a sneer behind the jest. He stood there, very solid and strong, with the black hair still wet on his bullet head, the flannel shirt wide open at his bronzed throat, and that little half-grin on his lips. Peter stared back at him with the odd mixture of hatred, defiance and admiration which he had always felt for his elder brother. His hand rose to finger his tie, a trick of his when he was nervous, and he broke into a laugh that he hoped sounded natural.

'You're lookin' grand,' Johnnie went on evenly, 'collar and tie and aw! You should have said you were coming. The lassies wid have stayed in for ye, nae doot. And Ah wid have bin in ma paraffin, tae. Ah widnae be surprised if the Donaldson woman wid have put off bairnin' for a wee while so that Mither cud be here tae greet ye instead of helpin' to bring another breadsnapper intae the world.'

'Aw, to hell with your kiddin', Johnnie! I was just out from the warehouse to see a customer for Mr Morgan, and being not far from here I thought I wid look in to see Mither before I went back. So she's away to the Donaldson woman? There's some will never learn sense. Eight of a family already and she forty-four or five if she's a day. ...She should ask some of the lassies what tae do to stop accidents, or mebbe how to poison that drunken old man of hers.'

Johnnie began to rub his hair vigorously with his towel and he replied at jerky intervals.

'Education, Peter – we're no' aw so educated as you. You'll be for Labour these days, mebbe – socialism by slow degrees – more schooling for the kids – an' less kids for the schools – what wey should the workin' classes have families they canny afford? I know – dumb brutes like yon Donaldson – folk who havenae the sense or the guts tae hold a respectable job – only the one pleasure in life, breeding fodder for the capitalist cannons. Oh, ay! Ah've heard it aw. Ah can almost talk the language.'

'If Ah'm anything,' his brother retorted, 'Ah'm a Communist, but Ah'm no' interested in politics at all. For all I care Donaldson and the like of him can go on havin' kids till he's played out. I'm only saying I wouldny be for having a big family myself.'

'No? Well, wait till you're married and then we'll see.'

'Sure. There's plenty time. No' sae much for you though, Johnnie, from what they tell me. I hear it's all fixed for you to marry Lizzie Ramsay in a week or two from now?'

'Who telt ye?' Johnnie asked the question with a scowl.

'I heard it first from Martha Ramsay a week last Saturday.'

'Did you? An' she wid have been prood tae gi'e ye the glad news, mebbe. Her sister – one o' the Ramsays o' Mathieson Street – merrit tae Razor King! and what did ye say to her, Peter? Did ye tell her ye were no' seein' so much of the family nowadays? Did ye make it clear that there's two kinds of Stark – yours and mine?'

In spite of himself, Peter felt the colour rising to his cheeks, for the sneer came perilously near the truth.

'I told her,' he said crisply, 'that I was glad. I said it wid likely be a fine thing for you both and that she would do well to make up her mind to it.'

'That was hellova nice of you. An' whit were you thinkin' yourself? Mebbe you were wunnerin' how such a fool as that brither o' yours ever came to get such a good-class bit stuff as Lizzie, eh? An' thinkin' it wid be like his bliddy nerve to set up hoose when he canny hope for a job? Ay, an' walkin' back to your fine friends, throwin' a chest an' saying, "By Christ, Ah'm glad Ah'm no' like him mysel'?" '

'What's the good of talking that wey, Johnnie? Is it my fault you an' me take different roads? Besides, you're wrong. Ah *am* glad you're tae be married. Ah'm no caring one way or the other whether you toil or whether you don't. An' I wid have telt Martha, if she hadny understood withoot the telling, that Lizzie is no' getting the worst o' the bargain.'

'What does that mean?' said the other ominously.

'Nothing; except that Razor King could take his pick of many a lass in Gorbals.'

'Mebbe that's what you meant. And mebbe it's no'. But let me tell *you* something, Peter lad. You think I'm Razor King and can never be anything else. You think you're hellova clever and I'm a mug. Well, there's more than one kind of mug. I've seen your kind before – plenty of them, likely fellahs, goin' to toil every day, kissin' the boss's backside when he throws them a good word; readin' books and newspapers; winchin' brainy bit stuffs wi' good clothes over a duff figure; keepin' aff the booze, talkin' and walkin' and dressin' and mebbe spewin' like a bliddy bourgeois – and dead sure, every one of 'em, that they're going to get on in the world.

'Ah'm no blamin' you; Ah'm sorry for you. What happens to them aw? They get married and they have kids. An' the wages doesny grow with the family. An' they take to drink a little later instead of sooner. An' the shop shuts or the yard shuts down or there's a bliddy strike. An' there they go, back to the dung heap, haudin' up the street corners, drawin' their money from the parrish, an' keepin' awa oot of the hoose all day, awa frae the auld wife's tongue and the kids that go crawlin' and messin' aroon the floor.'

Johnnie paused for breath. He had spoken with a queer gathering passion not directed so much at his brother as at life itself, and Peter, who had never heard him so eloquent, was too surprised to interrupt.

'That's what all your toil will bring ye,' the elder brother resumed. 'That and nothing else. Ah may be a mug, Peter, but Ah'm no such a bliddy mug as that. The ones that win are no' the toilers. You c'n use your brains. Leave me my weapons an' Ah'll finish far ahead of you! You think you're daein' fine now with your two-three pound a week while Ah've nothing but the buroo. But let me tell you, Mither sees more o' my money than she does of yours!'

'That be damned!' shouted Peter angrily. 'What you give her after you've paid for your booze widny pey for your keep.'

'You're a liar, but that's because you've got no sense. A razor king doesny *have* to pey for his drinks. There's more ways of making money than toiling for it. Ask Mither yoursel' if you canny believe me. Whit's more, Ah'm gaun tae take a job mysel' for a while. . . Ah c'n toil as well as you or any other bliddy fellah when Ah think it's worth ma while. But Ah'll no forget Ah'm Razor King. That's somethin' more than any job.'

'Oh, far more, right enough!' sneered Peter in his turn. 'A bliddy fine job, being Razor King – while it lasts! Wi' free holidays in Barlinnie an' aw! Christ! a great job for a gangster!'

Johnnie took a threatening step in his direction but checked himself.

'You mug!' he said bitterly. 'You should still be at the schule. You and your "gangsters!" Tell me this: are they no' *aw* gangsters who win in this stinkin' world? Look at Arthur Ross. Look at your own graftin' bliddy bosses! Look at the lousy policitians! What's jail worse than livin' outside it in Gorbals?

'You think yourself a hellova fellah,' continued Johnnie, 'but what about Bobbie Hurley? Mebbe you haveny heard that Bobbie and Lily are dancing at the Gaydom now, earnin' eight pound a week. And Bobbie was worse at school even than me!'

'That pimp! He can keep his bliddy money, the way he earns it!'

'Christ! Don't make me laugh! Whit's wrong with the dancing, then, that Mister . . . Peter . . . Stark widna soil his nice brown shoes by taking the floor?'

'An' the booking out?' retorted Peter. '*That's* a different kind of dancing, is it no'? Bobbie Hurley and Lily McKay! Whores, the pair of them, and booked to get married out of the profits! You can keep your pals.'

'By God! watch out who you're calling pals. Lily McKay might be worth more than that skinny bit stuff you're gaun wi'.'

'To hell with you! She might be worth more than that bandy-legged tart you're going to marry!'

The elder brother leapt into action at that taunt, his razors flashing, but Peter kept him off for a moment with a raised chair.

'You couldn't . . . fight . . . even me, wi'oot your weapons,' he gasped.

Johnnie uttered a furious oath and flung the razors across the room. Then he charged, head lowered and arms raised to guard it. The chair was dashed out of Peter's hands and his brother's fists drove home to chest and forehead sending him spinning across the room.

At that instant the door opened and Mrs Stark stood on the threshold. She uttered one loud cry and her elder son staggered to check his run with the boot drive at the end of it. He lurched on top of Peter, caught him by the shoulders and jerked him to his feet.

'That's how I floored the Plantation widoe,' he roared, 'one punch and a kick, and he was oot!'

Peter was breathing very hard, but his lips parted in a wry smile.

'It was . . . quick work,' he said. 'I'd like fine to have seen you!'

They stared at each other for a long moment and the scowls relaxed and at last there was something almost friendly in their gaze. Johnnie turned on his heel and went to the window.

But Mrs Stark had sat down suddenly and her face was grey.

'So you're home, Mither,' said Peter anxiously, matter-of-fact. 'An' how did you leave them aw at the Donaldsons?'

'Baith doin' fine,' she whispered. 'It wis a boy. Ay, the poor soul: it wis a *boy*!'

'A New Life'

from The Patriarch

CHAIM BERMANT (1929–)

Bermant has a sound reputation as a writer on many subjects extending beyond Glasgow and its tight little Jewish community centred on the south side of the city. Perhaps he is yet to win full critical acclaim, though, for work like The Patriarch, *a great sprawling dynastic epic with great heart and humour. Even within the scope of this one chapter, the reader encounters a vast sweep of Jewish and Glasgow life in the thirties and develops a knowledge of the network of relations and acquaintances of the Raeburn clan. The eponymous patriarch is Nahum Rabinowitz, or Raeburn, the name he took when he came to Glasgow in 1892 after escaping famine in his native Russia. The novel follows his life and career right through from then to 1968. More than this, in this thirties chapter we are given insights into such issues as: the tension between orthodox and modernist views of Judaism, some observations on the Jewish impact on Hollywood, and consequently on the cinema-going public here, and the gradual intrusion into the Glasgow scene of, at first distant, echoes of the rise of Fascism and Zionist action in Palestine.*

Nahum was in a long life both shipping magnate and cinema owner and the role of business in the 'Merchant City' is another recurring theme of the book. So too is the characters' differing degrees of assimilation to Glasgow and to Scotland as a whole. As Nahum is belatedly introduced to the world of theatre and concerts by Lotie, his new wife, we incidentally learn quite a lot about the cultural life of Glasgow in the thirties – such names as James Bridie make an appearance. Lotie is a keen fan of the land of Scotland and everything Scottish and, in a flash of the delightful humour that runs right through the book, she tries to persuade the synagogue board of management to wear Highland dress. Even Nahum, when he becomes a warden of the synagogue, refers to his new status as 'an elder of the Kirk'. Throughout, the dialogue and narrative sparkle, with humour never far away, and almost beg to be read aloud. Also, there is a feeling, from time to time, that Bermant has himself assimilated something of a distinctively Scottish brand of humour.

A NEW LIFE

There were what Nahum called 'wee difficulties' almost from the start. They had agreed that his house in Pollokshields was too large and gloomy for their own needs, and Nahum planned to buy a flat in the West End, but he naturally presumed that while they were looking for a suitable property, they would be staying in Pollokshields, but Lotie refused.

'Your aunt makes me nervous. She dislikes me, and I'm sure she would like to cast a spell on me.'

'She's too fat to be a witch,' said Nahum.

'Who said all witches must be thin?' And they finally arranged to stay in an hotel, which annoyed Nahum, for he disliked hotels and resented the expense, and when he tried to charge it to the company, he nearly fell out with Lomzer.

They quickly abandoned their search for flats, for they found nothing which Lotie regarded as even remotely suitable. They experienced the same difficulty when looking at houses, and Lotie suggested that they buy an old, ramshackle property on a suitable site, demolish it and build from scratch.

'Have you any idea what that would cost?'

'You gave me the impression you were comfortable.'

'I am comfortable, but not that comfortable.'

'I suppose I could find a few thousand pounds myself.'

'I thought you were penniless.'

'I am penniless, but not that penniless.'

'It would still be a waste of money. There're only the two of us. Who needs a palace?'

'We'd have Benny staying with us, and then one wants to have room for visiting relatives and friends.'

'That's what I'm afraid of. Once you have room for visiting relations, they don't come to visit, they come to stay. I already have a house which could be refurbished and refurnished to your taste, but you refuse to set foot in it because it already has visiting relatives in residence.'

'Why don't you sell it?'

'And what'll I do with Mother, dump her in the river?'

'No, but she won't live forever.'

'You don't know my mother.'

Nahum finally settled the matter – or thought he had settled it – by buying a semi-detached five-bedroom house in Newlands.

Lotie liked the house, for it overlooked green fields, and it had a sizable garden, but she thought it was a bit cramped.

'Cramped? It has five bedrooms and three public rooms. How many relatives are you expecting to stay?'

''It's not the number of rooms,' she said, 'It's the size of them.'

A few weeks later, she told Nahum that she had a small surprise for him. She had bought the adjoining property.

'Out of my own pocket,' she added, 'all we need to do is to knock down a wall and –'.

'For a penniless woman, you've got expensive tastes,' he said. 'We shall live in the house I bought, but if it proves too small, then we shall begin knocking down the walls.'

'But what about the half I bought?'

'It isn't a half, it's a whole.'

'But what shall we do with it?'

'We shall rent it out on a short lease.'

She was not happy about that, and as a compromise they decided to leave it empty for six months, in case they should require immediate possession. But then when they began to look at furniture she said: ''You know, this is silly. The sort of furnishing which would be suitable for a small house would not be suitable for a large one.'

'Lotie. We have bought the house, we shall live in it and if you don't want to furnish it to your tastes, I shall furnish it to mine, but I'm not going to spend the rest of my life arguing about accommodation.'

She looked at him as if she were seeing him – or, rather, hearing him – for the first time. A sternness had entered his tone which she had not noticed before. She was not too sure she liked it, but she was not at the moment disposed to argue.

With that settled, Nahum experienced a period of gladness he had never known before – not even during what he had termed his golden years – and he presumed that it had something to do with his age and Lotie's, and that one had to reach a certain pitch of maturity before one could experience true happiness. Sometimes, when he walked home from the office through a night of chill, impenetrable fog, he felt suffused with a golden glow which seemed to melt the cold around him, and he and Lotie would often go through a litany of regrets.

Why didn't he contact her when he first heard she was divorced?

Why didn't she contact him?

Why hadn't she gotten divorced earlier?

Why had she married Kagan at all?

Why hadn't they married when they first met?

It sometimes struck Nahum that he was possibly being unfair, for his marriage to Miri, certainly in the first years, had been happy and fruitful.

He had never known the serenity or contentment he experienced now, but it had been a more active, more boisterous sort of happiness, when the old were not so old, and the young were younger, and everybody was together, and death had yet to make it first inroads. And his earlier happiness had been tied to his business success. He was by no means a business failure now, but he was merely a businessman among other businessmen, a trifle richer, perhaps, but not a phenomenon, not a shipping magnate. Miri, moreover, had been in a houseful of people and had had to share his affection and attention with six growing children; he wasn't sure how his relationship with Lotie would have developed in the same circumstances.

She did not provide the same feeling of sensual fulfillment offered by Miri, but at his age he did not experience the same need to be fulfilled. Shyke had once told him that one could sleep with a queen or a skivvy, and the sensation was always the same, and that if there was any difference at all, it was probably in favour of the skivvy. There was, he found, something in that. He did not regard Lotie as a queen or Miri as a skivvy, but Miri's behaviour when they were alone together had sometimes shocked him, and the shock added something to the pleasure. Katya, too, in their first encounters, had been more exciting, but there a sense of guilt had added an extra dimension to desire. Jessie had been in the Katya class, and partly for the same reason. With Lotie, the experience was far more tender and more delicate, perhaps too delicate. There was no wild rush of bodies seeking fusion, but, rather, a gradual consummation of intimacy, and he ascribed it less to their age then to the nature of their relationship. They had so much to give each other that sex was but a pleasure among others, and, in retrospect, the fact that sex had played so large a part in his marriage to Miri suggested that their relationship perhaps had been otherwise deficient.

Lotie began to educate him. He had lived about forty years in Glasgow and had rarely set foot in a theatre or concert hall, except during some gala occasion on behalf of a charity. She now took him to the theatre almost weekly and to a concert at least once a month, and he enjoyed both, though the fare was often demanding. Shakespeare (which he had once seen in Yiddish) was, he admitted, wasted on him, but he enjoyed Shaw and a local Scottish playwright, James Bridie. He could not take Bach but enjoyed Tchaikovsky and Mendelssohn. By the way of reciprocity, he gave her a Jewish education, taught her the dietary laws and to keep meat dishes separate from milk ones. She complained that he had never mentioned such things when she had first known him, and he explained that he had been a bachelor then, and bachelors tend to be careless about such things, but his mother had kept a kosher home and so had Miri, and he was by now too used to kosher food to have a stomach for any other, at least in his own home. He also taught her how to light candles before the onset of the Sabbath at dusk on Fridays, and on Saturday mornings she accompanied him to synagogue. It was a pleasant walk through the leafy streets of Newlands and across the River Cart, and she enjoyed the service.

Nahum had never tried to define his religious beliefs. As a young man, he had been as devout as his father. In later years, he had allowed one observance after another to lapse, without consciously dropping any, and during his ship-owning years he had almost jettisoned Judaism altogether, though Miri still kept a kosher home, and he still found himself, from time to time, in synagogue for some state occasion or at a *bar mitzvah* or wedding. When Alex died, he went to synagogue thrice daily to say *kaddish*. He often asked himself why, because Alex had never, in his mature years, been a believer in any accepted sense of the word and had often expressed an indifference to Judaism and, indeed, all organised religion. Nor did Nahum himself believe that if he failed to say *kaddish*, Alex's soul would be consigned to purgatory or damnation, but he did find some comfort in being in the synagogue and uttering the ancient lines of the *kaddish*, even though he was no longer quite sure of their meaning. After the year of mourning was over, he continued to attend synagogue with fair regularity, and he was inevitably pulled into synagogue affairs, becoming first a member of the board of management and then, after he remarried, a synagogue warden, which meant that he had to acquire striped trousers, a frock coat and a top hat, but he felt good in the ensemble, and he looked good, certainly in Lotie's eyes. 'You're one of the few people who can wear this sort of outfit without looking as if you're in fancy dress,' she said.

There was a time when he had begun to verge on the portly, but he had suffered a loss of weight so drastic that when Sophie saw him in Palestine, she insisted that he see a doctor, but shock and worry had been the cause rather than ill health, and now that he was enjoying happier times, he began to put on weight again, until Lotie put him on a diet.

On Sundays, they would sometimes drive up to Crosshill and have tea with Jacob and his wife Gladys, who looked slightly less austere and forbidding now that she was married, and who was an excellent cook, but neither of them did justice to the plates she piled before them, for Lotie would peck at a cucumber sandwich and saw to it that Nahum had little more.

One Sunday they came for tea and found Jacob making the sandwiches.

'I'm sorry, I'm a bit behind,' he apologised. 'Gladys's been unwell and is resting.'

Lotie at once went up to see her, and when she came downstairs, she had the knowing smirk on her face which Nahum often noticed on women discussing a condition peculiar to their gender, and she imparted the news to Nahum when they drove home.

'She thinks she's pregnant.'

'What do you mean, she thinks? She's a doctor, and she should know.'

'But she's also a woman, and a woman of irregular habit, if you know what I mean.'

When it became clear that she was indeed pregnant, Nahum felt almost guilty about the good fortune he enjoyed and wondered what he had done to deserve it.

'All I need now,' he told Lotie, 'is to see Vicky happily married,' at which he thought he saw something like a shadow spread across her face.

A close, almost intimate friendship had developed between Lotie and Vicky. He had to travel down to London on business about once a month, and Lotie usually went with him and spent most of her time with Vicky. She showered her with expensive gifts, and when Nahum chided her for extravagance, she would say, 'But she looks so good in good things.'

One evening, à propos of nothing, Lotie asked him if it was true that he once nearly married a gentile, and he immediately sensed that there was more to the question than the mere desire for information. He said: 'You're not asking me because you want to know something, you're asking me because you want to tell me something. Out with it then, then, what is it?'

She hesitated, then grabbed the phone and told Vicky to come up on the next train.

'I knew it had something to do with Vicky the moment you raised that topic,' he said. 'She's marrying a *sheigatz*, isn't she?'

'Marrying a what?'

'A gentile. What sort of character is he?' His voice was calm and controlled.

'A very impressive sort, as a matter of fact.'

'You've met him?'

'Several times.'

'Then why didn't you tell me before?'

'I was going to, three months ago, the night you came home from synagogue to tell me you'd become an "elder of the Kirk", as you put it. My nerve failed.'

'Has she married him yet?'

'Not quite.'

'What do you mean, "not quite"? They're either married or they're not.'

'They're living together.'

'Phone her again and tell her to bring him up with her.'

'Why? What are you going to do?'

'What can I do? I'm, just curious to see what sort of man I'm going to have as my son-in-law.'

'You're not going to stand in her way?'

'You're got a curiously Victorian way of putting things. How can I stand in her way? She's twenty-three – come to think of it, the age you were when I wanted to marry you, except I'm not your mother, and I'm not going to drop dead in order to have my way.'

'You seem to be taking it all very philosophically.'

'I've always had the fear at the back of my mind ever since she went to London, and now that it has actually happened, it's something of a relief. In any case, in some ways the Jewish law is easier with women than men in these things. It means that her children, at least, will be Jewish.'

'Even if he doesn't convert?'

'Even if he doesn't convert? Why should he convert? She's only Jewish in name, but her children could become real Jews. Ask her to bring him with her, I'd like to meet him – I've a right to, don't you think?'

'You already have met him.'

'I've – ?' He looked at her wild-eyed for a moment, then put his hands to his head and gave a shriek which chilled her blood. 'No not Cameron, no – not young Cameron. Tell me, it's not Cameron, not Cameron, no.' And before she could answer, he had sunk down to the floor with his hands still to his head, swaying backwards and forwards as if the motion might purge the hated name from his head. It took her a few moments to pull herself together to call the doctor. She could not quite believe the scene before her was actually happening.

By the time the doctor came, Nahum had quieted down but was shivering convulsively, and Lotie helped him upstairs and put him to bed. The doctor gave him an injection, and he sank into sleep.

'Shock,' he said, 'keep him warm and see that he has complete rest. He should be all right in a day or two. I have a case like that almost every week these days. It's the *shiksa* syndrome.'

Lotie phoned Vicky to tell her what had happened and warned her not to show her face in Glasgow for the time being. She also phoned Hector.

She was making herself some coffee early the next morning when the door-bell rang, and Hector and Arabella appeared. She made them coffee and described in detail what had happened.

'The bitch,' said Arabella. 'What did she want to get married for, she was living with him, in any case. What else does she want?'

'She wants a family,' said Lotie. 'It isn't an unreasonable thing for a woman to want. He took it all in his stride till I mentioned Cameron, then he went berserk.'

'I was afraid that might happen.'

'Then you might have warned me.'

'She can't marry him, that all,' said Arabella.

'It's all right for you to say, but I've been through this sort of thing myself, and I don't think Vicky should make either the sacrifice or the mistake that I made.'

'Let them move to France or some other place where these things aren't noticed and have all the bastards they want,' said Arabella.

Nahum didn't stir until nearly noon, and when he opened his eyes and saw Arabella smiling affectionately at him, he didn't quite know where he was. She smoothed his hair, then kissed him on the lips.

'How do you come to be here?'

'I heard you were ill, so here I am.'

'Ill? Me?' And then the events of the night before returned to him, and he put his hand over his mouth.

'What happened to me, did I have a fit?'

'Or something like it. I couldn't believe it when Lotie told me, it's so unlike you.'

'Lotie? Where is Lotie?'

'Downstairs with Hector.'

'Is the whole family here?'

'No, only Hector and me.'

'I must have given her a terrible shock, poor dear.'

'We all got a terrible shock.'

'It's only when I heard the name Ca–Ca–I can't even bring myself to pronounce it.'

'Then don't.'

'You know, in my own way, I'm a fairly religious man–'

'I like that, *fairly* religious, you're a bloody fanatic.'

'Call me what you like. I have always believed in divine retribution, but, given my habits of mind, I have let myself assume that it's something you receive in the world to come. I'm wrong, you know; retribution comes to us in the here and now in the form of our fellow-men, and my retribution is Ca–Cameron.'

'What have you ever done to deserve retribution.?'

'Oh, Arabella, if only you knew.'

'Oh, Nahum, and what makes you think I don't know? So you fucked your aunt. It's not as if you've ever fucked your mother, though I suppose your aunt is the next best thing.'

'Please, Arabella, I hate to hear such words coming from your dear sweet mouth.'

'Is that why you ran for it when I invited you to fuck me?'

'I ran for it because I loved you.'

'You are an incurable romantic,' she said, reaching down between his sheets.

'Please, Ara,' he said between gasps, 'if I am, I don't want to be cured. And besides, Lotie's downstairs.'

'I know, and she knows I'm upstairs. She's a very understanding woman, your wife. Besides, she's got Hector with her. She looks very fetching in her negligée.' She stood up, unzipped her dress, pulled it over her head and got in beside him.

'For a sick man, you're in good shape,' she whispered and eased him inside her.

Some time later, when Lotie brought him up something to eat, he was fast asleep with his hands clasped across his chest and a look on his face so beatific that she thought he was dead and quickly called the doctor.

When he thought back on the events of what Lotie was to call 'Cameron night', and indeed, the following morning, he was almost convinced that they had never happened: the one part was too painful to contemplate; the other too heavenly to be true. Later, when he asked Arabella whether she had, in fact, gotten into bed with him, she feigned shock.

'What an indelicate suggestion! What sort of woman do you think I am?' But then she put her arms around him and whispered: 'You were great. If that was you in sickness, I'd be afraid to be with you in health.' But then, for all the years he had known Arabella, he was never quite sure how to take her, or be certain when she was joking and when she was not.

But whether 'Cameron night' and its sequel had happened or not, their effect was to purge him, at least temporarily, of his obsessive antagonism to Cameron, and a few weeks later Vicky and Cameron were married in a London registry office.

The following Passover, Nahum organised a large *seder* in his former Pollokshields home – because, as Lotie took pains to point out, none of the rooms in his own home in Newlands was large enough to accommodate all the guests – and, as if to confirm his admission to the womb of the family, he invited Cameron to come up with Vicky. Hector and Arabella also joined them, as did Jacob and Gladys. Lomzer was another guest, and, seating himself between Katya and her sister, he looked like some withered sacrificial animal hemmed in between two over-ornate caryatids. Gladys, in a green dress and an advanced stage of pregnancy, looked like one of the green hills of Somerset. Some women turn bovine in pregnancy, but she had acquired a bloom which she had lacked before. Her complexion had cleared, her eyes had softened, but, perhaps afraid she might spoil the effect by wearing glasses, she stumbled around as if she were blind. Cameron, in a large velvet skull-cap which came almost down to his ears, entered fully into the spirit of the occasion, followed the service which preceded the meal in the English translation of the *Hagadah*, asked knowledgeable questions and sang the traditional songs as if he had learned them in the cradle.

'He knows more than I do,' said Vicky proudly.

'That shouldn't be too difficult,' said Hector.

'I was stationed in Palestine for a number of years,' Cameron explained, 'and was usually invited to Jewish homes for the *seder*.'

Passover marks the exodus from Egypt and the beginning of Jewish nationhood, but to Nahum that year it was also a feast of reconciliation. Cameron seemed so amiable a fellow that he wondered how he could have harboured such fierce animosity against him for so long, and he had to remind himself that Cameron had betrayed his trust, something which should not be easily forgiven. But *had* Cameron betrayed his trust? They had not, after all, bought charges against him because they could offer no evidence which could have stood up in court. On the other hand, if he had not been a party to the fraud, he had shown a degree of negligence which was almost criminal in itself, but all that, as Nahum reminded himself, was twenty-five years ago, which was time enough to let bygones be bygones. He was glad to see Jacob – whom Lotie had nicknamed 'the Rabbi' and about whose attitude he was apprehensive – receive Cameron cordially, and even Benny, who normally had to summon courage to say 'good morning' to a stranger, engaged him in an animated conversation. Vicky, who in previous encounters had seem sullen and withdrawn, looked radiantly happy. He could easily imagine what his father would have thought of the match, but they were living in different times and in a different world, and they called for different attitudes.

About a month later Gladys had a daughter, whom she named Thelma, and Nahum, so to speak, became a grandfather in his own right. Some two years later, she gave birth to a son, Aaron. Cameron came up for the circumcision and took Nahum aside to tell him that Vicky was also expecting a child, and that if it was a boy, he, too would be circumcised. 'And not one of those clinical jobs in hospital,' he added, 'we'll give him the whole kosher works.'

Nahum found, as he had found during his 'golden days', that whenever he derived any special joy from his private world, external events intruded to darken them. For many years, events in Russia had preyed on his mind. There was a short period in 1917, after the March revolution, when he, in common with most other Jews, allowed himself to think that the dark days were finally over. Then came the October revolution and the Civil War, and the massacres, the famine, the disease. Nahum lost all contact with his sister and in the early twenties, after making his own abortive enquiries, approached some leading Scottish Communists – including John McLean, the honourary Russian Consul in Glasgow – to make enquiries on his behalf. They could do nothing for him, and some years later he arranged to travel to Russia to see for himself but was warned, as he had been born in Russia, he should not expect protection from his British passport if he were arrested. Alex went instead, and he was able to establish that Esther, her husband and her daughter had been last seen alive in Odessa in 1921, that all three had left town about the same time and that nothing had been heard of them since. It was Nahum's hope that they might have found their way to Poland, or perhaps even to Germany, but if so, why had they made no attempt to contact him?

Germany had never figured in Nahum's imagination on the same level as England or America, but it still represented decency, sufficiency and order, and he would have found it easier to be a patriot during the war if the enemy had been Russia, rather than Germany or Austria. He recalled how Wachsman had urged him to settle in Germany. 'It's a place which believes in hard work,' he said, 'it's the place to get on.' He had thus followed the rise of Hitler with disbelief and was assured by the reports he read everywhere that German good sense would assert itself, but the years passed without signs of such assertions, and in 1935 he found himself out again on a platform protesting against the treatment of the Jews. The hall was the same, the faces were mainly the same, the speeches were much the same, only the oppressor was different, and he still felt a trifle bewildered by the turn of events. Lotie felt particularly agitated, for her upbringing had been German. She had had a German governess and would fall asleep to German lullabies, and she still read German novels and poetry, and she had been rather more aware of her Germanic associations than her Jewish ones. 'What happens to people?' she kept asking. An emergency committee, much like those which had existed to help Russian Jewry, was formed on behalf of German Jewry, and again Nahum found himself on the executive board. He donated two hundred and fifty guineas and induced Lomzer, who thought he was being generous when he parted with half a crown, to do the same. Lotie, who continued to insist she was penniless and about whose means he was careful not to enquire, donated five hundred pounds.

Sophie, in the meantime, assailed all the members of the family with letters urging them to come to Palestine: 'If what is happening in Germany could happen in Germany, it could happen anywhere,' she wrote; 'if you don't come now of your own free will, you'll be chased out in another few years,' and she reminded Nahum that he had been a delegate to several Zionist congresses and was spoken of as 'a leading Zionist'. What is your Zionism about if you can't see your way to making your home in Zion?' she demanded. 'I know you've built up a good business and you're proud of it,' she went on. 'There's a man in this *moshav* who owned a department store in Düsseldorf. It's still there, but he doesn't know what happened to it, and he doesn't care. He packed his bags, left and is now a farmer, and he blesses the day he came. You're too old to become a farmer, but you're still in a position to sell out. Sell now before you have to give it away. It seems to me that history evolves its own compensations, and as some areas of the globe become uninhabitable for Jews, others open up, only people don't realise it and cling to their old ways and their old places. If your father had not faced ruin in Volkovysk, you'd probably still be in Russia – provided, of course, you had survived the wars and the famine – and what sort of life would you be leading now? Do you have to wait till you're ruined to do the sensible thing?'

Nahum had an uneasy feeling that there was force in her argument, and not only because he had some pretensions to being a Zionist and was indeed regarded as one of the leaders of British Zionism (if only because he was still a considerable donor to Zionist charities). He could not forget the shattered windows of his house – his own 'private pogrom', as he called it – when he was tried for trading with the enemy. He told himself that it had happened during the war and that no nation was in its right mind in wartime, but there were innumerable other incidents which, if he came to reflect upon them, made him doubt whether a Jew could ever be at ease in Britain. During his ship-owning days, he had developed the habit of going out with Colquhoun in the course of the morning for a coffee and a smoke in a nearby coffeehouse. He liked the ambience of panelled walls; the solid furniture; the smells of coffee, leather and tobacco; the friendly, convivial atmosphere, but once Colquhoun was gone, hardly anyone spoke to him, and it seemed to him that one had to have one's own private *goy* to gain entry to the *goyish* world. He also suspected – and Colquhoun thought the same – that Scottish banks treated his credit worthiness lightly and demanded the sort of guarantees which could only have been supplied by someone who didn't need their money in the first place, and it was this which kept him in thralldom to Kagan for so long. He had also entertained various colleagues from the shipping trade fairly lavishly at his home but had never been invited back, and after forty years in the country, there was still only one gentile with whom he was on really close terms. That was Jessie, and she had become virtually Jewish, if not by conversion then at least by immersion, and she, too, had written to him in much the same terms as Sophie.

In the cinema trade he moved largely in a Jewish world, though most of his employees were gentile. He was on good terms with them and was invited to their weddings, and sometimes even to christenings, and whenever he had something to celebrate, like a wedding, he always invited them back, but they were a source of discomfort. The young tended to get drunk and boisterous, the old looked around them uneasily, a little too careful to be on their best behaviour, and he wondered what they made of the abundant fare, the extravagant dress. He was conscious, perhaps a trifle too conscious, of the probe of critical eyes.

But even if he were disposed to take Sophie's argument seriously, he was too old to change his ways, to uproot himself and start a new life, and too many people were dependent on him – to say nothing of the sums he was giving to and raising for the emergency refugee appeal – and he wrote to Sophie:

> I don't know if you're right or wrong, though I have the unhappy feeling you may be right. Did I ever tell you I actually bought a plot of land in Palestine (I paid for it and have the receipt, though no one has been able to show me where it is), and there were a number of times when I thought of settling there before the war, after the war and again after poor Alex died, and I suppose if I'd gone out earlier, I might have done something with myself, but I've left it too late. I'm too old and too set in my ways. When things started going wrong in Russia, Father was too old – or felt too old – to go himself, and so he sent me. Well, although I didn't actually send you to Palestine, you still happen to be there, and Benny is talking about going out when he qualifies (if he qualifies – he has sat his anatomy exam five times). And, of course, poor Alex is on the Mount of Olives. So nearly half my family is already there, and more may follow. What more can you ask?

Special transports were being organised to bring Jewish children out of Germany, and Lotie asked whether they should adopt a child.

'I don't know if we're too old to have young children around the house,' she said, 'but wouldn't a young child be bored with two old crocks?'

'Not if they're in their second childhood,' said Nahum, 'and we do have the room to spare.'

They did not have it for long.

If Nahum had been less preoccupied, he might have noticed that old Lomzer was shaving more frequently and with great care – so that even his Adam's apple was free of stubble – that he changed his collar every day instead of every week (or perhaps every month), that his shirts were not too discoloured and that his trousers were pressed. It was only when he arrived one morning with a neatly furled umbrella on his arm and a brand-new hat on his head that Nahum looked up.

'Going to a wedding?'

'Somebody tell you?'

'Tell me what?'

'I'm getting married.'

'*You*?'

'Why not? You think you're the only one who can get married?'

'No, heaven forbid. I'm surprised, that's all.'

'What's so surprising?'

'Nothing, it's just – just that you gave no hint.'

'What do you want me to do, blow a whistle and tell the world I'm thinking of getting married?'

'No, no, but I thought as your partner–'

'My business partner. For business decisions I consult, for marriages I don't have to consult.'

'Look, let's not fall out over this. I'm delighted.'

'And if you weren't delighted, you think I wouldn't get married?'

'Just tell me one thing, who's the lucky woman.'

'Your aunt.'

'My *aunt*?'

'Your aunt, so from now on you can call me uncle.'

As a result, Nahum's mother came back to live with him.

Lotie at this time was active on many Jewish and non-Jewish charities, and one day, shortly before Christmas, Nahum found himself seated next to a churchman at a luncheon in aid of one of her causes. The conversation turned to the fate of German Jewry, and his neighbour, after murmuring the usual words of sympathy, then added: 'But, of course, you've got to ask yourself how much the Jews did to bring their troubles on themselves.'

At which Nahum, whose eyelids were beginning to droop, sat up: 'What do you mean?'

'Well, take a walk up Renfield Street or Sauchiehall Street and look at the cinema posters, and go inside the cinemas if you dare, and what do you find? Profanity, lewdness, debauchery, filth. This is supposed to be a Christian country, but everything it's supposed to stand for is being undermined. My Jewish friends – I was speaking to a rabbi about it only the other day – have the very same feelings. They shudder at these things. But that's not the worst of it. There was a time when these dens of iniquity were to be found only in the centres of town, but now they're everywhere, their insidious lights blinking at every corner, and there is no way of keeping the family and children away from them. There are schoolboys – aye, and even girls – who go to these places two or three evenings a week and sometimes even play truant to go in the afternoon. They are undermining Christian tradition and family life. They are polluting the atmosphere. They are poisoning the minds of the young.'

Nahum struggled to get a word in but could not.

The man, ruddy of face and heavy of jowl, with a large, angry mouth, bad teeth and stale breath, continued like a torrent: 'And they're Jewish, everyone – the people who make these films, the people who act in them, who write them, who distribute them, who show them, who finance them – Jews, everyone. Oh, I have nothing against the cinema, and, of course, I have nothing against Jews. Jews have been – and the cinema could be – a boon to mankind. It could be used to elevate, to improve taste, to raise educational standards, but instead it is being used to debauch, and it offers nothing more than a diet of smut. Now, I hold no brief for Herr Hitler. He has done some disgraceful things, but one thing you have to say for him – he has cleaned up the cinema. You can take your wife – aye, and your children – to any cinema in Germany and be certain that they will be exposed to nothing salacious or profane.' At which Nahum gave up any attempt at rebuttal, rose from his place and walked out of the room.

Lotie, who had been unable to attend because of ill heath, couldn't believe what he told her.

'He couldn't have known you were in the cinema trade,' she said.

'But don't you see, that makes it worse. If he'd known. I'd at least have admired his frankness, and, as a matter of fact, he is right in some ways. I'm not too proud of some of the films I show – but you should only see the ones I don't show. But they're not all trash, and, even if they were, they're no worse than some of the goings-on you used to have in the music halls. I've only been once to a music hall, and it was enough. Dirty songs, dirty stories, dirty gestures, scruffy-looking characters on stage and off, and a half-drunk audience. In the cinema, at least, they're sober, and even a bad film can be something of an education. You see something of the world – a good drama, good acting, good music, sometimes. Yes, you get smut, too, but it's nothing compared to the music halls.'

'Perhaps that's what he was complaining about.'

'And a clergyman, too. I'm beginning to think Sophie's right.'

He calmed down eventually but found the fact that he could be so upset by the stupid utterances of one stupid man extremely telling.

'A Russian Jew remains a Russian Jew,' said Lotie. 'He never feels secure, not even in America, and keeps looking over his shoulder and is liable to misconstrue almost anything said to him or about him.' She, for her part, claimed to feel perfectly at home in Britain or, rather, in Scotland. She was in love with the scenery of Scotland – its people, history, culture – and tried to persuade the board of management of the synagogue to don tam o'shanters and kilts for ceremonial occasions, and when they looked at her as if she were mad, she said: 'You're prepared to wear frock coats and top hats, which is English national dress, what objections can you have to Scottish national dress? After all, this is a *Scottish* synagogue.'

'And perhaps,' said a wizened little figure, 'you'll be maybe wanting us to blow the bag-pipes instead of the *shofar*.'

'And to toss the caber instead of shaking the *lulav*?' said another.

'And to eat haggis instead of *tzolen*t,' tittered a third.

She also tried to learn Gaelic, but with limited success.

Once, after a motoring holiday in the Highlands, she tried to persuade Nahum to buy a small country cottage somewhere in the hills – 'something tiny, three or four rooms, at most' – and even offered to pay for it out of her own resources, but Nahum felt it would be wrong to buy a second home while there were fellow Jews turning in all directions without a roof over their heads.

One evening, on the anniversary of Alex's death, Nahum stopped off on the way from work at a synagogue in the Gorbals. Lomzer, whom he was giving a lift home, came in with him. The service lasted about ten minutes, and they were crossing the road to the car when they were set upon by five or six youths, beaten, punched, kicked. Lomzer fell to the ground and hit his head against the kerb, and, as a crowd began to collect, the youths fled. The whole incident could not have taken more than a minute. Lomzer was rushed to hospital in an ambulance and allowed home after treatment. Nahum was only bruised, but he felt too shaken to drive and went home in a taxi. When he returned the next day to collect his car, he found his tyres missing.

Lotie had been away visiting friends in London. When she returned in the evening, he told her of the incident.

'Did no one come to your help?' she said.

'No one, not a soul.'

'And didn't they steal anything?'

'That's the frightening part of it. If it had been only robbery, well, these things happen, but we weren't set upon because anybody wanted our money; we were set upon because we were Jews.'

'Are non-Jews never attacked?'

'Maybe in gang wars. I don't belong to a gang, and, unless I'm very much mistaken, Lomzer doesn't, either. Why don't you want to face reality? We were attacked because we were Jews. Anyway, I should be grateful for it. It's a warning.'

'A warning.'

'A warning to get out. We're moving to Palestine. I know Jews are also being attacked in Palestine, but at least they're on their own soil, they can fight back.'

Lotie did not argue with him. She never did when he was excited, and she was confident that in a day or two he would forget all about it, but she became alarmed when a week passed and she found that he was still not only talking about Palestine, but that he was negotiating to sell his share of the company to Lomzer.

'You're not being serious?'

'I've never been so serious in my life. He's offering a good price, almost an extravagant price. I thought I'd have to haggle for the figure I had in mind, but he offered it right away, and I wondered if perhaps he knew something I didn't, or perhaps he's getting soft in his old age, but it so happens he's in sympathy with my plans – he said he'd have done the same if he was a younger man.'

'And it might have been a good idea if you were a younger man yourself, but darling, you're over sixty.'

'Just over sixty. Don't make me out to be an ancient.'

'But I love it here.'

'You'll love it there.'

'Amid all the fighting and riots?'

'They're bringing in a whole British Army to quiet things down, they're bringing in the air force. I assure you, by the time we're ready to go, it'll all be over.'

'But what'll you do there?'

'What am I doing here? I buy a cinema or build one. If I could build myself up from almost nothing twenty years ago–'

'Twenty years ago, you were twenty years younger.'

'You keep coming back to my age as if I've got a foot in the grave. I've never felt better. I feel ready to start afresh. I might even go back into shipping. I can't be the only Jew who feels as I feel. If they should all start making for Palestine, there'll be plenty of business for ships. In fact, I'm going to make enquiries about it tomorrow. I've always hankered to get back into ships. They're small change, cinemas, after ships.'

'What'll happen to your mother?'

'I've seen to that. Katya will be happy to look after her. Of course, I'll have to leave a bit of money aside to cover her costs – and she's a pretty sharp bargainer, is our Katya – but it's all settled.'

'Are you not afraid what she might do?'

'To my mother?'

'Your mother.'

'What could she do at her age?'

'Press a pillow over her face.'

'She's not that bad.'

Lotie was so unused to such enthusiasm or resolve in her husband that she felt unable to argue further. A few days later, while in Cooks' to work out her itinerary, she picked up a paper and found the front page filled with reports of large-scale fighting in Palestine. She showed it to Nahum.

'I've read it,' he said, 'and I've been listening to every news bulletin. I'm worried, but, apart from anything else, I want to see what's happening to Sophie, Yankelson and the children, but if you want, I'll go alone.'

'No,' she said grimly, 'I'm coming with you.'

7
THE HAMPDEN ROAR
Introduction

'Catch the red car to Mount Florida!' These are the directions given to Neil Munro's Jimmy Swan for getting to Hampden Park to see a football international. Jimmy has lived in Glasgow all his life and might be expected to know which tramcar to catch from the city centre to reach the great stadium – but Jimmy is a sensitive soul and much prefers singing in a choir to going to football matches. As a commercial traveller visiting many country towns and villages in Scotland just before the Great War, he uses talk about football, the players and the games, as part of his common currency of salesman's patter along with jokes and snatches from the music hall. The story *Jimmy's Sins Find Him Out* tells what happens when a country customer unexpectedly arrives in town and Jimmy's happy indifference to everything about football – apart from what he gleans from the sporting papers when he has to – is in danger of being revealed.

Mount Florida, a pleasant hilly suburb on Glasgow's South Side, has been for more than a century the scene of many great international sporting occasions (and not a few religious revivalist gatherings). Indeed for most of the year proceedings at Hampden are incredibly sedate (Robin Jenkins compares the vast edifice to a secular cathedral), as a tiny sprinkling of devotees gather on the mighty slopes to watch the Amateurs of Queen's Park playing at home. On big occasions like international and cup finals, however, the surrounding streets become clogged with thousands of intending spectators, and families and friends such as those following the Drumsagart Thistle (in Robin Jenkins's football novel) are wise to stick closely together, in case they are forcibly parted from each other, as happens to Jimmy Swan and his customer up from the country.

Curiously, this scene of intense sporting contests was once part of a more serious conformation, the Battle of Langside, in 1568. Following her escape from Loch Leven, Mary Queen of Scots' army, was making for the fortress of Dumbarton when it was intercepted by the forces of the Regent Moray, near to Mount Florida and overlooking the village of Langside. As the seventeenth-century historian, John Gibson, describes it:

> (Moray) crossed the bridge with his troops, and stood in order of battle at the village of Langside; the opposite lords were soon up with him and engaged; the victory was gained by the regent, though his army was inferior in number to the enemy. Upon his return to Glasgow, immediately after the battle, he made a present to the corporation of bakers of the ground which their mills at Partick are built, as a recompense for their diligence in preparing bread for the use of his army.

An early instance of an army marching on its stomach perhaps?

One of the most venerable of clichés is the comparison between football and war, and in Glasgow it is often heard. In his poem, *You Lived in Glasgow*, Iain Crichton Smith speaks of the 'divided city of the green and blue', although, somewhat surprisingly, the collective term for Celtic and Rangers – 'The Old Firm' – is actually quite innocuous and unwarlike. Perhaps the epithet 'Old Firm' is a gentle harking back to the city's mercantile past. More typically, however, the images we might have of the two clubs' grounds at Parkhead and Ibrox are great cauldrons, of skill certainly, but skill mixed with bigotry, and what most supporters get from the game is a lot less innocuous than entertainment or recreation. This is clear in our next piece, an often-quoted excerpt from *The Shipbuilders* by George Blake, which describes a clash of 'the green and blue' at Ibrox Park. We then return to Hampden for a refreshing item from the previously-mentioned novel by Robin Jenkins, *The Thistle and the Grail*, an amusing mock-epic tale of a progress to the final of the Scottish Junior Cup, Junior football being of a very different calibre from the Senior game.

Turning now to those other places of recreation, hospitality and entertainment known as inns and hotels, we remember that perhaps the most celebrated of these is 'The Saracen's Head', in what is now the less than fashionable surroundings of the Gallowgate, across the road from 'The Barras'. The Saracen's Head was visited by James Boswell and Dr Johnson and several other notable travellers in past centuries. Here is Bowell's account in which he seems to think well of the standards of accommodation and comfort:

> On our arrival at the Saracen's Head Inn, at Glasgow, I was made happy by good accounts from home; and Dr Johnson, who had not received a single letter since we left Aberdeen, found here a great many, the perusal of which entertained him much. He enjoyed in *imagination the comforts which we could now command, and seemed to be in high glee. I remember, he put a leg up on each side of*

> the grate and said with mock solemnity, by way of soliloquy, but loud enough for me to hear it, 'Here am I, an English man, sitting by a coal fire.'

The next lengthy extract chosen is very different, since it comes from one of the twentieth century's foremost English novelists, a man not known for his partiality to the Scots – Evelyn Waugh. In Officers and Gentlemen, the second novel in his *Sword of Honour* trilogy, comes an episode set in wartime Glasgow and presenting an evocative picture of a city thronged with a cast of military and camp-followers from 'a' the airts'. This reminds us that Glasgow is both city and port and that in wartime something like a million overseas servicemen entered Britain via the Tail of the Bank. Waugh's characters in this scene, set in November 1940, are not among his most prepossessing but represent the strong comic strain in this work of genius, published in 1955. We meet one particular smarmy individual called Trimmer, also known as Captain MacTavish, who has been training as a commando (something like Waugh's own wartime experience) on the west coast of Scotland. Trimmer is on leave, or 'rest and recreation' as the Americans would have it, and on arrival in Glasgow, 'went straight from the train to the station hotel' and there picks up Virginia, the ex-wife of the novel's central figure, Guy Crouchback.

There is a splendid cartoon drawing – one of the 'Home Front' series in the *Scottish Field* magazine of December 1941 – that with its congregation of assorted soldiery and Glasgow women, captures something of the cosmopolitan atmosphere of Waugh's novel and of Glasgow at this time. However, the cartoon shows the throng in a Glasgow tea-room, rather than an hotel, and a tea-room is really more typical of the city's social scene for much of the century. From 1875, when Stuart Cranston had created the first tea-room by setting aside tables for customers to drink tea in his tea-merchant's premises at the corner of Queen Street and Argyle Street, he was establishing a social trend. This trend was and is even today identified with those marvelous tea-rooms, such as the 'Willow' and the 'White Cockade', created by his better-known sister, Miss (Kate) Cranston.

By the time Neil Munro's Erchie Macpherson gave a rather waspish account of Miss Cranston's 'Willow Tea-room' in the *Glasgow Evening News* in 1904, the pattern was set. Tea-rooms were seen by Kate Cranston as emblems of the temperance movement and as temples to good design, employing people like Charles Rennie Mackintosh. Here is Erchie – a waiter, you may remember, and so someone with a professional interest – and his observations on Mackintosh's 'Room de Looks':

> It's the colour o' a goon Jinnet used to hae before we mairried: there's whit Jinnet ca's insertion on the table-cloths, and wee beads stitched a' ower the wa's the same as if somebody had done it themsels. The chairs is no' like any other chairs ever I clapped eyes on, but you could easy guess they were chairs. . . There was a wheen lassies wi' white frocks and tippets on for waitresses. and every yin o' them wi' a string o' big red beads roond her neck. 'Ye'll notice, Duffy', says I, 'that though ye canna get ony drink here, ye can tak' a fine bead onywye', but he didna see my joke.

The final item comes yet again from the pen of Neil Munro, in a chapter noted for examples of his fine gift for entertaining writing. It is one of the splendid journalist pieces collected under the heading *The Brave Days*; it shows an interesting side of Munro's adopted home and completes our picture of Kate Cranston, pioneer Glasgow business woman and patron of the arts.

'Jimmy's Sins Find Him Out'

from The Jimmy Swan Stories

NEIL MUNRO (1863–1930)

Jimmy Swan was the third of the comic characters brought to life by Neil Munro in the pages of the Glasgow Evening News. *Jimmy, the commercial traveller, made his first appearance in May 1911 and appeared occasionally until 1926. Perhaps not so popular as Erchie or Para Handy, the kindly, somewhat enigmatic character of Mr Swan, as he is generally known to his customers, has nevertheless attracted a group of readers who are enchanted by the subtle humour and vivid evocation of a long-lost world of small towns and draper's shops, with great enthusiasms like choral singing and soirée concerts. Munro developed a rich vein of story and sentiment in the commercial traveller or travelling salesman – a kind of gentle knight-errant figure.*

However, this particular story is set in Glasgow, which is Jimmy's home and also his business base – it is the location of the company he represents, Campbell and Macdonald's drapery warehouse. On this occasion one of his country customers has come to town in search of a ticket for a football match – an international to be played at the home of football, Hampden Park. It turns out that Jimmy has convinced the client in the course of his sales-patter that he is an expert on football. The truth is that, despite living in Ibrox near the home of Rangers FC, Jimmy knows next to nothing about football and instead has a poetic strain to his nature which makes him prefer an hour or so in Camphill listening to the birdsong.

As often, in the case of Munro's newspaper stories, this story had a strong element of topicality when written. It appeared in the 'The Looker-On's' regular Monday spot on the 6th April, 1914, two days after the international between Scotland and England. This was characteristic of Munro's method: to take a contemporary event or fashion and build an amusing tale around it. Incidentally, the match ended in a 3-1 victory for Scotland and the crowd, which did not include Jimmy Swan, numbered 105,000.

JIMMY'S SINS FIND HIM OUT

Mr James Swan picked up a bunch of violets, which he had been refreshing in a tumbler while he wrote out his expenses for the week, and placed it in his buttonhole. From a pocket he took a small case-comb, and, borrowing from Pratt, the office 'knut', the little mirror which Pratt kept always on his desk to consult as often as the Ready Reckoner, he went to the window and combed his hair.

'What side are sheds worn this season?' he asked Pratt, whom it was the joke of the office to treat with mock deference as arbiter of fashion, expert, and authority upon every giddy new twirl of the world of elegance.

'To the left,' said Pratt, without a moment's hesitation, and with the utmost solemnity; the parting of his own hair was notoriously a matter of prayerful consideration. He was a lank lad with a long neck; it looked as if his Adam's apple was a green one and was shining through – a verdant phenomenon due to the fact that he used the same brass stud for three years.

'Can't be done on the left,' said Mr Swan. 'That's the side I do my thinkin' on, and it's worn quite thin. I envy ye your head o' hair, Pratt; it'll last ye a life-time, no' like mine.'

Pratt, with the mirror restored to him, put it back in his desk with a final glance at it to see that his necktie was as perfectly knotted as it was three minutes ago; put on his hat and bolted from the office.

'They're a' in a great hurry to be off the day,' said Mr Swan to himself. 'I wonder what they're up to?'

'He was to find out in two minutes, to his own discomfiture.

At the foot of the stair which led to the upper warehouse he ran against Peter Grant of Aberdeen, who was in search of him.

'My jove!' said Grant, panting; 'I'm in luck! I was sure ye would be awa' to't, and I ran doon the street like to break my legs.'

'De-lighted to see ye, Mr Grant!' said Jimmy with a radiant visage. 'This is indeed a pleasant surprise! But ye don't mean to tell me ye came from Aberdeen this mornin'?'

'Left at a quarter to seven,' said Grant. 'I made up my mind last night to come and see it. And I says to myself', "If I can just catch Mr Swan before he goes to the field, the thing's velvet!" '

'De-lighted!' said Jimmy, and shook his hand again. But the feeling of icy despair in his breast was enough to wilt his violets.

His sin had found him out! There was only one inference to be drawn from Peter Grant's excited appearance; he had carried out the threat of a dozen years to come and see a Glasgow football match, and expected the expert company and guidance of C. & M.'s commercial traveller.

And Jimmy Swan had, so far as Grant was concerned, a reputation for football knowledge and enthusiasm it was impossible to justify in Glasgow, however plausible they seemed in a shop in Aberdeen. Grant, who had never seen a football match in his life, was a fanatic in his devotion to a game which for twenty years he followed in the newspapers. Jimmy in his first journeys to Aberdeen had discovered this fancy of his customer, and played up to it craftily with the aid of the *Scottish Referee*, which he bought on each journey North for no other purpose, since he himself had never seen a football match since the last cap of Harry M'Neill of the 'Queen's,' in 1881.

The appalling ignorance of Jimmy regarding modern football, and his blank indifference to the same, were never suspected by his customer, who from the traveller's breezy and familiar comments upon matches scrappily read about an hour before, credited him with knowing all there was to know about the national pastime.

When Jimmy was in doubt about the next move in a conversation with Grant, he always mentioned Quinn, and called him 'good old Jimmy'. He let it be understood that the Saturday afternoons when he couldn't get to Ibrox were unhappy – which was perfectly true, since he lived in Ibrox, though the Rangers' park was a place he never went near.

'I'll go and see a match some day!' Grant always said; he had said it for many years, and Jimmy always said, 'Mind and let me know when ye're comin', and I'll show ye fitba'.'

And now he was taken at his word!

What particular match could Grant have come for? Jimmy had lost sight of football, even in the papers, for the past three months.

With an inward sigh for a dinner spoiled at home, he took his customer to a restaurant for lunch.

'I want to see M'Menemy,' said Grant; 'it was that that brought me; he's a clinker!'

'And he never was in better form,' said Jimmy. 'Playin' like a book! He says to me last Monday, "We'll walk over them the same's we had a brass band in front of us, Mr. Swan!"'

'Will they win, do ye think?' Grant asked with great anxiety; he was so keen, the lunch was thrown away on him.

'Win!' said Jimmy. 'Hands down! The – the – the other chaps is shakin' in their shoes.'

So far he moved in darkness. Who M'Menemy was, and what match he was playing in that day, he had not the faintest ideas, and he played for safety. It was probably some important match. The state of the streets as they had walked along to the restaurant suggested a great influx of young men visitors; it might be something at Celtic Park.

He looked at Grant's square-topped hat and had an inspiration.

'If ye'll take my advice, Mr Grant,' said he, 'ye'll go and buy a kep. A hat like that's no use at a Gleska fitba' match; ye need a hooker. If ye wear a square-topped hat it jist provokes them. I'm gaun round to the warehouse to change my ain hat for a bunnet; I'll leave ye in a hat shop on the road and then I'll jine ye.'

'What fitba' match is on the day?' Jimmy asked a porter in the warehouse.

'Good Goad!' said the porter with amazement at him. 'It's the International against England.'

'Where is it played?' asked Jimmy.

'Hampden, of course!'

'What way do ye get to't, and when does it start?'

'Red car to Mount Florida; game starts at three; I wish to goodness I could get to't' said the porter.

Jimmy looked his watch. It was half-past one.

He found Grant with a headgear appropriate to the occasion, and wasted twenty minutes in depositing his hat at Buchanan Street left-luggage office. Another twenty minutes passed at the station bar, where Jimmy now discoursed with confidence on Scotland's chances, having bought an evening paper.

'Will ye no' need to hurry oot to the park?' Grant asked with some anxiety. 'There'l be an awfu' crood; twenty chaps wi bunnets came on at Steenhive.'

'Lot's of time!' said Jimmy with assurance. 'Well tak' a car. Come awa', and I'll show ye a picture-palace.'

It was fifteen minutes to three when they got to Hampden. A boiling mass of frantic people clamoured round the gates, which were shut against all further entrance, to the inner joy of Mr Swan, who lost his friend in the crowd and failed to find him.

'Where on earth were you till this time?' asked his wife when he got home to Ibrox two hours later.

'Out in the Queen's Park,' said Jimmy truthfully.

'Wi' luck I lost a man outside a fitba' match, and spent an hour in Camphill – no' a soul in't but mysel' – listenin' to the birds whistlin'.'

‘The Old Firm’

from The Shipbuilders

GEORGE BLAKE (1893–1961)

George Blake was born in Greenock on the River Clyde. After legal studies at Glasgow University and war service he went into journalism, working on the staff of the Glasgow Evening News, *whose editor at that time was Neil Munro. They remained friendly for years and Blake edited two collections of the older man’s journalistic pieces after Munro died in 1930.*

Blake’s 1935 novel The Shipbuilders *is the story of a Glasgow shipyard, ‘Pagan’s’, told mainly through the interwoven lives of the yard owner Leslie Pagan and the riveter Danny Shields. This excerpt focuses on the latter and is part of a longer section called ‘Saturday in Glasgow’. The episode revolves around a Saturday spent by Danny. In the morning he goes to his work, as was customary right up until after the last War, but because the only ship on order at Pagan’s yard is nearing completion, there is no real work for a riveter. Danny’s afternoon is spent in what we would now call a form of escapism, at Ibrox Park on the South Side, watching his team, Rangers, at home to their deadly rivals, Celtic. Set in the Depression years but characteristic of this particular confrontation at any time over more than a hundred years, the book presents a picture familiar to anyone brought up in the West of Scotland, and, as Blake tells us, even farther afield: ‘Blue for the Protestants of Scotland and Ulster, green for the Roman Catholics of the Free State’. The description of the game is in many ways intended as a form of social record, with the religious divide symbolised by the division of the supporters, or ‘enthusiasts’ into different areas of the ground: ‘All the social problems of a hybrid city were to be sublimated in the imminent clasp of mercenaries.’ There is more than just un undercurrent of violence, but Blake’s view seems to be that in this way, Danny and others like him find release or, more explicitly, ‘orgasm’.*

Only in one case is any of the ‘mercenaries’ actually named. Alan Morton, the ‘Wee Blue Devil’, who is described in some detail, was a real person and played all his career for Rangers in the city where he was born. He also won 31 caps on the left wing for Scotland in an era when there were few international matches, and he was a member of the famous 1928 ‘Wembley Wizards’. In the novel Morton is described in loving detail and

Blake perhaps shows his own true colours here – the novelist as fan perhaps? Or to quote an innocent (to modern ears) terracing chant from that era, aimed at a well-known Celtic goalkeeper:

Oh Baldy Shaw
He never saw,
Where Alan Morton
Pit the ba'!

THE OLD FIRM

These asperities were quite forgotten by the morning. They were too much the common currency of their domestic exchange to be remarkable in any event, and it so happened that the Friday evening passed very pleasantly for each of them.

A large tea inside him, including a black pudding of considerable size, Danny achieved peace of mind. The alcoholic anger melted from his consciousness and left him the friendly glow of repletion. Agnes did not return once to the obsession about Lizzie and Jim and the Pictures. Before the meal was over he was boasting to her of his unique immunity in the matter of the pay-off at Pagan's and she, after her fashion, was complimenting him on the distinction and exclaiming at her own luck. Then, when she had gone, Peter stayed behind and assisted in the filling up of the coupon, revealing a particularly helpful knowledge of the form in the South sub-section of the Third Division of the English League; and he stayed in while Danny went out for a final drink at half-past nine. Billy sat like a mouse by the fire, reading, and went to bed when he was told. Wee Mirren slept the evening through and stirred only when her mother returned at the back of eleven, her face flushed.

Agnes, too, had passed an agreeable time. She had seen Ronald Colman on the screen of one of the swell picture houses in Sauchiehall Street, and Jim had risen to balcony seats and ices. He had had his car parked in Holland Street, and after the show, had run them down to the lounge of the Adelphi for a round or two of drinks, in which Agnes's favourite wee ports figured pleasantly, and then had run her home as far as Partick Cross.

'Oh, and Dan!' she blurted out finally, 'They're awful keen for us to go out the morn's night. Not to the Pictures, but a wee supper. Jim's got a friend from England coming up, and they want to give him a night out. Could you not come after the match?'

A sudden shadow of resentment clouded Danny's mind. He could not like Lizzie and her husband, and he vaguely distrusted their influence on Agnes. But there some something in her eagerness that melted him, something that his Friday evening complaisance could not resist – and she had by an implication more cunning than he quite appreciated indicated that she would not nag him if he wished to go to the match.

'Ach to hell! I suppose we might as well,' said Danny.

If he regretted that desperate affability by breakfast time on Saturday, he did not confess the fact. There was never time for argument in the rush of getting to the Yard by eight o'clock, nor did Agnes ever quite emerge from sleep while he made his own breakfast, gulped it down, and hurried out. And on this great day of the Rangers–Celtic match at Ibrox, Danny was almost incapable of thinking beyond the thrills of the afternoon.

Anticipation of the game was indeed an obsession. An honest, keen workman, he found his labour in the Yard that morning an irritating irrelevance. If he worked hard, it was so that the hour of release might seem to come more quickly. Unhappily for him, his position as one who was there by favour, as a riveter for whom no task of riveting remained, was uneasy.

'I suppose I'll have to make work for you,' the foreman sneered. 'A riveter's no dammed use to me. Och, go and give old Tom a hand in the store there. We'll see on Monday. . .'

The man went off grumbling, and Danny was left with a double burden. He knew there was nothing for him to do in the Store that would keep him decently occupied; and the weakness of his supernumerary position had been emphasised. He greatly feared that particular foreman and his prejudices. What if the Major should forget the promise? A blue lookout indeed, and a nice come-down from the triumphs of yesterday!

These anxieties he quickly forgot in friendly chat with brosy old Tom, who had himself not sufficient work to keep him going, and his heart leaped when the foreman popped his head over the half-door of the store about eleven and called on Danny to run across to the engine-shop with a message to the foreman there. For this meant a licensed escape from the yard at a vital hour – and Danny had just remembered his need of something necessary to his enjoyment of the afternoon.

In their wisdom, the Magistrates of that part of the world in which Pagan's was situated had long ordained that public-houses should open at ten and close at noon on Saturdays. The ordinance was based on the theory that the working-man should not be tempted to squander his wages on strong drink on his way home, and had no doubt a bearing on public behaviour at the afternoon football games; but as the artisan had for many a day past been paid on Fridays it was only an interesting anachronism of local administration and bore hardly on such as Danny who desired refreshment in anticipation of other enjoyments. So the foreman's gruff order rejoiced him. It was easy to slip into Mackenzie's between Yard and engine-shop, swallow a quick half and half-pint, buy a flat half-mutchkin of whisky for the pocket and the cold vigil on the terraces, and time his return to the store almost as the whistle boomed the signal for the week-end release.

Thereafter there was nothing in the world for him but the Game. He hurried home, hurried through his washing and changing and eating, and, as if all the claims of family and hearth were nothing now, was out on the streets again half an hour before two o'clock, a unit of one of the stream of men converging from all parts of the city and from all its outliers on the drab embankments round an oblong of turf in Ibrox.

The surge of the stream was already apparent in the Dumbarton Road. Even though only a few wore favours of the Rangers blue, there was that of purpose in the air of hurrying groups of men which infallibly indicated their intention. It was almost as if they had put on uniform for the occasion, for most were attired as Danny was in decent dark suits under raincoats or overcoats, with great flat caps of light tweed on their heads. Most of them smoked cigarettes that shivered in the corners of their mouths as they fiercely debated the prospects of the day. Hardly one of them but had his hands deep in his pockets.

The scattered procession, as it were of an order almost religious, poured itself through the mean entrance to the Subway station at Partick Cross. The decrepit turnstiles clattered endlessly, and there was much rough, good-humoured jostling as the devotees bounded down the wooden stairs to struggle for advantageous positions on the crowded platform. Glasgow's subway system is of high antiquarian interest and smells very strangely of age. Its endless cables, whirling innocently over the pulleys, are at once absurd and fascinating, its signalling system a matter for the laughter of a later generation. But to Danny and the hundreds milling about him there was no strange spectacle here: only a means of approach to a shrine; and strongly they pushed and wrestled when at length a short train of toylike dimensions rattled out of the tunnel into the station.

It seemed full to suffocation already, but Danny, being alone and ruthless in his use of elbow and shoulder, contrived somehow to squeeze through a narrow doorway on to a crowded platform. Others pressed in behind him while official whistles skirled hopelessly without, and before the urgent crowd was forced back at last and the doors laboriously closed, he was packed tight among taller men of his kind, his arms pinned to his sides, his lungs so compressed that he gasped.

'For the love o' Mike . . .' he pleaded.

'Have ye no' heard ther's a fitba' match the day, wee man?' asked a tall humourist beside him.

Everybody laughed at that. For them there was nothing odd or notably objectionable in their dangerous discomfort. It was, at the worst, a purgatorial episode on the passage to Elysium.

So they passed under the River to be emptied in their hundreds among the red sandstone tenements of the South Side. Under the high banks of the Park a score of streams met and mingled, the streams that had come by train or tram or motor car or on foot to see the Game of Games.

Danny ran for it as soon as his feet were on the earth's surface again, selecting in an experienced glance the turnstile with the shortest queue before it, ignoring the mournful column that waited without hope at the Unemployed Gate. His belly pushed the bar precisely as his shilling smacked on the iron counter. A moment later he was tearing as if for dear life up the long flight of cindered steps leading to the top of the embankment.

He achieved his favourite position without difficulty: high on one of the topmost terraces and behind the eastern goal. Already the huge amphitheatre seemed well filled. Except where the monstrous stands broke the skyline there were cliffs of human faces, for all the world like banks of gravel, with thin clouds of tobacco smoke drifting across them. But Danny knew that thousands were still to come to pack the terraces to the point of suffocation, and, with no eyes for the sombre strangeness of the spectacle, he proceeded to establish himself by settling his arms firmly along the iron bar before him and making friendly, or at least argumentative, contact with his neighbours.

He was among enthusiasts of his own persuasion. In consonance with ancient custom the police had shepherded supporters of the Rangers to one end of the ground and supporters of the Celtic to the other: so far as segregation was possible with a great mob of human beings. For this game between Glasgow's two leading teams had more in it than the simple test of relative skill. Their colours, blue and green, were symbolic. Behind the rivalry of players, behind even the commercial rivalry of limited companies, was the dark significance of sectarian and racial passions. Blue for the Protestants of Scotland and Ulster, green for the Roman Catholics of the Free State; and it was a bitter war that was to be waged on that strip of white-barred turf. All the social problems of a hybrid city were to be sublimated in the imminent clash of mercenaries.

Danny was ready as the next man to fight a supporter of the other team, but he had no opportunity of doing so. They were solid for Rangers within a radius of twenty yards from where he stood, and time until the kick-off was pleasantly taken up with discussion of the miracles their favourites could perform. They needed no introductions to one another. Expertise was assumed. The anxiety was that the Rangers team, as announced and on form, could be relied on to beat the men from the East. It was taken for granted that the Rangers were in normal circumstances the superiors of the Celts; but here, it seemed, were special circumstances to render the issue of the afternoon's match peculiarly obscure.

Danny had some heartening exchanges with a man, smaller and older and grimmer than himself, who at his elbow smoked a clay pipe with a very short stem. The small man was not prepared to be unduly optimistic. Rangers were a fine bunch of boys, but the Celtic had been playing up great these last few Saturdays.

'It's a' in the melting-pot,' declared the small man, who had been reading the newspapers. 'I'm tellin' ye – it's a' in the bloody melting-pot.'

'Melting-pot, my foot!' Danny insisted gallantly. 'It's all in Alan Morton's left toe – out on the wing there. Wait till ye see the wee dandy.'

'Alan's fine,' the small man allowed gravely. 'Alan's a dandy. Alan's the best bloody outside left in fitba' the day. But I've been studying form, see?' He paused to let an attenuated dribble of saliva fall between his feet, and it took him a long time to wipe clean the stem of his short pipe. 'I've been studying form. Aye, I've been studying form – reading a' the papers, looking back a' the records – and it's like this. When ye've the Rangers here and the Celtic there and there's no much between them in the League–'

His discourse was interrupted by the irreverent voice of a youth behind. 'Does the wife know ye're out, old man?' it asked.

Laughter, half-friendly, half-derisive rose about them.

'I'll knock your block off, young fella,' said the old fellow, turning gravely on the youth and slowly removing the pipe from his wet mouth.

'Please, teacher, I'm sorry I spoke,' his tormentor assured him, mock-afraid.

They all laughed again; and so it went on – rough give-and-take, simple wisdom and facetious nonsense, passion and sentiment, hate and friendly laughter – while a brass band pumped out melody in the lee of the grandstand and press photographers hovered restlessly in anticipation of the appearance of the teams.

The Celtic came first, strangely attractive in their white and green, and there was a roar from the western end of the ground ('Hefty-looking lot o' bastards,' admitted the small, old man at Danny's side.) They were followed by a party of young men in light blue jerseys; and then it's seemed that the low-hanging clouds must split at the impact of the yell that rose to greet them from forty-thousand throats. The referee appeared, jaunty in his shorts and khaki jacket; the linesmen, similarly attired, ran to their positions. In a strange hush, broken only by the thud of footballs kicked by the teams uneasily practising, the captains tossed for ends. Ah! Rangers had won and would play with the sou'westerly wind, straight towards the goal behind which Danny stood in his eagerness.

This was enough to send a man off his head. Good old Rangers – and to hell with the Pope! Danny gripped the iron bar before him. The players trotted limberly to their positions. For a moment there was dead silence over Ibrox Park. Then the whistle blew, a thin, curt, almost feeble announcement of glory.

For nearly two hours thereafter Danny Shields lived far beyond himself in a whirling world of passion. All sorts of racial emotions were released by this clash of athletic young men; the old clans of Scotland lived again their ancient hatreds in this struggle for goals. Not a man on the terraces paused to reflect that it was a spectacle cunningly arranged to draw their shillings, or to remember that the twenty-two players were so many slaves of a commercial system, liable to be bought and sold like fallen women, without any regard for their feelings as men. Rangers had drawn their warriors from all corners of Scotland, lads from mining villages, boys from Ayrshire farms, and even an undergraduate from the University of Glasgow. Celtic likewise had ranged the industrial belt and even crossed to Ulster and the Free State for men fit to win matches so that dividends might accrue. But for such as Danny they remained peerless and fearless warriors, saints of the Blue or Green as it might be; and in delight in the cunning moves of them, in their tricks and asperities, the men on the terraces found release from the drabness of their own industrial degradation.

That release they expressed in ways extremely violent. They exhorted their favourites to dreadful enterprises of assault and battery. They loudly questioned every decision of the referee. In moments of high tension they raved obscenely, using a language ugly and violent in its wealth of explosive consonants – f's and k's and b's expressing the vehemence of their passions. The young man behind Danny, he who had chaffed his scientific neighbour, was notable in foulness of speech. His commentary on the game was unceasing, and not an observation could he make but one primitive Anglo-Saxon epithet must qualify every noun – and serve, frequently, as a verb. It was as if a fever of hate had seized that multitude, neutralising for the time everything gracious and kindly.

Yet that passionate horde had its wild and liberating humours. Now and again a flash of rough jocularity would release a gust of laughter, so hearty that it was as if they rejoiced to escape from the bondage of their own intensity of partisanship. Once in a while a clever movement by one of the opposition team would evoke a mutter of unwilling but sincere admiration. They were abundantly capable of calling upon their favourites to use their brawn, but they were punctilious in the observation of the unwritten laws that are called those of sportsmanship. They constituted, in fact, a stern but ultimate reliable jury, demanding of their entertainers the very best they could give, insisting that the spectacle be staged with all the vigour that could be brought to it.

The Old Firm – thus the evening papers conventionally described the meeting of Rangers and Celtic. It was a game fought hard and fearless and merciless, and it was but the rub of the business that the wearers of the Blue scored seven minutes from half-time.

The goal was the outcome of a movement so swift that even a critic of Danny's perspicacity could hardly tell just how it happened. What is it to say that a back cleared from near the Rangers' goal; that the ball went on the wind to the nimble feet of Alan Morton on the left wing; that the small but intense performer carried it at lightning speed down the line past this man in green-and-white and then that; that he crossed before the menace of a charging back, the ball soaring in a lovely curve to the waiting centre; and that it went then like a rocket into a corner of the Celtic net, the goalkeeper sprawling in a futile endeavour to stop it?

It was a movement completed almost as soon as it was begun and Danny did not really understand it until he read his evening paper on the way home. But it was a goal, a goal for Rangers, and he went mad for a space.

With those about him he screamed his triumph, waving his cap wildly above his head, taunting most foully those who might be in favour of a team so thoroughly humiliated as the Celtic.

From this orgasm he recovered at length.

'Christ!' he panted. 'That was a bobbydazzler.'

'Good old Alan!' screeched the young man behind. 'Ye've got the suckers bitched!'

'A piece of perfect bloody positioning,' gravely observed the scientist on Danny's left.

'Positioning, ma foot!' snorted Danny. 'It was just bloomin' good fitba! Will ye have a snifter, old fella?'

So they shared the half-mutchkin of raw whisky, the small man politely wiping the neck of the bottle with his sleeve before handing it back to Danny.

'That's a good dram, son,' he observed judicially.

Half-time permitted of discussion that was not, however, without its heat, the young man behind exploiting a critical theory of half-back play that kept some thirty men about him in violent controversy until the whistle blew again. Then the fever came back on them with redoubled fury – One–nothing for Rangers at half-time made an almost agonising situation; and as the Celtic battled to equalise, breaking themselves again and again on a defence grimly determined to hold its advantage, the waves of green hurling themselves on rocks of blue, there was a frenzy on the terraces.

When, five minutes before time, the men from the East were awarded a penalty kick, Danny's heart stopped beating for a space, and when the fouled forward sent the ball flying foolishly over the net, it nearly burst. The Rangers would win. 'Stick it, lads!' he yelled again and again. 'Kick the tripes out the dirty Papists!' The Rangers would win. They must win. . . A spirt of whistle; and, by God, they had won!

In immediate, swift reaction, Danny turned then and, without a word to his neighbours, started to fight his way to the top of the terracing and along the fence that crowned it to the stairs and the open gate. To the feelings of those he jostled and pushed he gave not the slightest thought. Now the battle was for a place in the Subway, and he ran as soon as he could, hurtling down the road, into the odorous maw of Copland Road station and through the closing door of a train that had already started on its journey northwards.

He even got a seat and was glad of it. Now he felt tired and flat after that long stand on a step of beaten cinders and nearly two hours of extreme emotional strain. It had been a hell of an afternoon, right enough! At Partick Cross he paused only to buy an evening paper before daring into the public-house nearest at hand. It was disappointing that the barman already knew the result, thanks to the daily miracle of the Press, and he saw in a glance at the stop-press that his coupon was burst again – Queen's Park down to St Mirren at home, the bunch of stiffs! But the accumulator looked good, his team having nine goals to their credit in two matches and a 2–1 victory as like as possible next Saturday. And there was the glory of telling with authority how Rangers, those shining heroes, had won at Ibrox that very afternoon.

Danny was happy and in his contentment thought kindly of Agnes at home. There remained in his mind the substance of his promise to her, and he did not linger unduly over his glass and pint. She too would welcome his news of victory, and he hurried home to tell her.

'My, that's fine, Dan!' she triumphed with him.' 'It must have been great. But I've left your good clothes ben in the room, and ye'd best go and change now. We're to be at the Commodore at six.'

The Final'

from The Thistle and the Grail

ROBIN JENKINS (1912–)

Published in 1954, The Thistle and the Grail, *by Robin Jenkins, is one of the cleverest comic novels to come from Scotland. The Thistle in question is Drumsagart Thistle, a junior football team from a small Lanarkshire town; the Grail that they are seeking is the Scottish Junior Cup. In this extract we follow the Thistle to Hampden Park for the Cup Final, and learn whether or not they are destined to win the 'Holy Grail'. It is difficult to say if Jenkins is using the pursuit of football success as a working out of the Arthurian legend in the manner of Bernard Malamud's baseball story* The Natural. *Perhaps Andrew Rutherford, the club chairman, is Arthur; perhaps one of the heroic knights Galahad and Percival is young Alec Elrigmuir the team's centre forward? It is difficult to say. What is certain is that Jenkins's notion of a comic novel, written around a small mining community and the gradually building suspense of a knock-out competition, is a great one. And the Thistle's striving to find the Grail must have a flaw, in the way that all the Arthurian tales have flaws; and this one is that Drumsagart Thistle only reached the Final by bending the rules. They appealed against being knocked out on dubious grounds and won the appeal.*

To make another comparison instead: there is something about the tumbling vitality and colour of this book that is reminiscent of a Bruegel painting. The large cast of characters, young and old – we seem to meet almost everyone in Drumsagart at one time or another – could well be drawn from Robin Jenkins's own experience of growing up in Lanarkshire. As the author of more than twenty novels, such as the acclaimed Guests of War *and* The Cone-Gatherers, *he brings all the elements of humour, vigour and rounded presentation of character to bear, most of all as the crowds make their way to the great cathedral of Hampden. A few readers may feel there is something lacking in the actual physical description of the action in the Final. It may not be totally recognisable as a football match as we know it, but perhaps that is because nowadays we have been 'desensitised' by the school of football journalism which gave the language 'a game of two halves' and 'shots nestling in the onion bag'.*

THE FINAL

Standing by the Cross, on the beautiful May afternoon, with the Town Hall clock striking three, Sergeant Elvan saw that he was the only human being at that precise moment on the main street. Not even on the dreichest, wettest Sunday in the murk of December had he seen the town so deserted. Yet the sunshine was warm and mellow, the leaves of the elms and poplars glittered in a pleasant breeze, yesterday's rain had laid the dust and cleansed the air, starlings and sparrows twittered in the trees, and high above an adjacent field a lark sang. It was an afternoon for old men to warm chilled bones on the benches in the fragrance of the flower-beds; for young mothers to push their prams with their sunburnt babies sleeping or chuckling at their own toes; for adventuring boys to be setting out for the pond under Drumsagart Hill to fish for minnows; for little girls to wear large white hats and very short dresses; for the philosophers at the University of the Unicorn to take off their caps and let the sweetness of the sun through to their bitter brains; for the matriarchs, grim, resolute, and compassionate, battered bulwarks against the incessant seas of despair, to stand at the doors of shops, clutching their purses, discussing prices and the latest births. Yet the street was as empty as if that morning, instead of old Davie Masters with the brush he sang to, Death had swept it.

The sergeant looked at the nearest flower-bed. In the midst of tall tulips, crimson, yellow, mauve, and pink, was an enormous many-headed thistle. It was not there through an accident of the wind or because of the negligence of the town council's gardeners; it had been carefully dug out of a field and replanted in that place. In every flower-bed was a similar thistle, a weed given royal supremacy over the lovely tulips. There was a clue here as to the vacuity of the street.

In George Rankin's butcher-shop window was another clue: a piece of silver cardboard cut into a peculiar shape. Across the street, in Robert Hutton the tailor's window, was still another hint: a large photograph draped with broad blue and thin red ribbons; it showed a dozen proud men with their arms folded and their knees bare. Further along, in Will Henderson's photographer's window, was another picture, this time of one footballer only, life-size, in colour: he had fair hair and had a ball at his feet. It was said that this spectacle in his window had brought Will more business in the last month than in the whole year previously.

The sergeant began to walk along the street. A cat ran miaowing out of a closemouth to rub itself against his legs. He bent down to stroke it.

'Whether they win or lose today,' he said, 'you'd be wise this night to find a cellar to hide in.' A bumble-bee hummed by to bury itself inside a red tulip. 'They'll be as thick as bees yonder,' he murmured, rather wistfully, as he went on; for he knew his own two boys would be buzzing as loudly as any. 'And to think,' he added, but without conviction, 'it's all based on fraud and trickery.'

Thicker than bees they were at Hampden Park that afternoon. Towards that famous Mecca they had been heading since one o'clock by bus, train, private car, taxi, motor-bike, lorry, van, invalid chair, bicycle, and foot. Stour was swirled up at all the entrances by feet anxious to get through the turnstiles early and so be able to take up a good position near the front. Beggars, blind, maimed, or imbecile, some with war medals, sang outside pay-boxes. Harry Link was one of them, with a Drumsagart blue-red rosette in one lapel and an Allanbank yellow-gold one in the other. Newspaper placards were everywhere, promising to tell that evening the whole story of the Final to those thousands hurrying to see it with their own eyes. Ice-cream barrows and carts were busy outside the gates. More mobile, and far more vociferous, were the sellers of chocolate and chewing-gum: their stereotyped cries – 'P.K., a penny a packet; Duncans' Hazelnut, penny a bar' – were as indigenous there as the cooing of doves in tranquil woods or the laughing hyenas in African prairies. Peddlers of rosettes were impartial, having on their trays both the Drumsagart and the Allanbank colours. In their shouting, though, was a hoarseness of desperation, for after the game, though one part of their stock would be snatched up, the other part would be as unsaleable as eggs marked rotten.

Those crowds swarming into Hampden were different in many ways from the usual crowds attending the important Senior matches there. They were made up largely of family parties, with many women and children. Being from various country towns and villages, they spoke in broader accents, with more Scots in their vocabulary than American. They were more sedately dressed. Their faces were redder, their hands thicker, their hair shorter, their humour more homely, their passions much less fierce. One old man, rolling along the pavement as if it was a ploughed field, saw a cartful of dung outside a house gate; it was being sold in bagfuls. He went over and sniffed at the dung, thrust a finger into it, and then announced to the scandalised merchants: 'By God, you've been gey sore on the sawdust.' He continued towards the football field, more indignant at the fraud perpetrated on the soil than on these city gardeners. That avenue had seen millions of football fans hurrying towards the shrine; his kind, however, was unusual, being met only once a year, in May, when the Junior Cup Final was played.

The contestants this year were Drumsagart Thistle and Allanbank Rangers from Ayrshire. Of course everybody from Allanbank came to see the Rangers win, and everybody came from Drumsagart prayed for a Thistle victory. The large majority of spectators at the outset were neutral. Some were there to support the team which had knocked their own team out of the competition; others to see that team itself suffer defeat. Many would make up their minds as soon as they saw the actual players on the field; Turk McCabe was to engage the sympathies of a large proportion of these for his side. A few would decide aesthetically: they would cheer the team with the bonnier strip. Still fewer would all during the game favour neither team but would applaud good play whoever was responsible. One section, small but violently outspoken, came not to support Allanbank but to revile, abuse, and asperse their opponents – in short, to wish them to the blackest corner of hell: these hailed from Muirvale and still burned for revenge for that infamous but successful protest.

A section of the vast grandstand had been reserved for Drumsagart fans able to pay the higher prices; another, at a judicious distance, for the affluent Allanbank. These sections from a little way off looked like gigantic rosettes in the rival colours, so many were the flamboyant favours sported: scarves, handkerchiefs, ties, tammies, and even blouses were in the sacred colours; at least one man wore a blazer in the Allanbank yellow and gold.

Of course the majority of Drumsagart people were not in the grandstand. They could not afford to be, for one reason; and for another, just as genuine, they deprecated the snobbery of sitting in comfort watching their team strive; they preferred to stand amongst their indigent fellows, who were, after all, the experts, the custodians of the inmost mysteries. There was, therefore, one part of the terracing which needed only the Mercat Cross to be erected in its midst to become another Drumsagart. Nat Stewart was there, out of his bed against the doctor's orders, his wife's tears, and his own premonitions of death. Others present were Rab Nuneaton, ashamed to be in Glasgow wearing his Drumsagart rags; Ned Nicholson, who had been offered a seat for the grandstand by Rutherford but who preferred to be with his cronies; Jock Saunders, with his crotcheted tie round a throat as eager to pulsate with cheers as anybody else's; Crutch Brodie, for whom a place at a crush barrier had been cleared, so that he could lean on it to take some weight off his leg; Nippy Henderson, who kept reminding everybody about the free dram at Malarkin's that night; and Tinto Brown, who was not there in body, being now two months buried in the paupers' corner of Drumsagart cemetery, but whom everybody felt to be there in spirit.

In the grandstand were many Drumsagart notabilities, present out of a sense of history rather than from any zest for football. They seldom attended the matches at home, but here at Hampden Park, Glasgow, this mighty open-air cathedral, where world-famous teams and personalities had appeared, here this afternoon it was Drumsagart's occasion; and Allanbank's, too, of course. Therefore the Provost was there, with his wife and daughter. Most of the councillors were present, among them Mr Lockhart, who, however, preferred to look on himself as a shepherd from other pastures. Nan was beside him, immensely interested and delighted; she kept assuring him the baby, in Nurse Brodie's charge, would come to no harm. He, too, was immensely thrilled, not so much by the actual scene around him as by an imaginary one, this tremendous bowl crammed to its full capacity of 140,000 souls, assembled not to watch football but to listen to the word of God and sing hymns. He did not presume to see himself as the preacher at so stupendous a conventicle: he had not done well enough at far humbler Drumsagart Park to justify that ambition; but he could readily see himself by the side of the inspired evangelist, a staunch lieutenant in the war against paganism. He was interrupted in this stirring by Nan's hand nipping his arm and her voice whispering, in excitement, glee, and malice: 'Look, Harold, yonder's Mr and Mrs Sowlas. For goodness sake, look at her hat. It's like a wreath.'

Margot Malarkin, in one of the most expensive seats, sat beside a man whom nobody knew, but whom everybody wished to know. He was elderly, about sixty perhaps, with silver hair and a pale hand oftener than not on her knee; but he gave off an aroma of wealth, with his clothes more suitable for Ascot than Hampden Park, and nothing was surer than that among the many cars in the car-park his would be the largest and the most magnificent.

Another couple to attract much attention were Mysie Dougary and John Watson, the bank-clerk. It was agreed, after inquisitive inspection, that Alec Elrigmuir still had a chance. He was known to be in love with her still; which was wonderful, which was as good as a story in the *People's Friend*, which helped the Thistle, for it inspired Alec to prodigious play (in the semi-final he had scored three goals), but which, all the same, confirmed the belief, now universally held though seldom uttered, that off the football field he was simpler than a man ought to be.

Archie Birkwood had brought his daughter and his wife. There, amidst all that laughter before the game began, she was given full licence; but, to his disappointment rather, she did not take advantage of it. She laughed, but temperately; she stood up and waved her hand to friends, but not as if she held in it the flag of victory.

Robbie Rutherford and his two boys had been sent complimentary tickets by the president. They were dressed in new clothes and already looked healthier from the change of house. Isa was at home looking after the sick girl.

The committee-men, of course, were in the best seats in the centre; and at the very altar, as it were, in the directors' box, was Andrew Rutherford, the president. With him he'd brought his wife and son, and also his brother-in-law Harry and his wife. It had been hoped for a time that Harry would buy his place on that eminence by supplying the pipe band with new accoutrements; but the warm possibility had turned to a cold doubt. Therefore he unmeritedly sat amongst the mighty, who included Glasgow's Lord Provost; while standing below in the enclosure, handy to an exit, were Bob McKelvie and his men in mufti, ready at the final whistle to dash out to their waiting bus, be rushed to Drumsagart, and there be waiting to greet the team with proud lament if beaten, with shrill and boisterous paeans if victorious. If they had got their new outfits they might have been out there strutting and piping to entertain this crowd of thousands, instead of the band of the King's Own Cameron Highlanders, which, though proficient enough, blew from duty rather than love.

To shrieks, bellows, and buglings of acclamation the teams trotted out side by side. They did not at once sprint towards their respective goals, but lined up leaving a lane between them, down which in a minute or so came walking the Lord Provost wearing his chain of office and accompanied by the Allanbank president, who presented his players, and by Andrew Rutherford, who presented his. The Provost had an amiable smile and a handclasp for each player; but for one he had an involuntary laugh. Turk McCabe had not shaved; his hair was cut close to the scalp; his shorts were so long as to be misnomers; and he wore an expression of simian melancholy. At the Provost's laughter he showed his two or three teeth in what was really reciprocal mirth, but which looked rather like resentment in the tree-tops. The Provost was a man of humour; outwardly impartial as his position demanded, he became at heart Turk's man and in the ensuing game applauded his every valiant rescue; which meant he was applauding often.

Presentations over, the teams made for the goals for some preliminary practice. Photographers waylaid one or two to snap them. Alec Elrigmuir had three snapping him like crocodiles at the same moment. It was noticed that when one approached Turk to confer on him this accolade of being photographed on the field of play, in the presence of forty thousand roaring devotees, he was repulsed either by word or glower, or by both, so precipitately did he run backwards in his retreat. The crowd roared appreciation of Turk's modesty. Without having so far kicked a ball, he was already a favourite. A thousand witticisms were launched as he set out on his usual circular canter. Many guessed this was his way of praying.

To the Allanbank's goalkeeper ran a boy in a yellow-and-gold jersey with a horseshoe of yellow-and-gold ribbons; to Sam Teem in the Drumsagart goal scooted the nephew of Ned Nicholson wearing a bright blue tall hat and carrying a thistle of the same colour almost as large as himself. Other worshippers leapt over the barriers to rush out on to the field and shake their champions' hands. Nathaniel Stewart was one of them. Despite the remonstrations of a policeman who followed him about, he insisted on shaking the hand of every Drumsagart player. To Alec Elrigmuir he said, 'Alec, son, I'll be dying soon. Win for me today, win for me today, and I'll die happy.' Alec politely said he would do his best. To Turk he merely said, 'Turk, for God's sake'; and Turk answered by winking.

Then the field was cleared of these interlopers, the coin was tossed up, Lachie Houston guessed wrongly, causing tremors in the hearts of his Drumsagart followers, the players took up positions, Alec Elrigmuir kicked off, and the great game, the Cup Final, was on at last.

Had one team, Drumsagart say, scored several goals early and prevented their opponents from retaliating, many souls that afternoon would have been spared the vertigo of suspense. Drumsagart souls would have kept on soaring, Allanbank souls plunging: there would have been no soarings, hoverings, and plungings in sick succession, time after time, while hands covered terrified eyes or teeth bit into scarves or eyes glistened or mouths watered or hands were clasped or legs stiffened or bottoms sprang off seats or seats were sprinkled with the tin-tacks of mortification.

It would have been known in advance that the dancing that evening on the wide pavements of Drumsagart would be natural and joyous, while the jigging in Allanbank's school playground would be half-hearted or hysterical. It would have been known, too, that the Drumsagart feast of ham and egg in the Town Hall would have the mustard of success, whereas the Allanbank boiled ham and tomato and lettuce would have lurking amidst it the maggot of disappointment. Above all, it would have been known that Drumsagart beer would be an elixir, preserving that time of bliss for ever; whereas in Allanbank pubs at the bottom of every glass would be found the frog of disenchantment, with its eyes wide open.

All that could have been known and prepared for had Drumsagart – or Allanbank, of course – scored those early goals.

But for a long time neither side could score, though one or other came very close to it almost every minute. Excitement ran among the players, teasing them into blunders that had the spectators shrieking, leaping to their feet, hammering their heads, moaning, laughing, and utterly silent. Alec Elrigmuir three times struck the cross bar with the ball, and once, from four yards, with the Allanbank goalkeeper flat on his face as if chewing daisies and the other Allanbank defenders reeling in horror at the anticipated blow, he hit the ball with all his juvenescent might and high over the bar it flew. Drumsagart howled, Allanbank smiled, Mysie Dougary turned like a wounded vixen on John Watson, who had, in company with thousands of Drumsagart well-wishers, cried: 'Oh you mug!' He was not a mug, she screamed, he was excited – that was all; he was worried too, but he would win the game in the end even if she had to go to the pavilion at half-time to tell him there was no need to worry any more. Young Watson scowled, for he was not so simple as Alec.

Among the Allanbank players excitement that hampered them had an ally, as grotesque as Puck and as supernatural in his endeavours. Turk McCabe, though his feet were still tender, played as though a goal scored against the Thistle would be his own death warrant, would be the signal for him to go back to the weird underworld from which he'd obviously come. Immortal though he was, he sweated, suffered, slaved, and bled more than any human. Not even the dragon guarding the Fleece in the woods of Colchis showed more devotion.

Half-time came without scoring; but three minutes after the restart Allanbank scored. While their followers were trying to express their glee, with voices, hands, eyes and lungs all inadequate, and while Drumsagart players and spectators alike were shivering at this first touch of the icy finger, Turk McCabe snatched the ball from an Allanbank foot, and instead of kicking it upfield as he'd done so often he began to charge towards the Allanbank goal as if he knew his immortality was fading and could be revived only by a goal nullifying that other. Allanbank players drew back, expecting him to pass the ball to one of his colleagues; they could not believe this freak had any virtue outside its own penalty area. But when he was within their own penalty area, and when at least three of them were hurtling themselves at him, he slipped the ball aside to Elrigmuir, who, football genius, was in the right place to kick it with wonderful élan past the Allanbank goalkeeper.

It was Drumsagart's turn now to find their rejoicing limited only by the coarseness of flesh. Mysie Dougary was on her feet, shrieking like any harridan and waving her tammy. Her rival, Margot Malarkin, shrieked too and dug her nails into her escort's knee in a way to bring tears of anguish to his mildly lewd eyes. Mrs Lockhart bounced up and down on her seat, so that her husband, remembering her fragility, was forced to chide her gently.

In the directors' box Hannah Rutherford was astonished and moved to see on her husband's face and hear in his voice a joy so spontaneous and innocent she knew, as deep in her heart she had suspected, there had been something a little false in his new delight in her company. Yet strangely she was not offended; rather did she feel an unprecedented pity for him and a fresh flow of affection. Perhaps it helped her to see on her other side that their son, too, was transformed by joy.

On the terracing, in Drumsagart corner, men who for years had disliked and distrusted one another were shaking hands. Even Rab Nuneaton, for whom friendly contacts had been so long loathsome, was taking any hand presented to him, and he was listening to yells of happiness in an unfamiliar voice that emerged from his own mouth.

On the field Turk and Alec were being pummelled by their team-mates. A congratulatory thumb poked into Turk's eye, a fist struck his scalp like a hammer; but brushing these off as if they were confetti, he shouted hoarsely 'The Cup! The Cup!' as if it was a mystical slogan.

Excitement that had made them clumsy in the beginning now made the players swift and fiery. The ball flew like hawk, skimmed the grass like hare, bounced like kangaroo; it had in it not mere air but the hopes, fears, frenzies, and ecstasies of that great crowd. It went everywhere – up on to the terracing even, into the grandstand, into this, that, and every section of the field – everywhere except into one or other of the goals.

Watches were in hands now; minutes, half-minutes, seconds were being counted. People anxious to be away early to avoid the homeward crush lingered, throwing backward glances, walking a step or two away, turning again, waiting, watching, groaning, sighing, and gasping. It would be a draw, everybody said; it would have to be refought next Saturday. Look, the referee was staring at his watch for the sixth or seventh time; his whistle was going to his mouth to blow for time-up. But look again. Look at young Alec Elrigmuir. He was on the ball, he was sidestepping the centre-half, dribbling past the right-back, swerving round that other player, and banging the ball well and truly past the goalkeeper.

Allanbank was stricken. Yellow-and-golden women wailed; children wept; and men whined: 'No. Offside. Time was up. Foul.' But there was no remedy. The referee was blowing his whistle for the end, no god descended, and all Drumsagart was abandoned to ecstasy and cacophony.

On the field the players were being punched and kissed by hordes of fanatically grateful followers; among these was Nat Stewart, so overwrought he found himself shaking the hand of an Allanbank player. On the terracing, when other more restrained Drumsagart rejoicers wished to shake hands with their Allanbank rivals the latter declined with shudders, saying never in sobriety could they be magnanimous enough.

In the grandstand the committee-men, captains in victory, were loving one another. Angus Tennant even, with devilment in his love, kissed Sam Malarkin's cheek, which tasted, he said afterwards, like a jujube. It was the kind of daft thing expected of Angus, but nobody could have anticipated it would put Sam into such a towering pet. Indeed, Sam's wan peevishness all that evening was to be attributed wrongly to the loss of whisky, as enervating to a publican as the loss of blood.

In the directors' box Rutherford showed no restraint. He kissed his wife, lifted up his son above his head as he'd done when the boy was an infant, shook hands rapturously with Harry, and slapped Mabel's bottom.

'We've done it, Hannah,' he cried. 'We've won the Cup.'

She smiled and nodded: her thought was, What money is it putting in your purse? But she did not, as formerly, sharpen that thought and wield it; she kept it blunted and sheathed; and she found, to her surprise, she had acted not so much virtuously as happily.

'I could greet,' he cried. 'I feel so pleased I could greet.'

It was Harry's turn to smile: his meant, So you're a wean yet, Andrew, in many ways? Well, weans are amenable, especially happy weans.

'If only old Tinto could hae been spared to see this,' cried Andrew.

Hannah noted that it was the old drunkard rather than his father he wished still alive.

Then the players, still in their shorts and jerseys, and with the grime and sweat of battle, came up the steps in single file. Lachie Houston led them. From the Lord Provost he received the Cup, which he immediately held on high, the silver grail at long last achieved, so that the Drumsagart people roared their homage. Then every player got handshakes of congratulation, first from the Provost, and immediately after from their president, who had words as well for them. 'Well done, boy. Champion work, Jim. Tom, you played like a hero,' and so on. He did not, as most did, praise Turk McCabe and Alec Elrigmuir above the rest; and the rest noticed it and were grateful.

He insisted on shaking the hands of the Allanbank players, too, though they seemed to think it was an act of supreme supererogation. To the Allanbank officials he was generous in his commiserations. They had to accept them, but one incontinently muttered: 'We should never have been playing you anyway: a poor Cup that's won by a protest.' Rutherford overheard and for a moment experienced his old dismay. 'That's true,' he said, to the person nearest him.

It was Hannah. She hadn't been attending. 'What's true, Andrew?'

He began to laugh and laid his hand on her shoulder. 'Never mind, Hannah. Whoever rejoices, there are bound to be some with sore hearts. We're just not built that we can all be happy together.'

She understood now, for all round were mourning Allanbank faces. 'No, but we that can manage to be happy, Andrew, are not to be expected to give it up till everyone joins us.'

'No, Hannah. That's right.'

It was at last, she thought, the formula they had been searching for for years, reconciling their different points of view. Hampden grandstand was a queer place to find it.

'Would you mind very much,' he asked, 'if I didn't go straight back home with you? I'd like to be in Drumsagart tonight and see the celebrations. Maybe you would like to come yourself? Maybe you would all like to come?'

'Not me, Andrew,' she said, smiling. 'But I've no objections if you want to go.'

'Thanks all the same, Andrew,' said Harry, 'but I think I'd be out of place in the celebrations. I've enjoyed myself here this afternoon, I've met some interesting and useful people, and the Thistle won. I think I can call it a day.'

'What about you, Gerald?' asked his father.

The boy gazed at his mother.

'It's up to you,' she said. 'It'll be a bit of a rabble there tonight, but surely your father can look after you.'

He saw she was no longer on his side against his father; and he felt sorry for himself.

'I don't know,' he muttered.

'It'll be great fun, Gerald,' said his father. 'There's to be dancing to the pipe band, and fireworks, and –'

'No. I want to go home.'

His father was disappointed. 'All right, son.' He looked at them all and laughed. 'Am I being thrawn?' he asked. 'Should I just go home too? Mind you, I'm the president.'

'You go to Drumsagart,' said Hannah. 'Likely it'll be your last visit there for a long time.'

So he went to Drumsagart, in the bus carrying the conquerors. Part of the roof had been slid back, and by standing on a seat a man could display the Cup to the passing world. That was a duty as much as a pleasure, but it was also less convenient than sitting comfortably in a seat; therefore it was honourably shared among the players. Only Turk refused: on the ground that it was a damned stupid way of travelling in a bus, one might as well be on a motor-bike. He had to be excused; his determined, surly common sense in the midst of the exultation was a pity, but it couldn't be helped: Turk was a force of nature, like a volcano, say, and if he chose to erupt that night after consuming gallons of whisky, so that Elvan and at least three bobbies dragged him to jail – why, then, it would all be part of the saga of the winning of the Cup.

The other hero, Alec Elrigmuir, was drunk already. He had to be restrained from climbing out on to the roof of the bus. Going through villages on the road home, he threw pennies to children, some of whom cheered and some of whom searched for clods to throw back. Everybody knew it was not just because he'd scored the winning goal, nor because six Senior clubs had begged him to play for them, but because Mysie Dougary had come shouting for him at the dressing-room door, had kissed him though he was naked from the waist up, and had called him her Sandy.

Rutherford sat amidst that busload of familiar men, noticing how happiness had purged them, as it had purged him, of all characteristic meanness and selfishness. This really was how men were, how they would wish to be always if circumstances allowed them. He had been wrong to think they had begun to respect and even like him because he had thrown away all his scruples about accepting their own standards of conduct and belief, which were the standards of pigs round a trough, every man for himself and to hell with the hindmost. Surely that respect and liking had been granted simply because he had given them a chance to respect and like him. Hitherto he had been too stiff, too remote, too entangled in prejudice and illusion. Here was the proof, his hand being shaken every minute, his back slapped, his part in the general victory loudly acknowledged.

When the bus, with dozens of vehicles following it, like coaches a great hearse, came into the main street there was Bob McKelvie ready with his swollen-cheeked men. To the shrill braggadocio of 'Scotland For Ever' that vast procession crawled along to the Town Hall, where from the lofty flagpole was flying a blue flag with a crimson thistle in the centre. Along each kerb were hundreds of townspeople waving, cheering, and laughing. Boys went wild, fencing each other with stolen tulips, or hooting at the team from the tops of trees. It was not thought likely even Sergeant Elvan would be at his normal work that evening.

It seemed to Rutherford from inside the bus, with tears almost in his eyes, that his native town, evergreen, deep-rooted, but sombre, had suddenly burst forth with bright flowers.

When the bus stopped at the Town Hall entrance the crowd began to roar for speeches; but for quite ten minutes more everybody had to wait in an explosive, sentimental, derisive, hilarious patience while Bob McKelvie and his pipers exhausted lungs and repertoire. When the last ululation had died away into the sunshine the speeches were made from the top of the bus. First was Lachie Houston, who let the Cup speak for him.

'Here it is, folks,' he shouted, and held it up.

The applause was excessive; at least so Mr Lockhart thought, now back at the manse, soothing the baby in his arms.

Alec Elrigmuir was called on. 'I'll tell you this,' he cried. 'I'm glad we won. And I'll tell you something else: me and Mysie are going to get married soon.'

Again the response was loud enough to waken all babies within half a mile and to make impossible the hushing of those not asleep. Mr Lockhart had to come away from the window, and found himself uttering the ungracious wish that Nan had stayed at home to attend to her fundamental duty instead of going out to see the fun, as she called it. It seemed she was fond of pipe music.

Wattie Cleugh spoke. 'This is a proud, proud day for Drumsagart,' he said, and went on saying it in a dozen different ways until at last even pride wearied.

Other players were shouted for: some refused; those who obliged were very brief. Turk at first was a refuser. The crowd kept roaring for him. At last he sprang up through the hole in the roof of the bus. When he was seen they cheered him so mightily that what he was roaring at them was not at first heard, although he kept repeating it, more and more vehemently. Then suddenly there was a hush. They were ready to listen to the blue-chinned scowling oracle.

'You're a shower of mugs,' he roared.

Apparently he could have chosen no more successful address: they cheered, whistled, clapped, and shrieked; one boy stole a great bang at the big drum.

Other committee-men spoke. Angus Tennant persevered in spite of the affectionate abuse flung at him, based mostly on the crookedness of his gaze and the fatness of his wife.

Then suddenly, at the end, when the band was getting ready to pipe the team into the Town Hall for the victory feast, there rose up a shout for the president, for Andrew Rutherford, for the man who'd got the protest.

He was afraid to speak, lest he should break the spell; yet he was afraid, too, not to speak, lest he should be admitting to himself that the spell, of friendliness, of neighbourly goodwill, was illusory; and there was always the danger that if he managed to find the right simple words someone would toss at him one disenchanting shout of spite or envy or contempt or even of hatred. Rab Nuneaton was in that crowd; so was Nippy Henderson; and many another who used, with good enough reason, to miscall him. Would one of them now, in the presence of the whole community, in the sunshine and the laughter, utter such a word?

No-one did. He found the right simple words. He was clapped as cordially as anyone else had been. When with the others he followed the pipers into the hall tears were again near his eyes.

It was a jubilant feast, even if the ham and eggs were a little cold, and Turk McCabe out of a morose silence jumped to his feet, hammered on the table for attention, passionately accused them all of having made use of him without ever having really been fond of him, and announced his intention of returning to England as soon as his mother was dead and buried.

The dancing afterwards on the pavement in the shadows of the trees became perhaps too boisterous as the males became drunker. These had all signs on their right wrists, conspicuous as they flung up their hands in corybantic extravagance. This sign was a tiny thistle in blue indelible ink, and it was proof not merely that the bearer was a true Thistle follower but also that he had been to collect his free dram of well-watered whisky at the Lucky Sporran, where four extra barmen had been engaged, and where the proprietor, in the midst of a bonanza of business, was pale and captious.

Jock Saunders was reminded of his pledge to creep on hands from the Cross to the Lucky Sporran and was challenged to make it good. He regretted he could not: it would make the knees of his trousers baggy. As these trousers had not been pressed for years, and indeed had knees not of the original cloth, his plea was accepted, amidst an uproar of appreciation like the simultaneous ripping of thousands of tight trousers.

Sergeant Elvan had been taken to the pictures by his wife; they almost had the place to themselves.

But Andrew Rutherford had to remember he no longer lived in Drumsagart; he was a visitor now, who had to keep his eye on the clock and his mind on the last bus. Therefore shortly after nine, during an impromptu concert round the Mercat Cross, at which he'd sung 'The Wee Cooper of Fife', he slipped away without saying goodbye to anyone, or at least to anyone alive. This might well be, as Hannah had hinted, his last visit here for a long time: the Drumsagart phase of his life might be ending; in that case he could hardly leave without saying farewell to his mother.

The cemetery lay out in the country among the fields, approached by quiet hedged roads. The bing of the now derelict Birkside Pit was close beside it, growing green like a hill. From the top of the bing the tombstones looked like the seagulls that were often to be seen in the neighbouring fields. Yet the white birds seldom came amongst the graves, perhaps because the geometrical paths and headstones, the decaying wreaths, and the general circumscription made too great a dissimilarity to the vast moving sea. Tits, sparrows, finches, starlings, and even the black crows, all earth-dwellers like man himself, found sanctuary there, fat worms, and crumbs left by picnicking mourners.

Rutherford met no-one on the way. Few people were so disorganised in their mourning as to be driven by it to huddle over a grave on a Saturday night. Most waited for the more propitious Sabbath when Christ in all the compassion of Sunday-school tracts might be imagined there, shaping promises with His mild bearded lips. This Saturday evening especially, with the celebrations in the town, nobody could be expected to languish there in loneliness.

Therefore as he went through the tall iron gates and made up the red path towards his mother's grave he saw no-one, only birds, butterflies, and on the green grass of one grave a black-beetle. He remembered how in boyhood, if someone had squashed such a beetle, everyone would spit, drawing a hand across his throat, and say: 'Not my grannie'. So far as he knew, boys still went through that ritual; but he had never found out what it meant.

For nearly half an hour he stood by his mother's grave, making no significant gesture, such as touching the small headstone, or plucking a blade of the grass, or reaching up for a leaf of the birch tree that grew near; thinking no important thoughts about himself and his leaving Drumsagart; revolving few memories of her. He just stood there, hat in hand, more still than the tree which the breeze stirred. Yet he did not feel this visit, this farewell, was being a failure: he had not come to weep, or pray, or beg for pity and forgiveness; he had come for a rest, a recuperation, a breathing space, and he was sure, as he softly walked away again, that he had found it.

He was almost at the gates again when he remembered there was Tinto Brown's grave to see, in the paupers' corner. He stopped, undecided. There was not much time to spare if he wanted to catch a bus to Glasgow and then a train to Helensburgh. Perhaps it would be better not to go away with the two graves confused in his mind. Yet would it not be unpardonable, on this night of victory, to be here so close to the friendless old man and not at least whisper the news to him? Whether Tinto would hear it or not, whether he was now a communicable creature of light and air, or whether he was a mess of rotting old flesh and bones under the heavy subsidised earth, all that really made no difference: the whisper would not merely be the supreme justification of football, it would also be the recognition of the dependence of human beings on one another, living and dead together. Yet he hesitated, unwilling to admit the true obstacle between him and Tinto's grave: there used to be a railing round the section owned by the parish for the burial of its paupers, and it had been removed through the agitation of Andrew's father.

Sharply he turned and hurried towards the low-lying obscure corner nearest to the pit bing. He thought he could hear faint sounds from the town: the spree was still on, and would continue after midnight. Tinto would have been foremost in it. All his life he had stood for the merry-making side of life. Many had disapproved of him, not really because they thought him wicked, but because, in spite of his coarseness, his drunkenness, and his lechery, he had represented a rebellion against the prevailing greyness, the sterile puritanism, and the inherited belief that exuberant joy was ungodly. True enough, the joy in the town tonight was exuberant; but Tinto had tried to make every day a day of Cup-winning: too much pleasure on earth weakened the promise of heaven and strengthened the threat of hell.

When he was amongst the paupers' graves, looking for the freshest one, he was smiling, as if he expected Tinto to be there to greet him, with a characteristic report on his new habitation and companions. When he found the grave therefore, and saw there was somebody sitting on the verge of grass round it, he stopped, shook his head hard, shivered, and laughed.

The apparition heard the laughter and turned, to reveal the face of Crutch Brodie streaming with tears and smiling. His cap was lying beside him, and his crutch: he looked like a war-victim begging by the side of a road; only the medals were missing.

Rutherford walked up to him. 'Well, it's yourself, Crutch,' he said.

Crutch touched his brow in a kind of salute; he was making to rise when Rutherford gently pushed him down.

'Sit where you are, Crutch,' he said, 'at Tinto's feet.'

'I just came to tell him the news,' said Crutch, with more cheerfulness than shame. 'I promised.'

'And do you think he's here to listen to you?'

'If what he believed himself is true, Mr Rutherford, no, he's not here; but I was never so dogmatic myself.'

'That's right, Crutch. It does no good to be dogmatic.'

'One thing I'm sure of all the same, Mr Rutherford: wherever he is, in whose hands, old Tinto's safe enough.'

Gazing down at the fat, shy, simple, elderly cripple in the shabby clothes, Rutherford felt a warm cleansing affection for him. there was, of course, no way by which to show it. The cap on the grave waited not for money but for faith and love. Rutherford knew it would wait there for the rest of his life, surely not in vain: just as the pound note would lie on the restaurant table.

Crutch laid his hand where Tinto's feet would have been. 'He said a lot he never meant. Nobody in Drumsagart should hae been offended. He loved the toon, Mr Rutherford.'

'I ken that, Crutch.'

'The Thistle never had a mair faithful supporter.'

'He was at every game, sun or rain.'

Crutch smiled, with regret and no rancour. 'When he was dying nobody came to see him.'

'I should have gone, Crutch.'

'He looked for you. He always had a good word to say for you, Mr Rutherford.'

'Yet I never went to see him.'

'He kent you had your ain troubles.'

For two or three minutes they were silent. Rutherford found himself shivering. The evening was turning chilly.

'One thing's often puzzled me, Crutch,' he said. 'How did he get the name Tinto? There's a hill called that, but what had it ever to do with him?

Crutch smiled. 'Did you think it was a nickname, Mr Rutherford? No, it was his true name, just as William's mine. His mither was called Jessie Tinto before she married Charlie Brown. Tinto he was from the womb, you might say, to the grave here.'

'I never knew that before,' said Rutherford, genuinely astonished and, at the same time, strangely dismayed. How much else of the old man had he not known? How shallow had his interest been!

'A lot of folk thought it was a nickname,' said Crutch reassuringly. 'It sounds like one. They made a fool of him at school.' Though he was smiling cheerfully, tears were again flowing. 'Well,' he went on, putting on his cap, 'I can't sit here all night. Tinto would be the first to say I was daft. I did what I promised. I told him all aboot the game. I'd better get back now. It'll take me an hour almost. I'm getting terribly slow at the hopping.' He made one or two slight efforts to rise, but failed. It was obvious that to rise up would require not only an exhausting but also an undignified struggle. He was reluctant to embarrass Rutherford.

'Give me your hand, Crutch,' said Rutherford.

Crutch did so, after a moment's hesitation. As gently as possible Rutherford pulled him up.

'Thanks,' said Crutch, 'thanks, Mr Rutherford.' He settled the crutch under his arm. 'I'm fine now. I'm slow but sure. You get on ahead. Don't have me making you miss your bus.'

'I'm not in as big a hurry as that, Crutch,' he said. 'I'll walk with you.'

'I take a wheen of rests, Mr Rutherford. Six hops and a puff, that's me now.'

'Then I'll take a puff along with you.'

'No.' Crutch, weeping, was agitated. 'No. Let me be, Mr Rutherford.'

Rutherford saw, with anguish and yet with love, that he would be doing the crippled man a kinder service by leaving him to manage himself than by insisting on accompanying him. It was another dismissal, another exclusion, but this time without contempt or coldness or animosity: it had its cause rather in that ultimate, irremediable loneliness of every human being, which might bring regret and sorrow but which also ought to bring profoundest sympathy, as it did here.

'God bless you, Crutch,' he said, and walked confidently away.

'On Leave in Glasgow'

from Officers and Gentlemen

EVELYN WAUGH (1903–1966)

Evelyn Waugh was born in Hampstead in London and had an unhappy spell as a schoolmaster in England before turning, first of all, to journalism and then to full-time writing on the strength of an immensely successful first novel, Decline and Fall *(1928). His wartime experience in the Royal Marines and the new type of unit known as a commando (the word came originally from the South African War), he used extensively in the trilogy of novels, collectively known as* Sword of Honour, *which appeared over nine years from 1952. This extract comes from the second volume* Officers and Gentlemen. *It includes an interlude in Scotland, during which the hero, Guy Crouchback, receives training in the British Armed Forces' embryo Commandos. Elsewhere in* Officers and Gentlemen *Waugh tells us:*

> *When the exotic name, 'Commando' was at length made free to the press it rapidly extended its meaning to include curates on motor bicycles. In 1940 a Commando was a military unit, about the size of a battalion, composed of volunteers for special service. They kept the badges of their regiments; no flashes or green berets then, nothing to display in inns.*

The training is on the fictitious Hebridean island of Mugg, which, we are told is on the West Coast lying near 'other monosyllabic protuberances', such as Rum, Muck and Eigg. In this chapter the reader meets again the dubious character Trimmer – calling himself McTavish, among other names – who is certainly not a gentleman and (because he is a con-man, or 'spiv') may not even be the officer he pretends to be. Trimmer (or McTavish) comes to Glasgow on leave and 'has a fling' with Crouchback's estranged wife Virginia in the station hotel – but which station hotel? Since we know roughly where the isle of Mugg is situated, train buffs might conjecture, firstly, that he came by train from Mallaig on the West Highland line, and secondly, that the hotel in question is the North British Hotel at Queen Street Station. But then again, it sounds rather more like the Central Hotel, what with 'the marble and mahogany halls above'; or could it even be the St Enoch's Hotel? What is certain is that Waugh gives as unmatched picture of the atmosphere of Glasgow in wartime:

> *Full, Dickensian fog enveloped the city. Day and night the streets were full of slow-moving, lighted trams and lorries and hustling coughing people. Sea-gulls emerged and suddenly vanished overhead. The rattle and shuffle and the hooting of motor-horns drowned the warnings of distant ships. Now and then the air-raid sirens rose above all.*

'ON LEAVE IN GLASGOW'

Neither character nor custom had fitted Trimmer to the life of a recluse. For a long time now he had been lying low doing nothing to call himself to the notice of his superiors. He had not reported the condition of his piece of artillery. So far there had been no complaints. His little detachment were well content; Trimmer alone repined as every day his need for feminine society became keener. He was in funds, for he was not admitted to the gambling sessions at the hotel. He was due for leave and at last he took it, seeking what he called 'the lights'.

Glasgow in November 1940 was not literally a *ville lumière*. Fog and crowds gave the black-out a peculiar density. Trimmer, on the afternoon of his arrival, went straight from the train to the station hotel. Here too were fog and crowds. All its lofty halls and corridors were heaped with luggage and thronged by transitory soldiers and sailors. There was a thick, shifting mob at the reception office. To everybody the girl at the counter replied: 'Reserved rooms only. If you come back after eight there may be some cancellations.'

Trimmer struggled to the front, leered and asked: 'Have ye no a wee room for a Scottish laddie?'

'Come back after eight. There may be a cancellation.'

Trimmer gave her a wink and she seemed just perceptibly responsive, but the thrust of other desperate and homeless men made further flirtation impossible.

With his bonnet on the side of his head, his shepherd's crook in his hand and a pair of major's crowns on his shoulders (he had changed them for his lieutenant's stars in the train lavatory), Trimmer began to saunter through the ground floor. There were men everywhere. Of the few women each was the centre of a noisy little circle of festivity, or else huddled with her man in a gloom of leave-taking. Waiters were few. Everywhere he saw heads turned and faces of anxious entreaty. Here and there a more hopeful party banged the table and impolitely shouted: 'We want service.'

But Trimmer was undismayed. He found it all very jolly after his billet on Mugg and experience had taught him that anyone who really wants a woman, finds one in the end.

He passed on with all the panache of a mongrel among the dustbins, tail waving, ears cocked, nose a-quiver. Here and there in his passage he attempted to insinuate himself into one or other of the heartier groups, but without success. At length he came to some steps and the notice: CHATEAU de MADRID. *Restaurant de grand luxe*.

Trimmer had been to this hotel once or twice before but he had never penetrated into what he knew was the expensive quarter. He took his fun where he found it, preferably in crowded places. Tonight would be different. He strolled down rubber-lined carpet and was at once greeted at the foot of the stairs by a head waiter.

'*Bon soir, monsieur*. Monsieur has engaged his table?'

'I was looking for a friend.'

'How large will monsieur's party be?'

'Two, if there is a party, I'll just sit here and have a drink.'

'*Pardon, monsieur*. It is not allowed to serve drinks here except to those who are dining upstairs.'

The two men looked at one another, fraud to fraud. They had both knocked about a little. Neither was taken in by the other. For a moment Trimmer was tempted to say: 'Come off it. Where did you get that French accent? The Mile End Road or the Gorbals?'

The waiter was tempted to say: 'This isn't your sort of place, chum. Hop it.'

In the event Trimmer said: 'I shall certainly dine here if my friend turns up. You might give me a look at the menu while I have my cocktail.'

And the head waiter said: '*Tout de suite, monsieur*.'

Another man deprived Trimmer of his bonnet and staff.

He sat at the cocktail bar. The decoration here was more trumpery than in the marble and mahogany halls above. It should have been repainted and re-upholstered that summer, but war had intervened. It wore the air of a fashion magazine, once stiff and shiny, which too many people had handled. But Trimmer did not mind. His acquaintance with fashion magazines had mostly been in tattered copies.

Trimmer looked about and saw that one chair only was occupied. Here in the corner was what he sought, a lonely woman. She did not look up and Trimmer examined her boldly. He saw a woman equipped with all the requisites for attention, who was not trying to attract. She was sitting still and looking at the half-empty glass on her table and she was quite unaware of Trimmer's brave bare knees and swinging sporran. She was, Trimmer judged, in her early thirties; her clothes – and Trimmer was something of a judge – were unlike anything worn by the ladies of Glasgow. Less than two years ago they had come from a *grand couturier*. She was not exactly Trimmer's type but he was ready to try anything that evening. He was inured to rebuffs.

A sharper eye might have noted that she fitted a little too well into her surroundings – the empty tank which had lately been lit up and brilliant with angel fish; the white cordings on the crimson draperies, now a little grimy, the white plaster sea-horses, less gay than heretofore – the lonely woman did not stand out distinctly from these. She sat, as it were, in a faint corroding mist – the exhalation perhaps of unhappiness or ill health, or of mere weariness. She drained her glass and looked past Trimmer to the barman who said: 'Coming up right away, madam,' and began splashing gin of a previously unknown brand into his shaker.

When Trimmer saw her face he was struck by a sense of familiarity; somewhere, perhaps in those shabby fashion-magazines, as he had seen it before.

'I'll take it over,' he said to the barman, quickly lifting the tray with the new cocktail on it.

'Excuse me, sir, *if* you please.'

Trimmer retained his hold. The barman let go. Trimmer carried the tray to the corner.

'Your cocktail, madam,' he said jauntily.

The woman took the glass, said 'Thank you' and looked beyond him. Trimmer then remembered her name.

You've forgotten me, Mrs Troy?'

She looked at him slowly, without interest.

'Have we met before?'

Often. In the *Aquitania*.'

'I'm sorry,' she said. 'I'm afraid I don't remember. One meets so many people.'

'Mind if I join you?'

'I am just leaving.'

'You could do with a rinse and set,' said Trimmer, adding in the tones of the *maître d'hôtel*, 'Madam's hair is *un peu fatigué, n'est-ce pas*? It is the sea-air.'

Her face showed sudden interest, incredulity, welcome.

'Gustave! It can't be you?'

'Remember how I used to come to your cabin in the mornings? As soon as I saw your name on the passenger list I'd draw a line through all my eleven-thirty appointments. The old trouts used to come and offer ten-dollar tips but I always kept eleven-thirty free in case you wanted me.'

'Gustave, how awful of me! How could I have forgotten? Sit down. You must admit you've changed a lot.'

'You haven't,' said Trimmer. 'Remember that little bit of massage I used to give you at the back of the neck. You said it cured your hangovers.'

'It did.'

They revived many fond memories of the Atlantic.

'Dear Gustave, how you bring it all back. I always loved the *Aquitania*.'

'Mr Troy about?'

'He's in America.'

'Alone here?'

'I came to see a friend off.'

'Boy friend?'

'You always were too damned fresh.'

'You never kept any secrets from me.'

'No great secret. He's a sailor. I haven't known him long but I liked him. He went off quite suddenly. People are always going off suddenly nowadays, not saying where.'

'You've got me for a week if you're staying on.'

'I've no plans.'

'Nor me. Dining here?'

'It's very expensive.'

'My treat, of course.'

'My dear boy, I couldn't possibly let you spend your money on me. I was just wondering whether I could afford to stand you dinner. I don't think I can.'

'Hard up?'

'Very. I don't quite know why. Something to do with Mr Troy and the war and foreign investments and exchange control. Anyway, my London bank manager has suddenly become very shifty.'

Trimmer was both shocked and slightly exhilarated by this news.

The barrier between hairdresser and first-class passenger was down. It was important to start the new relationship on the proper level – a low one. He did not fancy the idea of often acting as host at the Château de Madrid.

'Anyway, Virginia, let's have another drink here?'

Virginia lived among people who used Christian names indiscriminately. It was Trimmer's self-consciousness which called attention to his familiarity.

'Virginia?' she said, teasing.

'And I, by the way, am Major McTavish. My friends call me "Ali" or "Trimmer".'

'They know about your being a barber, then?'

'As a matter of fact they don't. The name Trimmer has nothing to do with that. Not that I'm ashamed of it. I got plenty of fun on the *Aquitania*, I can tell you – with the passengers. You'd be surprised, if I told you some of the names. Lots of your own set.'

'Tell me, Trimmer.'

For half an hour he kept her enthralled by his revelations, some of which had a basis of truth. The restaurant and foyer began to fill up with stout, elderly civilians, airmen with showy local girls, an admiral with his wife and daughter. The head waiter approached Trimmer for the third time with the menu.

'How about it, Trimmer?'

'I wish you'd call me "Ali".'

'Trimmer to me, every time,' said Virginia.

'How about a Dutch treat as we're both in the same boat?'

'That suits me.'

'Tomorrow we may find something cheaper.'

Virginia raised her eyebrows at the world 'tomorrow', but said nothing. Instead she took the menu card and without consultation ordered a nourishing but economical meal.

'*Et pour commencer*, some oysters? A little *saumon fumé*?'

'No,' she said firmly.

'Not keen on them myself,' said Trimmer.

'I am, but we're not having any tonight. Always read the menu from right to left.'

'I don't get you.'

'Never mind. I expect there are all sorts of things we don't "get" about one another.'

Virginia was looking her old self when she entered the restaurant: 'class written all over her' as Trimmer inwardly expressed it, and, besides, she gleamed with happy mischief.

At dinner Trimmer began to boast a little about his military eminence.

'How lovely,' said Virginia: 'all alone on an island.'

'There are some other troops there in training,' he conceded, 'but I don't have much to do with them. I command the defence.'

'Oh, damn the war,' said Virginia. 'Tell me more about the *Aquitania*.'

She was not a woman who indulged much in reminiscence or speculation. Weeks passed without her giving thought to the past fifteen years of her life – her seduction by a friend of her father's, who had looked her up, looked her over, taken her out, taken her in, from her finishing-school in Paris; her marriage to Guy, the Castello Crouchback and the endless cloudy terraces of the Rift Valley; her marriage to Tommy, London hotels, fast cars, regimental point-to-points, the looming horror of an Indian cantonment; fat Augustus with his cheque book always handy; Mr Troy and his taste for 'significant people' – none of this, as Mr Troy would say, 'added up' to anything. Nor did age or death. It was the present moment and the next five minutes which counted with Virginia. But just now in this shuttered fog-bound place, surrounded by strangers in the bright little room, surrounded by strangers in the blackness outside, miles of them, millions of them, all blind and deaf, not 'significant people'; now while the sirens sounded and bombs began to fall and guns to fire far away among the dockyards – now, briefly, Virginia was happy to relive, to see again from the farther side of the looking-glass, the ordered airy life aboard the great liner. And faithful Gustave who always kept his crowded hour for her, with his false French and his soothing thumb on the neck and shoulders and the top of the spine, suddenly metamorphosed beside her into a bare-kneed major with a cockney accent, preposterously renamed – Gustave was the guide providentially sent on a gloomy evening to lead her back to the days of sun and sea-spray and wallowing dolphins.

At that moment in London Colonel Grace-Groundling-Marchpole, lately promoted head of his most secret department, was filing the latest counter-intelligence:

> Crouchback, Guy, temporary Lieutenant Royal Corps of Halberdiers, now stationed with undefined duties at Mugg at HQX Commando. This suspect has been distributing subversive matter at night. Copy attached.

He glanced at *Why Hitler must win*.

'Yes, we've seen this before. Ten copies have been found in the Edinburgh area. This is the first from the islands. Very interesting. It links up the Box case with the Scottish Nationalists – a direct connexion from Salzburg to Mugg. What we need now is to connect Cardiff University with Santa Dulcina. We shall do it in time, I've no doubt.'

Colonel Marchpole's department was so secret that it communicated only with the War Cabinet and the Chiefs of Staff. Colonel Marchpole kept his information until it was asked for. To date that had not occurred and he rejoiced under neglect. Premature examination of his files might ruin his private, undefined Plan. Somewhere in the ultimate curlicues of his mind, there was a Plan. Given time, given enough confidential material, he would succeed in knitting the entire quarrelsome world into a single net of conspiracy in which there were no antagonists, merely millions of men working, unknown to one another, for the same end; and there would be no more war.

Full, Dickensian fog enveloped the city. Day and night the streets were full of slow-moving, lighted trams and lorries and hustling coughing people. Sea-gulls emerged and suddenly vanished overhead. The rattle and shuffle and the hooting of motor-horns drowned the warnings of distant ships. Now and then the air-raid sirens rose above all. The hotel was always crowded. Between drinking hours soldiers and sailors slept in the lounges. When the bars opened they awoke to call plaintively for a drink. The mêlée at the reception counter never diminished. Upstairs the yellow lights burned by day against the whitish-yellow lace which shut out half the yellow-brown obscurity beyond; by night against a frame of black. This was the scene in which Trimmer's idyll was laid.

It ended abruptly on the fourth day.

Trimmer had ventured down about midday into the murky hall to engage tickets for the theatre that evening. One of the suppliant figures at the reception-counter disengaged himself and jostled him.

'Sorry. Why, hullo, McTavish. What are you doing here?'

It was the second-in-command of his battalion, a man Trimmer believed to be far away in Iceland.

'On leave, sir.'

'Well, it's lucky running into you. I'm looking for bodies to take up north. Just landed at Greenock this morning.'

The Major looked at him more closely and fixed his attention on the badges of rank.

'Why the devil are you dressed like that?' he asked.

Trimmer thought quickly.

'I was promoted the other day, sir. I'm not with the regiment any more. I'm on special service.'

'First I've heard of it.'

'I was seconded some time ago to the Commandos.'

'By whose orders?'

'HOOHQ.'

The Major looked doubtful.

'Where are your men?'

'Isle of Mugg.'

'And where are you when you're not on leave?'

'Isle of Mugg, too, sir. But I'm nothing to do with the men now. I think they are expecting an officer to take over any day. I am under Colonel Blackhouse.'

'Well, I suppose it's all right. When is your leave up?'

'This afternoon, as a matter of fact.'

'I hope you've enjoyed it.'

'Thoroughly, thank you.'

'It's all very rum,' said the Major. 'Congratulations on your promotion, by the way.'

Trimmer turned to go. The Major called him back. Trimmer broke into a sweat.

'You're leaving your room here? I wonder if anyone else has got it.'

'I'm rather afraid they have.'

'Damn.'

Trimmer pushed his way forward to the hall porter. Instead of theatre tickets, it was train and ship he wanted now.

'Mugg? Yes, sir. You can just do it. Train leaves at 12.45.'

Virginia was sitting at the dressing-table. Trimmer seized his hair-brushes from under her hands and began filling his sponge-bag at the wash-handstand.

'What are you doing? Did you get the tickets all right?'

'I'm sorry, it's off.'

'Gustave!'

'Recalled for immediate service, my dear. I can't explain. War on, you know.'

'Oh God!' she said. 'Another of them.'

Slowly she took off her dressing-gown and returned to bed.

'Aren't you coming to see me off?'

'Not on your life, Trimmer.'

'What are you going to do?'

'I'll be all right. I'm going to sleep again. Good-bye.'

So Trimmer returned to Mugg. He had enjoyed his leave beyond all expectation, but it had left him with a problem of which he could see only one solution, and that a most unwelcome one.

While Trimmer was in Glasgow Tommy Blackhouse had been called to London. In his absence a lassitude fell on the Commando. In the brief hours of daylight the troops marched out to uninhabited areas and blazed away their ammunition into the snowy hillside and the dark sea. One of them killed a seal. Card playing languished and in the evenings the hotel lounge was full of silent figures reading novels – *No Orchids for Miss Blandish*, *Don't, Mr Disraeli*, the *Chartreuse de Parme* and other oddly assorted works of fiction passed from hand to hand.

Jumbo Trotter completed his work of filing and indexing the waste paper in the orderly-room. He had transformed himself for the time being into a Captain of the Home Guard, pending 'posting' to RNVR.

He and Guy sat in the orderly-room on the morning after Trimmer's return. They both wore their greatcoats and gloves. Jumbo was further muffled in a balaclava helmet. He had *Don't, Mr Disraeli* that morning and was visibly puzzled by it.

Presently he said:

'Did you see the letter from the laird?'

'Yes.'

'He seems to think the Colonel promised to give him some explosives. Doesn't sound likely.'

'I was there. Nothing was promised.'

'I rather like a bit of an explosion myself.'

He resumed his reading.

After a few minutes Guy shut *No Orchids for Miss Blandish*.

'Unreadable,' he said.

'Other fellows seemed to enjoy it. Claire recommended this book. Can't make it out at all. Is it a sort of skit on something?'

Guy turned over the papers in the 'pending' tray.

'What about Dr Glendening-Rees?' he asked. 'I don't think Colonel Tommy is going to be much interested in him.'

Jumbo took the letter and re-read it.

'Can't do anything until he comes back. Can't do very much then. This reads like an order to me. HOOHQ seem to send us every crank in the country. First Chatty Corner, now Dr Glendening-Rees. "Eminent authority on dietetics" . . . "original and possibly valuable proposal concerning emergency food supplies in the field" . . . "afford every facility for research under active service conditions". Can't we put him off?'

'He seems to have started. I dare say he'll liven things up a bit.'

A letter had lain on the table all the morning addressed in sprawling unofficial writing. The envelope was pale violet in colour and flimsy in texture.

'Do you think this is private?'

'It's addressed "OCX Commando", not to the Colonel by name. Better open it.'

It was from Trimmer.

'McTavish has put in an application to see Colonel Tommy.'

'The fellow who was chucked out of the Halberdiers? What does he want?'

'To join the Commando apparently. He seems very eager about it suddenly.'

'Of course,' said Jumbo tolerantly, 'there are lots of fellows who aren't quite up to the mark for *us*, who are quite decent fellows all the same. If you ask me, there are several fellows here already who wouldn't quite do in the Corps. Decent fellows, mind you, but not up to the mark.' Jumbo gazed before him, sadly, tolerantly, considering the inadequacy of No. X Commando.

'You know,' he said, 'they've issued NCOs with binoculars.'

'Yes.'

'I call that unnecessary. And I'll tell you something. There's one of them – Claire's CSM – queer looking fellow with pink eyes – they call him a "Corporal-Major" I believe. I overheard him the other day refer to these binoculars of his as his "opera glasses". Well, I mean to say – ' He paused for effect and continued on the original topic.

'I gather McTavish wasn't a great success in his own regiment. Sergeant Bane got it from his Sergeant that they threw him out of a window the day before embarking for Iceland.'

'I heard it was a horse-trough. Anyway, they knocked him about a bit. There was a lot of that sort of thing when I joined. Ink baths and so forth. No sense in it. Only made bad fellows worse.'

'Colonel Tommy's coming back tonight. He'll know what to do with him.'

Tommy Blackhouse returned as expected. He immediately called for the troop-leaders and said:

'Things are beginning to move. There's a ship coming for us tomorrow or the day after. Be ready to embark at once. She's fitted with ALCs. What are they, Eddie?'

'I don't know, Colonel.'

'Assault landing craft. These are the first lot made. You may have seen some of them on your Dakar jaunt, Guy. We start full-scale landing exercises at once. HOOHQ are sending observers so they had better be good. Issue maps to everyone down to Corporals. I'll give details of the scheme tomorrow.

'I haven't been so lucky with replacements. OCs don't seem as ready to play now as they were six weeks ago, but HOO have promised to bring us up to strength somehow. That's all. Guy, I shall want you.'

When the troop leaders had left, Tommy said:

'Guy, have you ever wondered why we are here?'

'No. I can't say I have.'

'I dare say nobody has. This place wasn't chosen simply for its bloodiness. You'll all know in good time. If you'd ever studied *Admiralty Sailing Directions* it might occur to you that there is another island with two hills, steep shingle beaches and cliffs. Somewhere rather warmer than this. The name doesn't matter now. The point is that these exercises aren't just a staff college scheme for Northland against Southland. They're the dress rehearsal for an operation. It won't do any harm if you pass that on. We've been playing about too long. Anything happen while I was away?'

'McTavish is very anxious to see you. He wants to join.'

'The wet Highlander who jammed his gun?'

'Yes, Colonel.'

'Right. I'll see him tomorrow.'

'He's no good, you know.'

'I can use anyone who's really keen.'

'He's keen all right. I don't quite know why.'

Ivor Claire occupied himself during the 'flap' in making elaborate arrangements for the safe-conduct of his pekinese, Freda, to his mother's care.

'Kate Cranstonish'

from The Brave Days

NEIL MUNRO (1863–1930)

It is perhaps inevitable that an anthology which takes Glasgow as its theme and subject should be to some extent dominated by the writings of Neil Munro. Elsewhere in this book the reader will encounter examples of his fiction and especially the humorous short stories that brought characters like Erchie MacPherson and Jimmy Swan to an adoring public. The journalism came first, however, and some of the finest moments of Munro's writing can be found in the collections of journalistic pieces first penned for the Glasgow Evening News *and subsequently edited by George Blake. This article about an attractive social phenomenon of the day comes from the collection known as* The Brave Days.

The article takes as its subject the person behind the most famous of Glasgow's celebrated 'art tea-rooms'. Miss Kate Cranston was one of those who occasionally fell under Munro's sharp eye and was the subject of his not always gentle satire; elsewhere, for instance, we quote from his story Erchie in An Art Tea-room. *Here he takes a more balanced view and gives a fine tribute to a person and an institution whose cultural impact and promotion of genuinely 'fine' art is still with us. Munro was a respected art critic as well as everything else and the very 'Room de Looks' that Erchie poked fun at is here called 'entrancing'. The author of Para Handy and* The New Road *was disparaging about his journalism – at one time he dismissed it as 'the jawbox' – but pieces such as these deserve quite a different evaluation.*

KATE CRANSTONISH

It is little more than thirty years since a Glasgow woman made a resounding name for herself in her native city by changing the whole conception of her sex as to what could be done to brighten up their afternoons. Till then it was a problem no one had seriously tried to solve for them.

After they had done their shopping in Sauchiehall Street or Buchanan Street there was nothing more for them to do but take the first tramcar home to Kelvinside or Pollokshields in time to arrange for the evening's meal or snatch a sustaining cup of tea in the too familiar and monotonous parlour with mother's bulrushes in vases in the corners.

For men the afternoon in town seemed to offer innumerable distractions even during intervals in business. They were always bright and merry when they came home, and often brought with them in the satchels which preceded the attaché case of later days some two-penny London buns or fruit-cakes as samples of the entertainment that had kept them late in old John Forrester's Gordon Street establishment.

All Glasgow men seemed to be in a conspiracy to precipitate their women back to their hearths and homes as soon as they had had a hurried glance at the warehouse windows, had picked the very stuff for the curtains, and realized the extortionate cost of those Frenchy-looking hats marked 'Chic' or 'À la Parisienne'.

Even quite nice gentlemen agreed that the home was the safest place for ladies in a city of tempting shops, and kept it dark from them that a brighter Glasgow movement was well under way in the business centres. As a matter of fact, 'Granny Black's', with its world-famed sixpenny teas, was obsolete years before those innocent ladies were allowed to find it was no longer the *dernier cri* in cafés.

It was an understood thing that licensed restaurants or hotels could never be *comme il faut* for fastidious ladies or their offspring. One never knew what orgies might be taking place there. The tradition of the early tea-room, too, was one of shabby furtive-looking shops in inconspicuous side streets, with a roll or two of beef, ham, and flypapers in the window; it was too manifestly the place for a hearty meal and made no parade of cream cookies and meringues.

Women occasionally cast a wistful eye on Lang's, 'Pie Smith's' and John Forrester's, but the laws of *purdah* put these establishments out of the question. They seemed to be strictly reserved for men, and to discourage sitting down.

It was the vendors of coffee in its dry state who first discovered that women were pining for some innocent equivalent to the afternoon assuagements of the men.

Cranston's in the Argyle Arcade and Queen Street, and Cooper's, for a time had been distilling tiny sample cups of coffee in their windows. The aroma, extending into the streets, appeared to have an irresistible attraction for the ladies, who began to buy their coffee by the ounce as an excuse for more frequent visits to town and the pleasure of free sampling.

From the gratuitous sample-counter quickly developed a sitting-room where coffee could be amply and leisurely enjoyed at a reasonable tariff, and the strain of shopping in town was relieved enormously. The Cranston family had one time been associated with the Crow Hotel, a famous hostelry which stood on the side of the present Merchants' House in George Square. According to *Who's Who in Glasgow* (1909), Miss Catherine Cranston was born there; the place of her retirement is in its immediate vicinity.

Miss Cranston, clever, far-seeing, artistic to her fingertips, and of a high adventurous spirit, was the first to discern in Glasgow that her sex was positively yearning for some kind of afternoon distraction that had not yet been invented. She mapped out a career for herself and became pioneer in a lunch-tea-room movement which in a few years made her name a household word. By general consent it was associated with the ideals and triumphs of the 'Glasgow School' of artists, then entering on international fame.

At the International Exhibition of 1901 in Kelvingrove her Tea-house and Tea-terrace had architectural and decorative innovations which created a sensation even among continental visitors. It meant the funeral knell of ugly and curly 'art nouveau' conventions in domestic decoration, and for the first time introduced a quite original note of surprise and gaiety into the mid-day 'snack' and its crockery and cutlery.

Miss Cranston's 'Groveries' establishment was, of course, only a temporary affair, which closed at the end of autumn, when the Exhibition itself ended, but by that time any lunch-tea-room of hers was assured of permanent popularity. She opened glorious ones in Sauchiehall Street and Buchanan Street, Argyle Street and Ingram Street, designed externally to attract the eye by architectural novelty, yet restrained and elegant.

They were deliberately conceived as houses of light refreshment most obviously for the pleasure of women and run wholly on 'temperance' lines. Even had the cocktail been in fashion at the time, it would have been unprocurable in any of the Cranston shops, which far more than made up for the absence of alcohol by features peculiar to themselves.

That wonderful woman appeared to have in view her own aesthetic gratification more than the rapid accumulation of a fortune on conventional restaurant lines. She was, herself, unique, vivacious, elegant, always with something of the *fête champêtre* in her costume, and the maids who served her tables took their note from her.

Miss Cranston brought to light the genius of a Glasgow architect, Charles Mackintosh, who died only in recent years and was the inspiring influence of a group of Glasgow artists, men and women, who made her tea-rooms homogeneous in structure, decoration, and furnishing. They were strangely beautiful the Cranston tea-rooms; women loved them, and

'Kate Cranstonish' became a term with Glasgow people in general to indicate domestic novelties in buildings and decorations not otherwise easy to define.

The top note in Miss Cranston's lunch-tea-rooms was struck by the one in Sauchiehall Street, which was popularly known as 'the room de luxe,' from the chamber which was its most admired and exciting feature. There even the cutlery and glass-ware had a character of their own, and thirty years ago no children's visit to the Circus was complete without a meal in this entrancing room de luxe, where everything was 'different,' and the whole atmosphere was one of gay adventure.

'Those Glasgow tea-rooms,' wrote Muirhead Bone, the etcher, in a London magazine, 'were things of extraordinary beauty and originality, and one cannot find any restaurants in London to-day comparable with them.'

With one or two exceptions they have recently disappeared or lost their identity with Miss Cranston's retirement into private life. But their influence is marked on nearly all Glasgow lunch-tea-rooms now, and the warehouses which now have lunch-tea-rooms of their own on the premises should be grateful for the inspiration of the pioneer, Kate Cranston.

8
THE REVOLUTIONARY MOMENT
Introduction

Religion and politics have long been intertwined in the history of the city, as in the history of Scotland as a whole. In the long years of the Reformation and of the Convenanting Wars, and in much of the eighteenth century, for example, religion was the very stuff and substance of politics, with various forms of national and local forms of clerical government and administration being experimented with. In this respect, however, the focus of activity was more often than not elsewhere on the national stage – not in Glasgow. Scotland's parliament, when it met, usually sat in Edinburgh, as did the body which often surpassed it in importance, the General Assembly of the Church of Scotland. This absence from centre-stage could have its advantages, as is shown in the chapter 'The Bishop's Burgh' where it is described how Glasgow's beautiful cathedral church managed to escape destruction by religious zealots. There was one occasion, nevertheless, one defining moment when the Assembly met at Glasgow in the same cathedral, and when this meeting had a direct effect on national events. This came in 1638, not long after the signing of the National Covenant in Greyfriars Church in Edinburgh, with these words:

> Everyone of us underwritten protest that after examination of our owne consciences, in matters of true and false Religion, we are now thoroughly resolved on the Truth, by the Word and Spirit of God . . . we abhorre and detest all contrary Religion and Doctrine . . . even as they are now damned and confuted by the word of God, and Kirk of Scotland.

The Covenant subsequently began to be subscribed in places throughout the land, including the city of Glasgow. Charles I was on the throne, but events at the Glasgow Assembly in November were to shake his realm to its foundations. Glasgow was now emphatically centre-stage. This first excerpt describes this momentous gathering and comes from John Buchan's splendid biography of James Graham, Marquis of Montrose.

In the turmoil of religious and political opinion that followed, Charles was defeated by the Covenanting party, but a few years later Montrose, the first signatory of the Covenant, had taken up arms against its party and in favour of the King. He won several amazing victories in 1645 and August of that year found him in the immediate vicinity of Glasgow on his way to Kilsyth, which battle briefly made him master of Scotland. The city was in general dominated by those of the Covenanting persuasion, but Gibson's eighteenth-century history of Glasgow suggests the sensible apprehension felt by the city fathers, aroused by the presence of a threatening Highland army:

> [Montrose had] encamped with his army in the vicinity of the town, and had sent a message to the magistrates, demanding a certain number of bonnets, shoes, and other necessaries, with some money for the use of his army; the magistrates and town council had waited upon them, to endeavour to get him to abate somewhat in his demands; the marquis had detained them to dinner, and had granted them the abatement they demanded; upon taking leave of him, some of them kissed his hand, and out of the abundance of their zeal wished him success; an account of this was soon sent to the covenanters . . .

Montrose fell; so did his king, and the surge of political and religious strife drove on in both kingdoms. For a period the Cromwellian armies occupied Scotland. An administrative official, Thomas Tucker, left this favourable impression of the city during the lull in hostilities in 1655. It shows the relationship between Glasgow and the Highlands in a more favourable light than was sometimes the case:

> This towne, seated in a pleasant and fruitfull soyle, and consisting of four streets, handsomely built in the form of a cross, is one of the most considerablest burghs of Scotland, as well for the structure as trade of it. The inhabitants [all but the students of the college which is here] are traders and dealers: with their neighbours the Highlanders, who come hither from the isles and western parts; in summer by the Mull of Cantyre, and in winter by the Torban [Tarbert] to the head of Loch Fyne [which is a small neck of sandy land, over which they usually draw their small boats into the Firth of Dunbarton] and so pass up in the Clyde with pladding, dry hides, goat, kid, and deer skins, which they sell and purchase with their price such commodities and provisions as they stand in need of . . .

The extreme covenanters, like Habbakuk Muckleworth in Scott's *Old Mortality*, from which the next extract comes, were destined to disintegrate into several sects of various hues of conviction and appetites for martyrdom. Many indeed joined the ranks of the martyrs in the bloody aftermath of the Battle of Bothwell Bridge, a handful of miles from the city, in 1679. In the same novel Cuddie Headrigg says in a masterpiece of evasion, when asked whether he had been present at the battle: 'I'll no' say but it may be possible that I might hae been there.'

In the Union of 1707, which Glasgow opposed, even if it benefited from it, religion did not play so important a role. In Scotland as a whole, however, religious issues remained at the forefront of the series of Jacobite insurrections which were to follow. Glasgow's opinion was strongly Hanoverian and anti-Jacobite, but its sole direct involvement came in 1746 when the Young Pretender's army occupied the city on its return north from Derby. Gibson's History, published only thirty years later, makes it clear that Glasgow's policy of supporting what he called 'Revolution-principles' (i.e. support for the Revolution of 1688 and the Protestant Succession) could have led to something worse than occupation:

> During the time of the rebellion, the citizens of Glasgow gave proof of their attachment to Revolution-principles, by raising two battalions, of 600 men each, for the service of government; and for their activity in favour of the present family, they would have suffered most severely, had it not been for the interposition of Mr Cameron of Lochiel; a resolution had been taken by the rebels to plunder and burn the city of Glasgow, and had not Mr Cameron threatened to withdraw his clan, if this resolution should be put in practice, it is probable that Glasgow would have been destroyed.

For the next 200 years, Glasgow was to resume its position as a place some way off-stage from national political events – although as the city grew to dwarf all others in Scotland it became the focus of tremendous social and economic change. In 1820 the so-called 'Radical War' led to the execution of a weaver, James Wilson, on Glasgow Green and the hasty repression of others. No political revolution in Glasgow then; no religious revolution either, as had been the case in 1638 – although Thomas Chalmers, a reforming minister of St John's parish, succeeded for a time in building a radical programme of poor relief. Chalmers's views strike us as nationalist as well as egalitarian:

> If England will so idolise her own institutions as be unwilling to part with even the most vicious she must be let alone, since she will have it so. But let her not inoculate with the virus of her own gangrene those countries which have the misfortune to border on her territory and be subject to her sway; and more especially, let not the simple

> and venerated parochial system of our land lie open to the crudities, or be placed at the disposal of a few cockney legislators.

By the twentieth century the separation of politics from religion was pretty marked, although there were occasions, especially in Glasgow, when Irish-style issues intruded, but this does not mean that religion ceased to be important in many people's lives. As recently as the 1950s, for example, the readership of the Glasgow *Evening News* and *Daily Record* was assumed to have enough bible knowledge to appreciate the fine comic verses of the Glasgow poet, W.D. Cocker. These poems were based on Scriptural stories like Moses, Ruth, Daniel and The Deluge, the story of Noah, which we include here.

Despite that, in this most secular of centuries much of the Glaswegian's energies, love of debate and argument was now concentrated on politics, and especially the brand of radical political reform which earned the epithet 'Red Clydeside'. For a while, in the first thirty-odd years of the century Glasgow seemed again at the heart of political affairs, on the verge of initiating a political revolution in the same way as had happened in 1638. There follows a pair of extracts which show different facets of Red Clydeside. These are an extract from John Buchan's Mr Standfast, a novel partly set in Glasgow in 1917, followed by Tom Johnston's journalistic piece in the magazine *Forward*.

Then on 31st January, 1919 came the flash point. The '40 Hours' Strike' by many of the Scottish trade unions led to a massive demonstration in George Square, the unfurling of the Red Flag and the retaliatory bringing in of troops by the Liberal Coalition Government. Tanks were held ready in Duke Street's Meat Market. In years to come there were claims that the 1917 Bolshevik Revolution had come close to repetition in Scotland, but within a few days the strike was called off. The forces of labour in Scotland and Glasgow resumed their preferred method of change through industrial action rather than violence. As John Wheatley argued: 'A bloody revolution is far too slow, whether viewed from the standpoint of democracy or expediency. I prefer the ILP policy of relying more upon brains than bullets.' Even by 3rd February, when the following account was printed in the London Times, the crisis was deemed to have passed:

> Thousands of soldiers wearing steel helmets and full service kit were brought into Glasgow yesterday morning, and the hooligan element responsible for the bottle-throwing, window-smashing and looting on Friday has disappeared from the streets. I do not think there will be any recurrence of disorder. Those who now speak for the strikers – Shinwell has been arrested at his home in Govan, and with

> Kirkwood and Gallagher is detained under remand at Duke Street prison – instead of talking of unconstitutional methods are asking the authorities to prove one instance of illegal conduct by the men. In their paper the *Strike Bulletin*, today they say – 'It seems as if the Government want an opportunity to use arms against the workers on the Clyde, but we can assure them the workers have no desire or intention of providing such an opportunity. The workers are well aware of what the Government want and are not so foolish as to fall into the trap set so carefully to ensnare them.'
>
> This is ingenious, but it may serve the purpose of restraining young hotheads from rash action. The looters, who serve one purpose of the revolutionary movement behind the strike itself, may be trusted to keep in hiding while the troops guard the city.

Very much the establishment view, but while there is mention of 'the revolutionary movement' the Government appears to have been as reticent about using force as anyone. In Scottish terms it now looks that 1919, rather than the General Strike of 1926, marked the high water mark in radical politics.

This section of the anthology concludes with an extract from Catherine Gavin's *Clyde Valley*, which gives an interesting version of politics and religion in thirties Glasgow, and finally the poem *James Maxton* by Tom Scott. Maxton is a suitable figure to end with, since his sincerity won the respect of all and, although his ambitions were never realised and his brand of socialism increasingly isolated, to some extent his spirit lives on.

'Revolution in the Air'

from Montrose

JOHN BUCHAN (1875–1940)

The first of two extracts from the works of John Buchan in this section is about a moment in seventeenth-century Scottish history which probably comes as close as any to outright revolution – the General Assembly of the Church of Scotland held in the Cathedral of St Mungo in Glasgow in November 1638. Characteristically, the elements of religion and politics were thoroughly mixed in this intensely dramatic event, and adding to the drama was the setting within the Cathedral, where new galleries were constructed and extra seating brought in to accommodate the crowds of official and unofficial observers.

The build-up to the Assembly can be traced through the many contentious events of the reign of Charles I, and in particular his religious policy and attempts to reintroduce episcopacy to Scotland. In 1637, the imposition of Laud's Revised Prayer Book, *with its challenge to Presbyterian forms of worship, lit the fuse that led on to the signing of the National Covenant in Greyfriars Kirkyard in Edinburgh on 28th February, 1638. The Covenant avoided the language of outright revolt, but radical elements increasingly came out against the King's government, and there was open confrontation with the King's Commissioner, the Duke of Hamilton, at the Assembly. After Hamilton's departure the Assembly went on to depose the bishops and the Prayer Book was condemned as being 'heathenish, Popish, Jewish and Arminian'. The actions of the Assembly were confirmed by Parliament and the civil war known as the First Bishops' War followed soon afterwards. Buchan's mention of the Tables is a reference to the committee, consisting of four members from each of the Estates of Parliament (Nobles, Clergy and Burgesses), set up to oppose Charles in 1637 and instrumental in the drawing up of the Covenant.*

In this excerpt Buchan adds to the reader's knowledge of a number of the leading figures of the time. These include, obviously, Montrose, who is the subject of this biography; Alexander Henderson, a leading minister on the Covenanters' side; and Archibald, eighth Earl of Argyll, to whom he devotes a long and introspective passage. Buchan chooses here to develop the figure of Argyll – he intends to set the two noblemen, Montrose and the head of Clan Campbell, over against each other and in so doing to heighten the dramatic tension. From now on, there is a special edge to the narrative and the work as a whole develops and grows. It is possible to see why Buchan's biographical writings have retained a widespread critical esteem which has not quite happened in the case of his fictional works. Maurice Lindsay, for example, asserts that Montrose *(and* Walter Scott, *another of his biographies) 'stylish in presentation, warm and perceptive in their sympathies, make up the really significant part of his contribution to our literature.'*

REVOLUTION IN THE AIR

The Assembly which met in Glasgow in November was a legal gathering, sanctioned by the king, and duly presided over by Hamilton, the royal commissioner. The issues between sovereign and people had been narrowed. Charles had surrendered all the earlier objects of strife – the liturgy, the book of canons, and an irresponsible episcopate. It appeared that he was prepared to accept a moderate episcopacy responsible to a General Assembly, the original constitution of the Reformed Kirk in Scotland. But with the people at large the controversy had now gone far beyond the articles of the National Covenant. Episcopacy in any form had become suspect, because it had been made the instrument of an assault upon both civil and religious freedom. To Charles, as to Hamilton, some form of episcopate was an essential corollary of a monarchy. To them it appeared that the control over the Kirk given by bishops appointed by the king was the only safeguard against an anarchical theocracy; to the Scottish people it seemed that so long as this channel for arbitrary government was left unblocked there was no security against further encroachments upon their liberties. The historian may admit that there was reason in both views, but it was certain that the Assembly, the first held for twenty years, would demand the complete removal of the latter menace.

It met on the 21st day of November, in the old Cathedral of Glasgow, one of the few ancient churches in Scotland which had escaped the destroying zeal of the Reformers. Glasgow was then a clean little city of some 12,000 inhabitants, clustered about its college and cathedral above the shining links of the Molendinar burn. The Assembly was a packed one, since the Tables, as appeared during the proceedings, had exercised a rigorous veto over the delegates. Of these there were some 240, 142 being ministers, and 98 laymen, ruling elders appointed by presbyteries. The Privy Council attended, and there were numerous assessors. Hamilton had striven to regulate the body by a proclamation – completely disregarded – against the presence of retainers and the bearing of arms. The nobles and barons appeared each with his usual 'tail', and not a few of the clerical members had swords and pistols, ostensibly to defend themselves on the journey against a certain John Macgregor, a bandit who professed a distaste for the Covenant and a liking for the king.

The crowd at the opening was so great that the town guard had the utmost difficulty in opening a way for the members to their seats. The Glasgow populace attended in great numbers, and their behaviour in the kirk shocked the decorous soul of Mr Robert Baillie. 'It is here alone where, I think, we might learn from Canterbury, yea, from the Pope, from the Turks, or pagans, modesty and manners. . . . Our rascals without shame, in great numbers, made such dinn and clamour in the house of the true God, that if they minted to use the like behaviour in my chamber, I could not be content till they were down the stairs.' Hamilton sat uneasily on a high chair of state, and below him the Lords of the Privy Council – conspicuous among them the lean aquiline face and the red hair of Lorn, now, by his father's death, Earl of Argyll, and a figure of interest to every man, since he had not declared himself. In front of them was a chair for the Moderator, and a table for the Clerk. Then came a long bench at which were seated the nobles and barons elected by the presbyteries, and at which sat Montrose as an elder, representing his own presbytery of Auchterarder. At the end of the church a platform had been erected for the eldest sons of peers, and in tiers on both sides were the seats of the clerical and burgess members. The 'rascal multitude', including many women, occupied the aisles and galleries. It was a strange form of ecclesiastical assembly, for among the black gowns of the ministers were the slashed and laced doublets of the laity, and the gleam of many swords.

Alexander Henderson was unanimously elected Moderator, and Wariston, Clerk. The first step was to verify the commissions of the members, and Hamilton found cause to question the legality of many. His objection to the presence of laymen was without substance, as their admission was in accordance with the letter and spirit of Presbyterianism. With better reason he protested against the method of electing these laymen, and the way in which the Tables had supervised the appointments. A test case was that of Lord Carnegie, Montrose's brother-in-law, who had been nominated by the presbytery of Brechin, but disallowed by the Tables, and Erskine of Dun named in his stead.

Montrose had been the chief mover in the matter, and, when Wariston inadvertently read the letter of the Tables, Hamilton seized upon the irregularity. Montrose hotly defended it, and thereby came into conflict not only with Southesk, his father-in-law, but with Mr David Dickson, who questioned his action. The young man was in a high temper, and in the cause he had chosen was prepared to respect neither kinsman nor cleric.

The Assembly waved aside the royal commissioner's doubts as to its competence and constitution, and proceeded to the business at the back of every member's head – the abolition of episcopacy. The bishops had refused to acknowledge the court or to appear before it, and, when their formal declinature had been handed in, Hamilton decided to dissolve the Assembly. On the morning of 28th November, after recapitulating the king's concessions, he declared the Assembly illegal owing to the method of its election, and 'discharged their further proceedings under pain of treason.' He was answered in moderate language by Rothes and Henderson, but the latter refused to accept the dissolution. 'All that are here know the reasons of the meeting of this Assembly, and, albeit we have acknowledged the power of Christian kings for convening of Assemblies, yet that may not derogate from Christ's right; for He has given divine warrants to convoke Assemblies whether magistrates consent or not.' Then arose Mr David Dickson, who said, looking towards Hamilton, 'that that nobleman was very much to be commended for his zeal and faithfulness to his master the king, and sticking close by what he thought for his credit and interest; and he craved leave to propose his example for the Assembly's imitation. They had a better master, Christ the King of Kings, to serve, and his credit and honour to look after according to their commission and trust; and therefore he moved that, having this in their eye, they might sit still and do their Master's work faithfully.' In this high mood the Assembly saw Hamilton depart. It was a moment which von Ranke has compared to that scene a century and a half later, when the new French National Assembly for the first time withstood the commands of its king.

Before leaving for the south, Hamilton summoned the members of the Privy Council together and counselled them to do their duty by the king. One or two withdrew, declaring that they were on the popular side, and among them was Argyll, who, the day before, when Hamilton dissolved the Assembly, had defended the legality of the lay element and announced his adhesion to the Covenanting cause. Hamilton wrote to Charles and to Laud announcing the failure of his mission, and urging the necessity of speeding on the armed preparations. In his letter to the king of 27th

November he provided his master with certain character-studies of the Scots nobility. Two of his comments are worth noting: Argyll 'will prove the dangerousest man in this state'; of the Covenanting leaders there was 'none more vainly foolish than Montrose.'

The Assembly resumed its sittings on the 29th, with Argyll as the solitary Privy Councillor. It sat till 20th December, and, says Burnet, 'went on at a great rate, now that there were none to curb them.' It pronounced the last six General Assemblies invalid; condemned the service book, the book of canons, and the Court of High Commission; annulled the Articles of Perth; declared episcopacy to be utterly abjured and cast out of the Kirk; established a press censorship, under the control of Wariston; and, in a mood of startling enlightenment, prohibited salmon-fishing on Sundays.

The whole Scottish hierarchy was deposed, and most of its members excommunicated as well. The bishops had declined to appear, so there was no defence; the Aberdeen doctors were not there to raise their voices, which Baillie thought might have induced a more moderate temper. Undoubtedly there had been much laxness of conduct on the part of the bishops, and certain scandals; but many of the charges were absurd, and few were supported by evidence which would have satisfied a court of law. The fact of holding episcopal office was held sufficient to afford presumptive proof of moral delinquencies. Episcopacy and its ministrants were abolished root and branch, and certain dubious historical dogmas were affirmed, against which Baillie, to his honour, protested. He had been impressed by Hamilton's conduct in the commissioner's chair, and had wept at his withdrawal; he may be taken as the type of the moderate Covenanter, who was against episcopacy as a system, but did not think it necessarily forbidden by the reformed faith. But the ministerial leaders, with the support of the lay members, would be content with no half-hearted condemnation. On the day when the prelates were sentenced, Henderson preached the sermon, long known as 'The Bishops' Doom'; but the passage of Scripture selected by the reader may have had an ominous ring in other ears than Mr Robert Baillie's. 'These things I have spoken to you that you should not be offended. They shall put you out of the synagogue; yea, the time cometh that whosoever killeth you will think that he doeth God service.'

The Assembly had clearly gone beyond its legal powers. When the king's commissioner dissolved it, under the Act of 1592, it ceased to exist at law. Henderson's act had all the significance which von Ranke has claimed for it; in the words of his most recent biographer, it 'spelt revolution'. The Assembly claimed to repeal the laws of the land, and it proceeded to carry its edicts into action. The treatment of the bishops was as harsh as it was irregular, but revolutions are not considerate of individual rights. Our judgment of its doings must be based upon the assumption that it was a definite revolt against the king's authority. It sought, indeed, to be a modified revolution. A treasonable sermon by Mr George Gillespie was condemned by implication by the Moderator; Argyll warned them, and Henderson repeated his warning, against any disrespect to 'so good and gracious a prince'; and at the end an address was drawn up to his Majesty, humbly asking him to confirm their acts in the Parliament presently to be summoned. But a revolution is a hard thing to delimit, and it has a fatal habit of producing a reaction in kind. The doings of 1638 were exactly paralleled by the Act Rescissory of 1661, which blotted out twenty-three years of legislation and re-established episcopacy. One form of violence was to be matched by another.

The Gods alone
Remember everlastingly; they strike
Remorselessly, and ever like for like.
By their great memories the Gods are known.

Yet to judge the protagonists at Glasgow with the cold-blooded retrospective reason of history is to do grave injustice. The implications of their actions were not present to the minds of the best of the clergy and laity. These revolutionaries were still royalists almost to a man. They opposed, not the monarchy, but the dogma of 'no bishop, no king', which would impair the royal authority by making it dependent upon a particular ecclesiastical form. Their mark was Laud rather than Charles. Among them were many fanatics of Presbytery, but there was also those who were lukewarm enough towards Presbyterian claims, but enthusiastic for Scottish liberties, and who considered that the people should have the church they wanted. Such men had a well-founded distrust of an episcopate as the gate by which autocracy had often entered the sheepfold. It is to be remembered that few Scots believed in divine right, that the nation had never known an unquestioned monarchy like that of the Tudors in England, and that they had been in the habit of frequently taking up arms to read their kings a lesson. While professing in all honesty their love for Charles, they were prepared to chasten him. They demanded that the nation's liberties should be safeguarded, and the proof of that would be the grant of the Kirk the nation preferred. On such a policy it was possible to unite for the moment the gross and wary sagacity of Rothes, the young enthusiasm of Montrose, and the profound and subtle ambition of the latest convert, Argyll.

To one who studies such portraits as exist of the chief figures in the Scotland of that epoch, there must come a sense of disappointment. Few convey the impression of power which is found among the Puritans and Cavaliers of England. There is Hamilton, self-conscious, arrogant, and puzzled; Lanark, his brother, dark, sullen, and stupid; Huntly, a peacock head surmounting a splendid body; Rothes, heavy-chinned, goggle-eyed, Pickwickian; Glencairn, weak and rustical; old Leven, the eternal bourgeois; the Border earls, but one remove from the Border prickers; Wariston, obstinate and crack-brained; James Guthrie, lean and fanatical. But there are three exceptions. One is the haunting face of Montrose, whose calm eyes do not change from the Jameson portrait of his boyhood to the great Honthorst of his prime. The second is the face of Alexander Henderson, yellow from the fevers of the Leuchars marshes, lined with thought, and burning with a steady fire. The third is that of Archibald, eighth Earl of Argyll. We see him at nineteen, in his marriage clothes, his reddish hair falling over his collar, his grey-blue eyes with ever so slight a cast in them; we see him in his twenty-fourth year, with the air and accoutrements of a soldier; in the Castle Campbell portrait, unfortunately burned in the Inveraray castle fire of 1877, he is in armour, but the face has a scholar's pallor and a curious melancholy; in the familiar Newbattle picture, painted in his late forties, he is in sober black with the skull-cap of a divine on his head, the features are drawn with ill-health and care, the mouth is compressed and secret, the nose is pendulous, and the cast in the eyes has become almost a deformity. But at whatever period we take it, it is a face of power, with intellect in the broad brow, and resolution in the tight lips and heavy chin.

In every national crisis there is some personal antagonism, where the warring creeds seem to be summed up in the persons of two protagonists – Caesar and Pompey, Pym and Strafford, Fox and Pitt. So were to stand those present allies, Montrose and Argyll, secular types of conflicting temperaments and irreconcilable views. The head of the great house of Campbell was now some thirty-four or thirty-five years of age, eight years the senior of Montrose. He had the widest possessions of any Highland chief except Huntly, and at his back by far the most powerful clan, for he lived close to the Lowlands, and could put 5,000 men into the field. His father, to whom the sobriquet of Gilleasbuig Gruamach – 'Gillespie the Sullen' – properly belonged, was an odd character and led an odd life. He was defeated at Glenrinnes in 1594 by the Gordons, but later added to his possessions by subduing the Macdonalds of Islay and Kintyre. But his fortune was not commensurate with his lands; he fell deeply into debt, married a Catholic second wife, joined the Church of

Rome, and had to flee the country. He was permitted to return, and lived some ten years in England before his death. His first wife was a daughter of the house of Morton, so his son had in his veins the unaccountable Douglas blood. Like the father, the son had an unhappy childhood, for he lost his mother in his infancy, and during his youth was perpetually at variance with his wandering sire. He had to fight hard during his minority for his rights, and the experience must have made him wary and distrustful, and taught him diplomacy and dissimulation. Charles is said to have assisted him against his vindictive parent, and Clarendon reports some dubious gossip about the old man warning the king against his son, 'for he is a man of craft, subtlety, and falsehood, and can love no man, and if ever he finds it in his power to do you a mischief, he will be sure to do it.'

What is clear is that in his youth he was deeply in debt, and found his great estates less of a boon than an incumbrance. He determined to husband and increase his fortune, and there is record of a curious venture to annex an imaginary island beyond the Hebrides. He took his part in policing the Highlands, and in 1636 brought to justice the outlaw Patrick Macgregor, who is famous in balladry as Gilderoy. With high politics he did not meddle. He defended the laird of Earlston against the Bishop of Galloway, and befriended Samuel Rutherford when brought before the Court of High Commission, but his motive may well have been only friendship to his kinsfolk, the Kenmures. These incidents did not predispose him to love the bishops, and in 1637 he convened a meeting of Rothes, Traquair, and other noblemen, to protest against the 'pride and avarice of the prelates seeking to overrule the haill kingdom.' But up to 1638 we may regard him as principally occupied with family troubles and the care of his estates, a little suspect by Presbytery as the son of a Catholic and the brother-in-law of Huntly, well regarded by the king in spite of his father's warnings, and with no special predilection towards the Kirk. He was one of the few nobles who, in the summer of 1638, took the king's alternative covenant at the request of Hamilton.

In this mood he attended the Glasgow Assembly. There it would appear that he underwent a profound spiritual experience, and in the theological sense was 'converted'. It was the habit of Alexander Henderson during the sittings to hold meetings at night for prayer and counsel. 'I find,' says Wodrow, who must have been repeating a tradition handed down in the ministry, 'that their meetings were remarkably countenanced of God, and that the Marquis of Argyll, and several others who sometimes joined in them, dated their conversion, or a knowledge of it, from those times.' It was this change of heart, and not the discovery that the Covenant was the side of the majority, that determined Argyll's course. He was an acute judge of popular opinion, but it was something more than policy that took him over to the Covenant side. For from that day this man, who in the past had been wholly concerned with his worldly possessions, and had held himself conspicuously aloof from the Kirk, became a religious enthusiast, a fanatic; and no mortal, however consummate an actor, could simulate such enthusiasm as Argyll revealed during the remainder of his troubled life.

'Bothwell Brig'

from Old Mortality

WALTER SCOTT (1771–1832)

Our excerpt from Old Mortality *describes the Battle of Bothwell Bridge in 1679. This was close to Glasgow, there was a considerable Covenanting party in the city and some of the victorious Royal forces under Charles II's bastard son Monmouth came there after the battle. In his introduction to the 'Penguin Classics' edition of the novel, Angus Calder gives this measured verdict on what is among Scott's starkest and most rapidly developed narratives:*

> Old Mortality *is a book written about an abortive revolution by a man who lived in a period which historians now often call the 'Age of Revolution'. Based on events in late seventeenth-century Scotland which, without it, would never have been widely known outside that country, and which, in spite of it, are now mostly forgotten, it yet remains painfully vivid.*

To which we might add that it is some time since anything of these events was known inside Scotland, widely or not. Scott's novel, which is not always strictly accurate in its description of events but is almost Shakespearean in its dramatic compression and heightening of the action, shows the Covenanters, mainly from the south-west of Scotland, winning a victory at Drumclog in June but provoking a savage response at Bothwell Bridge within the space of the same month. The leader of the small Royalist force beaten at Drumclog turns out to be the immensely dramatic, enigmatic – and possibly favoured by Scott – John Graham of Claverhouse, Viscount Dundee, 'Bluidy Clavers' and 'Bonny Dundee' in one person. After Drumclog, Dundee had beaten off a force of Covenanters at the Tolbooth Steeple at the Cross of Glasgow.

Against Claverhouse and other historical Royalists like the ferocious Dalyell of the Binns, Scott sets the fictional hero Morton, who is with but not wholly of the Covenanting side. The personal story of Morton is never allowed to detract from the broad sweep of events and Scott encourages the reader to see the faults and 'bloody bigots' on both sides. The immensely complicated and shifting pattern of groups on the Covenant side is certainly not totally sympathetic in its treatment, and the assorted

Cameronians and other sects, Scott suggests, may be martyrs but are not all saints.

Morton's personal fate at the end of the book is a happy one; to talk of the Covenanters or 'original whigs' of the south-west, however, Bothwell Bridge means the crushing of the rising. Eventually their gravestones will fall under the care of 'Old Mortality', the old Cameronian of a later age who wanders from graveyard to graveyard and who begins the tale:

> *In the language of Scripture, he left his house, his home, and his kindred, and wandered about until the day of his death, a period of nearly thirty years. During this long pilgrimage, the pious enthusiast regulated his circuit so as annually to visit the graves of the unfortunate Covenanters, who suffered by the sword, or by the executioner, during the reigns of the two last monarchs of the Stewart line.*

BOTHWELL BRIG

When Morton had left the well-ordered outposts of the regular army, and arrived at those which were maintained by his own party, he could not but be peculiarly sensible of the difference of discipline, and entertain a proportional degree of fear for the consequences. The same discords which agitated the counsels of the insurgents, raged even among their meanest followers; and their picquets and patrols were more interested and occupied in disputing the true occasion and causes of wrath, and defining the limits of Erastian heresy, than in looking out for and observing the motions of their enemies, though within hearing of the royal drums and trumpets.

There was a guard, however, of the insurgent army, posted at the long and narrow bridge of Bothwell, over which the enemy must necessarily advance to the attack; but, like the others, they were divided and disheartened; and, entertaining the idea that they were posted on a desperate service, they even meditated withdrawing themselves to the main body. This would have been utter ruin; for, on the defence or loss of this pass the fortune of the day was most likely to depend. All beyond the bridge was a plain open field, excepting a few thickets of no great depth, and, consequently, was ground on which the undisciplined forces of the insurgents, deficient as they were in cavalry, and totally unprovided with artillery, were altogether unlikely to withstand the shock of regular troops.

Morton, therefore, viewed the pass carefully, and formed the hope, that by occupying two or three houses on the left bank of the river, with the copse and thickets of alders and hazels that lined its side, and by blockading the passage itself, and shutting the gates of a portal, which, according to the old fashion, was built on the central arch of the bridge of Bothwell, it might be easily defended against a very superior force. He issued directions accordingly, and commanded the parapets of the bridge, on the farther side of the portal, to be thrown down, that they might afford no protection to the enemy when they should attempt the passage. Morton then conjured the party at this important post to be watchful and upon their guard, and promised them a speedy and strong reinforcement. He caused them to advance videttes beyond the river to watch the progress of the enemy, which outposts he directed should be withdrawn to the left bank as soon as they approached; finally, he charged them to send regular information to the main body of all that they should observe. Men under arms, and in a situation of danger, are usually sufficiently alert in appreciating the merit of their officers. Morton's intelligence and activity gained the confidence of these men, and with better hope and heart than before, they began to fortify their position in the manner he recommended, and saw him depart with three loud cheers.

Morton now galloped hastily towards the main body of the insurgents, but was surprised and shocked at the scene of confusion and clamour which it exhibited, at the moment when good order and concord were of such essential consequence. Instead of being drawn up in line of battle, and listening to the commands of their officers, they were crowding together in a confused mass, that rolled and agitated itself like the waves of the sea, while a thousand tongues spoke, or rather vociferated, and not a single ear was found to listen. Scandalized at a scene so extraordinary, Morton endeavoured to make his way through the press to learn, and, if possible, to remove, the cause of this so untimely disorder. While he is thus engaged, we shall make the reader acquainted with that which he was some time in discovering.

The insurgents had proceeded to hold their day of humiliation, which, agreeably to the practice of the puritans during the earlier civil war, they considered as the most effectual mode of solving all difficulties, and waiving all discussions. It was usual to name an ordinary week-day for this purpose, but on this occasion the Sabbath itself was adopted, owing to the pressure of the time and the vicinity of the enemy. A temporary pulpit, or tent, was erected in the middle of the encampment; which, according to the fixed arrangement, was first to be occupied by the Reverend Peter Poundtext, to whom the post of honour was assigned, as the eldest clergyman present. But as the worthy divine, with slow and stately steps, was advancing towards the rostrum which had been prepared for him, he was prevented by the unexpected apparition of Habakkuk Mucklewrath, the insane preacher, whose appearance had so much startled Morton at the first council of the insurgents after their victory at Loudon-hill. It is not known whether he was acting under the influence and instigation of the Cameronians, or whether he was merely compelled by his own agitated imagination, and the temptation of a vacant pulpit before him, to seize the opportunity of exhorting so respectable a congregation. It is only certain that he took occasion by the forelock, sprung into the pulpit, cast his eyes wildly round him, and, undismayed by the murmurs of many of the audience, opened the Bible, read forth as his text from the thirteenth chapter of Deuteronomy, 'Certain men, the children of Belial, are gone out from among you, and have withdrawn the inhabitants of their city, saying, let us go and serve other gods, which you have not known;' and then rushed at once into the midst of his subject.

The harangue of Mucklewrath was as wild and extravagant as his intrusion was unauthorized and untimely; but it was provokingly coherent, in so far as it turned entirely upon the very subjects of discord, of which it had been agreed to adjourn the consideration until some more suitable opportunity. Not a single topic did he omit which had offence in it; and, after charging the moderate party with heresy, with crouching to tyranny, with seeking to be at peace with God's enemies, he applied to Morton, by name, the charge that he had been one of those men of Belial, who, in the words of his text, had gone out from amongst them, to withdraw the inhabitants of his city, and to go astray after false gods. To him, and all who followed him, or approved of his conduct, Mucklewrath denounced fury and vengeance, and exhorted those who would hold themselves pure and undefiled to come up from the midst of them.

'Fear not,' he said, 'because of the neighing of horses, or the glittering of breastplates. Seek not aid of the Egyptians, because of the enemy, though they may be numerous as locusts, and fierce as dragons. Their trust is not as our trust, nor their rock as our rock; how else shall a thousand fly before one, and two put ten thousand to the flight! I dreamed it in the visions of the night, and the voice said, "Habakkuk, take thy fan and purge the wheat from the chaff, that they be not both consumed with the fire of indignation and the lightning of fury." Wherefore, I say, take this Henry Morton – this wretched Achan, who hath brought the accursed thing among ye, and made himself brethren in the camp of the enemy – take him and stone him with stones, and thereafter burn him with fire, that the wrath may depart from the children of the Covenant. He hath not taken a Babylonish garment, but he hath sold the garment of righteousness to the woman of Babylon – he hath not taken two hundred shekels of fine silver, but he hath bartered the truth, which is more precious than shekels of silver or wedges of gold.'

At this furious charge, brought so unexpectedly against one of their most active commanders, the audience broke out into open tumult, some demanding that there should instantly be a new election of officers, into which office none should hereafter be admitted who had, in their phrase, touched of that which was accursed, or temporized more or less with the heresies and corruptions of the times. While such was the demand of the Cameronians, they vociferated loudly, that those who were not with them were against them – that it was no time to relinquish the substantial part of the covenanted testimony of the Church, if they expected a blessing on their arms and their cause; and that, in their eyes, a lukewarm Presbyterian was little better than a Prelatist, an Anti-Covenanter, and a Nullifidian.

The parties accused repelled the charge of criminal compliance and defection from the truth with scorn and indignation, and charged their accusers with breach of faith, as well as with wrong-headed and extravagant zeal in introducing such divisions into an army, the joint strength of which could not, by the most sanguine, be judged more than sufficient to face their enemies. Poundtext, and one or two others, made some faint efforts to stem the increasing fury of the factious, exclaiming to those of the other party, in the words of the Patriarch, – 'Let there be no strife, I pray thee, between me and thee, and between thy herdsmen and my herdsmen, for we be brethren.' No pacific overture could possibly obtain audience. It was in vain that even Burley himself, when he saw the dissension proceed to such ruinous lengths, exerted his stern and deep voice, commanding silence and obedience to discipline. The spirit of insubordination had gone forth, and it seemed as if the exhortation of Habakkuk Mucklewrath had communicated a part of his frenzy to all who heard him. The wiser, or more timid part of the assembly, were already withdrawing themselves from the field, and giving up their cause as lost. Others were moderating a harmonious call, as they somewhat improperly termed it, to new officers, and dismissing those formerly chosen, and that with a tumult and clamour worthy of the deficiency of good sense and good order implied in the whole transaction. It was at this moment when Morton arrived in the field and joined the army, in total confusion, and on the point of dissolving itself. His arrival occasioned loud exclamations of applause on the one side, and of imprecation on the other.

'What means this ruinous disorder at such a moment?' he exclaimed to Burley, who, exhausted with his vain exertions to restore order, was now leaning on his sword, and regarding the confusion with an eye of resolute despair.

'It means,' he replied, 'that God has delivered us into the hands of our enemies.'

'Not so,' answered Morton, with a voice and gesture which compelled many to listen; 'it is not God who deserts us, it is we who desert him, and dishonour ourselves by disgracing and betraying the cause of freedom and religion. – Hear me,' he exclaimed, springing to the pulpit which Mucklewrath had been compelled to evacuate by actual exhaustion – 'I bring from the enemy an offer to treat, if you incline to lay down your arms. I can assure you the means of making an honourable defence, if you are of more manly tempers. The time flies fast on. Let us resolve either for peace or war; and let it not be said of us in future days, that six thousand Scottish men in arms had neither courage to stand their ground and fight it out, nor prudence to treat for peace, nor even the coward's wisdom to retreat in good time and with safety. What signifies quarrelling on minute points of church-discipline, when the whole edifice is threatened with total destruction? O, remember, my brethren, that the last and worst evil which God brought upon the people whom he had once chosen – the last and worst punishment of their blindness and hardness of heart, was the bloody dissensions which rent asunder their city, even when the enemy were thundering at its gates!'

Some of the audience testified their feeling of this exhortation, by loud exclamations of applause; others by hooting, and exclaiming – 'To your tents, O Israel!'

Morton, who beheld the columns of the enemy already beginning to appear on the right bank, and directing their march upon the bridge, raised his voice to its utmost pitch, and, pointing at the same time with his hand, exclaimed, – 'Silence your senseless clamours, yonder is the enemy! On maintaining the bridge against him depend our lives, as well as our hope to reclaim our laws and liberties. – There shall at least one Scottish-man die in their defence. – Let any one who loves his country follow me!'

The multitude had turned their heads in the direction to which he pointed. The sight of the glittering files of the English Foot-Guards, supported by several squadrons of horse, of the cannon which the artillerymen were busily engaged in planting against the bridge, of the plaided clans who seemed to search for a ford, and of the long succession of troops which were destined to support the attack, silenced at once their clamorous uproar, and struck them with as much consternation as if it were an unexpected apparition, and not the very thing which they ought to have been looking out for. They gazed on each other, and on their leaders, with looks resembling those that indicate the weakness of a patient when exhausted by a fit of frenzy. Yet when Morton, springing from the rostrum, directed his steps towards the bridge, he was followed by about an hundred of the young men who were particularly attached to his command.

Burley turned to Macbriar – 'Ephraim,' he said, 'it is Providence points us the way, through the worldly wisdom of this latitudinarian youth. – He that loves the light, let him follow Burley!'

'Tarry,' replied Macbriar; 'it is not by Henry Morton, or such as he, that our goings-out and our comings-in are to be meted; therefore tarry with us. I fear treachery to the host from this *nullifidian* Achan. – Thou shalt not go with him. Thou art our chariots and our horsemen.'

'Hinder me not,' replied Burley; 'he hath well said that all is lost, if the enemy win the bridge – therefore let me not. Shall the children of this generation be called wiser or braver than the children of the sanctuary? – Array yourselves under your leaders – let us not lack supplies of men and ammunition; and accursed be he who turneth back from the work on this great day!'

Having thus spoken, he hastily marched towards the bridge, and was followed by about two hundred of the most gallant and zealous of his party. There was a deep and disheartened pause when Morton and Burley departed. The commanders availed themselves of it to display their lines in some sort of order, and exhorted those who were most exposed to throw themselves upon their faces to avoid the cannonade which they might presently expect. The insurgents ceased to resist or to remonstrate; but the awe which had silenced their discords had dismayed their courage. They suffered themselves to be formed into ranks with the docility of a flock of sheep, but without possessing, for the time, more resolution or energy; for they experienced a sinking of the heart, imposed by the sudden and imminent approach of the danger which they had neglected to provide against while it was yet distant. They were, however, drawn out with some regularity; and as they still possessed the appearance of an army, their leaders had only to hope that some favourable circumstance would restore their spirits and courage.

Kettledrummle, Poundtext, Macbriar, and other preachers, busied themselves in their ranks, and prevailed on them to raise a psalm. But the superstitious among them observed, as an ill omen, that their song of praise and triumph sunk into 'a quaver of consternation', and resembled rather a penitentiary stave sung on the scaffold of a condemned criminal, than the bold strain which had resounded along the wild heath of Loudon-hill, in anticipation of that day's victory. The melancholy melody soon received a rough accompaniment; the royal soldiers shouted, the Highlanders yelled, the cannon began to fire on one side, and the musketry on both, and the bridge of Bothwell, with the banks adjacent, were involved in wreaths of smoke.

As e'er ye saw the rain doun fa',
Or yet the arrow from the bow,
Sae our Scots lads fell even down,
And they lay slain on every knowe.
Old Ballad

Ere Morton or Burley had reached the post to be defended, the enemy had commenced an attack upon it with great spirit. The two regiments of Foot-Guards, formed into a close column, rushed forward to the river; one corps, deploying along the right bank, commenced a galling fire on the defenders of the pass, while the other pressed on to occupy the bridge. The insurgents sustained the attack with great constancy and courage; and while part of their number returned the fire across the river, the rest maintained a discharge of musketry upon the further end of the bridge itself, and every avenue by which the soldiers endeavoured to approach it. The latter suffered severely, but still gained ground, and the head of their column was already upon the bridge, when the arrival of Morton changed the scene; and his marksmen, commencing upon the pass a fire as well aimed as it was sustained and regular, compelled the assailants to retire with much loss. They were a second time brought up to the charge, and a second time repulsed with still greater loss, as Burley had now brought his party into action. The fire was continued with the utmost vehemence on both sides, and the issue of the action seemed very dubious.

Monmouth, mounted on a superb white charger, might be discovered on the top of the right bank of the river, urging, entreating, and animating the exertions of his soldiers. By his orders, the cannon, which had hitherto been employed in annoying the distant main body of the presbyterians, were now turned upon the defenders of the bridge. But these tremendous engines, being wrought much more slowly than in modern times, did not produce the effect of annoying or terrifying the enemy to the extent proposed. The insurgents, sheltered by copsewood along the bank of the river, or stationed in the houses already mentioned, fought under cover, while the royalists, owing to the precautions of

Morton, were entirely exposed. The defence was so protracted and obstinate, that the royal generals began to fear it might be ultimately successful. While Monmouth threw himself from his horse, and, rallying the Foot-Guards, brought them on to another close and desperate attack, he was warmly seconded by Dalzell, who, putting himself at the head of a body of Lennox-Highlanders, rushed forward with their tremendous war-cry of Loch-sloy. The ammunition of the defenders of the bridge began to fail at this important crisis; messages, commanding and imploring succours and supplies, were in vain dispatched, one after the other, to the main body of the presbyterian army, which remained inactively drawn up on the open fields in the rear. Fear, consternation, and misrule, had gone abroad among them, and while the post on which their safety depended required to be instantly and powerfully reinforced, there remained none either to command or to obey.

As the fire of the defenders of the bridge began to slacken, that of the assailants increased, and in its turn became more fatal. Animated by the example and exhortations of their generals, they obtained a footing upon the bridge itself, and began to remove the obstacles by which it was blockaded. The portal-gate was broke open, the beams, trunks of trees, and other materials of the barricade, pulled down and thrown into the river. This was not accomplished without opposition. Morton and Burley fought in the very front of their followers, and encouraged them with their pikes, halberds, and partisans, to encounter the bayonets of the Guards, and the broadswords of the Highlanders. But those behind the leaders began to shrink from the unequal combat, and fly singly, or in parties of two or three, towards the main body, until the remainder were, by the mere weight of the hostile column as much as by their weapons, fairly forced from the bridge. The passage being now open, the enemy began to pour over. But the bridge was long and narrow, which rendered the manoeuvre slow as well as dangerous; and those who first passed had still to force the houses, from the windows of which the Covenanters continued to fire. Burley and Morton were near each other at this critical moment.

'There is yet time,' said the former, 'to bring down horse to attack them, ere they can get into order; and, with the aid of God, we may thus regain the bridge – hasten thou to bring them down, while I make the defence good with this old and wearied body.'

Morton saw the importance of the advice, and, throwing himself on the horse which Cuddie held in readiness for him behind the thicket, galloped towards a body of cavalry which chanced to be composed entirely of Cameronians. Ere he could speak his errand, or utter his orders, he was saluted by the execrations of the whole body.

'He flies!' they exclaimed – 'the cowardly traitor flies like a hart from the hunters, and hath left valiant Burley in the midst of the slaughter!'

'I do not fly,' said Morton. 'I come to lead you to the attack. Advance boldly, and we shall yet do well.'

'Follow him not! – Follow him not!' – such were the tumultuous exclamations which resounded from the ranks; 'he hath sold you to the sword of the enemy!'

And while Morton argued, entreated, and commanded in vain, the moment was lost in which the advance might have been useful; and the outlet from the bridge, with all its defences, being in complete possession of the enemy, Burley and his remaining followers were driven back upon the main body, to whom the spectacle of their hurried and harassed retreat was far from restoring the confidence which they so much wanted.

In the meanwhile, the forces of the King crossed the bridge at their leisure, and, securing the pass, formed in line of battle; while Claverhouse, who, like a hawk perched on a rock, and eyeing the time to pounce on its prey, had watched the event of the action from the opposite bank, now passed the bridge at the head of his cavalry, at full trot, and, leading them in squadrons through the intervals and round the flanks of the royal infantry, formed them in line on the moor, and led them to the charge, advancing in front with one large body, while other two divisions threatened the flanks of the Covenanters. Their devoted army was now in that situation when the slightest demonstration towards an attack was certain to inspire panic. Their broken spirits and disheartened courage were unable to endure the charge of the cavalry, attended with all its terrible accompaniments of sight and sound; the rush of the horses at full speed, the shaking of the earth under their feet, the glancing of the swords, the waving of the plumes, and the fierce shouts of the cavaliers. The front ranks hardly attempted one ill-directed and disorderly fire, and their rear were broken and flying in confusion ere the charge had been completed; and in less than five minutes the horsemen were mixed with them, cutting and hewing without mercy. The voice of Claverhouse was heard, even above the din of conflict, exclaiming to his soldiers – 'Kill, kill – no quarter – think on Richard Grahame!' The dragoons, many of whom had shared the disgrace of Loudon-hill, required no exhortations to vengeance as easy as it was complete. Their swords drank deep of slaughter among the unresisting fugitives. Screams for quarter were only answered by the shouts with which the pursuers accompanied their blows, and the whole field presented one general scene of confused slaughter, flight, and pursuit.

About twelve hundred of the insurgents who remained in a body a little apart from the rest, and out of the line of the charge of cavalry, threw down their arms and surrendered at discretion, upon the approach of the Duke of Monmouth at the head of the infantry. That mild-tempered nobleman instantly allowed them the quarter which they prayed for; and, galloping about through the field, exerted himself as much to stop the slaughter as he had done to obtain the victory. While busied in this humane task he met with General Dalzell, who was encouraging the fierce Highlanders and royal volunteers to show their zeal for King and country, by quenching the flame of the rebellion with the blood of the rebels.

'Sheathe your sword, I command you, General!' exclaimed the Duke, 'and sound the retreat. Enough of blood has been shed; give quarter to the King's misguided subjects.'

'I obey your Grace,' said the old man, wiping his bloody sword and returning it to the scabbard; 'but I warn you, at the same time, that enough has *not* been done to intimidate these desperate rebels. Has not your Grace heard that Basil Olifant has collected several gentlemen and men of substance in the west, and is in the act of marching to join them?'

'Basil Olifant?' said the Duke; 'who, or what is he?'

'The next male heir to the last Earl of Torwood. He is disaffected to government from his claim to the estate being set aside in favour of Lady Margaret Bellenden; and I suppose the hope of getting the inheritance has set him in motion.'

'Be his motives what they will,' replied Monmouth, 'he must soon disperse his followers, for this army is too much broken to rally again. Therefore, once more, I command that the pursuit be stopped.'

'It is your Grace's province to command, and to be responsible for your commands,' answered Dalzell, as he gave reluctant orders for checking the pursuit.

But the fiery and vindictive Grahame was already far out of hearing of the signal of retreat, and continued with his cavalry an unwearied and bloody pursuit, breaking, dispersing, and cutting to pieces all the insurgents whom they could come up with.

Burley and Morton were both hurried off the field by the confused tide of fugitives. They made some attempt to defend the streets of the town of Hamilton; but, while labouring to induce the fliers to face about and stand to their weapons, Burley received a bullet which broke his sword-arm.

'May the hand be withered that shot the shot!' he exclaimed, as the sword which he was waving over his head fell powerless to his side. 'I can fight no longer.'

Then turning his horse's head, he retreated out of the confusion. Morton also now saw that the continuing his unavailing efforts to rally the fliers could only end in his own death or captivity, and, followed by the faithful Cuddie, he extricated himself from the press, and, being well mounted, leaped his horse over one or two enclosures, and got into the open country.

From the first hill which they gained in their flight, they looked back, and beheld the whole country covered with their fugitive companions, and with the pursuing dragoons, whose wild shouts and halloo, as they did execution on the groups whom they overtook, mingled with the groans and screams of their victims, rose shrilly up the hill.

'It is impossible they can ever make head again,' said Morton.

'The head's taen aff them, as clean as I wad bite it aff a sybo!' rejoined Cuddie. 'Eh, Lord! see how the broadswords are flashing! War's a fearsome thing. They'll be cunning that catches me at this wark again. But, for God's sake, sir, let us mak for some strength!'

Morton saw the necessity of following the advice of his trusty squire. They resumed a rapid pace, and continued it without intermission, directing their course towards the wild and mountainous country, where they thought it likely some part of the fugitives might draw together, for the sake either of making defence, or of obtaining terms.

'The Deluge'

W.D. (WILLIAM DIXON) COCKER (1882–1970)

The Lord took a staw at mankind,
A righteous an' natural scunner;
They were neither to haud nor to bind,
They were frichtit nae mair wi' his thun'er.

They had broken ilk edic' an' law,
They had pitten his saints to the sword,
They had worshipped fause idols o' stane;
'I will thole it nae mair,' saith the Lord.

'I am weary wi' flytin' at folk;
I will dicht them clean oot frae my sicht;
But Noah, douce man, I will spare,
For he ettles, puir, chiel, to dae richt.

So he cried unto Noah ae day,
When naebody else was aboot,
Sayin': 'Harken, my servant, to Me
An' these, my commands, cairry oot:

'A great, muckle boat ye maun build,
An ark that can float heich an' dry,
Wi' room in't for a' yer ain folk
An' a hantle o' cattle forby.

'Then tak' ye the fowls o' the air,
Even unto big bubbly-jocks;
An' tak' ye the beasts o' the field:
Whittrocks, an' foumarts, an' brocks.

'Wale ye twa guid anes o' each,
See that nae cratur rebels;
Dinna ye fash about fish;
They can look efter theirsels.

'Herd them a' safely aboard,
An' ance the Blue Peter's unfurled,
I'll send doun a forty-day flood
And de'il tak' the rest o' the world.'

Sae Noah wrocht hard at the job,
An' searched to the earth's farthest borders,
An' gethered the beasts an' the birds
An' tell't them to staun' by for orders.

An' his sons, Ham an' Japheth an' Shem,
Were thrang a' this time at the wark;
They had fell'd a wheen trees in the wood
An' biggit a great, muckle ark.

This wasna dune juist on the quate,
An' neebours would whiles gether roun';
Then Noah would drap them a hint
Like: 'The weather is gaun to break doun.'

But the neebours wi' evil were blin'
An' little jaloused what was wrang,
Sayin': 'That'll be guid for the neeps,'
Or: 'The weather's been drouthy ower lang.'

Then Noah wi' a' his ain folk,
An' the beasts an' the birds got aboard;
An' they steekit the door o' the ark,
An' they lippened theirsels to the Lord.

Then doun cam' a lashin' o' rain,
Like the wattest wat day in Lochaber;
The hailstanes like plunkers cam' stot,
An' the fields turned to glaur, an' syne glabber.

An' the burns a' cam' doun in a spate,
An' the rivers ran clean ower the haughs,
An' the brigs were a' soopit awa',
An' what had been dubs becam' lochs.

Then the folk were sair pitten aboot,
An' they cried, as the weather got waur:
'Oh! Lord, we ken fine we ha'e sinn'd
But a joke can be cairried ower faur!'

Then they chapp'd at the ark's muckle door,
To speer gin douce Noah had room;
But Noah ne'er heedit their cries,
He said: 'This'll learn ye to soom.'

An' the river roar'd loudly an' deep;
An' the miller was droon't in the mill;
An' the watter spread ower a' the land,
An' the shepherd was droon't on the hill.

But Noah, an' a' his ain folk,
Kep' safe frae the fate o' ill men,
Till the ark, when the flood had gi'en ower,
Cam' dunt on the tap o' a ben.

An' the watters row'd back to the seas,
An' the seas settled doun and were calm.
An' Noah replenished the earth–
But they're sayin' he took a guid dram!

'Andrew Amos'

from Mr Standfast

JOHN BUCHAN (1875–1940)

It is 1917. Richard Hannay, the hero of The Thirty Nine Steps *and* Greenmantle, *now a Brigadier on the Western Front, has been pulled out of France by Intelligence who want to recruit his help to stop a damaging leak of information from Britain to Germany. Hannay's search for the leak starts in the Garden City of Biggleswick in the Home Counties, where he meets the first of his secret allies and his future wife, Mary Lamington, and encounters a wide range of anti-war activists whom Buchan depicts in characters ranging from the eccentric to the obnoxious.*

Hannay, passing himself off as Cornelius Brand, a South African mining engineer and pacifist, follows the trail to Red Clydeside where he will meet Abel Gresson, an American industrial agitator known to be linked to the German spy ring. Hannay/Brandt arrives at the Glasgow home of Andrew Amos, Border radical turned shop steward and undercover agent for British Intelligence. Amos, with a reputation for 'whunstane common sense' claims to represent the bulk of the Glasgow workers and like 'the average man on the Clyde . . . hates just three things, and that's the Germans, the profiteers, as they call them, and the Irish' – The Easter Rising of 1916 and the exemption of Ireland from conscription adding fuel to the never distant fires of sectarian tensions in the Glasgow and West of Scotland of the period.

Among his other experiences in Glasgow Hannay attends an uproarious political meeting formed to create a Glasgow branch of a British Council of Workmen and Soldiers. This Russian-inspired body reflects the persistently radical nature of Glasgow politics, but the gathering descends into chaos, more than a little reminiscent of the Lloyd George gathering in the following extract.

The novel's title is taken from John Bunyan's seventeenth-century spiritual classic – The Pilgrim's Progress *– which Hannay, and his fellow agents of British Intelligence use as a form of code book.*

ANDREW AMOS

I took the train three days later from King's Cross to Edinburgh. I went to the Pentland Hotel in Princes Street and left there a suitcase containing some clean linen and a change of clothes. I had been thinking the things out, and had come to the conclusion that I must have a base somewhere and a fresh outfit. Then, in well-worn tweeds and with no more luggage than a small trench kit-bag, I descended upon the city of Glasgow.

I walked from the station to the address which Blenkiron had given me. It was a hot summer evening, and the streets were filled with bareheaded women and weary-looking artisans. As I made my way down the Dumbarton Road I was amazed at the number of able-bodied fellows about, considering you couldn't stir a mile on any British front without bumping up against a Glasgow battalion. Then I realized that there were such things as munitions and ships, and I wondered no more.

A stout and dishevelled lady at a close-mouth directed me to Mr Amos's dwelling. 'Twa stairs up. Andra will be in noo, havin' his tea. He's no yin for overtime. He's generally hame on the chap of six.' I ascended the stairs with a sinking heart, for like all South Africans I have a horror of dirt. The place was pretty filthy, but at each landing there were two doors with well-polished handles and brass plates. On one I read the name of Andrew Amos.

A man in his shirt-sleeves opened to me, a little man without a collar, and with an unbuttoned waistcoat. That was all I saw of him in the dim light, but he held out a paw like a gorilla's and drew me in.

The sitting-room, which looked over many chimneys to a pale yellow sky against which two factory stalks stood out sharply, gave me light enough to observe him fully. He was about five feet four, broad-shouldered, and with a great towsy head of grizzled hair. He wore spectacles, and his face was like some old-fashioned Scots minister's, for he had heavy eyebrows and whiskers which joined each other under his jaw, while his chin and enormous upper lip were clean-shaven. His eyes were steely grey and very solemn, but full of smouldering energy. His voice was enormous and would have shaken the walls if he had not had the habit of speaking with half-closed lips. He had not a sound tooth in his head.

A saucer full of tea and a plate which had once contained ham and eggs were on the table. He nodded towards them and asked me if I had fed.

'Ye'll no eat onything? Well, some would offer ye a dram, but this house is staunch teetotal. I doot ye'll have to try the nearest public if ye're thirsty.'

I disclaimed any bodily wants, and produced my pipe, at which he started to fill an old clay. 'Mr Brand's your name?' he asked in his gusty voice. 'I was expectin' ye, but Dod! man, ye're late!'

He extricated from his trousers pocket an ancient silver watch, and regarded it with disfavour. 'The dashed thing has stoppit. What do ye make the time, Mr Brand?'

He proceeded to prise open the lid of his watch with the knife he had used to cut his tobacco, and, as he examined the works, he turned the back of the case towards me. On the inside I saw pasted Mary Lamington's purple-and-white wafer.

I held my watch so that he could see the same token. His keen eyes, raised for a second, noted it, and he shut his own with a snap and returned it to his pocket. His manner lost its wariness, and became almost genial.

'Ye've come up to see Glasgow, Mr Brand? Well, it's a steerin' bit, and there's honest folk bides in it, and some not so honest. They tell me ye're from South Africa. That's a long gait away, but I ken something about South Africa, for I had a cousin's son oot there for his lungs. He was in a shop in Main Street, Bloomfountain. They called him Peter Dobson. Ye would maybe mind of him.'

Then he discoursed of the Clyde. He was an incomer, he told me, from the Borders, his native place being the town of Galashiels, or, as he called it, 'Gawly'. 'I began as a power-loom tuner in Stavert's mill. Then my father dee'd and I took up his trade of jiner. But it's no world nowadays for the sma' independent business, so I cam to the Clyde and learned a shipwright's job. I may say I've become a leader in the trade, for though I'm no an official of the Union, and not likely to be, there's no man's word carries more weight than mine. And the Goavernment kens that, for they've sent me on Commissions up and down the land to look at wuds and report on the nature of the timber. Bribery, they think it is, but Andrew Amos is not to be bribit. He'll have his say about ony Goavernment on earth, and tell them to their face what he thinks of them. Ay, and he'll fight the case of the workin'-man against his oppressor, should it be the Goavernment or the fatted calves they ca' Labour Members. Ye'll heard tell o' the shop stewards, Mr Brand?'

I admitted I had, for I had been well coached by Blenkiron in the current history of industrial disputes.

'Well, I'm a shop steward. We represent the rank and file against office-bearers that have lost the confidence o' the workin'-man. But I'm no socialist, and I would have ye keep mind of that. I'm yin o' the older Border radicals, and I'm not like to change. I'm for individual liberty and equal rights and chances for all men. I'll no more bow down before a

Dagon of a Goavernment official than before the Baal of a feckless Tweedside laird. I've to keep my views to mysel', for thae young lads are all drucken-daft with their wee books about Cawpital and Collectivism and a wheen long senseless words I wouldna fyle my tongue with. Them and their socialism! There's more gumption in a page of John Stuart Mill than in all that foreign trash. But, as I say, I've got to keep a quiet sough, for the world is gettin' socialism now like the measles. It all comes of a defective eddication.'

'And what does a Board radical say about the war?' I asked.

He took off his spectacles and cocked his shaggy brows at me. 'I'll tell ye, Mr Brand. All that was bad in all that I've ever wrestled with since I cam to years o' discretion – Tories and lairds and manufacturers and publicans and the Auld Kirk – all that was bad, I say, for there were orra bits of decency, ye'll find in the Germans full measure pressed down and running over. When the war started, I considered the subject calmly for three days, and then I said: 'Andra Amos, ye've found the enemy at last. The ones ye fought before were in a manner o' speakin' just misguided friends. It's either you or the Kaiser this time, my man!'

His eyes had lost their gravity and had taken on a sombre ferocity. 'Ay, and I've not wavered. I got word early in the business as to the way I could serve my country best. It's not been an easy job, and there's plenty of honest folk the day will give me a bad name. They think I'm stirrin' up the men at home and desertin' the cause o' the lads at the front. Man, I'm keepin' them straight. If I didna fight their battles on a sound economic isshue, they would take the dorts and be at the mercy of the first blagyird that preached revolution. Me and my like are safety-valves, if ye follow me. And dinna you make ony mistake, Mr Brand. The men that are agitating for a rise in wages are not for peace. They're fighting for the lads overseas as much as for themselves. There's not yin in a thousand that wouldna sweat himself blind to beat the Germans. The Goavernment has made mistakes, and maun be made to pay for them. If it were not so, the men would feel like a moose in a trap, for they would have no way to make their grievance felt. What for should the big man double his profits and the small man be ill set to get his ham and egg on Sabbath mornin'? That's the meaning o' Labour unrest, as they call it, and it's a good thing, says I, for if Labour didna get its leg over the traces now and then, the spunk o' the land would be dead in it, and Hindenburg could squeeze it like a rotten aipple.'

I asked if he spoke for the bulk of the men.

'For ninety per cent in any one ballot. I don't say that there's not plenty of riff-raff – the pint-and-a-dram gentry and the soft-heads that are aye reading bits of newspapers, and muddlin' their wits with foreign whigmaleeries. But the average man on the Clyde, like the average man in ither places, hates just three things, and that's the Germans, the profiteers, as they call them, and the Irish. But he hates the Germans first.'

'The Irish!' I exclaimed in astonishment.

'Ay, the Irish,' cried the last of the old Border radicals. 'Glasgow's stinkin' nowadays with two things, money and Irish. I mind the day when I followed Mr Gladstone's Home Rule policy, and used to threep about the noble, generous, warm-hearted sister nation held in a foreign bondage. My Goad! I'm not speakin' about Ulster, which is a dour, ill-natured den, but our own folk all the same. But the men that will not do a hand's turn to help the war and take the chance of our necessities to set up a bawbee rebellion are hateful to Goad and man. We treated them like pet lambs and that's the thanks we get. They're coming over here in thousands to tak the jobs of the lads that are doing their duty. I was speakin' last week to a widow woman that keeps a wee dairy down the Dalmarnock Road. She had two sons, and both in the airmy, one in the Cameronians and one a prisoner in Germany. She was telling me that she could not keep goin' any more, lacking the help of the boys, though she had worked her fingers to the bone. "Surely it's a crool job, Mr Amos,' she says, "that the Goavernment should tak baith my laddies, and I'll maybe never see them again, and let the Irish gang free and tak the bread frae our mouth. At the gasworks across the road they took on a hundred Irish last week, and every yin o' them as young and well set up as you would ask to see. And my wee Davie, him that's in Germany, had a weak chest, and Jimmy was troubled wi' a bowel complaint. That's surely no justice!" . . .'

He broke off and lit a match by drawing it across the seat of his trousers. 'It's time I got the gas lichtit. There's some men coming here at half-ten.'

As the gas squealed and flickered in the lighting, he sketched for me the coming guests. 'There's Macnab and Niven, two o' my colleagues. And there's Gilkison of the Boiler-fitters, and a lad Wilkie – he's got consumption, and writes wee bits in the papers. And there's a queer chap o' the name o' Tombs – they tell me he comes frae Cambridge and is a kind of professor there – anyway he's more stuffed wi' havers than an egg wi' meat. He telled me he was here to get at the heart o' the workin'-man, and I said to him that he would hae to look a bit further than the sleeve o' the workin'-man's jaicket. There's no muckle in his head, poor soul. Then there'll be Tam Norie, him that edits our weekly paper – *Justice for All.* Tam's a humorist and great on Robert Burns, but he hasna the balance o' a dwinin' teetotum. . . . Ye'll understand, Mr Brand, that I keep my mouth shut in such company, and don't express my own views more than is absolutely necessary. I criticize whiles, and that gives me a name for whunstane common sense, but I never let my tongue wag. The feck o' the lads comin' the night are not the real workin'-man – they're just the froth on the pot, but it's the froth that will be useful to you. Remember they've heard tell o' ye already, and ye've some sort o' reputation to keep up.'

'Will Mr Abel Gresson be here?' I asked.

'No,' he said. 'No yet. Him and me havena yet got to the point o' payin' visits. But the men that come will be Gresson's friends and they'll speak of ye to him. It's the best kind of introduction ye could seek.'

The knocker sounded, and Mr Amos hastened to admit the first comers. These were Macnab and Wilkie: the one a decent middle-aged man with a fresh-washed face and a celluloid collar; the other a round-shouldered youth, with lank hair and the large eyes and luminous skin which are the parks of phthisis. 'This is Mr Brand, boys, from South Africa,' was Amos's presentation. Presently came Niven, a bearded giant, and Mr Norie, the editor, a fat dirty fellow smoking a rank cigar. Gilkison of the Boiler-fitters, when he arrived, proved to be a pleasant young man in spectacles who spoke with an educated voice and clearly belonged to a slightly different social scale. Last came Tombs, the Cambridge 'professor,' a lean youth with a sour mouth and eyes that reminded me of Launcelot Wake.

'Ye'll no be a mawgnate, Mr Brand, though ye come from South Africa,' said Mr Norie with a great guffaw.

'Not me. I'm a working engineer,' I said. 'My father was from Scotland, and this is my first visit to my native country, as my friend Mr Amos was telling you.'

The consumptive looked at me suspiciously. 'We've got two-three of the comrades here that the cawpitalist Government expelled from the Transvaal. If ye're our way of thinking, ye will maybe ken them.'

I said I would be overjoyed to meet them, but at the time of the outrage in question I had been working on a mine a thousand miles farther north.

Then ensued an hour of extraordinary talk. Tombs in his sing-song namby-pamby University voice was concerned to get information. He asked endless questions, chiefly of Gilkison, who was the only one who really understood his language. I thought I had never seen any one quite so fluent and so futile, and yet there was a kind of feeble violence in him like a demented sheep. He was engaged in venting some private academic spite against society, and I thought that in a revolution he would be the class of lad I would personally conduct to the nearest lamp-post. And all the while Amos and Macnab and Niven carried on their own conversation about the affairs of their society, wholly impervious to the tornado raging around them.

It was Mr Norie, the editor, who brought me into the discussion.

'Our South African friend is very blate,' he said in his boisterous way. 'Andra, if this place of yours wasn't so dammed teetotal and we had a dram apiece, we might get his tongue loosened. I want to hear what he's got to say about the war. You told me this morning he was sound in the faith.'

'I said no such thing,' said Mr Amos, 'As ye ken well, Tam Norie, I don't judge soundness on that matter as you judge it. I'm for the war myself, subject to certain conditions that I've often stated. I know nothing of Mr Brand's opinions, except that he's a good democrat, which is more than I can say of some o' your friends.'

'Hear to Andra,' laughed Mr Norie. 'He's thinkin' the inspector in the Socialist State would be a waur kind of awristocrat then the Duke of Buccleugh. Weel, there's maybe something in that. But about the war he's wrong. Ye ken my views, boys. This war was made by the cawpitalists, and it has been fought by the workers, and it's the workers that maun have the ending of it. That day's comin' very near. There are those that want to spin it out till Labour is that weak it can be pit in chains for the rest o' time. That's the manoeuvre we're out to prevent. We've got to beat the Germans, but it's the workers that has the right to judge when the enemy's beaten and not the cawpitalists. What do you say, Mr Brand?'

Mr Norie had obviously pinned his colours to the fence, but he gave me the chance I had been looking for. I let them have my views with a vengeance, and these views were that for the sake of democracy the war must be ended. I flatter myself I put my case well, for I had got up every rotten argument and I borrowed largely from Launcelot Wake's armoury. But I didn't put it too well, for I had a very exact notion of the impression I wanted to produce. I must be seen to be honest and in earnest, just a bit of a fanatic, but principally a hard-headed business man who knew when the time had come to make a deal. Tombs kept interrupting me with imbecile questions, and I had to sit on him. At the end Mr Norie hammered with his pipe on the table.

'That'll sort ye, Andra. Ye're entertainin' an angel unawares. What do ye say to that, my man?'

Mr Amos shook his head. 'I'll no deny there's something in it, but I'm not convinced that the Germans have got enough of a wheepin'.' Macnab agreed with him; the others were with me. Norie was for getting me to write an article for his paper, and the consumptive wanted me to address a meeting.

'Wull ye say a' that over again the morn's night down at our hall in Newmilns Street?' We've got a lodge meeting o' the I.W.B., and I'll make them pit ye in the programme.' He kept his luminous eyes, like a sick dog's fixed on me, and I saw I had made one ally. I told him I had come to Glasgow to learn and not to teach, but I would miss no chance of testifying to my faith.

'Now, boys, I'm for my bed,' said Amos, shaking the dottle from his pipe. 'Mr Tombs, I'll conduct ye the morn over the Brigend works, but I've had enough clavers for one evening. I'm a man that wants his eight hours' sleep.'

The old fellow saw them to the door, and came back to me with the ghost of a grin in his face.

'A queer crowd, Mr Brand! Macnab didna like what ye said. He had a laddie killed in Gallypoly, and he's no lookin' for peace this side the grave. He's my best friend in Glasgow. He's an elder in the Gaelic kirk in the Cowcaddens, and I'm what ye call a freethinker, but we're wonderful agreed on the fundamentals. Ye spoke your bit verra well, I must admit. Gresson will hear tell of ye as a promising recruit.'

'It's a rotten job,' I said.

'Ay, it's a rotten job. I often feel like voamiting over it mysel'. But it's no for us to complain. There's waur jobs oot in France for better men. . . . A word in your ear, Mr Brand. Could ye not look a bit more sheepish? Ye stare folk ower straight in the een, like a Hieland sergeant-major up at Maryhill Barracks.' And he winked slowly and grotesquely with his left eye.

He marched to a cupboard and produced a black bottle and a glass. 'I'm blue-ribbon myself, but ye'll be the better of something to tak the taste out of your mouth. There's Loch Katrine water at the pipe there. . . . As I was saying, there's not much ill in that lot. Tombs is a black offence, but a dominie's a dominie all the world over. They may crack about their Industrial Workers and the braw things they're going to do, but there's a wholesome dampness about the tinder on Clydeside. They should try Ireland.'

'Supposing,' I said, 'there was a really clever man who wanted to help the enemy. You think he could do little good by stirring up trouble in the shops here?'

'I'm positive.'

'And if he were a shrewd fellow, he'd soon tumble to that?'

'Ay.'

'Then if he still stayed here he would be after bigger game – something really dangerous and damnable?'

Amos drew down his brows and looked me in the face. 'I see what ye're ettlin' at. Ay! That would be my conclusion. I came to it weeks syne about the man ye'll maybe meet the morn's night.'

Then from below the bed he pulled a box from which he drew a handsome flute. 'Ye forgive me, Mr Brand, but I aye like a tune before I go to my bed. Macnab says his prayers, and I have a tune on the flute, and the principle is just the same.'

So that singular evening closed with music – very sweet and true renderings of old Border melodies like 'My Peggy is a young thing', and 'When the kye come hame'. I fell asleep with a vision of Amos, his face all puckered up at the mouth and a wandering sentiment in his eye, recapturing in his dingy world the emotions of a boy.

The widow-woman from next door, who acted as housekeeper, cook, and general factotum to the establishment, brought me shaving water next morning, but I had to go without a bath. When I entered the kitchen I found no one there, but while I consumed the inevitable ham and egg, Amos arrived back for breakfast. He brought with him the morning's paper.

'The *Herald* says there's been a big battle at Eepers,' he announced.

I tore open the sheet and read of the great attack of July 31st which was spoiled by the weather. 'My God!' I cried. 'They've got St Julien and that dirty Frezenberg ridge . . . and Hooge...and Sanctuary Wood. I know every inch of the dammed place. . . .'

'Mr Brand,' said a warning voice, 'that'll never do. If our friends last night heard ye talk like that ye might as well tak the train back to London. . . . . They're speakin' about ye' in the yards this morning. Ye'll get a good turn-out at your meeting the night, but they're sayin' that the polis will interfere. That mightna be a bad thing, but I trust ye to show discretion, for ye'll not be muckle use to onybody if they jyle ye in Duke Street. I hear Gresson will be there with a fraternal message from his lunattics in America. . . . I've arranged that ye go down to Tam Norie this forenoon and give him a hand with his bit paper. Tam will tell ye the whole clash o' the West country, and I look to ye to keep him off the drink. He's aye arguin' that writin' and drinkin' gang thegither, and quotin' Robert Burns, but the creature has a wife and five bairns dependin' on him.'

I spent a fantastic day. For two hours I sat in Norie's dirty den, while he smoked and orated, and, when he remembered his business, took down in shorthand my impressions of the Labour situation in South

Africa for his rag. They were fine breezy impressions, based on the most wholehearted ignorance, and if they ever reached the Rand I wonder what my friends there made of Cornelius Brand, their author. I stood him dinner in an indifferent eating-house in a street off the Broomielaw, and thereafter had a drink with him in a public-house, and was introduced to some less reputable friends.

About tea-time I went back to Amos's lodgings, and spent an hour or so writing a long letter to Mr Ivery. I described to him everybody I had met, I gave highly-coloured views of the explosive material on the Clyde, and I deplored the lack of clear-headedness in the progressive forces. I drew an elaborate picture of Amos, and deduced from it that the Radicals were likely to be a bar to true progress. 'They have switched their old militancy,' I wrote, 'on to another track, for with them it is a matter of conscience to be always militant.' I finished up with some very crude remarks on economics culled from the table-talk of the egregious Tombs. It was the kind of letter which I hoped would establish my character in his mind as a laborious innocent.

Seven o'clock found me in Newmilns Street, where I was seized upon by Wilkie. He had put on a clean collar for the occasion and had partially washed his thin face. The poor fellow had a cough that shook him like the walls of a powerhouse when the dynamos are going.

He was very apologetic about Amos. 'Andra belongs to a past worrld,' he said. 'He has a big repittation in his society, and he's a fine fighter, but he has no kind of Vision, if ye understand me. He's an auld Gladstonian, and that's done and damned in Scotland. He's not a modern, Mr Brand, like you and me. But tonight ye'll meet one or two chaps that'll be worth your while to ken. Ye'll maybe no go quite as far as them, but ye're on the same road. I'm hoping for the day when we'll have oor Councils of Workmen and Soldiers like the Russians all over the land and dictate our terms to the pawrasites in Pawrliament. They tell me, too, the boys in the trenches are comin' round to our side.'

We entered the hall by a back door, and in a little waiting-room I was introduced to some of the speakers. They were a scratch lot as seen in that dingy place. The chairman was a shop-steward in one of the Societies, a fierce little rat of a man, who spoke with a cockney accent and addressed me as 'Comrade.' But one of them roused my liveliest interest. I heard the name of Gresson, and turned to find a fellow of about thirty-five, rather sprucely dressed, with a flower in his buttonhole. 'Mr Brand,' he said, in a rich American voice which recalled Blenkiron's. 'Very pleased to meet you, sir. We have come from remote parts of the globe to be present at this gathering.' I noticed that he had reddish hair, and small bright eyes, and a nose with a droop like a Polish Jew's.

As soon as we reached the platform I saw that there was going to be trouble. The hall was packed to the door, and in all the front half there was the kind of audience I expected to see – working-men of the political type who before the war would have thronged to party meetings. But not all the crowd at the back had come to listen. Some were scallawags, some looked like better-class clerks out for a spree, and there was a fair quantity of khaki. There were also one or two gentlemen not strictly sober.

The chairman began by putting his foot in it. He said we were there to-night to protest against the continuation of the war and to form a branch of the new British Council of Workmen and Soldiers. He told them with a fine mixture of metaphors that we had got to take the reins into our own hands, for the men who were running the war had their own axes to grind and were marching to oligarchy through the blood of the workers. He added that we had no quarrel with Germany half as bad as we had with our own capitalists. He looked forward to the day when British soldiers would leap from their trenches and extend the hand of friendship to their German comrades.

'No me!' said a solemn voice. 'I'm not seekin' a bullet in my wame,' – at which there was laughter and cat-calls.

Tombs followed and made a worse hash of it. He was determined to speak, as he would have put it, to democracy in its own language, so he said 'hell' several times, loudly but without conviction. Presently he slipped into the manner of the lecturer, and the audience grew restless. 'I propose to ask myself a question –' he began, and from the back of the hall came – 'and a damned sully answer ye'll get.' After that there was no more Tombs.

I followed with extreme nervousness, and to my surprise got a fair hearing. I felt as mean as a mangy dog on a cold morning, for I hated to talk rot before soldiers – especially before a couple of Royal Scots Fusiliers, who, for all I knew, might have been in my own brigade. My line was the plain practical, patriotic man, just come from the colonies, who looked at things with fresh eyes, and called for a new deal. I was very moderate, but to justify my appearance there I had to put in a wild patch or two, and I got these by impassioned attacks on the Ministry of Munitions. I mixed up a little mild praise of the Germans whom I said I had known all over the world for decent fellows. I received little applause, but no marked dissent, and sat down with deep thankfulness.

The next speaker put the lid on it. I believe he was a noted agitator, who had already been deported. Towards him there was no lukewarmness, for one half of the audience cheered wildly when he rose, and the other half hissed and groaned. He began with a whirlwind abuse of the idle rich, then of the middle classes (he called them the 'rich man's flunkeys'), and finally the Government. All that was fairly well received, for it is the fashion of the Briton to run down every Government and yet to be very averse to parting with it. Then he started on the soldiers and slanged the officers ('gentry pups' was his name for them), and the generals, whom he accused of idleness, of cowardice, and of habitual intoxication. He told us that our own kith and kin were sacrificed in every battle by leaders who had not the guts to share their risks. The Scots Fusiliers looked perturbed, as if they were in doubt of his meaning. Then he put it more plainly. 'Will any soldier deny that the men are the barrage to keep the officers' skins whole?'

'That's a bloody lee,' said one of the Fusilier Jocks.

The man took no notice of the interruption, being carried away by the torrent of his own rhetoric, but he had not allowed for the persistence of the interrupter. The Jock got slowly to his feet, and announced that he wanted satisfaction 'If ye open your dirty gab to blagyird honest men, I'll come up on that platform and wring your neck.'

At that there was a fine old row, some crying out, 'Order', some 'Fair Play', and some applauding. A Canadian at the back of the hall started a song, and there was an ugly press forward. The hall seemed to be moving up from the back, and already men were standing in all the passages and right to the edge of the platform. I did not like the look in the eyes of these newcomers, and among the crowd I saw several who were obviously plain-clothes policemen.

The chairman whispered a word to the speaker, who continued when the noise had temporarily died down. He kept off the army and returned to the Government, and for a little sluiced out pure anarchism. But he got his foot in it again, for he pointed to the Sinn Feiners as examples of manly independence. At that pandemonium broke loose, and he never had another look in. There were several fights going on in the hall between the public and courageous supporters of the orator.

Then Gresson advanced to the edge of the platform in a vain endeavour to retrieve the day. I must say he did it uncommonly well. He was clearly a practised speaker, and for a moment his appeal, 'Now, boys, let's cool down a bit and talk sense,' had an effect. But the mischief had been done, and the crowd was surging round the lonely redoubt where we sat. Besides, I could see that for all his clever talk the meeting did not like the look of him. He was as mild as a turtle dove, but they wouldn't stand for it. A missile hurtled past my nose, and I saw a rotten cabbage envelop the baldish head of the ex-deportee. Some one reached out a long arm and grabbed a chair, and with it took the legs from Gresson. Then the lights suddenly went out, and we retreated in good order by the platform door with a yelling crowd at our heels.

It was here that the plain-clothes men came in handy. They held the door while the ex-deportee was smuggled out by some side entrance. That class of lad would soon cease to exist but for the protection of the law which he would abolish. The rest of us, having less to fear, were suffered to leak into Newmilns Street. I found myself next to Gresson, and took his arm. There was something hard in his coat pocket.

Unfortunately there was a big lamp at the point where we emerged, and there for our confusion were the Fusilier Jocks. Both were strung to fighting pitch, and were determined to have some one's blood. Of me they took no notice, but Gresson had spoken after their ire had been roused, and was marked out as a victim. With a howl of joy they rushed for him.

I felt his hand steal to his side-pocket. 'Let that alone, you fool,' I growled in his ear.

'Sure, mister,' he said, and the next second we were in the thick of it.

It was like so many street fights I have seen – an immense crowd which surged up around us, and yet left a clear ring. Gresson and I got against the wall on the side-walk, and faced the furious soldiery. My intention was to do as little as possible, but the first minute convinced me that my companion had no idea how to use his fists, and I was mortally afraid that he would get busy with the gun in his pocket. It was that fear that brought me into the scrap. The Jocks were sportsmen every bit of them, and only one advanced to combat. He hit Gresson a clip on the jaw with his left, and but for the wall would have laid him out. I saw in the lamplight the vicious gleam in the American's eye and the twitch of his hand to his pocket. That decided me to interfere and I got in front of him.

This bought the second Jock into the fray. He was a broad, thickset fellow, of the adorable bandy-legged stocky type that I had seen go through the Railway Triangle at Arras as though it were blotting-paper. He had some notion of fighting, too, and gave me a rough time, for I had to keep edging the other fellow off Gresson.

'Go home, you fool,' I shouted. 'Let this gentleman alone. I don't want to hurt you.'

The only answer was a hook-hit which I just managed to guard, followed by a mighty drive with his right which I dodged so that he barked his knuckles on the wall. I heard a yell of rage and observed that Gresson seemed to have kicked his assailant on the shin. I began to long for the police.

Then there was that swaying of the crowd which betokens the approach of the forces of law and order. But they were too late to prevent trouble. In self-defence I had to take my Jock seriously, and got in my blow when he had overreached himself and lost his balance. I never hit any one so unwillingly in my life. He went over like a poled ox, and measured his length on the causeway.

I found myself explaining things politely to the constables. 'These men objected to this gentleman's speech at the meeting, and I had to interfere to protect him. No, no! I don't want to charge anybody. It was all a misunderstanding.' I helped the stricken Jock to rise and offered him ten bob for consolation.

He looked at me sullenly and spat on the ground. 'Keep your dirty money,' he said. 'I'll be even with ye yet, my man – you and that red-headed scab. I'll mind the looks of ye the next time I see ye.'

Gresson was wiping the blood from his cheek with a silk handkerchief. 'I guess I'm in your debt, Mr Brand,' he said. 'You may bet I won't forget it.'

I returned to an anxious Amos. He heard my story in silence, and his only comment was – 'Well done the Fusiliers!'

'It might have been worse, I'll not deny,' he went on. 'Ye've established some kind of claim upon Gresson, which may come in handy. . . Speaking about Gresson, I've news for ye. He's sailing on Friday as a purser on the *Tobermory*. The *Tobermory's* a boat that wanders every month up the West Highlands as far as Stornoway. I've arranged for ye to take a trip on that boat, Mr Brand.'

I nodded. 'How did you find out that?' I asked.

'It took some finding,' he said drily, 'but I've ways and means. Now I'll not trouble you with advice, for ye ken your job a well as me. But I'm going north myself the morn to look after some of the Ross-shire wuds, and I'll be in the way of getting telegrams at the Kyle. Ye'll keep that in mind. Keep in mind, too, that I'm a great reader of the *Pilgrim's Progress* and that I've a cousin of the name of Ochterlony.'

'The Dilution of Labour – Mr Lloyd George in Glasgow'

from Forward 1st January, 1916

During the First World War a serious munitions supply crisis affected the British forces. A Ministry of Munitions was created in May 1915. A reflection of the importance of the post was the appointment of the Chancellor of the Exchequer, David Lloyd George, to head the new Ministry.

One of the measures that was proposed to increase the supply of arms and armaments was the employment of factories and shipyards of workers who had not gone through the normal process of trade and craft apprenticeships. This 'dilution of labour', as it was called, brought in to occupations previously reserved to time-served craftsmen a wide range of workers, male and female, from an unskilled background. These dilution proposals aroused great suspicions on the part of the skilled workers and their shop stewards, even though senior Trade Union representatives had been involved in drawing up the proposals. Two fears seem to have been to the forefront of the workers' minds; first, that the employment of dilutee labour would simply boost the already swollen wartime profits of the factory owners, and secondly, that despite being introduced as an emergency measure the undermining of the traditional craft apprenticeship system would continue into peace-time.

David Lloyd George, one of the great political orators of the age, went out to the industrial areas of Britain to seek to reassure munitions workers that they had nothing to fear from the Munitions of War Act which gave effect to the dilution scheme. Glasgow, as one of the great centres of war production, was an essential stop on this tour. John Buchan has Richard Hanny in Mr Standfast *(see our previous extract) reflect: 'As I made my way down the Dumbarton Road I was amazed at the number of able-bodied fellows about, considering that you couldn't stir a mile on any British front without bumping up against a Glasgow battalion. Then I realized that there were such things as munitions and ships, and I wondered no more.'*

Lloyd George's meeting in the St Andrew's Halls on 25th December did not go to plan. (Christmas Day was then, and for many years after, a normal working day for most industrial workers.) The original meeting date had been unilaterally changed by the Ministry from Thursday evening to Saturday morning, and almost everyone then worked on a Saturday morning, so production was lost and the Ministry of Munitions had to pay those attending for their lost wages. Lloyd George, and the chairman of the meeting, Arthur Henderson MP, the Cabinet's adviser on labour issues, swiftly lost, if indeed they ever held, the sympathy of the meeting, and as the report shows, the meeting swiftly degenerated into chaos.

The report comes from a Scottish socialist weekly, Forward, *founded in 1906 by a young Kirkintilloch man, Tom Johnston. Johnston was deeply hostile to the War and took delight in publishing his reporter Tom Hutchinson's highly entertaining account of the meeting, rather than the bland censored report produced by the official information machine. This decision, and the disrespectful treatment of Lloyd George reported so enthusiastically in* Forward, *aroused the ire of the Minister. As Johnston later wrote in his memoirs: 'All this was too much for Mr Lloyd George, who completely lost his sense of proportion, and ordered a complete raid of all copies of the* Forward *in every newsagent's shop in Scotland; he even had the police search the homes of known purchasers.'* Forward *was shut down for five weeks, but Johnston's view was that the publicity occasioned by the Government's action was advertising worth thousands of pounds to the magazine.*

Lloyd George survived his roasting at the hands of the Glasgow workers, moving on to become Secretary of State for War in July 1916 and Prime Minister in December 1916. Tom Johnston became a Labour Member of Parliament in 1922 and Secretary of State for Scotland in the coalition government during the Second World War. The Glasgow workers continued to acquire the reputation for intransigence and radicalism summed up in the phrase 'Red Clydeside' – a reputation which came to a head with the '40 hours' strike and the George Square demonstration of 1919.

THE DILUTION OF LABOUR – MR LLOYD GEORGE IN GLASGOW

The best-paid munitions worker in Britain, Mr Lloyd George (almost £100 per week), visited the Clyde last week in search of adventure.

He got it.

His meeting with the Clyde workers was to have taken place in the St Andrew's Halls, on the Thursday night, but to everybody's great surprise, the newspapers on Thursday morning announced that the meeting was 'off' until Saturday morning. The announcement excused itself by saying that the postponement from a night meeting, when men were not all working, to a forenoon meeting, when all the men should be working, was to suit the convenience of all concerned!

Not even Mr Sexton Blake, the eminent detective could unravel *that*!

After all the arrangements had been made for the Thursday meeting, Messrs Lorimer (Blacksmiths), Bunton (ASE), and Sharp (Boilermakers), had been summoned by telegraph to Newcastle to meet Mr Lloyd George. Mr Sharp did not go, but Messrs Lorimer and Bunton went, and were informed by Mr Lloyd George that he had changed his mind about the Thursday meeting, that he intended first to visit the workshops, and that the meeting would be postponed to Saturday (Xmas) morning.

The Committee of Trades Representatives responsible for the Thursday meeting, met on Thursday evening, and after two hours discussion, decided by 29 votes to 7 not to have anything to do with the Saturday meeting, owing to the shortness of time and their inability to secure a thoroughly representative gathering.

This resolution was again put to the meeting, and by 34 votes to 3 re-affirmed. It was then resolved unanimously that before any future meeting was arranged for the Ministry of Munitions that an aggregate meeting of shop stewards and trade union officials be held, for the purpose of discussing and formulating a policy to be pursued at any future meeting with Mr Lloyd George. Immediately after these decisions had been arrived at, someone had telephoned the result to Mr Lloyd George's party, who viewed the decision so seriously that they desired to discuss the matter with the delegates at once. In a few minutes the Rt. Hon. Arthur Henderson, MP, and three Government officials, appeared on the scene, and the whole business was reopened. After a statement from Mr Henderson, questions were asked, and some were answered. It was then moved by Mr Bunton (ASE) and seconded by Bailie Whitehead (Brassfinishers), that the meeting rescind their previous resolutions agreed to, but by 20 votes to 13 the meeting refused to rescind their previous decisions, and therefore the Saturday meeting was declared off as an Official Representative Trade Union Meeting. The hour was now 11.45 p.m., and the delegates went home, but through the night letters were delivered at their homes and offices, signed by 'Murray, of Elibank', asking them to meet at the Central Station Hotel on Friday morning at 10 o'clock, and hear an appeal from Lord Murray as to reasons why they should reconsider their decision of the previous evening.

Less than half the delegates turned up at the Friday morning meeting, the absentees being chiefly men at work. It transpired that, despite the decision of the previous evening, the following were willing to go on with the Saturday meeting – Bunton (Engineers), Whitehead (Brassfinishers), Lorimer (Blacksmiths), and Gardiner (Painters).

The remaining unions, nearly 30 in total, agreed to remain loyal to the decisions arrived at on the previous evening.

Saturday's meeting, then, was not representative of all the Clyde unions. The other unions have drafted a circular to their members explaining why they refused to take part in the Saturday meeting.

On this phase of the whole strange business, the only comments necessary are relief that such a large proportion of Union officials refused to be jockeyed about at the sweet will of the Ministry of Munitions – where so many showed dignity and refused to be overawed by the politicians, it may be even unfair to single out Councillor George Kerr, of the Workers' Union, for specially honourable mention – and a comment of surprise that a Ministry of Munitions that openly boasts of the economies it is securing, should have actually cancelled an evening meeting that cost no expenses in workers' wages or in production, and substituted therefor a forenoon meeting, which, to the extent that it was attended by munition workers, *diminished production*, and cost the country 6/- per head in wages – this 6/- being the sum the unions are to pay each member attending the meeting; the unions are to be remembered by the Ministry of Munitions. In hard cash – uselessly spent hard cash – HERE GOES ONE THOUSAND POUNDS.

THE SATURDAY MEETING

Wild Scenes

Mr Lloyd George says Ramsay MacDonald 'is one of my greatest personal friends'

But does not speak on Munitions Act

Thanks Socialist for Appealing for Hearing for Him

Break-up in Disorder

On Saturday morning the St Andrew's Hall was fairly well filled. An official account of the meeting has been issued by the Censor and published in the Press. The account of Mr Lloyd George's speech summarised very fairly the points he made, though the language has been 'touched up' – at any rate, some of his graceful periods (in the Press reports) did not reach reporters in the audience.

The comments which preface the official Press report are misleading, inasmuch as they give the impression that only a small minority of the audience was hostile to the Munitions Act. The report is also unfair as it cuts out Mr Lloyd George's loudly-cheered expression of his friendship for Ramsay MacDonald, and his thanks to the Convener of the Parkhead Shop Steward (Mr Kirkwood) for rising and appealing for a hearing to him, when the interruptions threatened to overwhelm him altogether.

The Censor has passed an official report of the meeting, issued by the Press Association – probably with the idea of preventing publication of news about munitions, guns, etc., going to the enemy, as might have been the case, if the ordinary newspaper reports had been permitted. We have no desire to touch the military or 'preparedness' side of the speech, but the purely political side must not go misrepresented. It is simply stupid to go about deluding people that only an insignificant minority, and not the vast overwhelming majority of the meeting was angry, and the journalist, whoever he was, who drew up the report and omitted the political reference to Ramsay MacDonald and the efforts of the Socialists to secure a hearing for Mr George is really *not* playing a patriotic part.

• • •

We are all for free speech, and free speech not only for ourselves, but for our opponents. We, therefore, associate ourselves wholeheartedly with the Socialist effort to secure Mr George a hearing, and regret that a mean-spirited press report should seek to convey the impression that it was the Socialists (called 'Syndicalists') who sought to break up the meeting.

The meeting began with a storm of hissing and booing, and the Chairman (Mr Henderson) suffered a running fire of interruption. In our opinion he would have done better to have explained the admirable part he played in getting Jas. Marshal, of Parkhead, released from jail, rather than to attempt, as he did, a rather general patriotic appeal. Here is the sort of thing he suffered:

I am delighted to have the opportunity of appearing in this hall with the Minister of Munitions – [what about the hall for the workers?] – to lay before you the great issue of the present moment so far as the war is concerned. [Ay! and profits.] You are all aware of the fact that we are engaged in probably the greatest war – [at hame] – that ever the old country has been concerned with . . . The issue that was raised in August, 1914, when the neutrality – [Oh! Heavens, how long have we to suffer this?] – of a brave and independent people was trodden on in the most shameful way. [That's enough.]

When we began the war – [we don't want to hear that. Get to the Munitions Act] – I am endeavouring to show you that the country was not prepared, and the fact that we were not prepared – [loud interruption: Cut it short! Come away wi' Davy!] . . . Mr Lloyd George [loud booing and hissing] – will presently address you – [more booing and hissing and some cheering] – on the importance of the dilution of labour.

The scheme of dilution that Mr Lloyd George will recommend to you did not come from any employer. It came from a Committee – [interruption] – upon which there were seven trade unionists. [Traitors: Give their names: Was John Hodge one o' them?]

I am quite prepared to give you their names. I do not want to hold anything back. The first name I will give you is the Chairman of the ASE [Booing and hissing.] My friends may jeer at his name, but he has been elected Chairman since this scheme of dilution came up. [Dirty.] Another member of the Committee was Mr Kaylor – re-elected to the Executive. [Away with him.] Also Mr Duncan, who, I believe, is still connected with the ASE. Another member was the Secretary of the Steam Engine Makers, and another was Miss Macarthur. [Miss Macarthur's the best man o' the lot.] I am quite disposed to agree with my friend. She certainly knows to deal with women workers. [Soft soap.]

What is it they ask you to do? I will be done directly. [Hear, hear!] They only ask you to enable the skill of the worker to be utilised during this crisis in the best interests of the state. [Yes, in the interests of the Capitalists.]

We must have the workers necessary to equip the vast army. [What about the unemployed army after the war?] The whole position will be restored to you after the war. [Question: Don't think!] It appears to me if the position is so safeguarded that you have everything restored to you after the war – [Why don't you put it in the Bill.] It is already in the Bill. I am afraid some people do not read Acts of Parliament. They only read the criticisms, the false criticisms people make for their own advantage.

I want to say here in the most emphatic terms that the safeguarding of the trade union position is already in an Act of Parliament. And I want to tell you it was put there by MR RAMSAY MACDONALD [Great cheering.]

I hope you all believe in freedom of speech. [What about the action of the Glasgow Magistrates?] [You've made a bloomer that time, Arthur!] [Great commotion.] . . . Now I am going to call upon Mr Lloyd George, and I am quite sure, however, much you may differ with him, you are prepared to give him that hearing to which his responsible position entitles him. [He has got to apologise first.]

Mr Lloyd George was sent to organise munitions, and no man has had a harder task. [Tripe: Nonsense.] If we win this war, as I believe we shall, much of the credit will be due to him. [Commotion.] After he has stated his case I am going to ask for questions, and if you do not waste too much time I think we will have sufficient time to answer all the questions that are sent up. I must ask that the questions be sent up in writing. [No, no: We're had again.] Surely in a crisis like this Mr Lloyd George is entitled to see the questions he is going to answer. I hope you will take note, and get your questions ready, and Mr Lloyd George will do his best to give satisfaction.

• • •

On rising to speak Mr Lloyd George was received with loud and continued booing and hissing. There was some cheering, certainly, and about a score of hats were waved in the area, but the meeting was violently hostile. Two verses of 'The Red Flag' were sung before the Minister could utter a word. Owing to the incessant interruption and the numerous altercations going on throughout the hall, it was quite impossible to catch every word of Mr George's speech.

'My first duty,' he said, 'is to express regret to you because I could not address the meeting on Thursday.' [Leave that alone.] At this stage a delegate in the area stood upon a seat and endeavoured to speak. He only got the length of saying 'Mr Lloyd George' when apparently he was pulled down. There were loud cries of 'Free Speech', and someone shouted: 'This is a meeting of trade union officials, not police officials', evidently hinting at the surprisingly large force of police in the hall. 'This is the only opportunity we have,' shouted another, 'they on the platform will never give us the opportunity.' The Chairman appealed for quietness, and again gave the order of procedure. It was only proper, he said, that they should accept the ruling.

Mr Lloyd George tried to resume: 'I have to express my regret at the alteration of the arrangement – [What about the Conference at Bristol? and loud cries of 'apologise'] I have addressed many meetings in Scotland and have never seen Scotsmen deny the rights of free speech. The vast majority are in favour of it.' Amidst the general commotion Mr Lloyd George was understood to say that he stood with the Socialists against the South African War. He continued:

> I thought a small nation was being oppressed, and I did not care whether it was being oppressed by our own people or by a foreign land . . . Let me put this to you, friends: whilst we are comfortable at home on Christmas day – [interruption: No sentiment!; We're here for business!] – there are hundreds of thousands of our fellow-countrymen, some of them our sons, some of them our brothers, in the trenches facing death. [You're here to talk about the dilution of labour.] It's on their behalf and at their written request that I come here to put before the workmen of Glasgow their appeal for help.
>
> We need a very large number of heavy guns and projectiles, and I am going to put to you a business proposition. [For the exploiters.] Do you think these men in the trenches are exploiters? [Don't hedge. The shipowners are doing their bit.] Do let me state the facts. [We know them.] We have started great national factories; state-owned and state-controlled; every timber and nail in them belonging to the state. My friends, these are great Socialist factories. [Violent interruption.] Believe me, the whole of them owned by the State, erected by the State, no profit made by any Capitalist, because they don't belong to the Capitalist.
>
> What is the issue? Does anyone deny that these factories we are building are State factories? [A voice: 'Yes'.] If you deny that you would deny anything.
>
> I will ask any man representing you in the House of Commons – and surely there is someone you trust ['No!' and laughter.] Not even Mr Ramsay MacDonald? ['Yes, yes!' Loud cheers given for Ramsay MacDonald.] Mr MacDonald is one of my greatest personal friends, and whether he is for the war or against the war not one single word will fall from my lips against Mr MacDonald. You get Mr Ramsay MacDonald – [What about the hall for him?] He will tell you they are national factories.
>
> Mr Thomas, one of the most distinguished members of the Socialist Party and as good a Socialist to-day as he ever was – [What about Jaurés?] – took the matter of shells in hand. He called to his

assistance the French women and brought them into the factories. With what result? The German invasion was rolled back, and the Germans have no more chance of conquering any French territory than they have of conquering the kingdom of heaven.

Is it too much to ask the British workmen to help his comrades in the field? [No; what about the Munitions Act?] France will never forget it. Whatever scheme the French workman puts forward in the future for better treatment, he will have the ear, the willing ear of millions of French men and women, who will remember the gallant and devoted service he rendered to his country. [Cries of 'Hurry up' and commotion.]

[Mr Kirkwood apparently had been appealed to for help, and he made an appeal to the meeting to hear the speaker. This was duly acknowledged by Mr Lloyd George.]

Mr Kirkwood, he said, did not restrain himself from telling me what he thought about the Munitions Act and about me, but at any rate, he knows the value of free speech, and I am very grateful to him for his assistance in obtaining order.

I have but one word more to say. I want to talk to you in all sincerity as a man brought up in a worker's house. I know as much about the life of the worker as any man here. The responsibility of a Minister of the Crown in a great war is not an enviable one. ['The money's good', and laughter.] I can assure you it is no laughing matter.

There will be unheard-of changes in every country in Europe, changes that go to the root of our social system. You Socialists watch them. It is convulsion of nature; not merely a cyclone that sweeps away the ornamental plants of modern society and wrecks the flimsy trestle-bridges of modern civilisation. It is more. It is an earthquake that upheaves the very rocks of European life.

And to go on chaffering about a regulation here and the suspension of a custom there is just haggling with an earthquake. Workmen; may I make one appeal to you? [Interruption.] Lift up your eyes above the mist of suspicion and distrust. Rise to the height of the great opportunity now before you. If you do, you will emerge after this war is over into a future which has been the dream of many a great leader. [Cheers, loud hissing and booing.]

At the close of the address, Mr Lloyd George proceeded to answer the written questions which had been handed up from the body of the hall. He promised to reply to them all if he possibly could, but he had an engagement at 12 o'clock, and if he failed to get through them the remaining answers would be published. At 11.45, however, Mr John Muir, of the Clyde Workers' Committee, got up on the seat and demanded an opportunity of stating the case for the workers. This, he said, had been promised, and he was not going to wait any longer. Both Mr Lloyd George and Mr Henderson appealed to him to resume his seat, but Mr Muir was determined not to be put off till Mr George had to leave. As it was impossible to hear either the Minister or Mr Muir, the Chairman closed the proceedings, and the meeting broke up in disorder.

'The River of Words'

from Clyde Valley

CATHERINE GAVIN (1907–)

This chapter from Catherine Gavin's 1938 novel tells the story of a fictional by-election for a parliamentary seat in the Glasgow Exchange division (or constituency). The candidate on whom much of the novel focuses is Major Kennedy Carmichael, son of a viscount, who is the chosen candidate of what is known as the Constitutional (largely Conservative) Party. All of this amounts to a thinly fictionalised version of the political scene at the time of the 'National' Government of 1931, which came to power briefly under the uneasy leadership of Ramsay MacDonald after the failure of his Labour Party (here called Socialists) to hold on to office. MacDonald is briefly described in the novel as 'Hamish Macrobert ("From Herd-laddie to Prime Minister")' and the same sense of betrayal felt by real-life Labour supporters is shown by their fictional counterparts when the character known as Mr Paidle says: 'I fund it verra hard to swally Macrobert. Here, if it was his Government got us all into the mess and had to be chucked oot, whit wey does he get to go on bein' Prime Minister with the new lot?'

Working for public-school educated Kennedy Carmichael during the election campaign is the book's heroine, a young journalist turned novelist called Lenny Gordon, who becomes infatuated with him, although he is already married to a wife, Audrey, of good background. Strong meat for a novel in these days, this intensely felt affair is shown against an impressionistic background of various twentieth-century religious issues as well as national politics. Although there are passages of melodramatic overstatement, in general the book presents an entertaining account of an election, and of various classes and types of voters and party-workers (incidentally reminding us that Tories once had a substantial working-class following).

Elsewhere in the novel there are also interesting descriptions of the shipbuilding industry during the Depression, and an account of the building and launch of a great Cunard ocean liner, No. 999, as a means of getting the workers of Clydeside (or 'Clyde Valley') back to work after long stretches of catastrophic unemployment. This is of course very close to the historic facts, with, instead, No. 534 being the real ship later christened

'Queen Mary'. *In* Clyde Valley *a later sequence describes the maiden trip down-river of the newly-launched Cunarder bearing the name* 'Victoria'.

'THE RIVER OF WORDS'

The time began when everybody talked endlessly and at once. The West of Scotland Constitutional Union talked, through its mouthpieces, Messrs Macfayden and Gillespie, who favoured the candidate with pieces of elementary information on the danger of doing anything suggestive of bribery and corruption; and the necessity of depositing £150 with the Sheriff on nomination day. Finding that Kennedy's replies were curt enough they turned to the more repaying task of terrorising Mr Paidle, who had been appointed Election Agent and was so alarmed by the honour that he assailed the candidate, the chairman, all the members of committee and any stray voluntary workers, with requests for help and sharing of responsibility.

The committee talked, about their new candidate's good looks and high-handed ways, and about all the people they would rather have had instead of him, and about how different from his father he was: preferring to ignore the inescapable fact that as their last balance sheet had shown a liability of £72. 10s. 11½d. they were in no position to call the tune, but must support a candidate who could pay the piper – put down £600 for election expenses and square the deficit in the funds as well.

The Socialists talked a great deal. Their candidate was Willie Ferguson, who had been returned at the elections of 1921, 1925, and 1930 and claimed on that account to be 'the reel member for the division'. No man could say exactly what Mr Ferguson had done for Exchange during his ten years as a Member. Its manufactures were carpets, footwear, and soft goods; its interests included all sorts of general trading, the fruit and vegetable markets, as well as the Glasgow Stock Exchange, being within its boundaries; but Mr Ferguson's activities had been concentrated upon Distressed Fishermen, Dispossessed Crofters and Oppressed Miners. Thereby he showed his wisdom, having earned a luscious reputation as the Puir Fowk's Champion without running up against the big business interests in his own division.

By many of the business men, indeed, he was dubbed 'harmless' or 'a decent enough soul', and with their favour in view he had had a hard struggle with himself when his leader, Hamish Macrobert, joined the Constitutionalists in 1931. He would have been glad to follow the illustrious example and play for safety, but his Committee assured him that by so doing he would cease to be their candidate, and forced him to fight in the orthodox Labour interest, with the result that he was defeated by Sir Frederick Carmichael. The lesson had been salutary. Mr Ferguson lost interest in the country folk and began to attack the Government on behalf of the east-enders. In the means test he had a weapon ready to his hand.

Nevertheless the by-election caught Mr Ferguson at the moment when, snake-like. he had sloughed off half his old skin but had not yet emerged glittering in the new one.

Peter Clifton talked a lot. He was Audrey's only brother, who had had the good fortune to be born in December 1900 and so had escaped the Great War by the narrowest margin of time, for Peter had not felt called upon to falsify his age and leave the playing-fields of Eton for Flanders. He was an aimless, cheery soul, a noted gentleman rider who had once come in second in the Grand National, and his sole object in being an MP was 'to learn something about it, what?' before he succeeded his father in the Upper House. As he represented a hard-riding West Country division, where many of the farmers were his father's tenants, and gave him a hearty welcome at their annual political meetings, he was obviously well-fitted to advise Kennedy on the approach to a Scottish industrial area.

And down at the Tap o' Newton Kirsten and John talked a great deal more about this election than any one before. Kirsten, like most of the fisher population, was a Liberal, John was a Tory; neither cared to sink their party distinctions as a Constitutionalist. 'It's as bad as the Union o' the Kirks,' Kirsten had said – and that had been enough, for though she had attended Crawford Kirk since her marriage, she was, as she said 'a UP at hert.' The Exchange by-election, however, roused no party antagonisms. Their interest in it was purely on Lenny's account.

She had become Major Carmichael's political private secretary without any special arrangement, indeed he had never even discussed her position at Carmichael & Hewitt's; she was there, she had nothing to do, she understood something of the constituency routine – very well, she should help in the election.

'And ye're lucky saft,' Kirsten said vigorously. 'What do you ken aboot politics? Ha' done with the whole hypothec and look for anither job.'

But when Lenny suggested that she might look for a newspaper job in London, her father objected.

'Nae lassie o' mines,' said old John, 'gaes awa' to bide her lane in that unchancy place. Bide still wi' yer brither; a' this political work will maybe settle down. And it's good pay.'

Three-pound-ten a week, indeed, seemed riches to the shepherd. He laid great importance, too, on Lenny's life with her brother. Dr George Gordon was now lecturing on Surgery at Glasgow University, after spending two years in a famous Viennese clinic. He lived in a comfortable private hotel near the University, and allowed Lenny, who had a tiny bedroom next to his big one, to share his sitting-room and bathroom in exchange for darning his socks and looking after his clothes. As he liked to remark, without him her home life would not have been so comfortable, and their old father thought that at least she was protected.

Lenny talked about the election less than any one, and did more. She was general factotum at the dingy office in Spindle Street, and acted as liaison officer between Kennedy and the Press. She directed the activities of the Canvass Corps, a bevy of London girls whom Audrey had collected, who went about the more respectable streets in Exchange and said brightly, 'I do hope you're voting for Major Carmichael, he's the *most* marvellous person!' They worked hard from 2.30 to 4.30 every day, and faithfully attended Kennedy's evening meetings, wearing blue satin bows in their hair. This, with their smart fur coats and make-up, reduced audiences to frenzy and necessitated their protection by Peter Clifton and his friends. After a few nights it was thought to be simpler if Peter took them straight to the Fleur-de-Lis without bothering to go to the meetings at all. Canvassing during the other hours of the day was done less decoratively and rather more efficiently by some working men of the committee.

Lenny's was a twelve-hour day. and she grudged the extra work at a time when her second book, *Facing Both Ways*, had just reached the engrossing stage. She took the election excitement home with her and could not concentrate on her hero and heroine. For the first time in her life, she found it hard to 'make up a story'. While she was on the *Gazette* she could turn out copy against time, with the roar of the presses in her ears. Then, she could sub. a page of 'Womens Topics', including recipes, fashions, and a short – a very short – article on 'The Girlhood of our Beloved Queen', write a stick-and-a-half of rhyming couplets to help a colleague struggling with 'Piggy-Wee's Children's Corner', attend a fashionable wedding to report a highly original toilette of white satin, pearl necklace, and lilies – and at the end of the day walk home with her head in the clouds, inventing situations for a heroine whose ideals were the ideals of Wordsworth and Keats.

Now, she sat over her gas-fire at midnight, chewing her pencil blankly and cursing Kennedy Carmichael and his politics for interrupting her evenings.

Kennedy was cursing politics too. Like all his kind, he had applauded and voted for the Constitutional Government when it took office during a great economic crisis. He had always been a Tory, any adolescent leanings towards Fabianism having been killed over the regimental port, so that he felt the Tory Party had done its bit towards 'saving the country' by giving up its name and its identity to merge, as the Constitutional Party, with a number of converted Liberals and place-seeking Socialists. It was odd that among the die-hards, these adjectives were never transposed, nor were those who had turned from their original faith ever given credit in private for the 'public-spiritedness' so stridently attributed to them in public.

Even Mr Paidle had his doubts.

'I must say, Major,' he cheeped, 'I fund it verra hard to swally Macrobert. Here, if it was his Government got us all into the mess and had to be chucked oot, whit wey does he get to go on bein' Prime Minister with the new lot?'

Kennedy was nonplussed. He had also found it hard to swallow Hamish Macrobert ('From Herd-laddie to Prime Minister') but obviously his duty now was to support him. 'Anyway, Paidle,' he said, 'I really haven't got time to wrestle with *your* political doubts!' And Mr Paidle held his tongue.

The candidate's days were full, but he had no lack of helpers, all those who aimed at being candidates themselves at no distant date, rushing forward with offers to address meetings for him, in the hopes that they might bask in the light of national publicity which beats upon a by-election. Sir Alistair Veitch, indeed, a former Lord Provost who had been Mr Fentie's favourite as candidate (Sir Alistair was also a soft-goods manufacturer, able to put many a 'good thing' in Mr Fentie's way if he chose) declined to give up his evenings to the Cause; but as Sir Alistair had never been known to utter two consecutive grammatical sentences in his life, the cause of oratory at least did not suffer by his absence.

On the other hand, Lord Lomond, who had been timidly favoured by the Exchange Women's Committee, was modestly certain that the better man had been chosen, and since he also had been at Winchester, though ten years later than Kennedy Carmichael, he rallied to the Old School Tie.

The members of the Beaconsfield Club, as usual, swore to perform mighty deeds of valour at the East End meetings, and as usual, remained in their armchairs to criticise the candidate. Seventy-eight of them volunteered to send cars to drive voters to the poll, and nineteen actually kept their word.

'What like a body is the Major's wife?' asked Mrs Murdoch's husband one evening when his spouse was preparing to set out for one of the first election meetings.

'Real nice; some highty-tighty,' was the terse rejoinder. Mrs Murdoch did not approve of her husband's taking an interest, however slight, in politics, in view of the fact that he suffered long spells of unemployment, during which his vigorous wife described him as 'a perfect scunner, soss, sossin' at the fireside'. One of the results of his enforced intimacy with the domestic scene sat on his knee now in the person of a nine-months-old baby, born to his wife when her youngest was sixteen and she herself not far short of fifty. This event, hailed as a miracle by the matrons of their own and adjacent stairs, had completed the overthrow of Mrs Murdoch's never very stable temperament. Thenceforth she regarded her husband as the mother of the child, obliged him to give it blue milk in unsavoury bottles, change its garments and push its pram on Glasgow Green, while she attended her Church Guild, Orange Lodge, Eastern Star, and Constitutional Committees.

Like all the other members of the Exchange Committee, and 70 per cent of their fellow-believers throughout Britain, she had been perplexed by the change in the party name. 'A Tory I was born and a Tory I'll dee,' she had been wont to proclaim. Tory was a good word, a short word, a word with a class-conscious grandeur about it, truly irritating to the Opposition; the new one was difficult to pronounce and impossible to spell. Even Mr Paidle used three alternatives.

Mrs Murdoch pondered the intricacies of the party system for about three of her twenty-minutes' tramp to the school in which the first of that night's meetings was to be held. The other seventeen she gave more pleasurably to the personalities of the occasion: to the Major, God bless his handsome face, to Mr Fentie, a perfeck gentleman, and Mr Paidle, a perfeck goat – and to Mistress Carmichael, real nice but some highty-tighty.

Actually Audrey had been very nice to all 'the workers' as they styled themselves. The trouble was that she could not adapt to the present need the attitude of pleasant yet off-hand interest which her father's tenants and her own servants liked so much. The cool tones of her voice, the poses of her body, would have been exactly right in a country constituency: the Exchange Division of Glasgow wanted something at once redolent of Buckingham Palace and of luxuriant womanhood. 'Vote for my *husband*, because I love him and freely give him to your service!' – there was the peroration which the Exchange wanted from its candidate's wife. Audrey, when she spoke at all, asked them to vote for the Constitutional Government and English liberties.

To hell with the English, said Exchange.

Audrey was scarcely more fortunate with that section of the division which would have hesitated to let such a word cross its genteel lips, and which only aspired to emulate the English in all things.

'The Honourable Mrs Carmichael is to be there.' 'And is your Papa the Viscount keeping some better?' 'Your brother, the Honourable Peter, was at school with my boy David' – these were the phrases spoken of and to Audrey in the early stages of the Exchange by-election, by ladies who usually preferred to forget that the Exchange existed. They were very important ladies – and they knew it – for if they rallied from their suburban strongholds to vote by virtue of the qualifications of their husbands' business premises, it was possible that they might turn the scale. Certainly they had done so in the desperate struggle of 1919, when bus-loads and car-loads of startled matrons were rushed up at the eleventh hour from Bearsden, Milngavie, Helensburgh and Bridge of Weir; and they had helped to give Sir Frederick Carmichael the comfortable majority of exactly 4,500 votes, which remained like a bank balance for his son to draw upon.

On this occasion there was no doubt whatever about the loyalty of the business men's wives to the Constitutional cause. When they might shake hands daily with a Viscount's daughter, whose picture appeared regularly in the *Prattler* and the *Onlooker*, their exertions began long before polling-day. 'The workers' at the Central Committee Rooms were augmented by a band of furry ladies, and canvass cards, envelopes and glue-pots were scattered in all directions.

This atmosphere of sycophancy was genuinely new to Audrey, and she could not conceal her dislike of it: Kennedy and she, never a very united couple, came closer in their mutual disgust for the backstairs side of the election.

'I wish I'd known more about politics before this show began,' Kennedy confessed one evening when they were having supper in the Fleur-de-Lis after two election meetings.

Audrey nodded. 'I think I know what you mean,' she said slowly. 'It was rather awkward to-night, when that man tackled you about wages in the carpet factory. . . . Still, you really can't be expected to know details like that.'

'Miss Gordon thinks I can,' said her husband dryly.

'Did she say so? What impertinence!'

'No – she looked it. I never knew any girl who can look a reproof as she can.'

'Reproof indeed,' exclaimed Audrey. 'I'm getting rather tired of that young woman's airs and graces. I wish she'd get on with her job and take some of her reproofs to herself!'

'Oh – well.' Kennedy signalled to the waiter. 'There's something in this particular instance. I really should know all about their wage-scales and what-not. Must ask Paidle to make out a list for me. One thing I've learnt – the dole figures.' And the waiter respectfully tendered the bill.

'Total number of unemployed, do you mean?' Mrs Carmichael was examining her carefully un-made-up face in her little mirror. Kennedy did not reply and she looked up quickly. He was studying the bill, his mouth rather set. 'Kennedy!'

'Yes, my dear. Er – I meant the dole itself. Fifteen and nine a week for a man, and all that.' And very slowly he took out his note-case. It had been a modest little supper, for the foul air of the schoolroom where the meetings were held had taken away their appetite. Some sherry, scrambled eggs and coffee had been all they wanted. And the total stared up at him on the white slip – the price of one meal, or a whole week's livelihood – fifteen shillings and nine pence.

From that night Kennedy's thoughts and Kennedy's speeches took a new turn. Till then he had proceeded on the happy assumption that his side was entirely right and the other side entirely wrong; that the gaunt men and women who came to his meetings and shrieked out, 'How wud ye like to keep a bairn on twa shillin's a week?' were paid agitators or types of the eternally discontented; that the east end of Glasgow was a suburb of Moscow.

Now, he struggled into the small hours of one frozen January morning to write a speech which would at once express his sympathy with the have-nots and explain exactly the world and national developments which had brought increased unemployment, and might under the Constitutional Government bring back prosperity to the West of Scotland.

It was not a good speech, nor was it well delivered, for Kennedy was much more nervous when offering his own opinions than when parroting off one of the 'Speeches Readymade' with which the West of Scotland Constitutional Union thoughtfully supplied its speakers in such emergencies. True, the 'Speeches Readymade' were prepared by an astute gentleman in London and too often dealt solely with English problems, but that, while irritating to those who had to listen to them, was of little account to those who delivered them, who were more than thankful to use 'material' so nicely arranged in predigested paragraphs which only required to be joined by conjunctions for immediate use.

Kennedy's speech on 'Unemployment', then, was a failure, as such speeches, even by Cabinet Ministers and economists tended to be at that time. He was harassed by steady interruptions about the means test and the dole cuts, but he was reported (without the interruptions) in the next day's *Glasgow Messenger* to the considerable mystification of breakfasting die-hards and the delight of his cousin, Janet Frew, who arrived at his Central Committee Rooms early in the forenoon.

'Janet, you devil!' Kennedy sprang up with more animation than 'the workers' were accustomed to, and seized the hands of a tall woman in furs. 'Janet, where have you been? I thought you were coming to help me.'

'I waited till I thought you were worth helping,' said Mrs Frew coolly. 'Till you stopped beating the party drum and began playing your own tune.'

Audrey, who had been talking to Mr Paidle, came forward and dabbed her lips at the newcomer's ear. '*Dear* Janet,' she said 'always so outspoken! So sweet of you to come down, but do you know, honestly, I don't think there's very much for you to *do*.'

'Victory is certain, then?' said Janet quizzically. 'All right! I kept out of the way till all the envelopes were addressed. Nobody ever reads election literature anyway. And I won't canvass – the *Messenger* says you've got a beauty chorus on that job, Audrey! I don't mind speaking at an odd women's meeting – though I draw the line at the rough stuff.'

'The women's meetings can be pretty rough,' Kennedy remarked ruefully. 'I don't seem to be able to reason with 'em somehow.'

Janet looked amused. 'Poor Kennedy,' she said lightly. 'You've put yourself in a spot where you simply *have* to use your brains. What does it feel like?'

Into the nonplussed silence which followed there came the sound of a door opening, and Lenny Gordon entered with a packet of letters. Audrey, who disliked her, was nevertheless glad to use her to create a diversion – to introduce her and explain her to Mrs Frew distracted Janet's attention, and Janet seemed to be in her most sarcastic mood.

At the same time the arrival of Kennedy's cousin – who had indeed allowed the first week of the by-election campaign to pass before she appeared on the scene – seemed to Audrey a good excuse to relax her own efforts. She was heartily sick of the sycophancy of one set of women and in her secret heart a little afraid of the passion of the other. When

Kennedy was trying to get a hearing in a wild meeting, when men were shaking their fists in each other's faces and women were pressing closer and closer to the platform, their white faces distorted with brute rage, Audrey sat with a chilly little smile, which, though she did not know it, only fanned the mob's hostility, but which served to mask her inward fear of revolution.

Besides, the end of January brought a spell of good hunting weather and Audrey had an invitation to ride with the Cart Vale Hunt. So she left Janet Frew to take her place in the Exchange, and drove into Renfrewshire three days a week, to join the Glasgow business men riding at fourteen stone and sawing at their horses' mouths, and their ladies, whose horsemanship had been learnt late in life on livery stable hacks. And Audrey, who was one of the best riders in her native Somerset, gave them some fine performances in these crisp winter days – she lived then, with the wind from the Firth of Clyde in her nostrils, and the thunder of hooves in her ears, and she led the field consistently, which was a little galling for the Cart Vale.

That was how she came to be twenty miles away, dining in Renfrewshire, on the night she was most needed, in the last week of the election, when the inevitable muddle of times and places left an entire audience of three hundred souls, all precious in God's sight but singularly valueless in each other's, to cramp and chafe in an overheated school hall, with as many more, denied admission, prowling and pressing in the playground, and no speaker at all to address them – neither the candidate, nor his wife, nor his cousin, nor his brother-in-law, nor any of the odd dozen or so of voluntary speakers who as a rule were clamouring to catch the reporters' attention. Only Mr Paidle and Lenny Gordon represented Kennedy's cause, and it was Lenny who got up pale and trembling, after twenty minutes of worry, indecision and growing alarm, to face the worst beast in the world – the mob – for the first time in her life.

There were a few jeers and cat-calls, when she began, a few profanely worded orders to go on home and play with her doll's house, but she went on steadily, in a queer mixture of quotations, morsels of politics, such as she had heard daily for three weeks, and her father's aphorisms on good government. Indeed what struck Janet and Kennedy most – for they arrived shortly after she began, and stood silent and unseen behind the platform door to listen – was that this speech, unlike all the others delivered in the by-election, dealt neither with past deeds nor present promises, but with a future – a future reminiscent of Plato's Republic and Augustine's City of God, tinged with a girl's idealism and described in words which, though they came haltingly, were so forceful, so vivid, that they caught and held a gathering of men and women quite untrained to concentrate.

At the end she fell back on the poets, and gave them 'the Parliament of man, the Federation of the world', sweeping from Tennyson to Burns and a language more familiar to her listeners, as she pleaded for a better understanding between class and class, nation and nation:

> That man to man, the warld o'er
> Shall brithers be for a' that!

Kennedy came forward smiling in a great roar of applause, but his cousin knew that it was all for Lenny – that there was a fire in this pale girl, now hiding her shaking hands in her pockets, that could blaze through the hastily conceived, ill-constructed and loosely argued speech to inflame an audience. And she told Kennedy as they drove out of the Exchange that night, that Lenny Gordon was his trump card.

But as it happened she was wrong. The next morning the headlines announced that the Constitutional Government would subsidize the resumption of work on the great Cunarder, No. 999, and a wave of thankfulness passed from Clydebank all over Scotland. Hundreds of men would start work at once, scores of subsidiary trades would benefit. Wages would pour like a revitalizing stream through the shops; and families in the east end and the west end of Glasgow, without the remotest chance of benefiting directly or indirectly from the Government's action, rejoiced that February morning and felt that the Constitutionalists had done a fine thing and that the country was up and out of the mire at last.

'Money for jam!' purred the political organizers and so indeed it proved. On the four nights which remained of his campaign, Major Carmichael had only to mention the Cunarder to elicit a burst of frantic cheering. On a wave of optimism, of renewed faith in the Government, he went forward to the polls, and on the night of the 19th of February he was returned for the Exchange Division of Glasgow by a majority of 921 votes.

James Maxton

from Chapman, Spring 1987

TOM SCOTT (1918–1995)

Made by the Clyde and unmade by the Thames,
His words were mair volcanic nor his deeds.
We honour his passion, honour his noble aims
Mair nor aucht he achieved for Scotland's needs.
Mithered by Glescae, frae her iron dugs
He sucked his love o the sufferan human race:
Grieved owre the scabbit bairn in its bed o bugs,
And kendlet his ire ilka stairvan face.

Born o a man-made wasterie o stane,
He wrocht to make yon desart burgeon green,
Gar new sang braird frae its mirk hert o pain;
And his vision-torkit mind and hauntit een
Clawcht sicht o, throu ilk beelan Glescae slum,
The lineaments o New Jerusalem.

Index of Authors

Acknowledgements

Bell, J. J., 'Hullo Glesca Hielanders' from *Courtin' Christina,* Birlinn.

Bermant, Chaim, Chapter 29, 'A New Life', from *The Patriarch*, out of print.

Blake, George, Chapter 4, 'The Old Firm', from *The Shipbuilders*. Reprinted by permission of B&W.

Blake, George, part of Chapter 1, *The Shipbuilders.* Reprinted by permission of B&W.

Buchan, John, 'Divus Johnston' from *The Runagates Club*. The publisher acknowledges the Estate of John Buchan.

Buchan, John, Chapter 4, 'Andrew Amos' from *Mr Standfast*. The publisher acknowledges the Estate of John Buchan.

Buchan, John, pp 82–92, 'Revolution in the Air', from *Montrose*. The publiher acknowledges the Estate of John Buchan.

Cocker, W. D., *The Deluge*. The publisher acknowledges the Estate of W. D. Cocker.

Gavin, Catherine, Chapter 3, 'The River of Words', from *Clyde Valley*, out of print.

Hutcheson, William J. F., 'Twin-Screw Set' from *Mungo's Tongues.* Reprinted by permission of Mainstream.

Jenkins, Robin, pp 277–296, 'The Final', from *The Thistle and the Grail.* Reprinted by permission of Edinburgh University Press.

MacGill, Patrick, Chapters 24 & 25, *The Rat-Pit*, Birlinn.

McArthur, Alexander & Long, H. Kingsley, Chapter 8, *No Mean City*. Reprinted by permission of Transworld.

McCrone, Guy, pp 8–9, 'The West End' from *Aunt Bel.* Reprinted by permission of B&W.

Morton, H. V., 'The Launch' and 'The Board Room' from *In Search of Scotland*. The publisher acknowledges the Estate of H. V. Morton.

Muir, James Hamilton, *Shipbuilding from Glasgow in 1901*, out of print.

Munro, Neil, 'Jimmy's Sins Find Him Out', from *Erchie & Jimmy Swan*, Birlinn, 1996.

Munro, Neil, 'Kate Cranstonish', from *Brave Days.* The publisher acknowledges the Estate of Neil Munro.

Munro, Neil, 'The Adventures of a Country Customer' from 'Jimmy Swan, the Joy Traveller', in *Erchie & Jimmy Swan*, Birlinn, 1996

Munro, Neil, Chapter X, 'Harbour Life' from *The Clyde, River and*

Firth. The publisher acknowledges the Estate of Neil Munro.
Niven, Frederick, Chapters 1 & 2, *The Staff at Simson's*, out of print.
Scott, Tom, 'James Maxton'. Reprinted by permission of *Chapman*.
Smith, Iain Crichton, Chapter 1, *The Tenement,* out of print.
Waugh, Evelyn, Chapter 8, pp 248–256, 'On Leave in Glasgow', from *Officers and Gentlemen*. Reprinted by permission of Methuen.